Butler 38

HATA

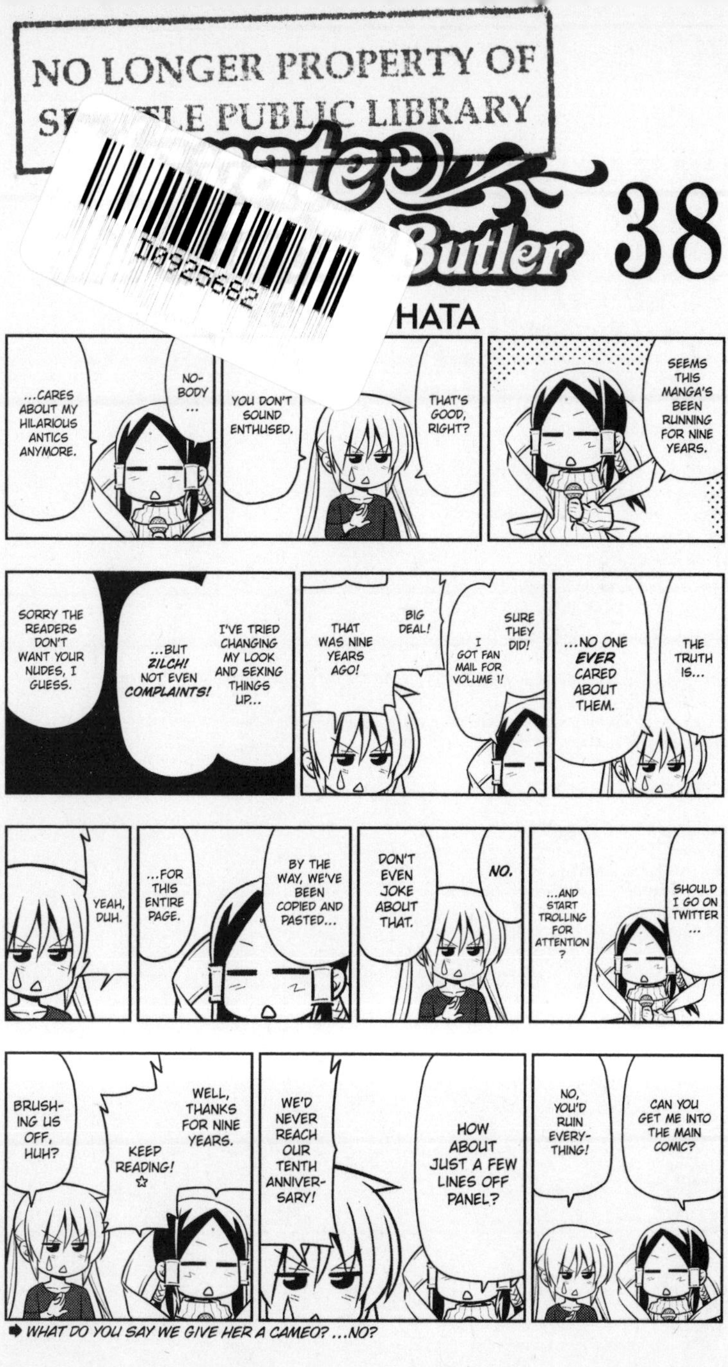
SEEMS THIS MANGA'S BEEN RUNNING FOR NINE YEARS.
THAT'S GOOD, RIGHT?
YOU DON'T SOUND ENTHUSED.
NO-BODY ...
...CARES ABOUT MY HILARIOUS ANTICS ANYMORE.
THE TRUTH IS...
...NO ONE *EVER* CARED ABOUT THEM.
SURE THEY DID!
I GOT FAN MAIL FOR VOLUME 1!
BIG DEAL!
THAT WAS NINE YEARS AGO!
I'VE TRIED CHANGING MY LOOK AND SEXING THINGS UP...
...BUT *ZILCH!* NOT EVEN *COMPLAINTS!*
SORRY THE READERS DON'T WANT YOUR NUDES, I GUESS.
SHOULD I GO ON TWITTER ...
...AND START TROLLING FOR ATTENTION ?
NO.
DON'T EVEN JOKE ABOUT THAT.
BY THE WAY, WE'VE BEEN COPIED AND PASTED...
...FOR THIS ENTIRE PAGE.
YEAH, DUH.
CAN YOU GET ME INTO THE MAIN COMIC?
NO, YOU'D RUIN EVERY-THING!
HOW ABOUT JUST A FEW LINES OFF PANEL?
WE'D NEVER REACH OUR TENTH ANNIVER-SARY!
WELL, THANKS FOR NINE YEARS.
KEEP READING! ☆
BRUSH-ING US OFF, HUH?

➡ *WHAT DO YOU SAY WE GIVE HER A CAMEO? ...NO?*

HAYATE THE COMBAT BUTLER
VOL. 38
Shonen Sunday Edition

STORY AND ART BY
KENJIRO HATA

HAYATE NO GOTOKU! Vol. 38
by Kenjiro HATA

Original Japanese edition published by SHOGAKUKAN.
English translation rights in the United States of America, Canada, the United Kingdom and Ireland arranged with SHOGAKUKAN.

Translation/John Werry
Touch-up Art & Lettering/John Hunt
Design/Yukiko Whitley
Editor/Shaenon K. Garrity

Printed in the U.S.A.

Published by VIZ Media, LLC
P.O. Box 77010
San Francisco, CA 94107

10 9 8 7 6 5 4 3 2 1
First printing, September 2021

VIZ MEDIA
viz.com

shonensunday.com

ratings.viz.com
RATED T+ OLDER TEEN

PARENTAL ADVISORY
HAYATE THE COMBAT BUTLER is rated T+ for Older Teen and is recommended for ages 16 and up. This volume contains fantasy violence and crude humor.

Hayate
the Combat Butler

38

KENJIRO HATA

38

CONTENTS

Episode 1:
"Kyoto and Ise: Conclusion (Night 7)— Hinagiku and Chiharu's Wholesome Walk"

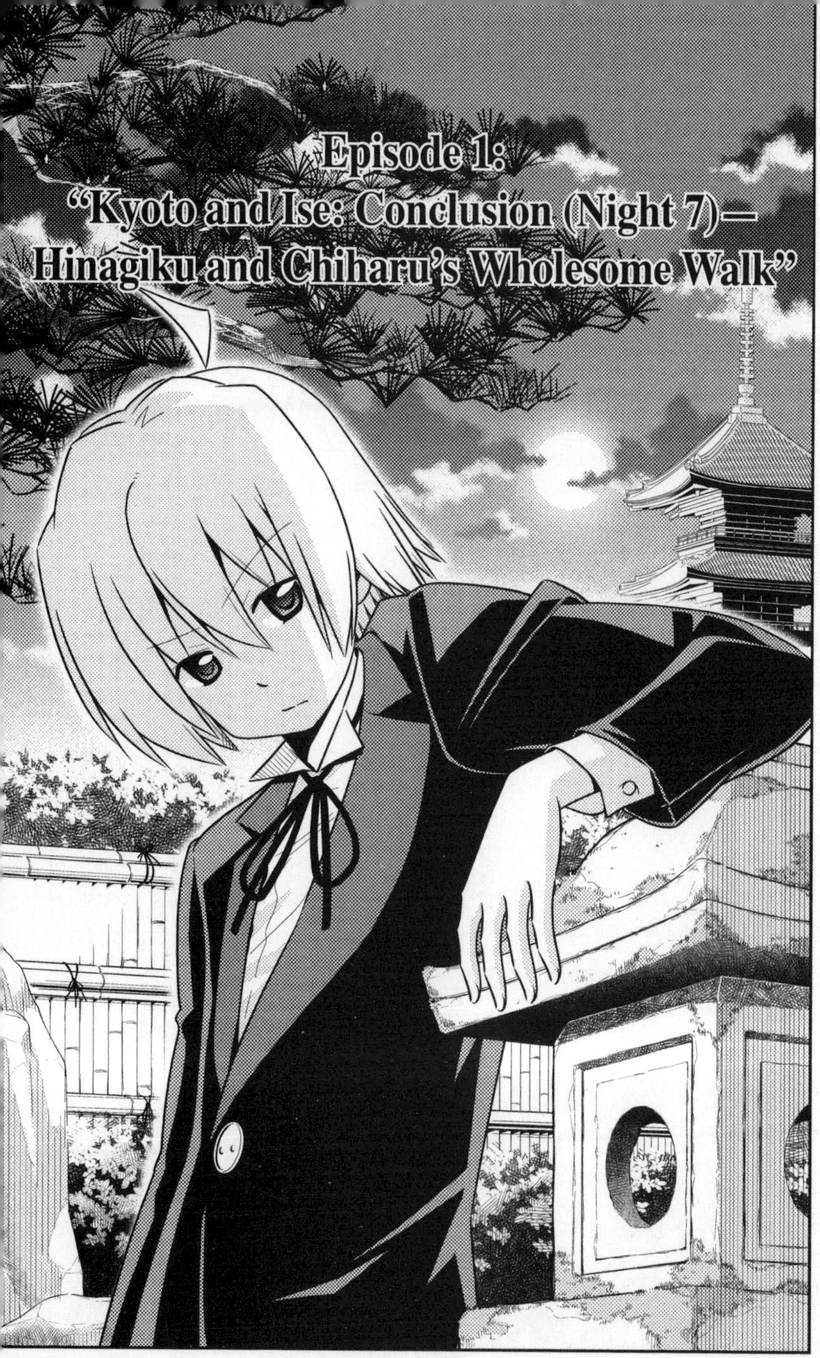

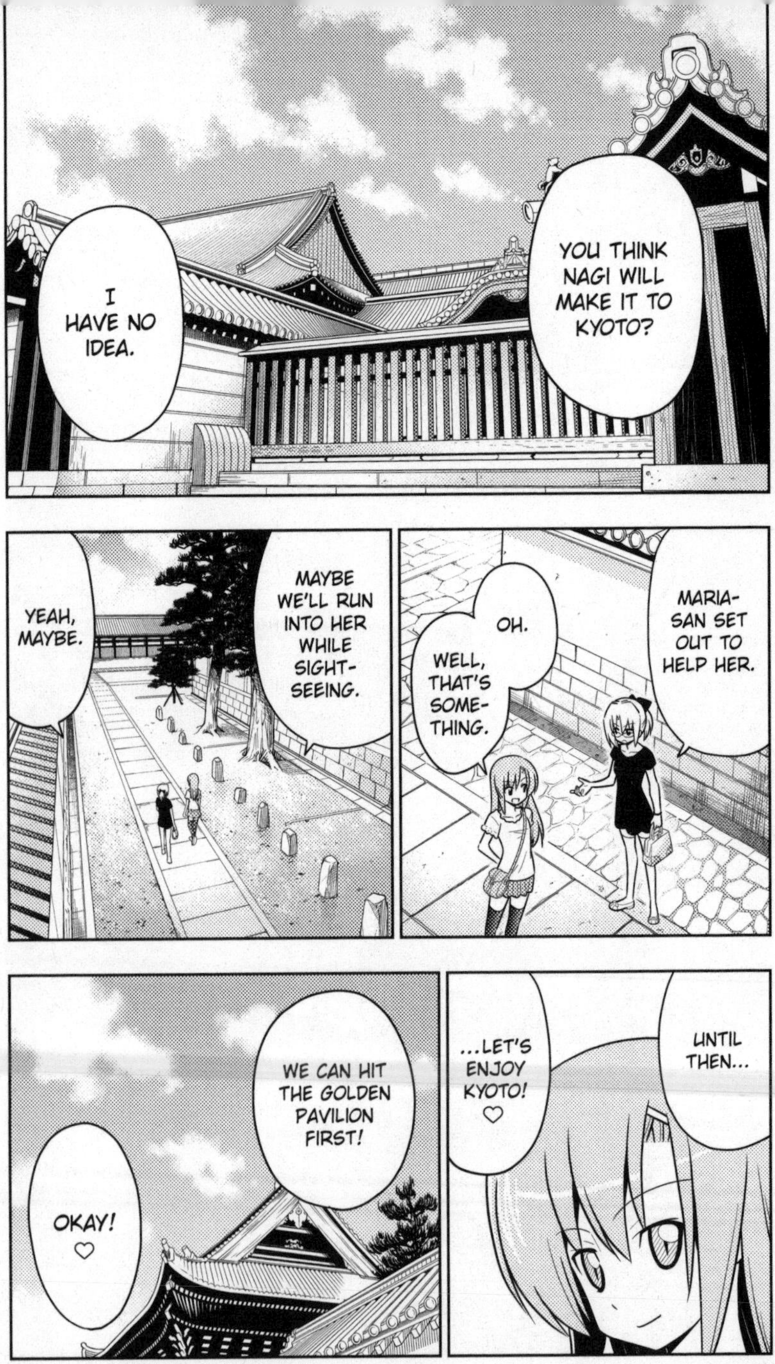
YOU THINK NAGI WILL MAKE IT TO KYOTO?
I HAVE NO IDEA.
MARIA-SAN SET OUT TO HELP HER.
OH.
WELL, THAT'S SOME-THING.
MAYBE WE'LL RUN INTO HER WHILE SIGHT-SEEING.
YEAH, MAYBE.
UNTIL THEN...
...LET'S ENJOY KYOTO! ♡
WE CAN HIT THE GOLDEN PAVILION FIRST!
OKAY! ♡

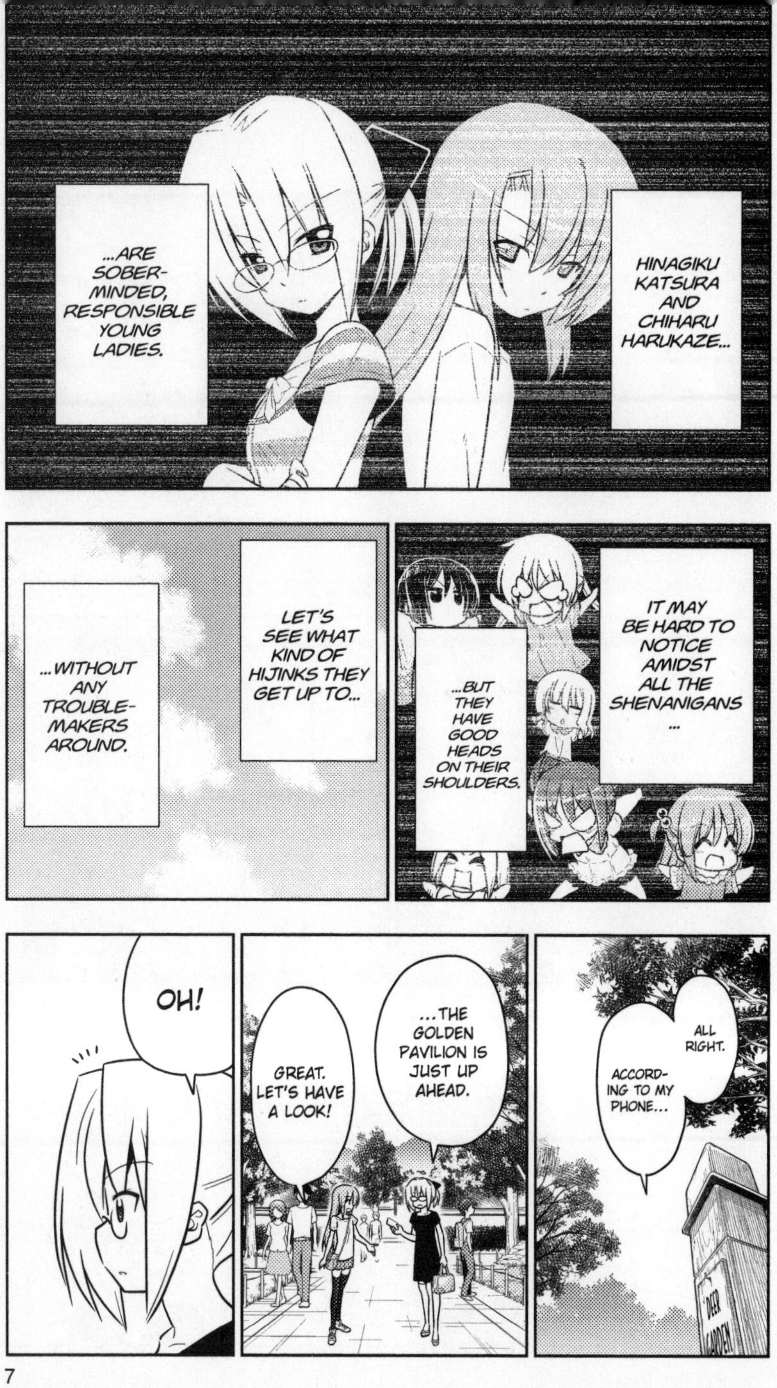
HINAGIKU KATSURA AND CHIHARU HARUKAZE...
...ARE SOBER-MINDED, RESPONSIBLE YOUNG LADIES.
IT MAY BE HARD TO NOTICE AMIDST ALL THE SHENANIGANS...
...BUT THEY HAVE GOOD HEADS ON THEIR SHOULDERS.
LET'S SEE WHAT KIND OF HIJINKS THEY GET UP TO...
...WITHOUT ANY TROUBLE-MAKERS AROUND.
ALL RIGHT.
ACCORDING TO MY PHONE...
DEER GARDEN
...THE GOLDEN PAVILION IS JUST UP AHEAD.
GREAT. LET'S HAVE A LOOK!
OH!

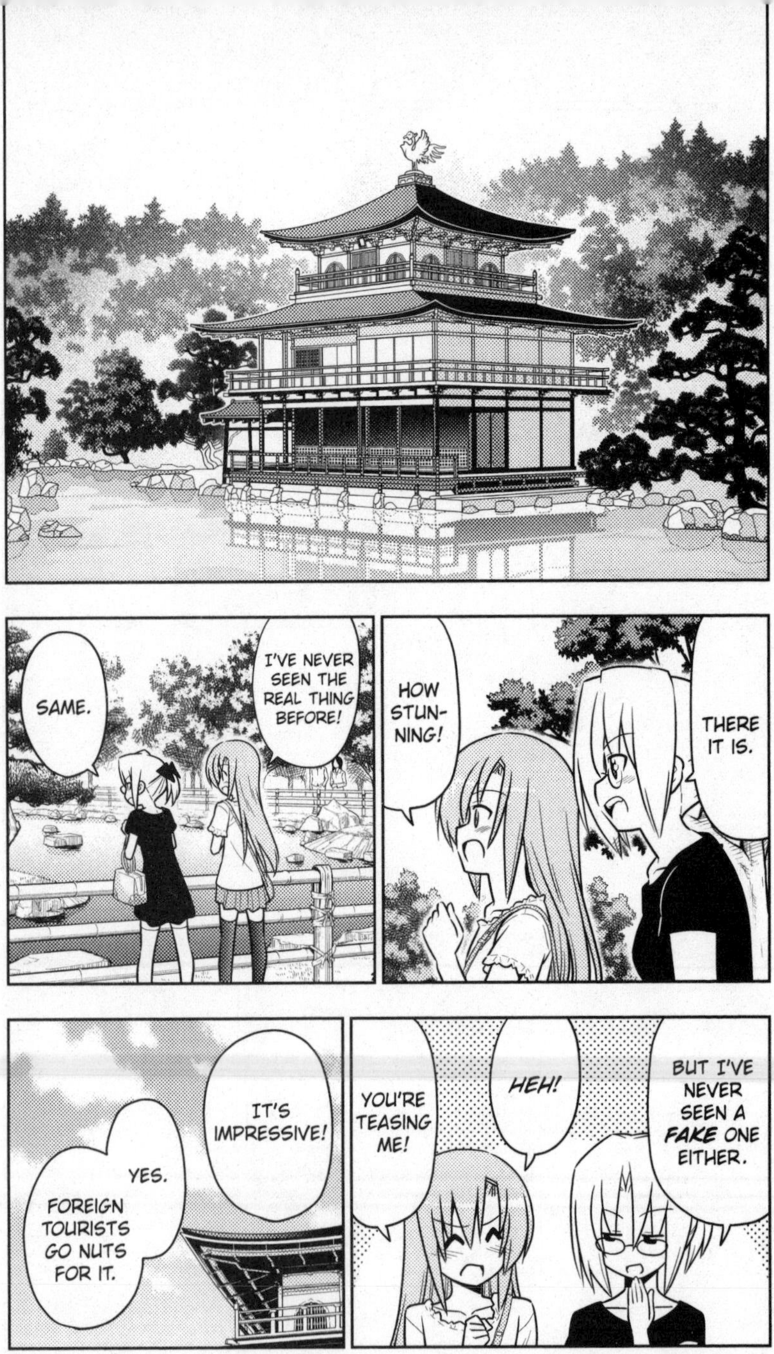
THERE IT IS.
HOW STUN-NING!
I'VE NEVER SEEN THE REAL THING BEFORE!
SAME.
BUT I'VE NEVER SEEN A **FAKE** ONE EITHER.
HEH!
YOU'RE TEASING ME!
IT'S IMPRESSIVE!
YES. FOREIGN TOURISTS GO NUTS FOR IT.

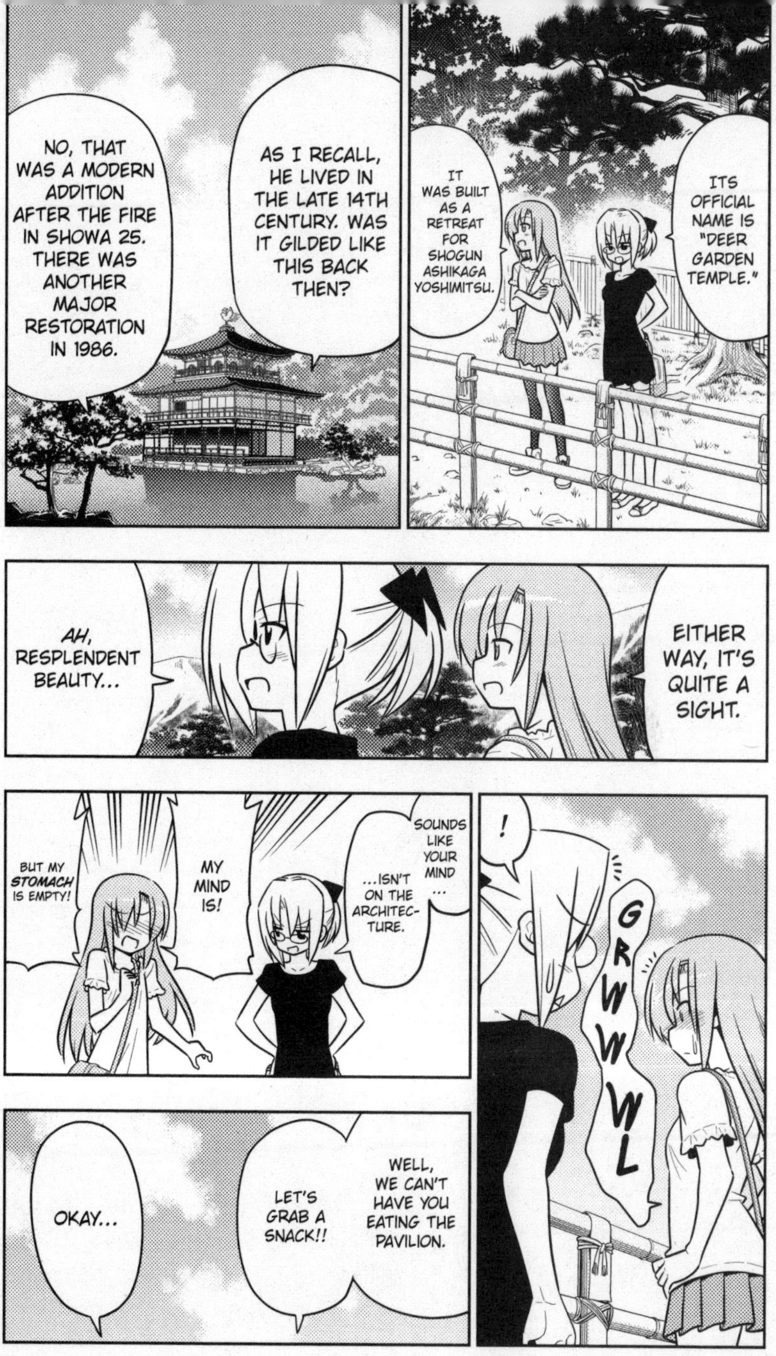
ITS OFFICIAL NAME IS "DEER GARDEN TEMPLE."
IT WAS BUILT AS A RETREAT FOR SHOGUN ASHIKAGA YOSHIMITSU.
AS I RECALL, HE LIVED IN THE LATE 14TH CENTURY. WAS IT GILDED LIKE THIS BACK THEN?
NO, THAT WAS A MODERN ADDITION AFTER THE FIRE IN SHOWA 25. THERE WAS ANOTHER MAJOR RESTORATION IN 1986.
EITHER WAY, IT'S QUITE A SIGHT.
AH, RESPLENDENT BEAUTY...
!
GRWWWL
SOUNDS LIKE YOUR MIND ...
...ISN'T ON THE ARCHITECTURE.
MY MIND IS!
BUT MY *STOMACH* IS EMPTY!
WELL, WE CAN'T HAVE YOU EATING THE PAVILION.
LET'S GRAB A SNACK!!
OKAY...

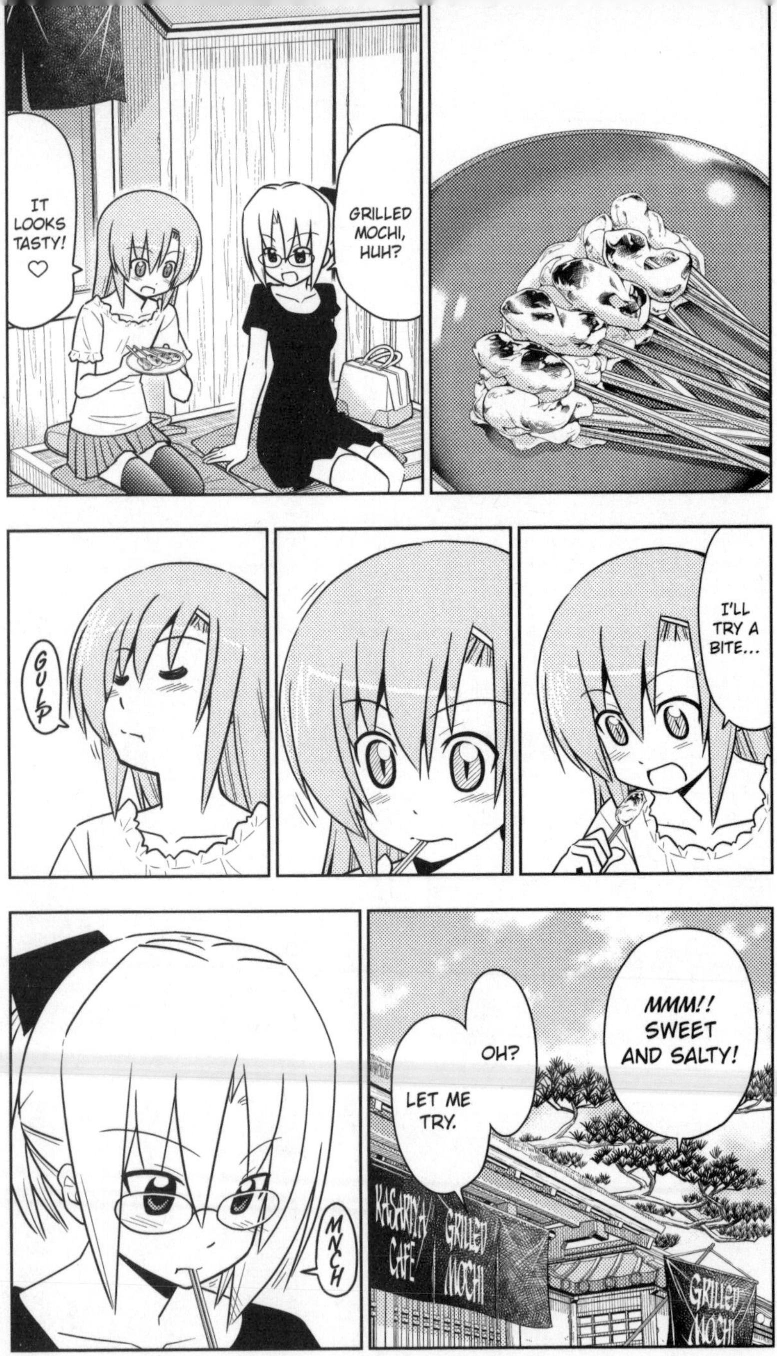
GRILLED MOCHI, HUH?
IT LOOKS TASTY! ♡
I'LL TRY A BITE...
GULP
MMM!! SWEET AND SALTY!
OH? LET ME TRY.
KASARIYA CAFE
GRILLED MOCHI
GRILLED MOCHI
MNCH

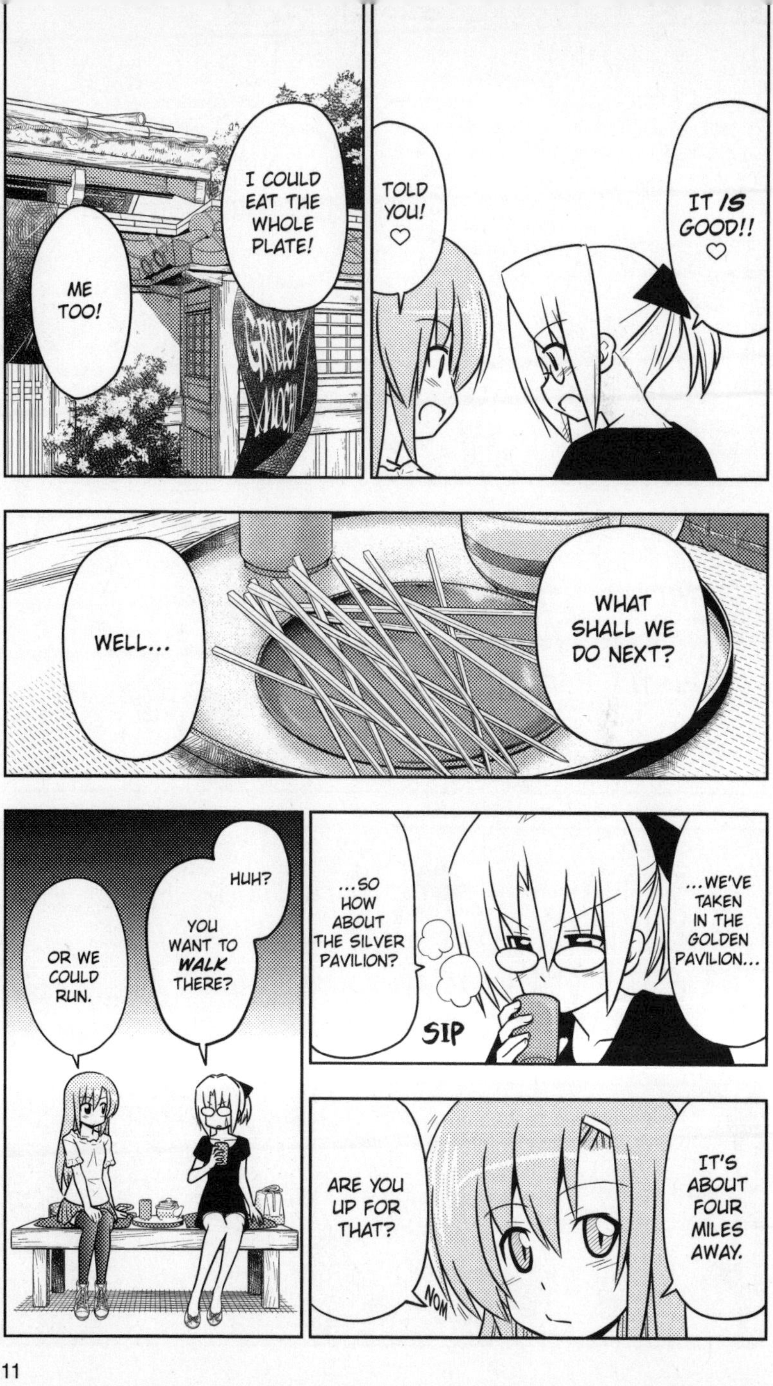
IT *IS* GOOD!! ♡
TOLD YOU! ♡
I COULD EAT THE WHOLE PLATE!
ME TOO!
GRILLED MOCHI
WHAT SHALL WE DO NEXT?
WELL...
...WE'VE TAKEN IN THE GOLDEN PAVILION...
...SO HOW ABOUT THE SILVER PAVILION?
SIP
IT'S ABOUT FOUR MILES AWAY.
ARE YOU UP FOR THAT?
NOM
HUH?
YOU WANT TO ***WALK*** THERE?
OR WE COULD RUN.

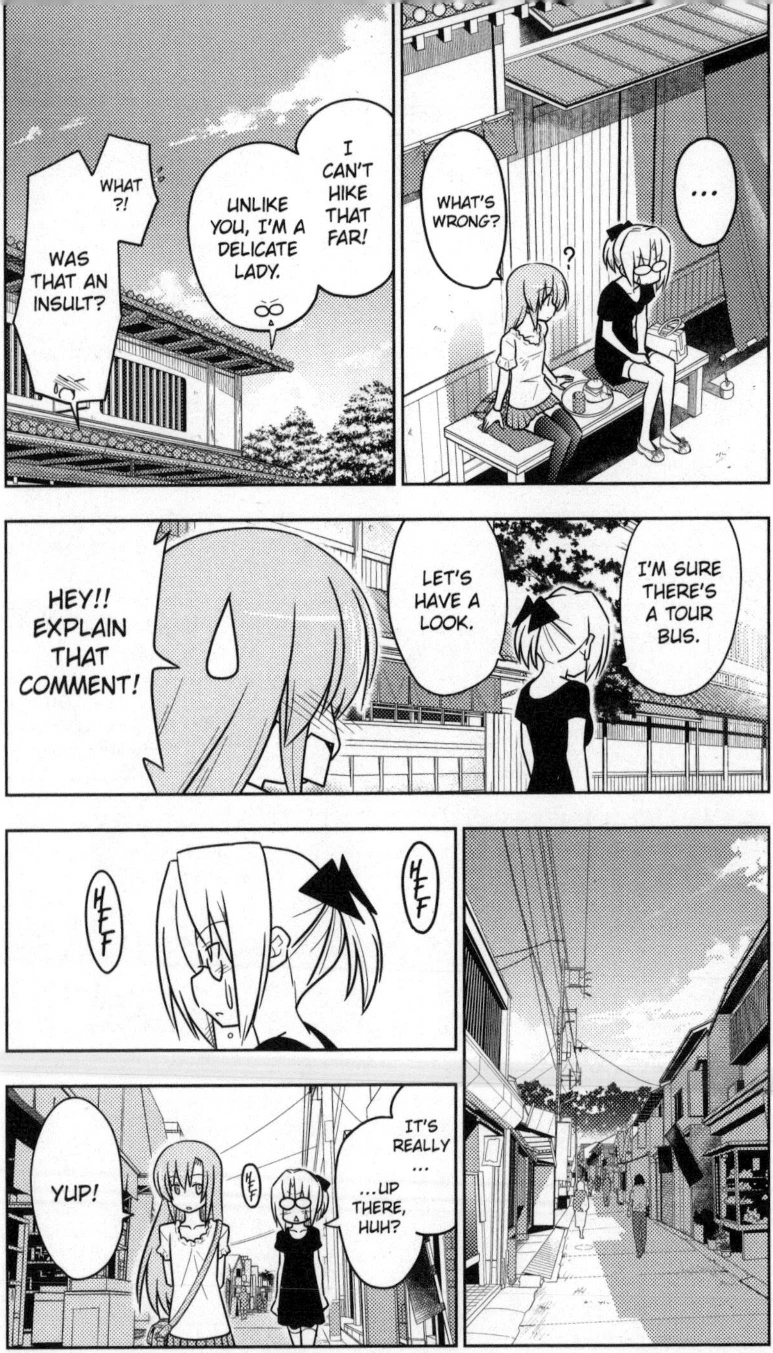
...
WHAT'S WRONG?
?
I CAN'T HIKE THAT FAR!
UNLIKE YOU, I'M A DELICATE LADY.
WHAT ?!
WAS THAT AN INSULT?
I'M SURE THERE'S A TOUR BUS.
LET'S HAVE A LOOK.
HEY!! EXPLAIN THAT COMMENT!
HEF
HEF
IT'S REALLY ...
...UP THERE, HUH?
HEF
YUP!

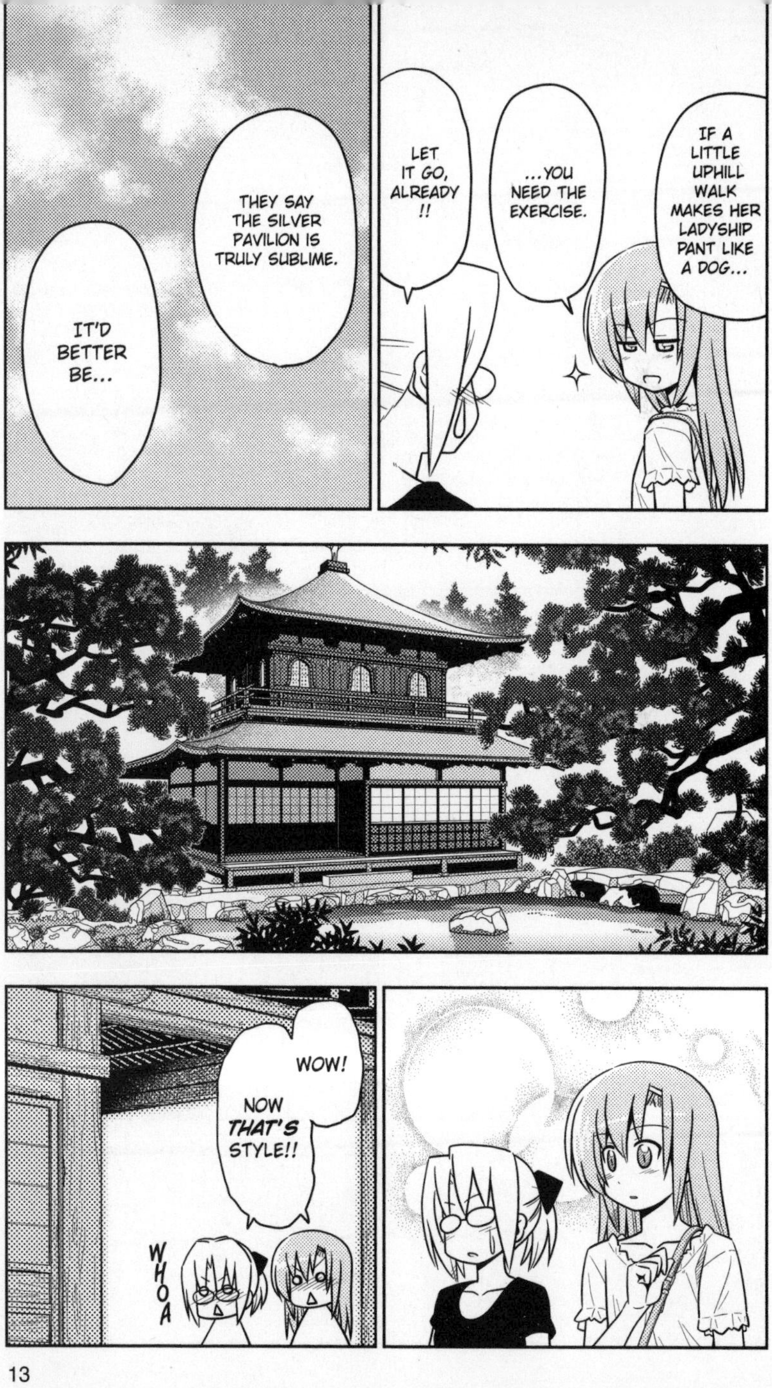
IF A LITTLE UPHILL WALK MAKES HER LADYSHIP PANT LIKE A DOG...
...YOU NEED THE EXERCISE.
LET IT GO, ALREADY !!
THEY SAY THE SILVER PAVILION IS TRULY SUBLIME.
IT'D BETTER BE...
WOW!
NOW *THAT'S* STYLE!!
WHOA

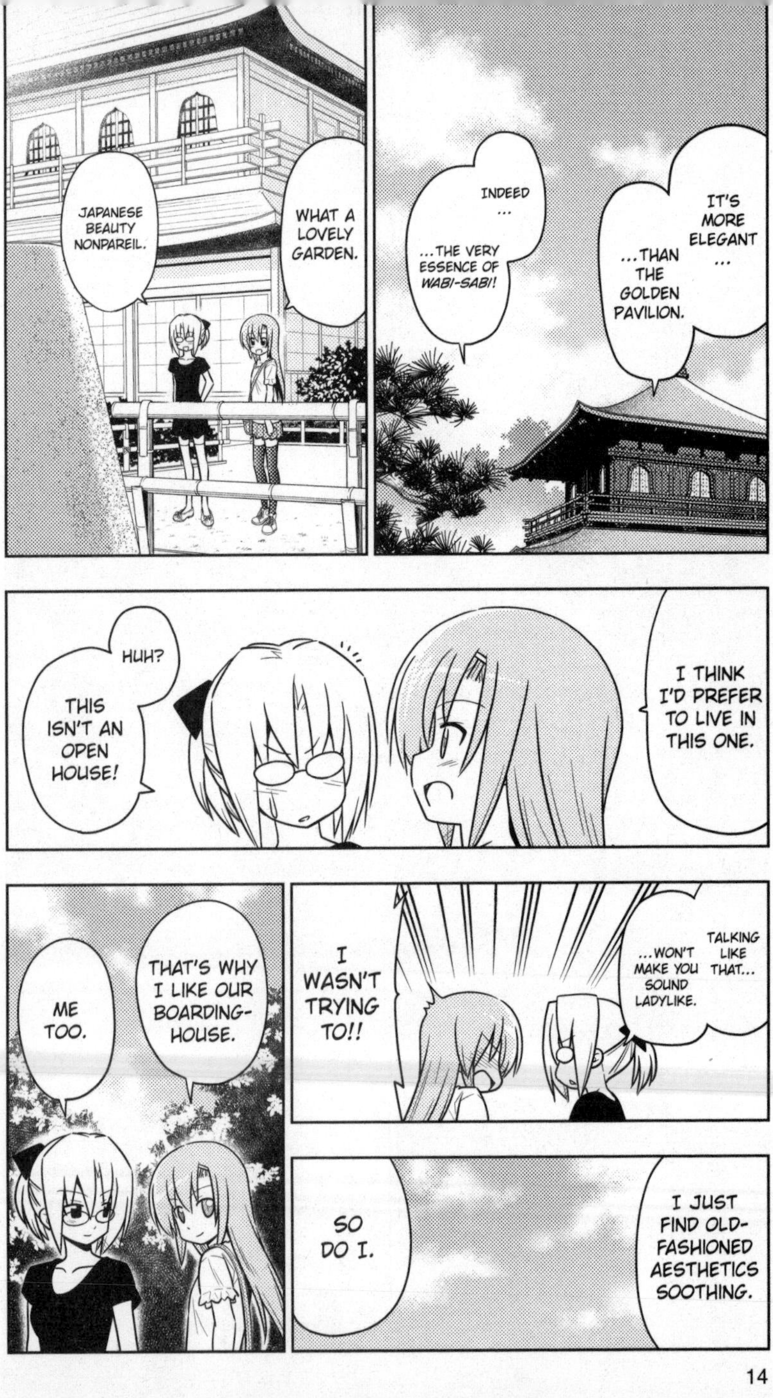
IT'S MORE ELEGANT...
...THAN THE GOLDEN PAVILION.
INDEED...
...THE VERY ESSENCE OF *WABI-SABI*!
WHAT A LOVELY GARDEN.
JAPANESE BEAUTY NONPAREIL.
I THINK I'D PREFER TO LIVE IN THIS ONE.
HUH?
THIS ISN'T AN OPEN HOUSE!
TALKING LIKE THAT...
...WON'T MAKE YOU SOUND LADYLIKE.
I WASN'T TRYING TO!!
I JUST FIND OLD-FASHIONED AESTHETICS SOOTHING.
SO DO I.
THAT'S WHY I LIKE OUR BOARDING-HOUSE.
ME TOO.

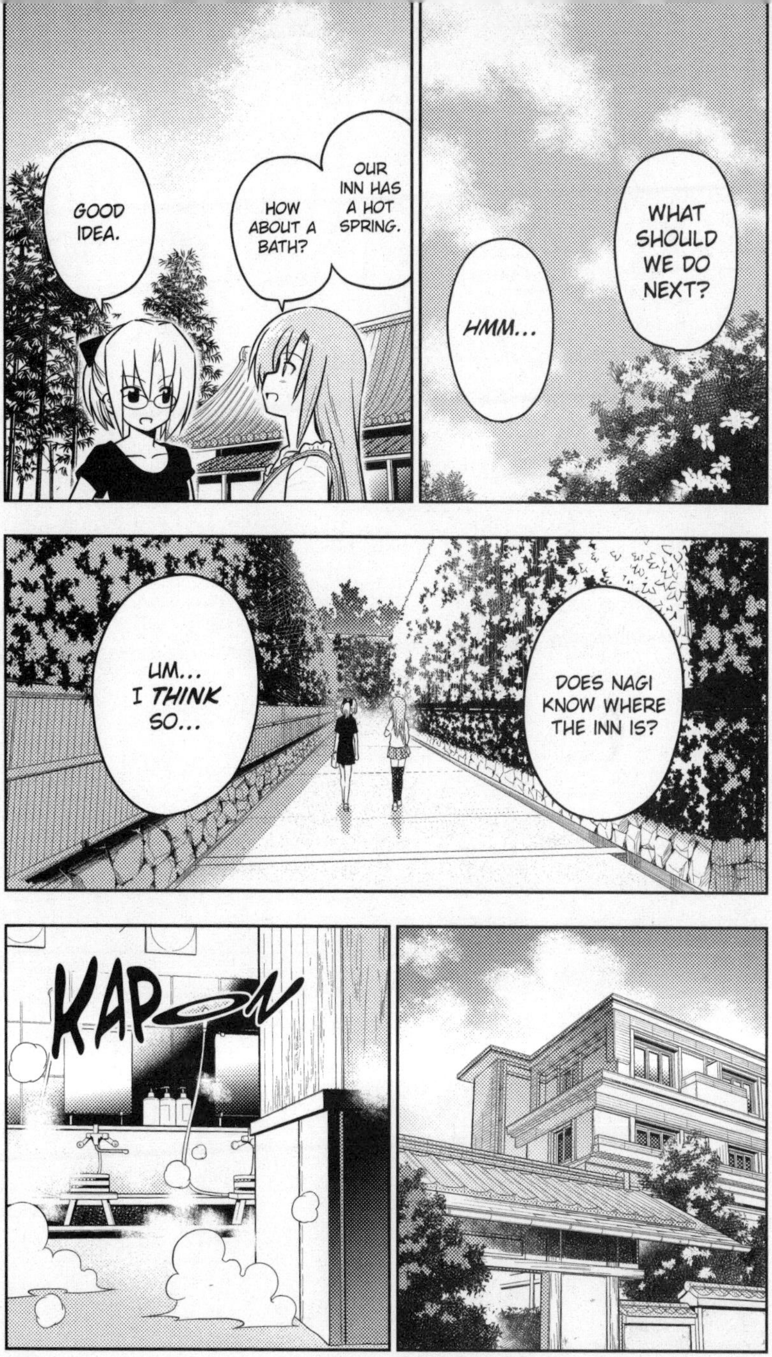
WHAT SHOULD WE DO NEXT?
HMM...
OUR INN HAS A HOT SPRING.
HOW ABOUT A BATH?
GOOD IDEA.
DOES NAGI KNOW WHERE THE INN IS?
UM... I *THINK* SO...
KAPON

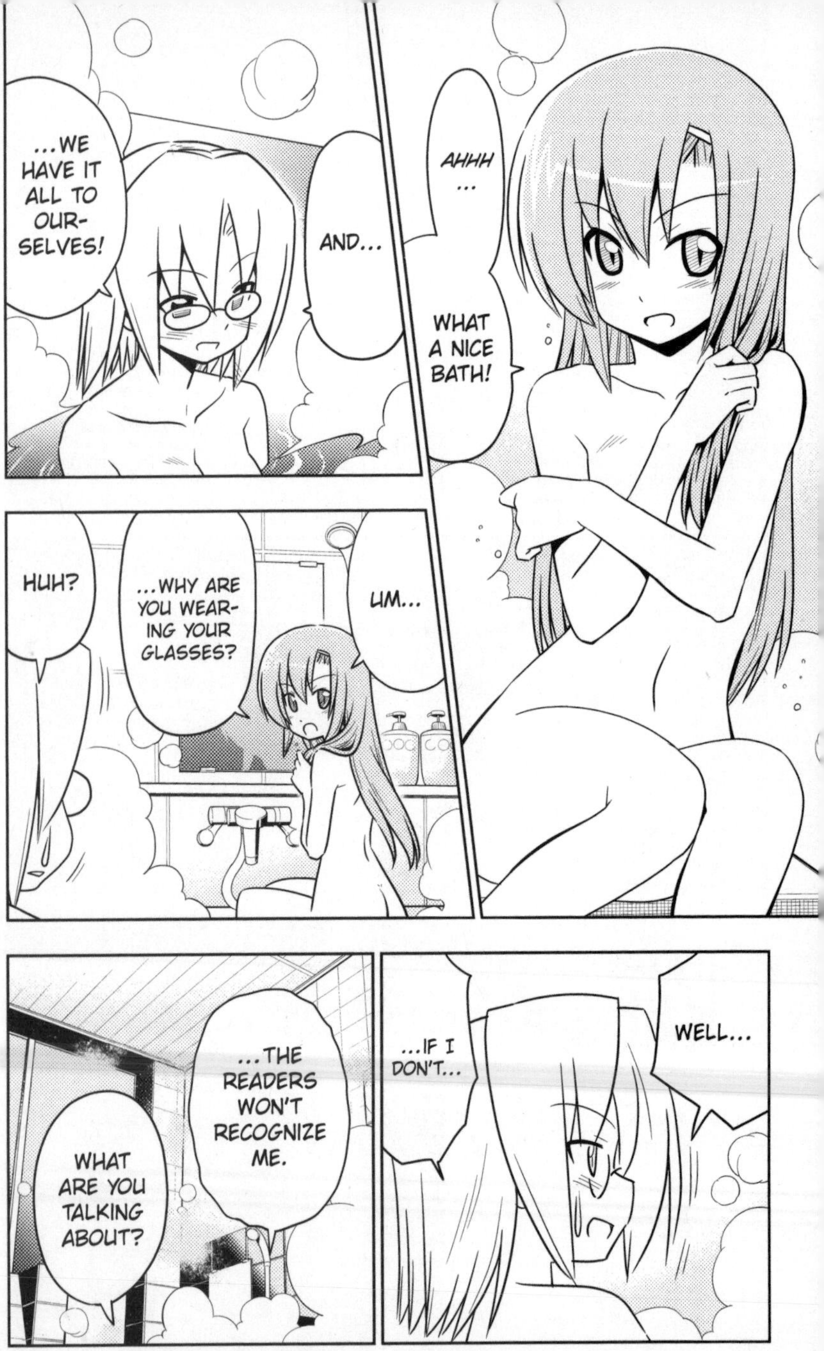
AHHH...
WHAT A NICE BATH!
AND...
...WE HAVE IT ALL TO OURSELVES!
UM...
...WHY ARE YOU WEARING YOUR GLASSES?
HUH?
WELL...
...IF I DON'T...
...THE READERS WON'T RECOGNIZE ME.
WHAT ARE YOU TALKING ABOUT?

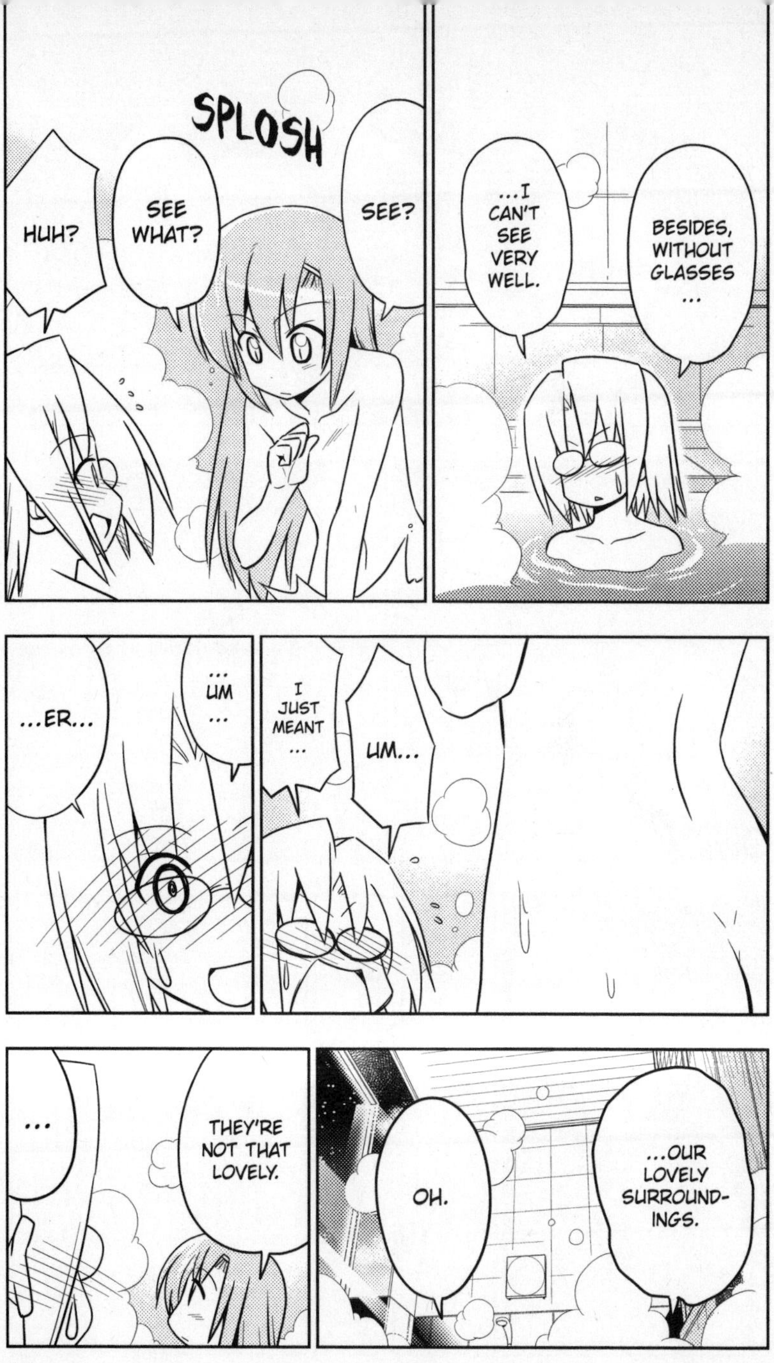
BESIDES, WITHOUT GLASSES ...
...I CAN'T SEE VERY WELL.
SEE?
SPLOSH
SEE WHAT?
HUH?
UM...
I JUST MEANT ...
... UM ...
...ER...
...OUR LOVELY SURROUND-INGS.
OH.
THEY'RE NOT THAT LOVELY.
...

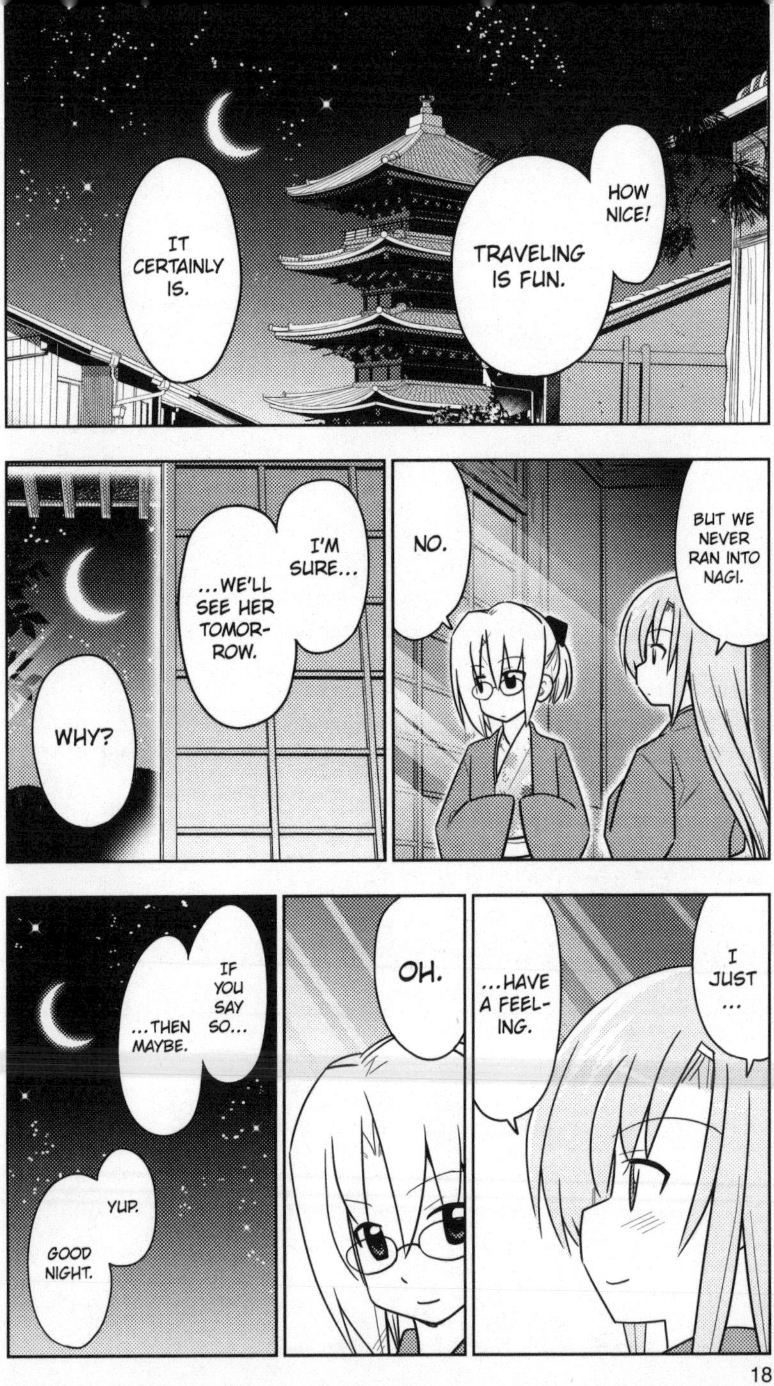
HOW NICE!
TRAVELING IS FUN.
IT CERTAINLY IS.
BUT WE NEVER RAN INTO NAGI.
NO.
I'M SURE...
...WE'LL SEE HER TOMOR-ROW.
WHY?
I JUST ...
...HAVE A FEEL-ING.
OH.
IF YOU SAY SO...
...THEN MAYBE.
YUP.
GOOD NIGHT.

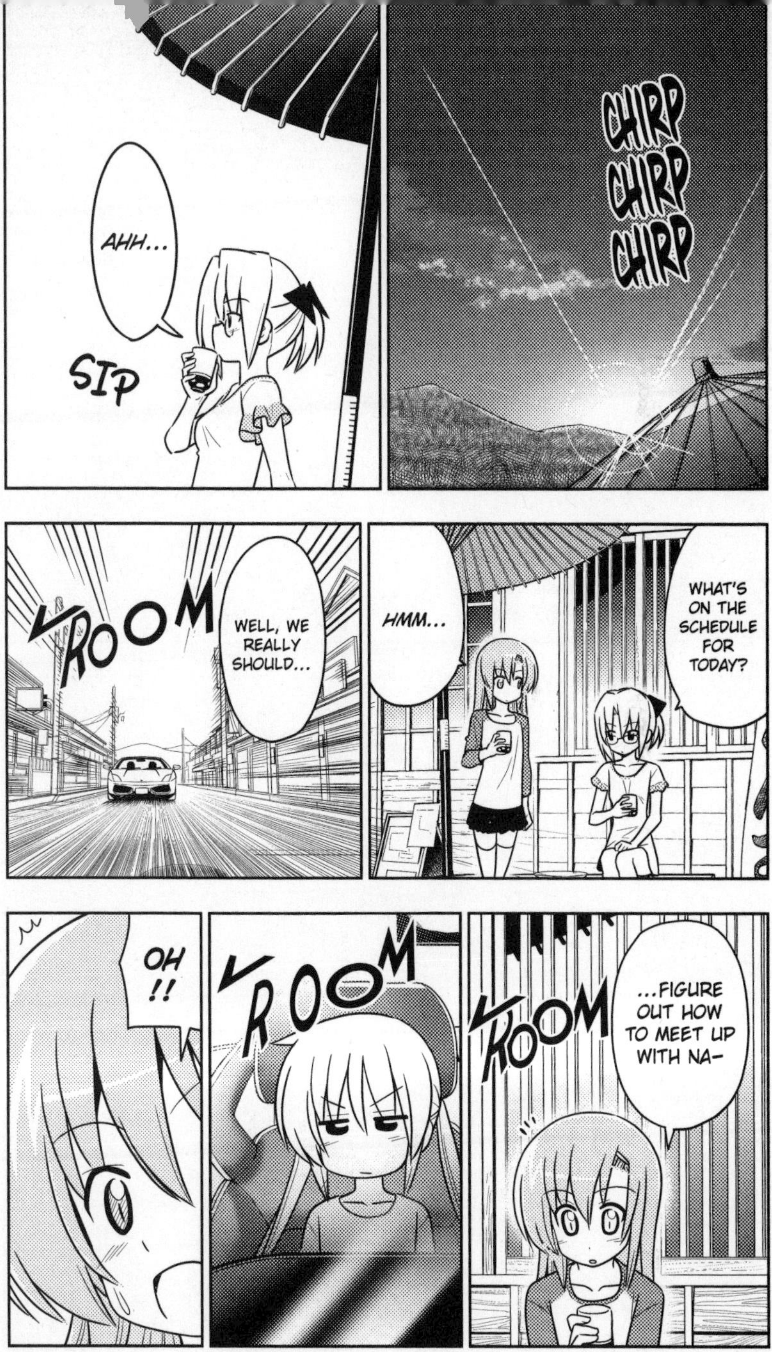
CHIRP
CHIRP
CHIRP
AHH...
SIP
WHAT'S ON THE SCHEDULE FOR TODAY?
HMM...
WELL, WE REALLY SHOULD...
VROOM
...FIGURE OUT HOW TO MEET UP WITH NA-
VROOM
VROOOM
OH!!

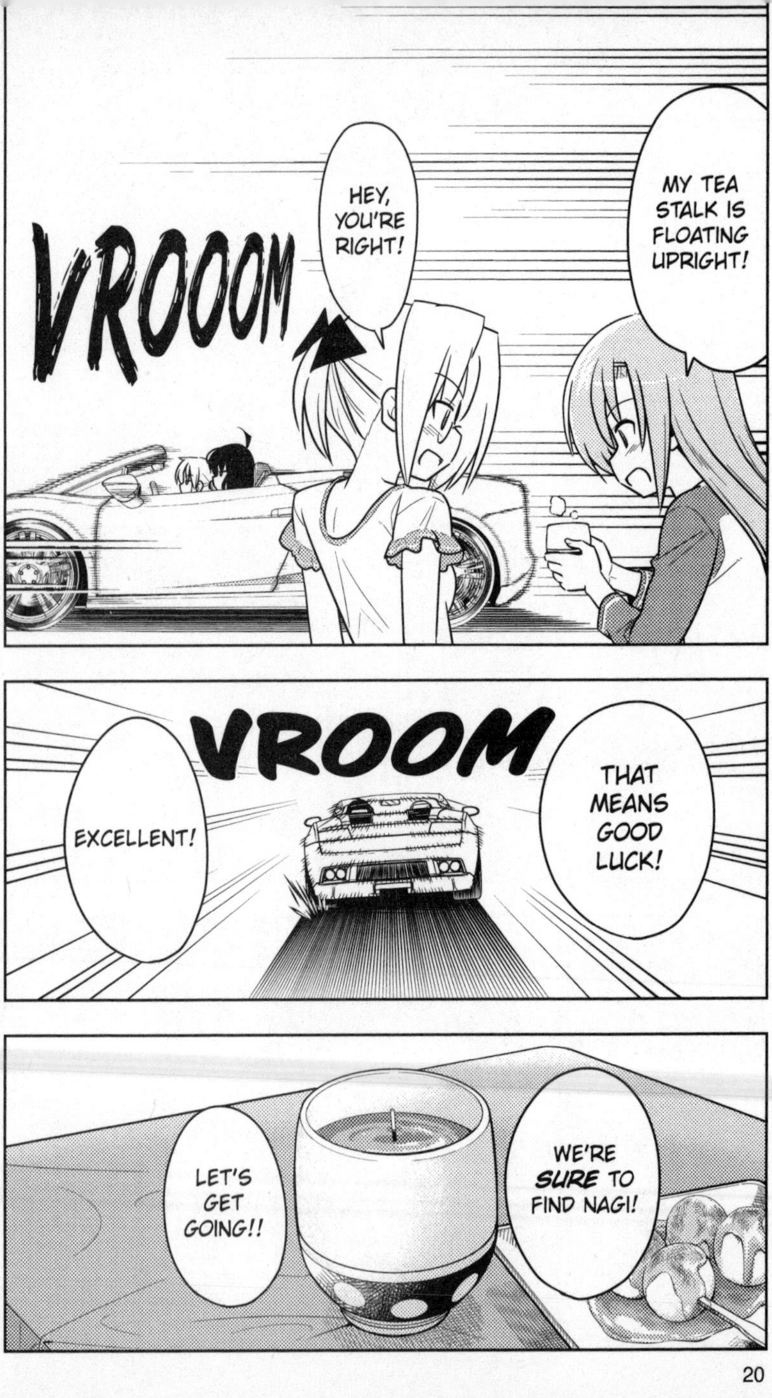
MY TEA STALK IS FLOATING UPRIGHT!
HEY, YOU'RE RIGHT!
VROOOM
THAT MEANS GOOD LUCK!
VROOM
EXCELLENT!
WE'RE SURE TO FIND NAGI!
LET'S GET GOING!!

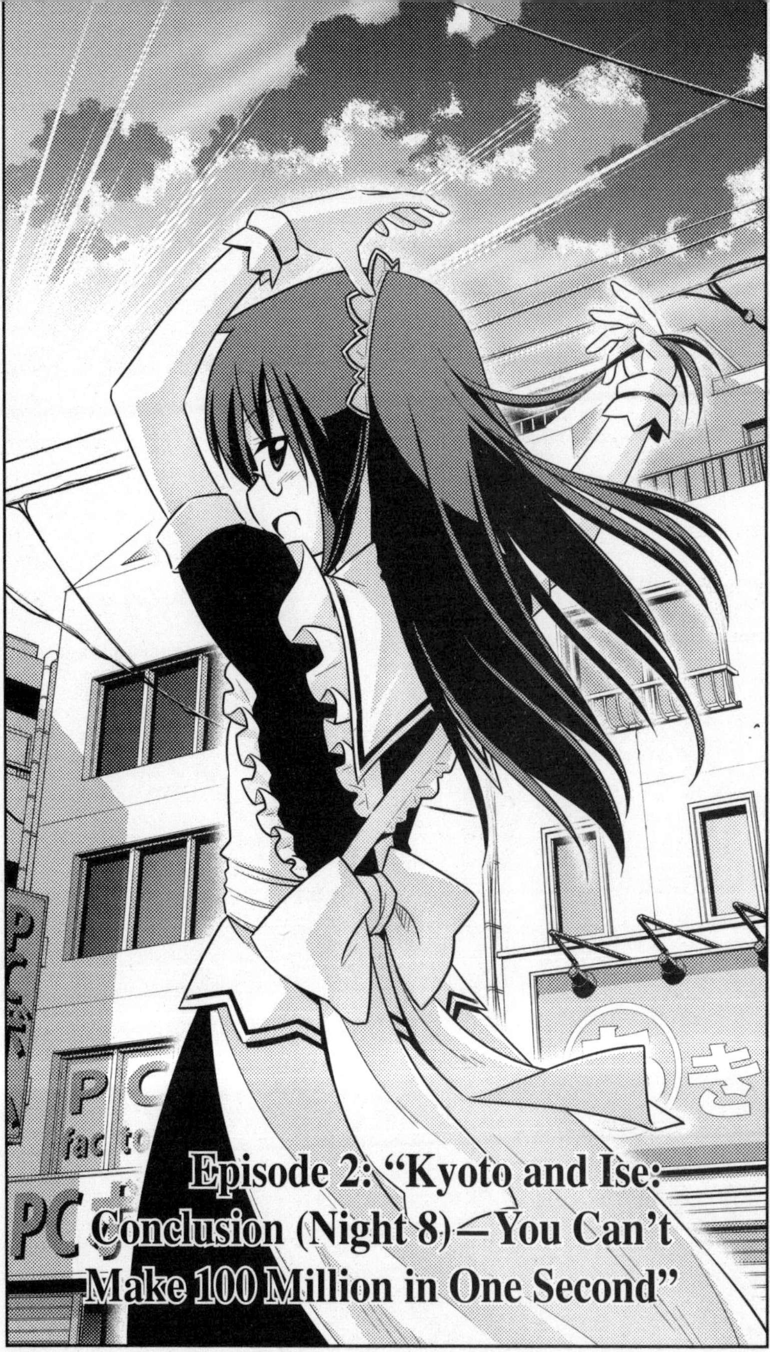

Episode 2: "Kyoto and Ise: Conclusion (Night 8)—You Can't Make 100 Million in One Second"

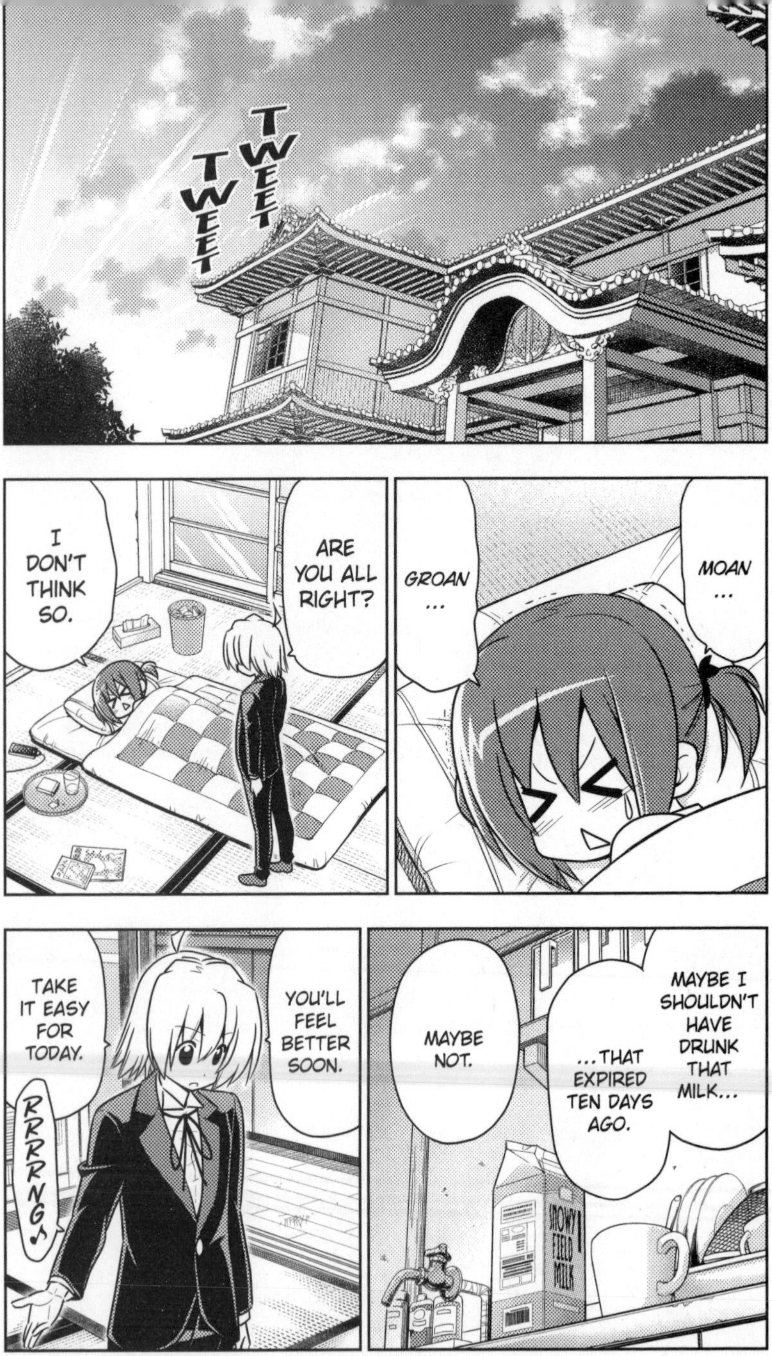
TWEET
TWEET
MOAN...
GROAN...
ARE YOU ALL RIGHT?
I DON'T THINK SO.
MAYBE I SHOULDN'T HAVE DRUNK THAT MILK...
...THAT EXPIRED TEN DAYS AGO.
MAYBE NOT.
SNOWY FIELD MILK
YOU'LL FEEL BETTER SOON.
TAKE IT EASY FOR TODAY.
RRRRNG♪

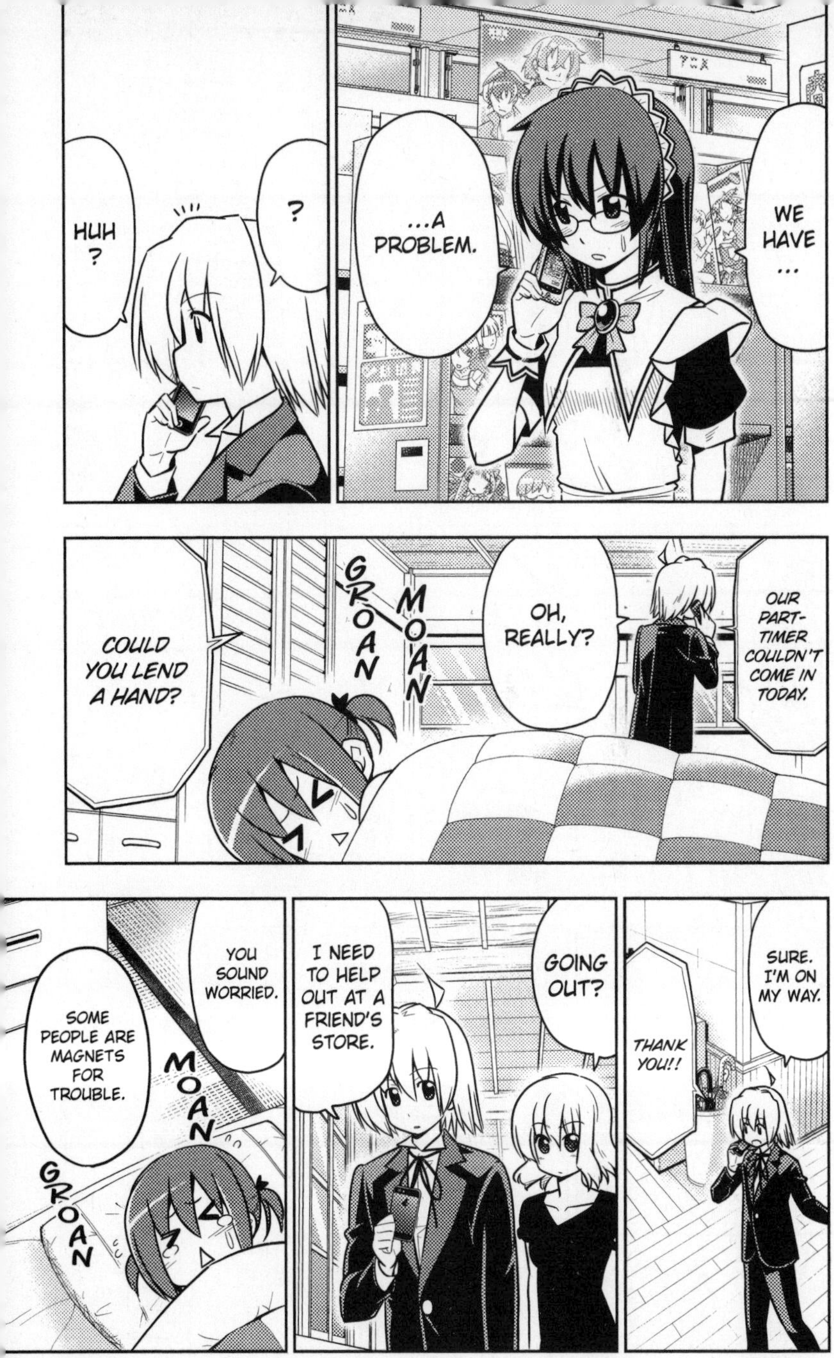
WE HAVE...
...A PROBLEM.
?
HUH?
OUR PART-TIMER COULDN'T COME IN TODAY.
OH, REALLY?
MOAN
GROAN
COULD YOU LEND A HAND?
SURE. I'M ON MY WAY.
THANK YOU!!
GOING OUT?
I NEED TO HELP OUT AT A FRIEND'S STORE.
YOU SOUND WORRIED.
SOME PEOPLE ARE MAGNETS FOR TROUBLE.
MOAN
GROAN

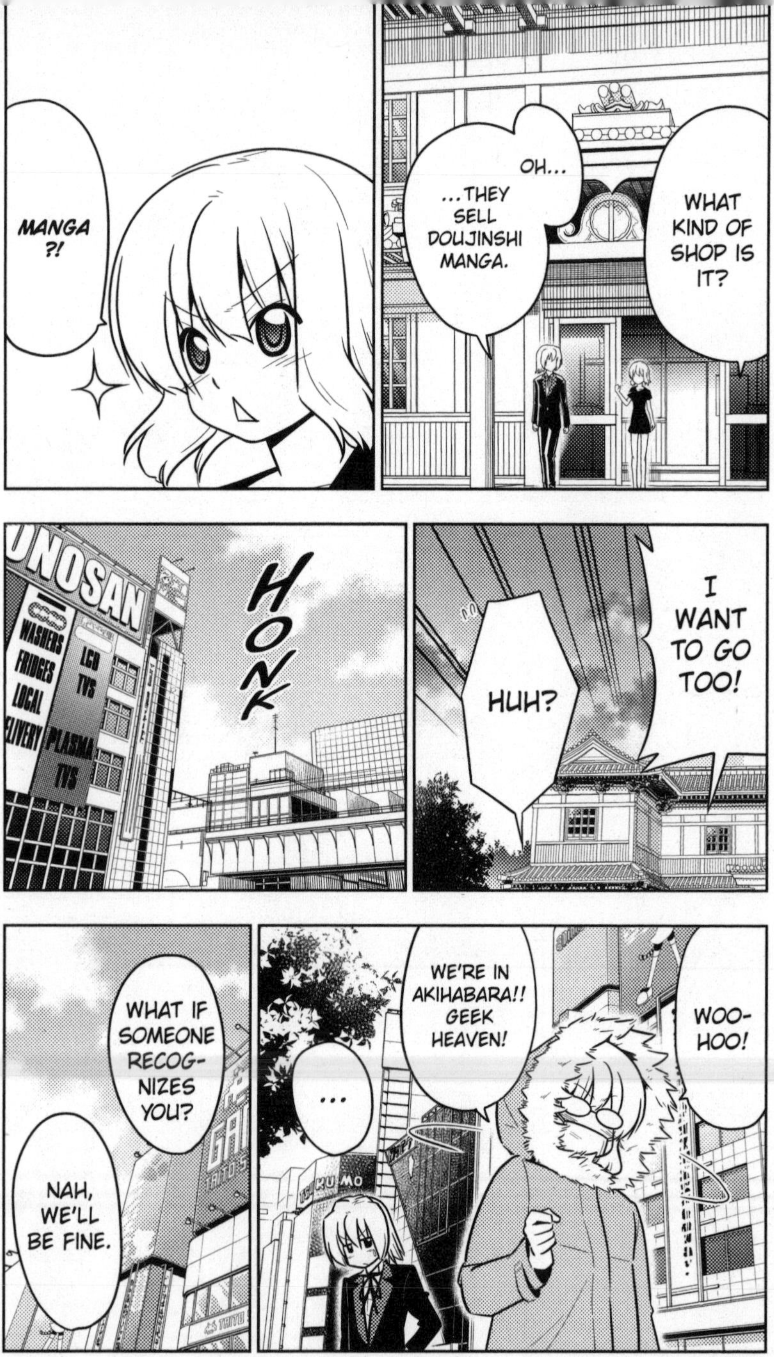
WHAT KIND OF SHOP IS IT?
OH...
...THEY SELL DOUJINSHI MANGA.
MANGA?!
I WANT TO GO TOO!
HUH?
HONK
UNOSAN
WASHERS
FRIDGES
LOCAL
LCD TVS
PLASMA TVS
WOO-HOO!
WE'RE IN AKIHABARA!! GEEK HEAVEN!
...
WHAT IF SOMEONE RECOG-NIZES YOU?
NAH, WE'LL BE FINE.

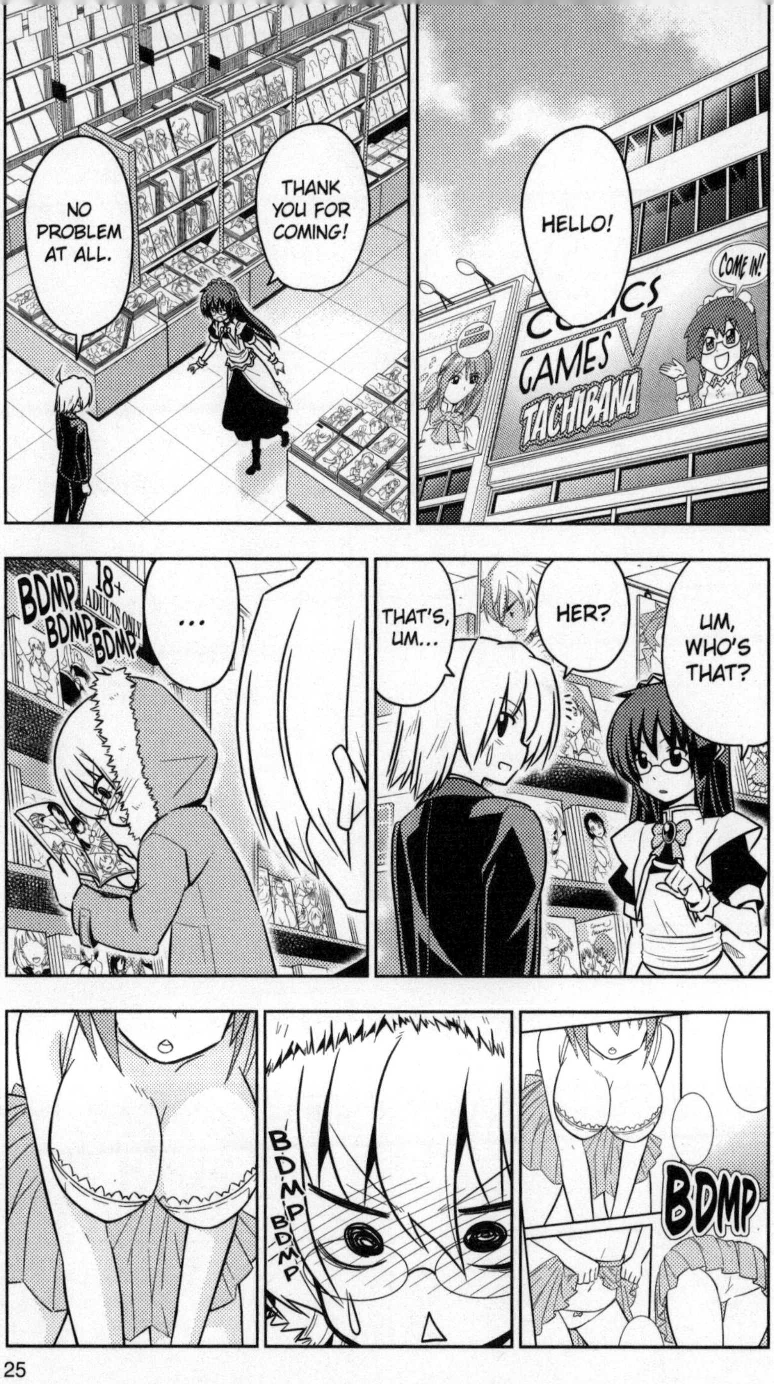
HELLO!
GAMES V
TACHIBANA
COME IN!
THANK YOU FOR COMING!
NO PROBLEM AT ALL.
UM, WHO'S THAT?
HER?
THAT'S, UM...
...
18+ ADULTS ONLY
BDMP BDMP BDMP
BDMP
BDMP BDMP

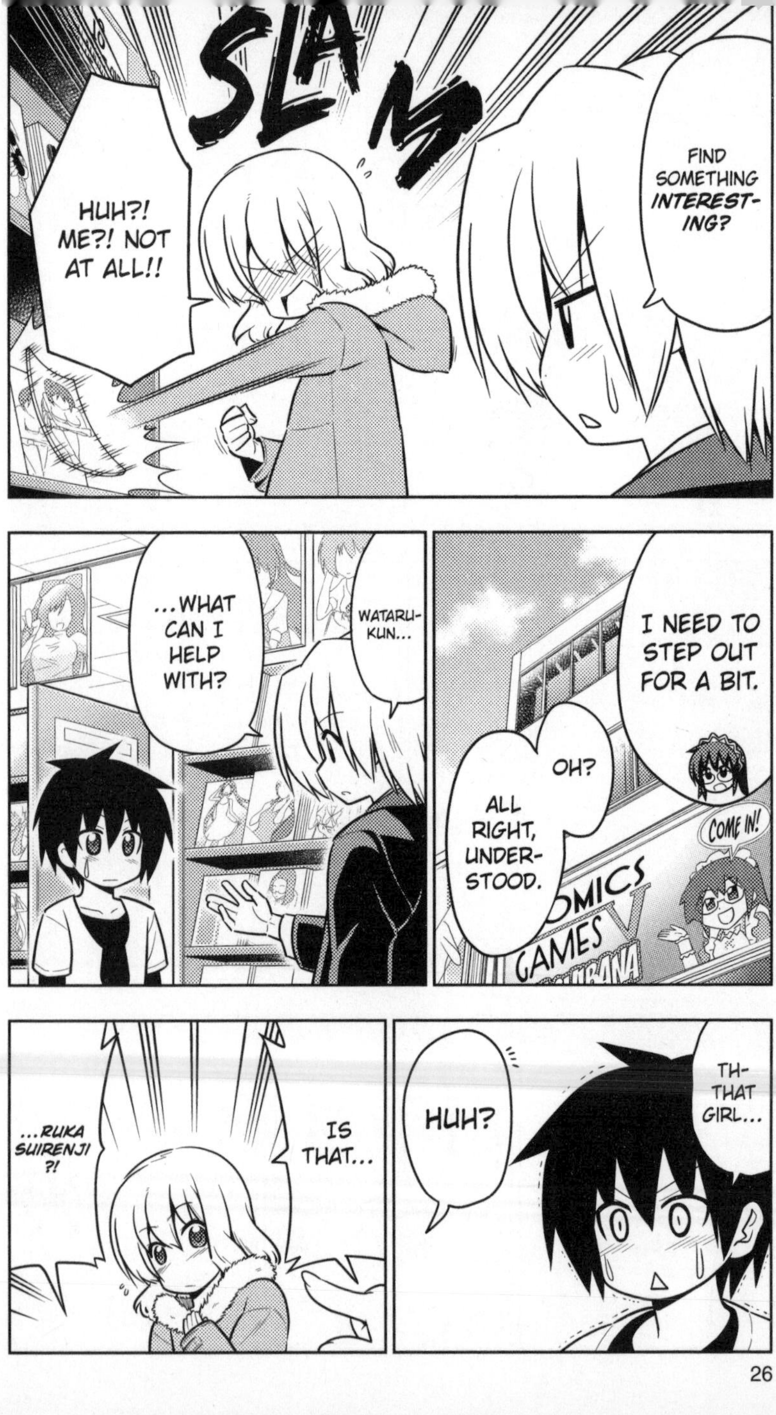
FIND SOMETHING INTERESTING?
SLAM
HUH?! ME?! NOT AT ALL!!
I NEED TO STEP OUT FOR A BIT.
OH? ALL RIGHT, UNDERSTOOD.
COME IN!
COMICS
GAMES
WATARU-KUN...
...WHAT CAN I HELP WITH?
TH- THAT GIRL...
HUH?
IS THAT...
...RUKA SUIRENJI?!

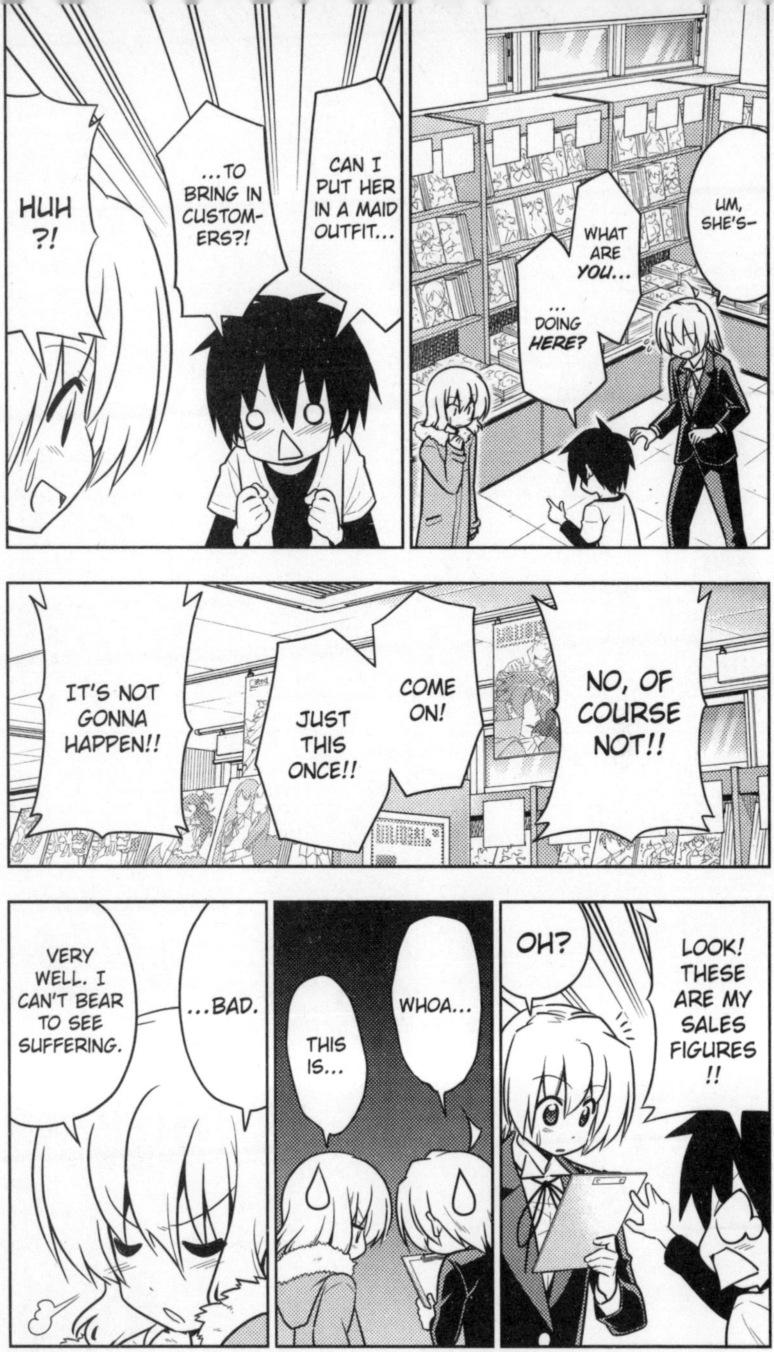
UM, SHE'S-
WHAT ARE *YOU*...
...DOING *HERE*?
CAN I PUT HER IN A MAID OUTFIT...
...TO BRING IN CUSTOM-ERS?!
HUH ?!
NO, OF COURSE NOT!!
COME ON!
JUST THIS ONCE!!
IT'S NOT GONNA HAPPEN!!
LOOK! THESE ARE MY SALES FIGURES !!
OH?
WHOA...
THIS IS...
...BAD.
VERY WELL. I CAN'T BEAR TO SEE SUFFERING.

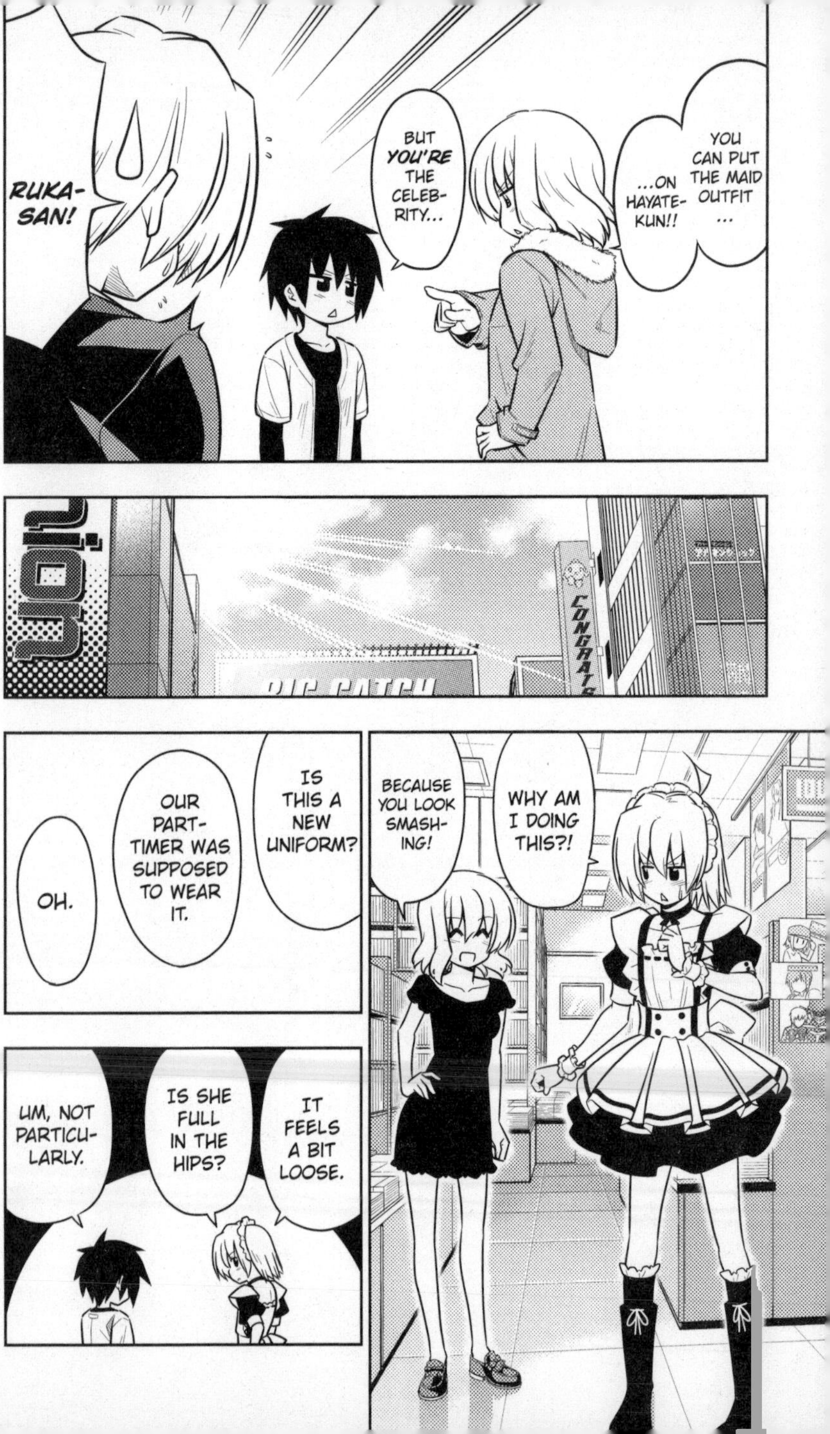
YOU CAN PUT THE MAID OUTFIT ...
...ON HAYATE-KUN!!
BUT *YOU'RE* THE CELEBRITY...
RUKA-SAN!
WHY AM I DOING THIS?!
BECAUSE YOU LOOK SMASHING!
IS THIS A NEW UNIFORM?
OUR PART-TIMER WAS SUPPOSED TO WEAR IT.
OH.
IT FEELS A BIT LOOSE.
IS SHE FULL IN THE HIPS?
UM, NOT PARTICULARLY.

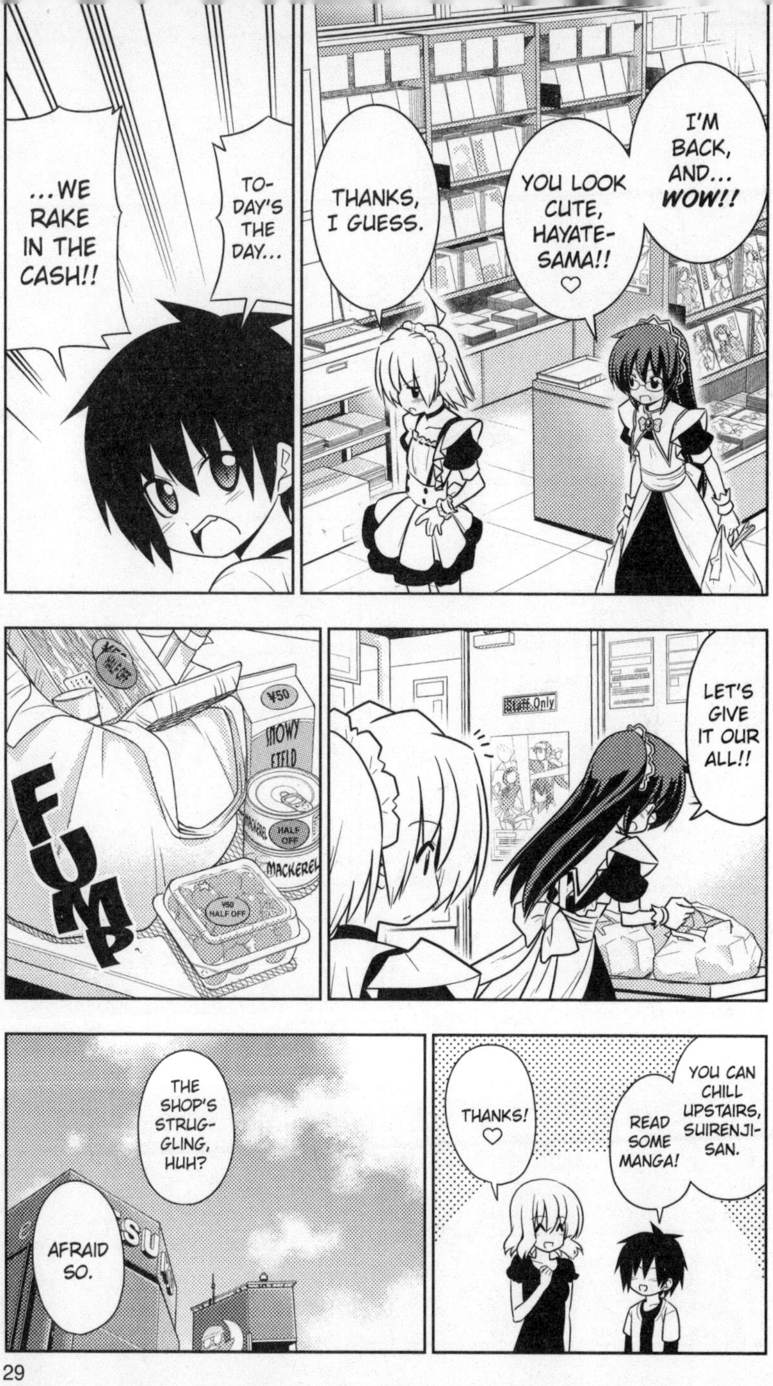
I'M BACK, AND... **WOW!!**
YOU LOOK CUTE, HAYATE-SAMA!! ♡
THANKS, I GUESS.
TO-DAY'S THE DAY...
...WE RAKE IN THE CASH!!
LET'S GIVE IT OUR ALL!!
Staff Only
FUMP
¥50
HALF OFF
MACKEREL
¥50 HALF OFF
YOU CAN CHILL UPSTAIRS, SUIRENJI-SAN.
READ SOME MANGA!
THANKS! ♡
THE SHOP'S STRUG-GLING, HUH?
AFRAID SO.

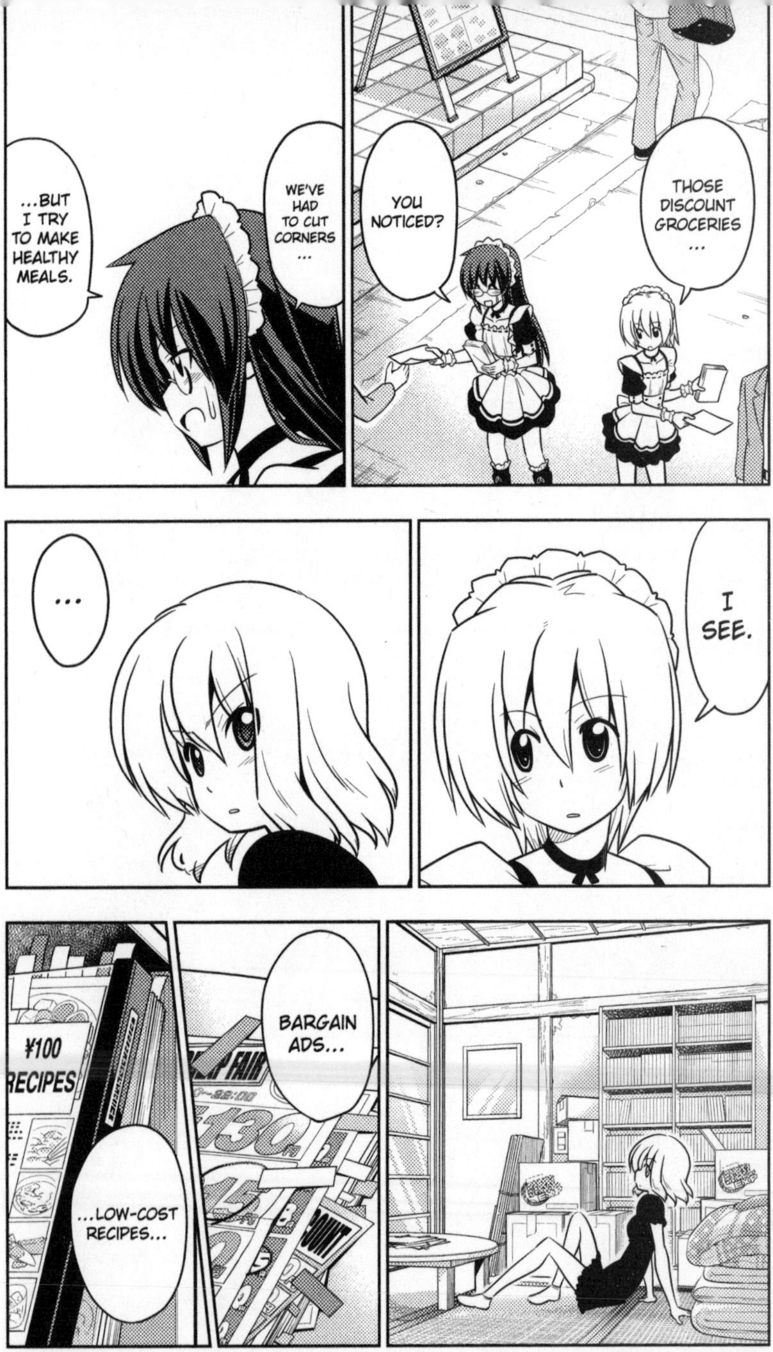
THOSE DISCOUNT GROCERIES ...
YOU NOTICED?
WE'VE HAD TO CUT CORNERS ...
...BUT I TRY TO MAKE HEALTHY MEALS.
I SEE.
...
BARGAIN ADS...
¥100 RECIPES
...LOW-COST RECIPES...

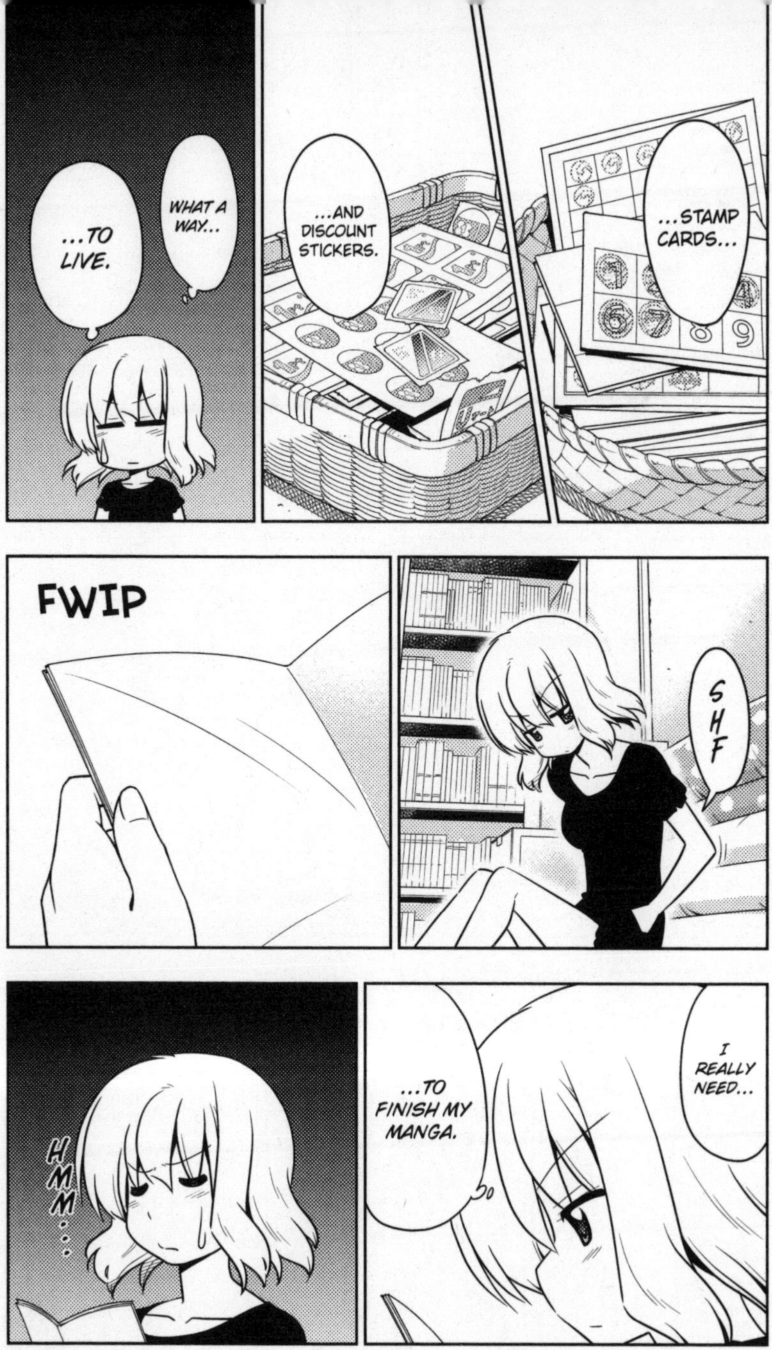
...STAMP CARDS...
...AND DISCOUNT STICKERS.
WHAT A WAY...
...TO LIVE.
SHF
FWIP
I REALLY NEED...
...TO FINISH MY MANGA.
HMM...

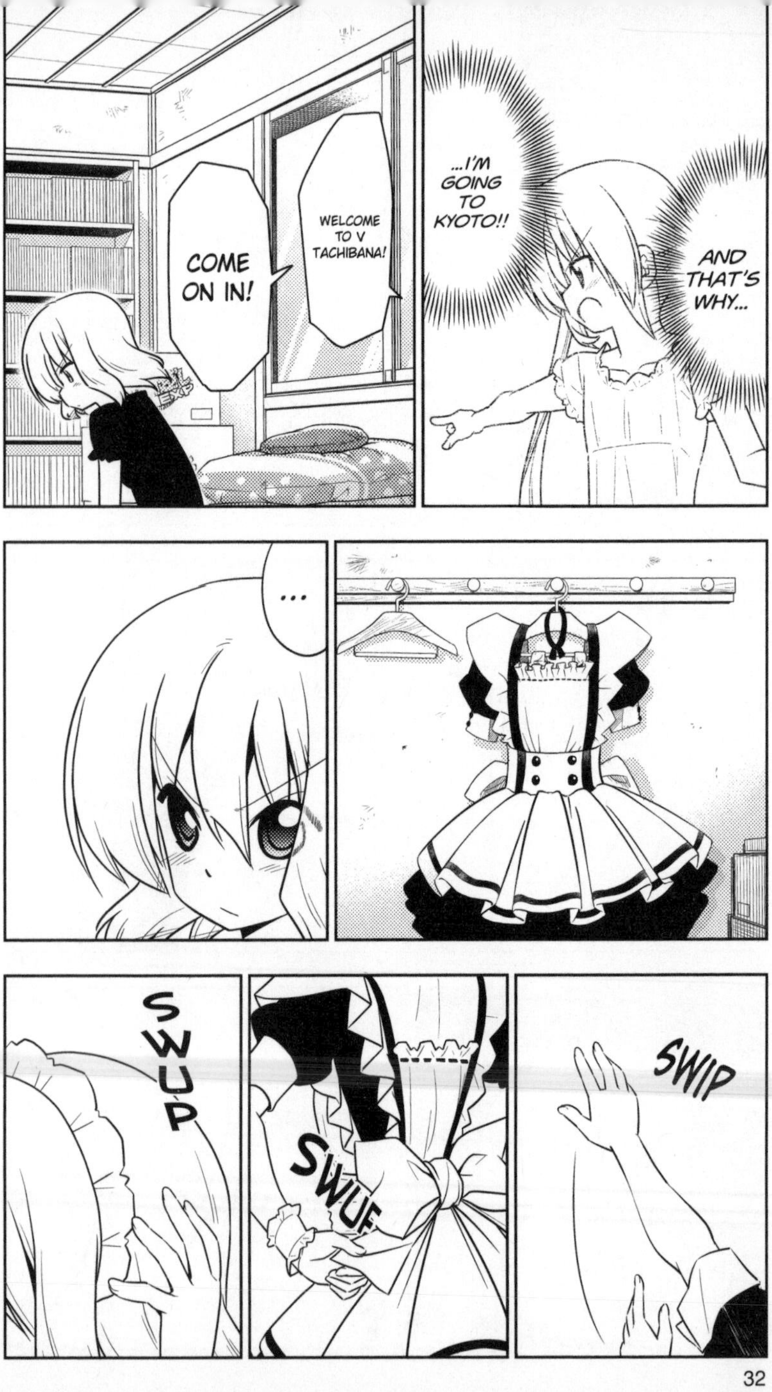
AND THAT'S WHY...
...I'M GOING TO KYOTO!!
WELCOME TO V TACHIBANA!
COME ON IN!
...
SWIP
SWUF
SWUP

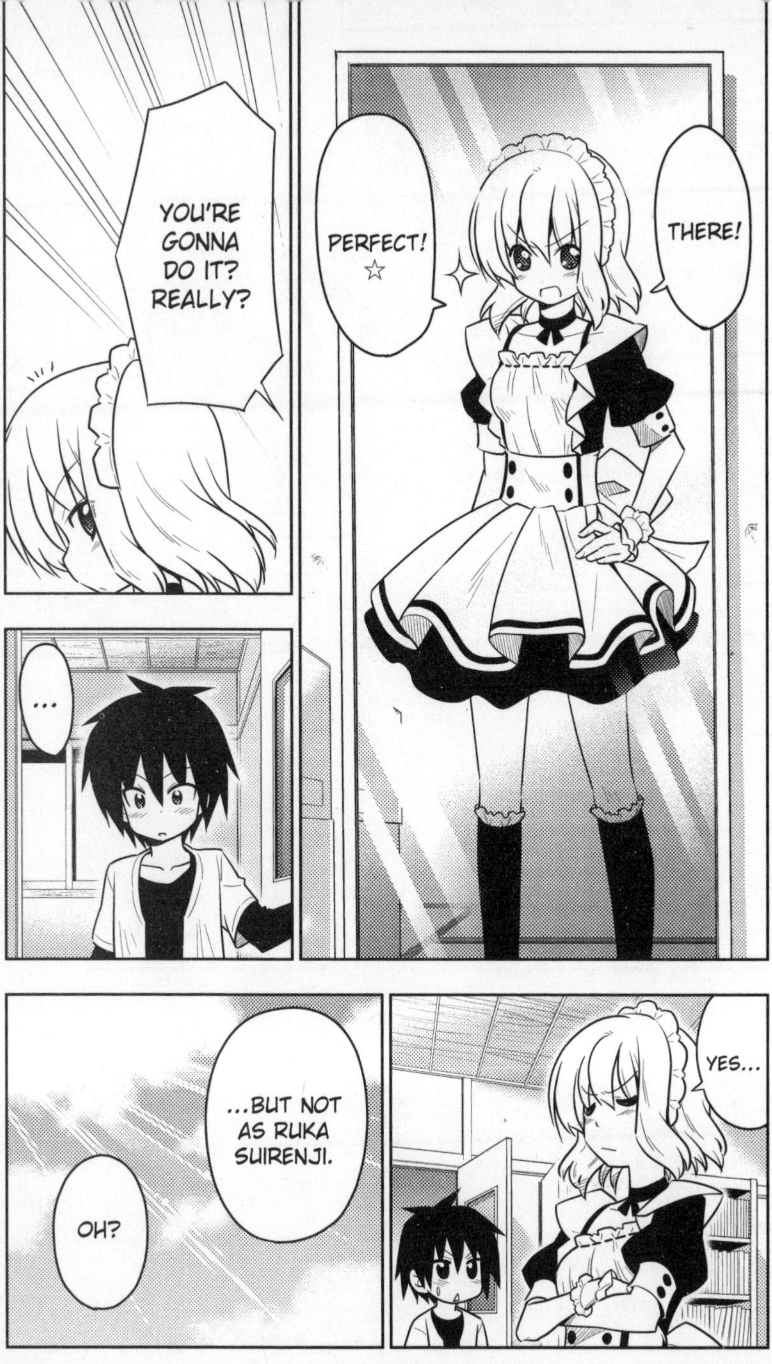
THERE!
PERFECT! ☆
YOU'RE GONNA DO IT? REALLY?
...
YES...
...BUT NOT AS RUKA SUIRENJI.
OH?

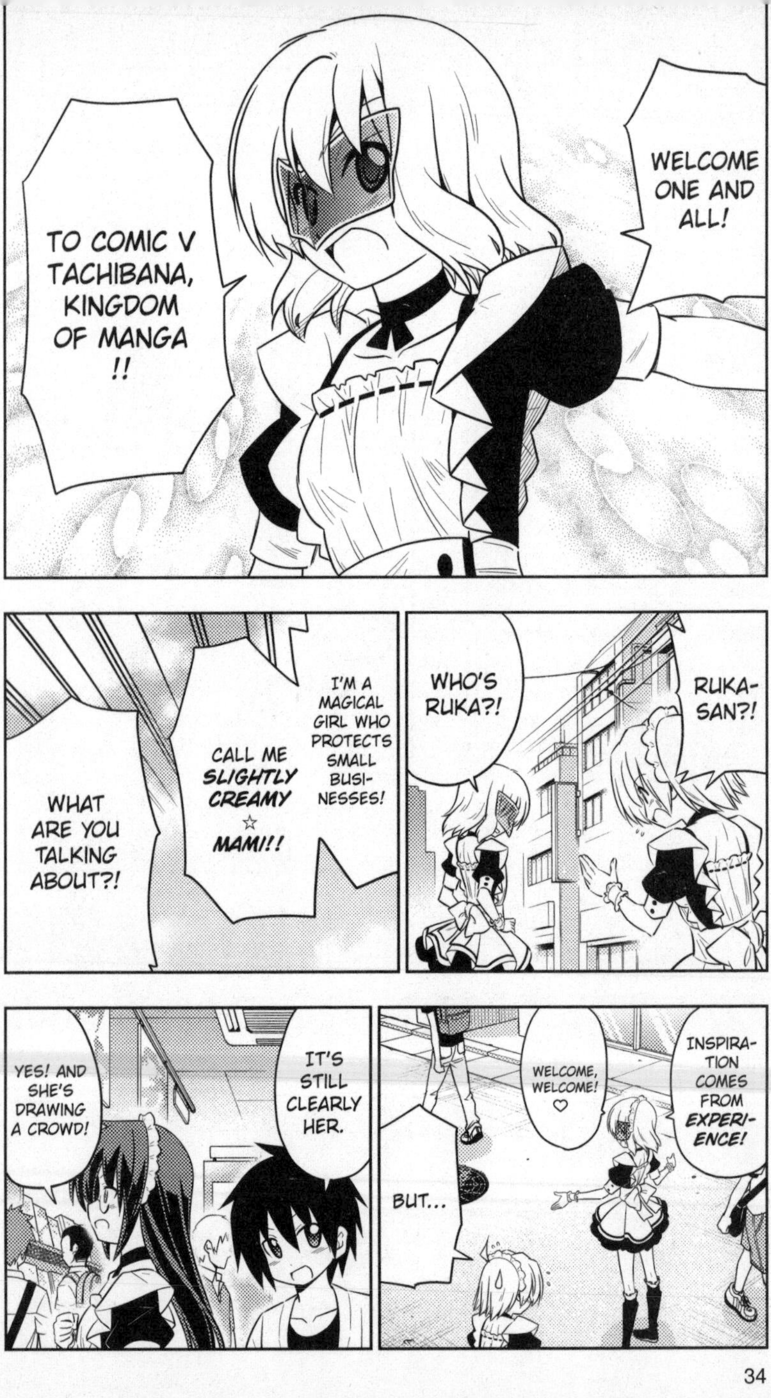
WELCOME ONE AND ALL!
TO COMIC V TACHIBANA, KINGDOM OF MANGA !!
RUKA-SAN?!
WHO'S RUKA?!
I'M A MAGICAL GIRL WHO PROTECTS SMALL BUSINESSES!
CALL ME *SLIGHTLY CREAMY* ☆ *MAMI!!*
WHAT ARE YOU TALKING ABOUT?!
INSPIRATION COMES FROM *EXPERIENCE!*
WELCOME, WELCOME! ♡
BUT...
IT'S STILL CLEARLY HER.
YES! AND SHE'S DRAWING A CROWD!

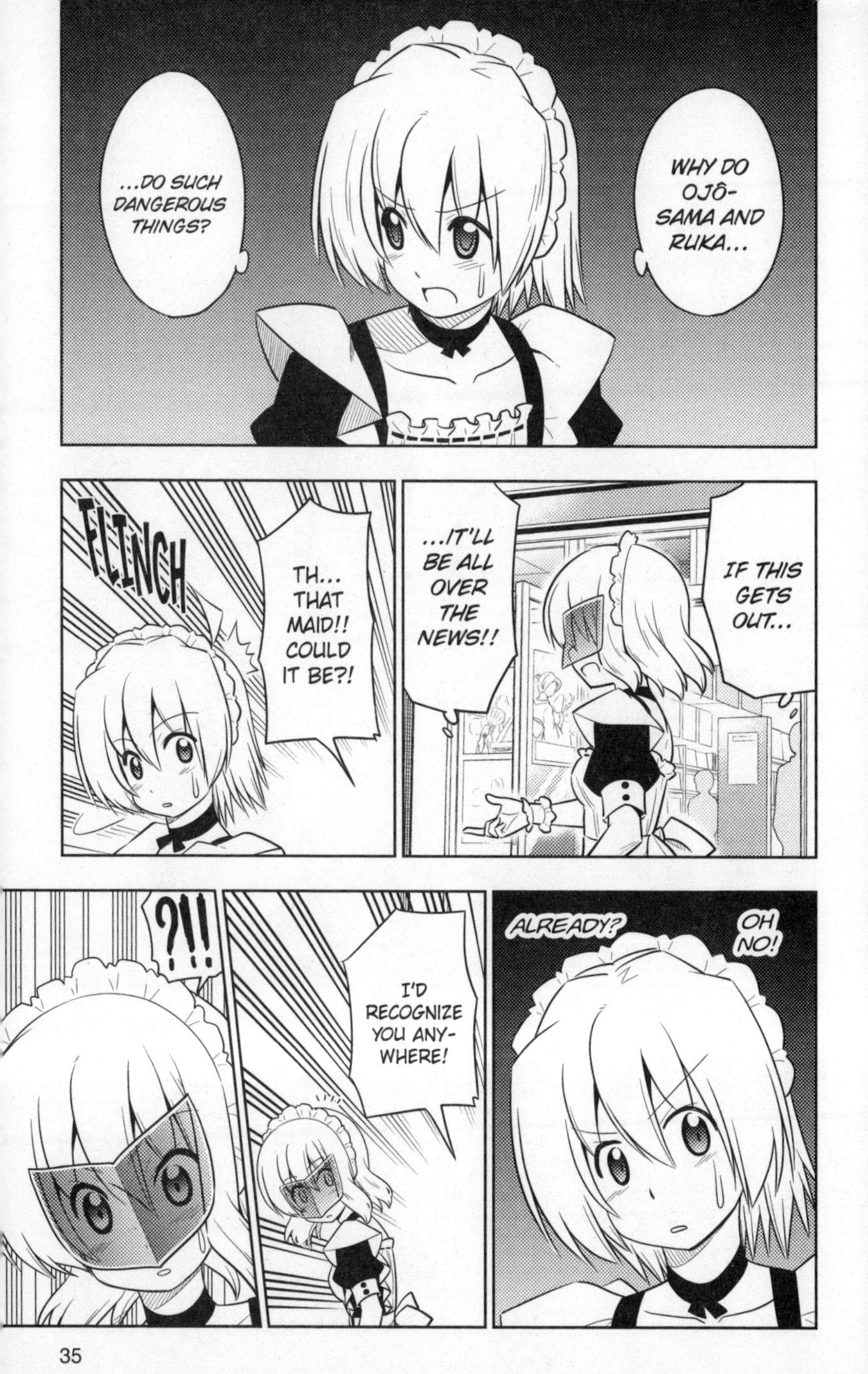
WHY DO OJÔ-SAMA AND RUKA...
...DO SUCH DANGEROUS THINGS?
IF THIS GETS OUT...
...IT'LL BE ALL OVER THE NEWS!!
FLINCH
TH... THAT MAID!! COULD IT BE?!
OH NO!
ALREADY?
I'D RECOGNIZE YOU ANY-WHERE!
?!!

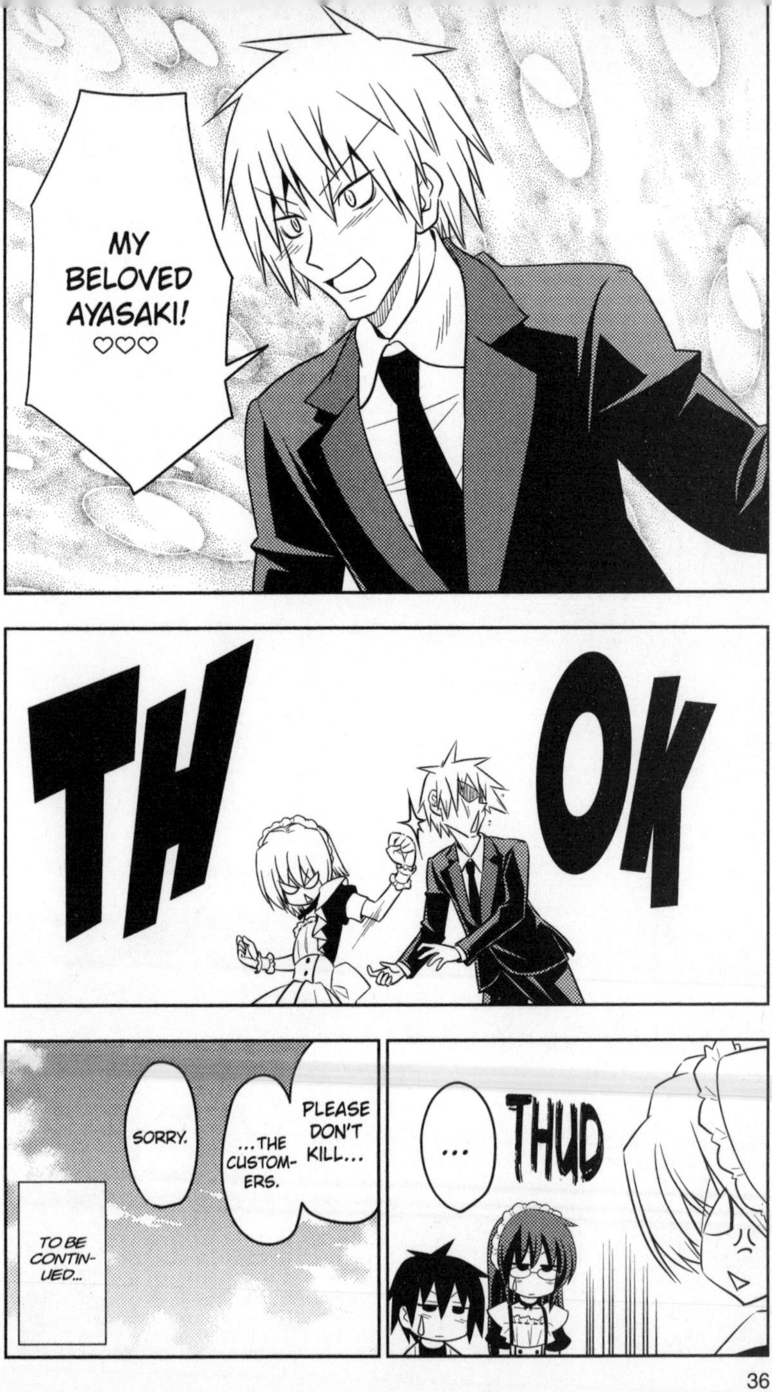
MY BELOVED AYASAKI! ♡♡♡
TH
OK
...
THUD
PLEASE DON'T KILL...
...THE CUSTOMERS.
SORRY.
TO BE CONTINUED...

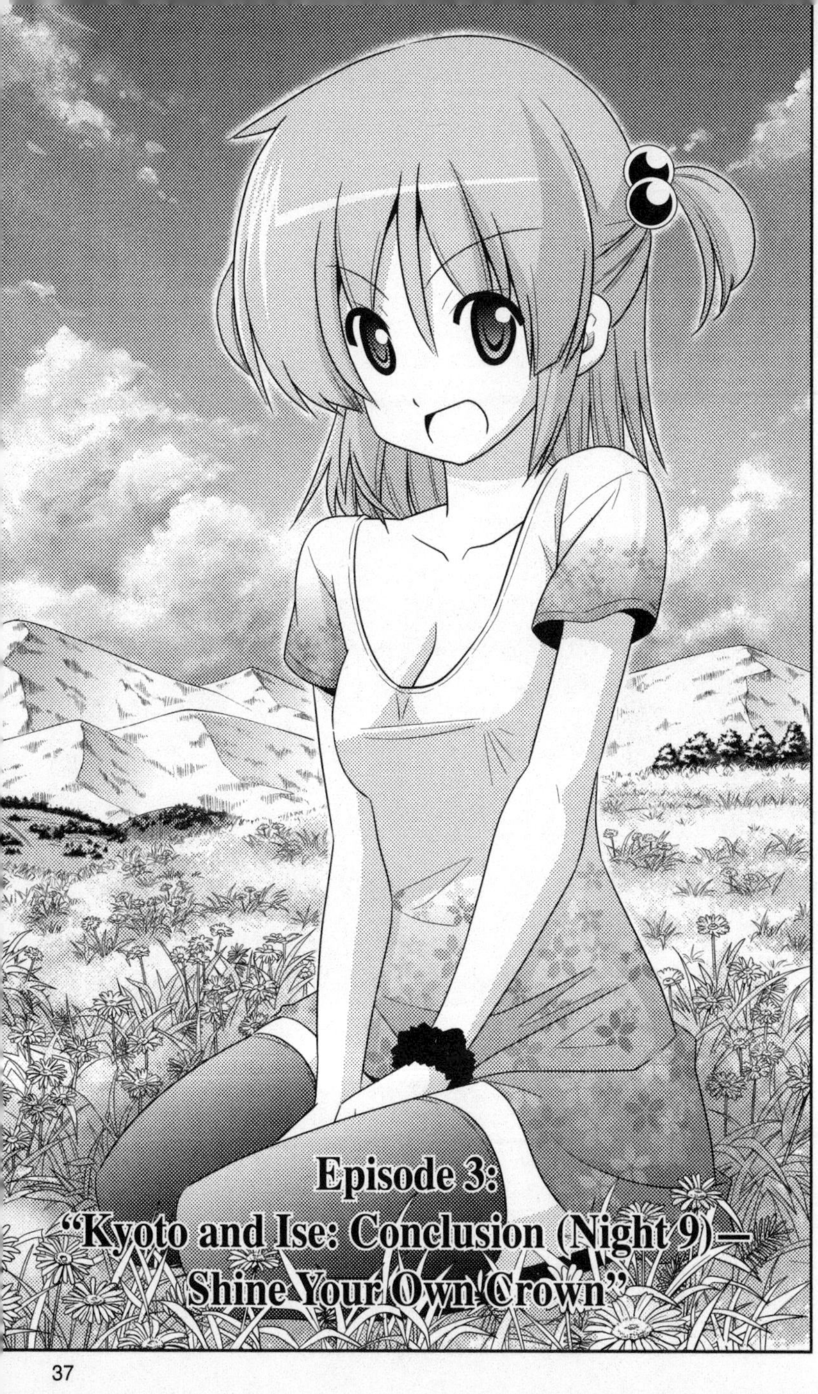
Episode 3:
"Kyoto and Ise: Conclusion (Night 9) —
Shine Your Own Crown"

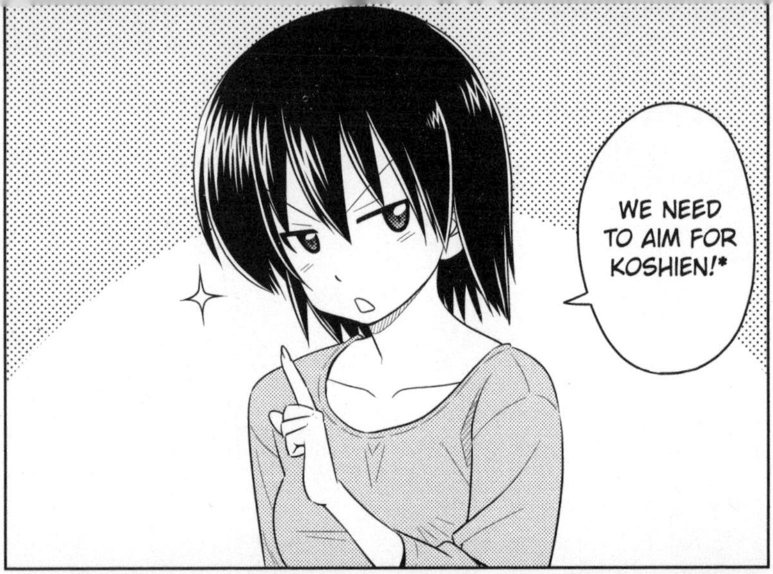
WE NEED TO AIM FOR KOSHIEN!*

*JAPAN'S NATIONAL HIGH SCHOOL BASEBALL CHAMPIONSHIP.

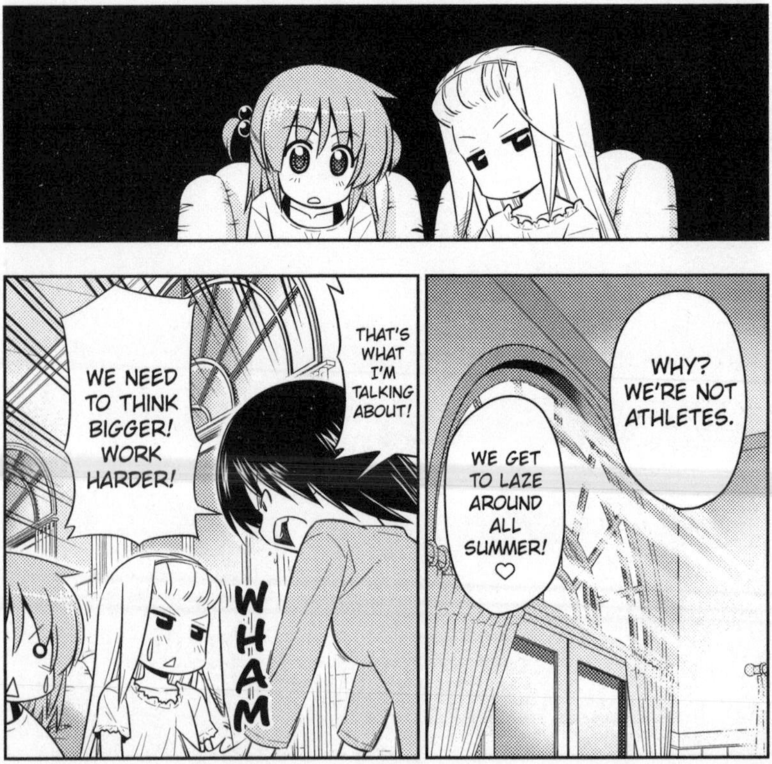
WHY? WE'RE NOT ATHLETES.
WE GET TO LAZE AROUND ALL SUMMER! ♡
THAT'S WHAT I'M TALKING ABOUT!
WE NEED TO THINK BIGGER! WORK HARDER!
WHAM

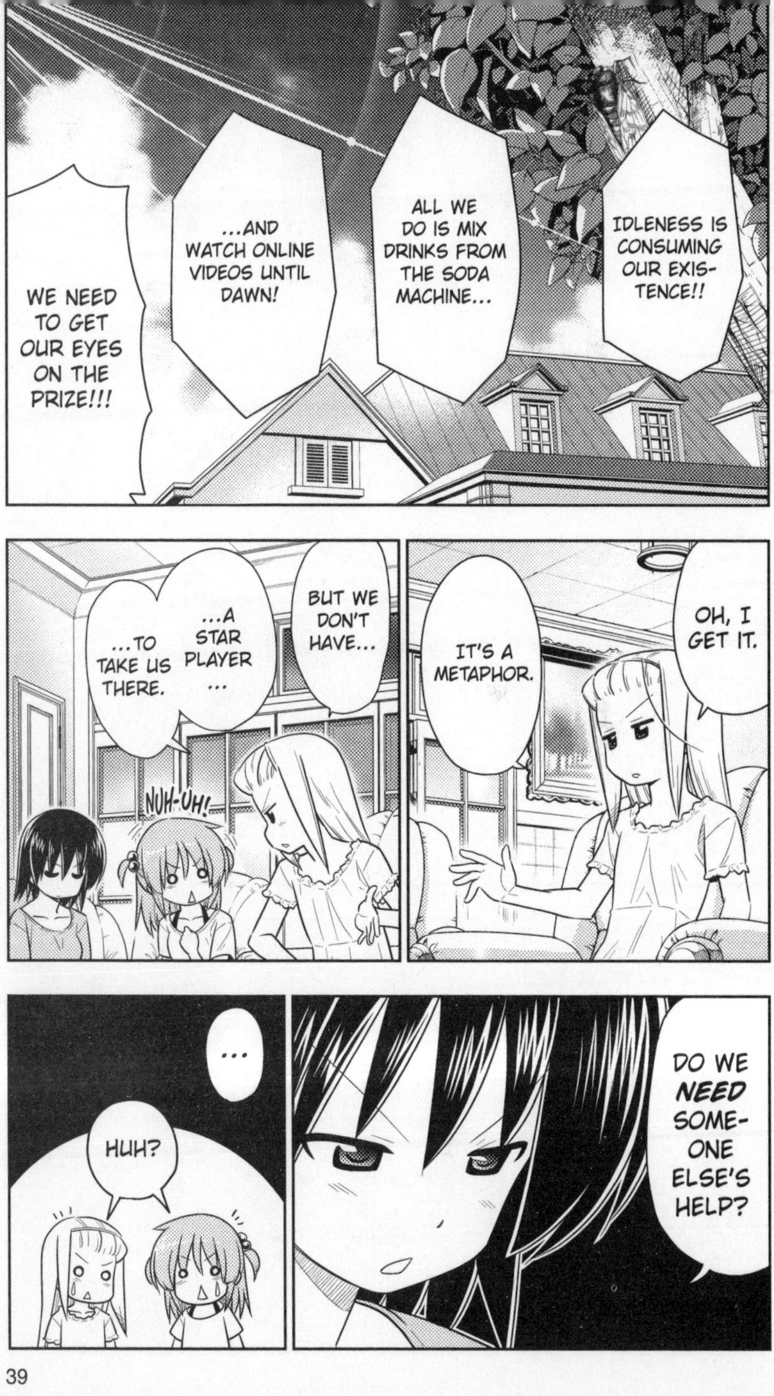
IDLENESS IS CONSUMING OUR EXIS-TENCE!!
ALL WE DO IS MIX DRINKS FROM THE SODA MACHINE...
...AND WATCH ONLINE VIDEOS UNTIL DAWN!
WE NEED TO GET OUR EYES ON THE PRIZE!!!
OH, I GET IT.
IT'S A METAPHOR.
BUT WE DON'T HAVE...
...A STAR PLAYER...
...TO TAKE US THERE.
NUH-UH!
DO WE **NEED** SOME-ONE ELSE'S HELP?
...
HUH?

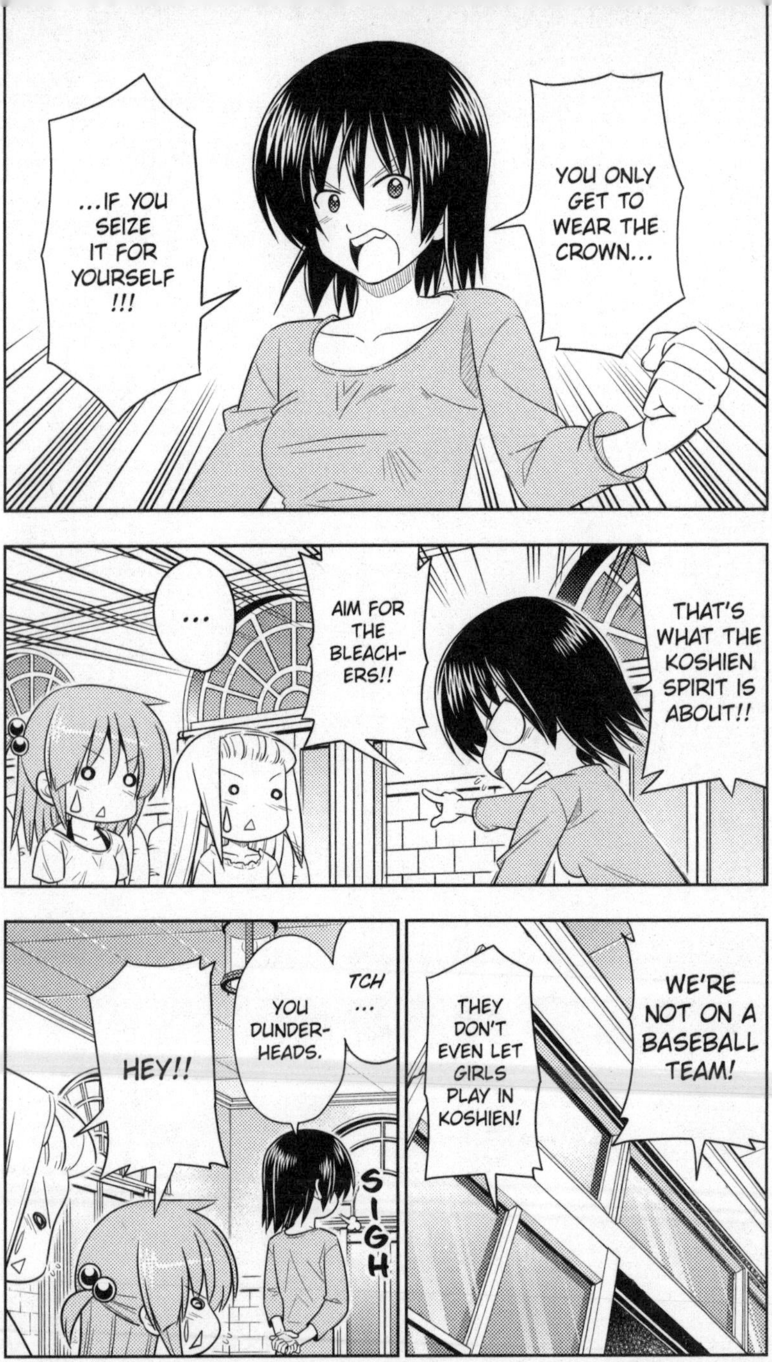

YOU ONLY GET TO WEAR THE CROWN...
...IF YOU SEIZE IT FOR YOURSELF!!!
THAT'S WHAT THE KOSHIEN SPIRIT IS ABOUT!!
AIM FOR THE BLEACH-ERS!!
...
WE'RE NOT ON A BASEBALL TEAM!
THEY DON'T EVEN LET GIRLS PLAY IN KOSHIEN!
TCH ...
YOU DUNDER-HEADS.
HEY!!
SIGH

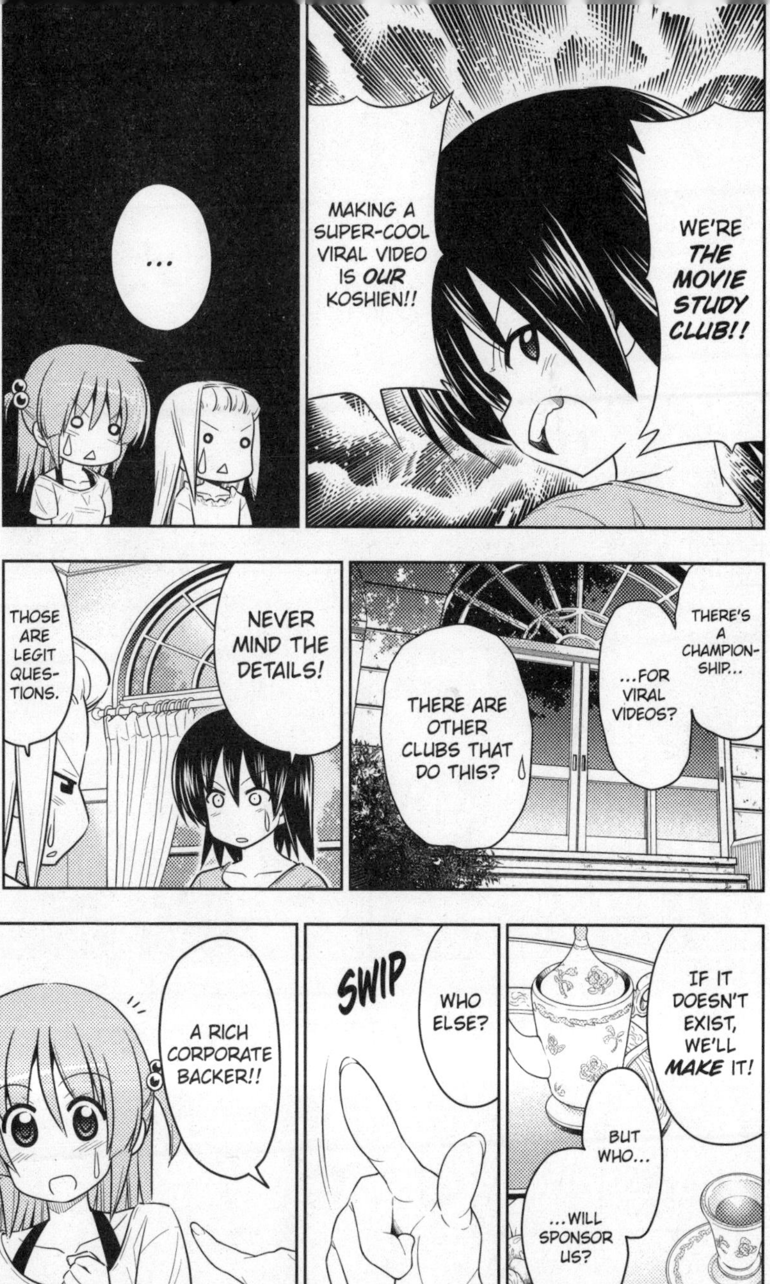
WE'RE THE MOVIE STUDY CLUB!!
MAKING A SUPER-COOL VIRAL VIDEO IS OUR KOSHIEN!!
...
THERE'S A CHAMPIONSHIP...
...FOR VIRAL VIDEOS?
THERE ARE OTHER CLUBS THAT DO THIS?
NEVER MIND THE DETAILS!
THOSE ARE LEGIT QUESTIONS.
IF IT DOESN'T EXIST, WE'LL MAKE IT!
BUT WHO...
...WILL SPONSOR US?
WHO ELSE?
SWIP
A RICH CORPORATE BACKER!!

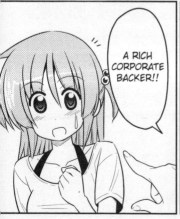

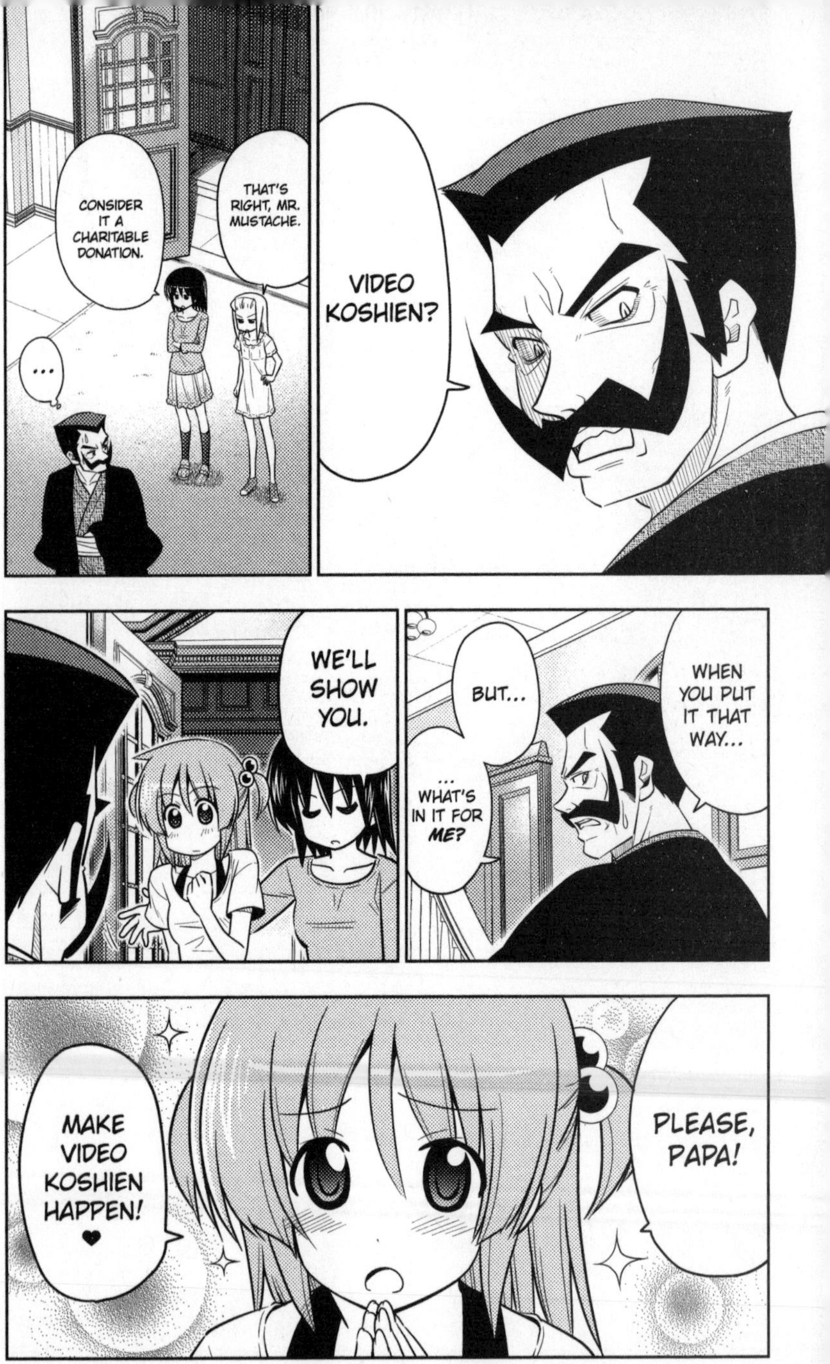
VIDEO KOSHIEN?
THAT'S RIGHT, MR. MUSTACHE.
CONSIDER IT A CHARITABLE DONATION.
...
WHEN YOU PUT IT THAT WAY...
BUT...
...WHAT'S IN IT FOR *ME*?
WE'LL SHOW YOU.
PLEASE, PAPA!
MAKE VIDEO KOSHIEN HAPPEN! ❤

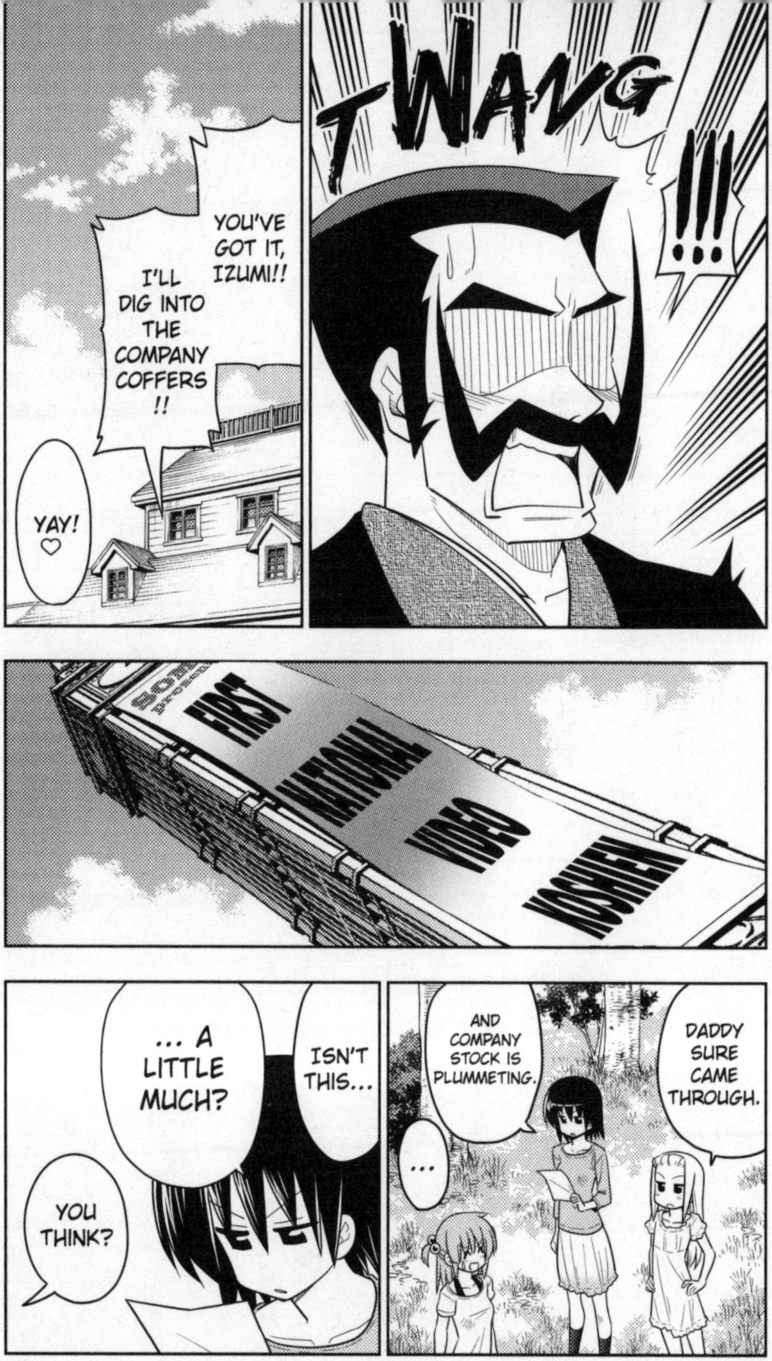
TWANG
!!!
YOU'VE GOT IT, IZUMI!!
I'LL DIG INTO THE COMPANY COFFERS!!
YAY! ♡
FIRST NATIONAL VIDEO KOSHIEN
DADDY SURE CAME THROUGH.
AND COMPANY STOCK IS PLUMMETING.
...
ISN'T THIS...
... A LITTLE MUCH?
YOU THINK?

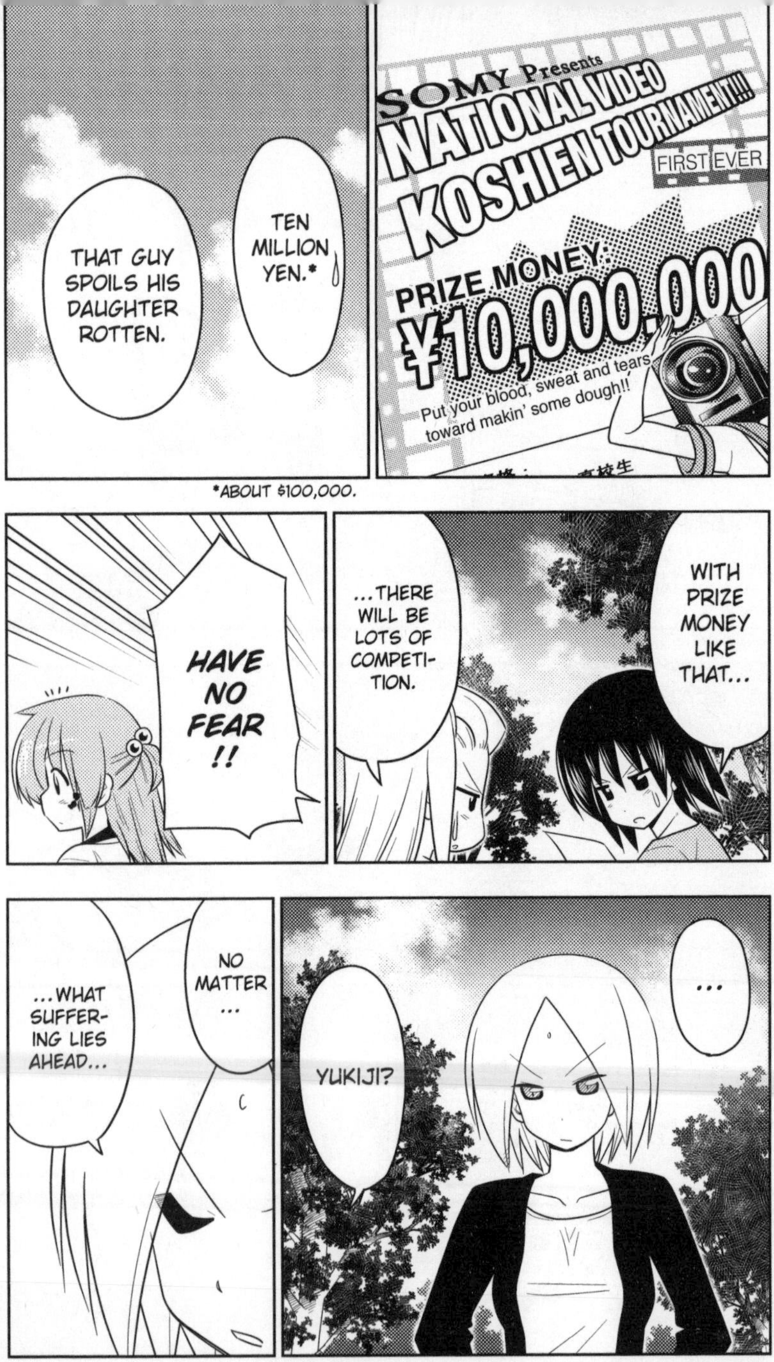
SOMY Presents
NATIONAL VIDEO KOSHIEN TOURNAMENT!!!
FIRST EVER
PRIZE MONEY: ¥10,000,000
Put your blood, sweat and tears toward makin' some dough!!
TEN MILLION YEN.*
THAT GUY SPOILS HIS DAUGHTER ROTTEN.
WITH PRIZE MONEY LIKE THAT...
...THERE WILL BE LOTS OF COMPETITION.
HAVE NO FEAR!!
...
YUKIJI?
NO MATTER...
...WHAT SUFFERING LIES AHEAD...

*ABOUT $100,000.

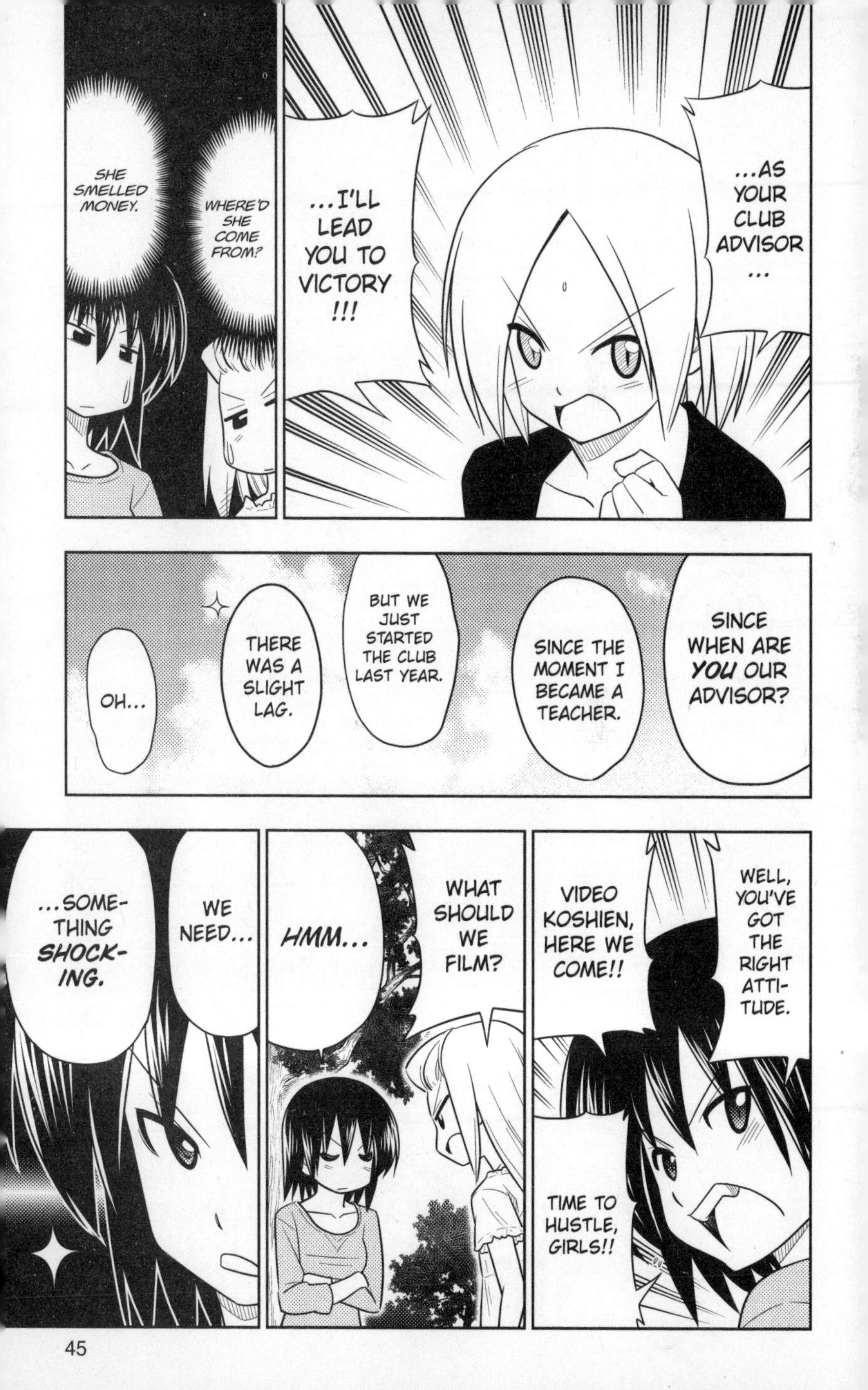
...AS YOUR CLUB ADVISOR...
...I'LL LEAD YOU TO VICTORY!!!
WHERE'D SHE COME FROM?
SHE SMELLED MONEY.
SINCE WHEN ARE *YOU* OUR ADVISOR?
SINCE THE MOMENT I BECAME A TEACHER.
BUT WE JUST STARTED THE CLUB LAST YEAR.
THERE WAS A SLIGHT LAG.
OH...
WELL, YOU'VE GOT THE RIGHT ATTITUDE.
VIDEO KOSHIEN, HERE WE COME!!
TIME TO HUSTLE, GIRLS!!
WHAT SHOULD WE FILM?
HMM...
WE NEED...
...SOMETHING *SHOCKING.*

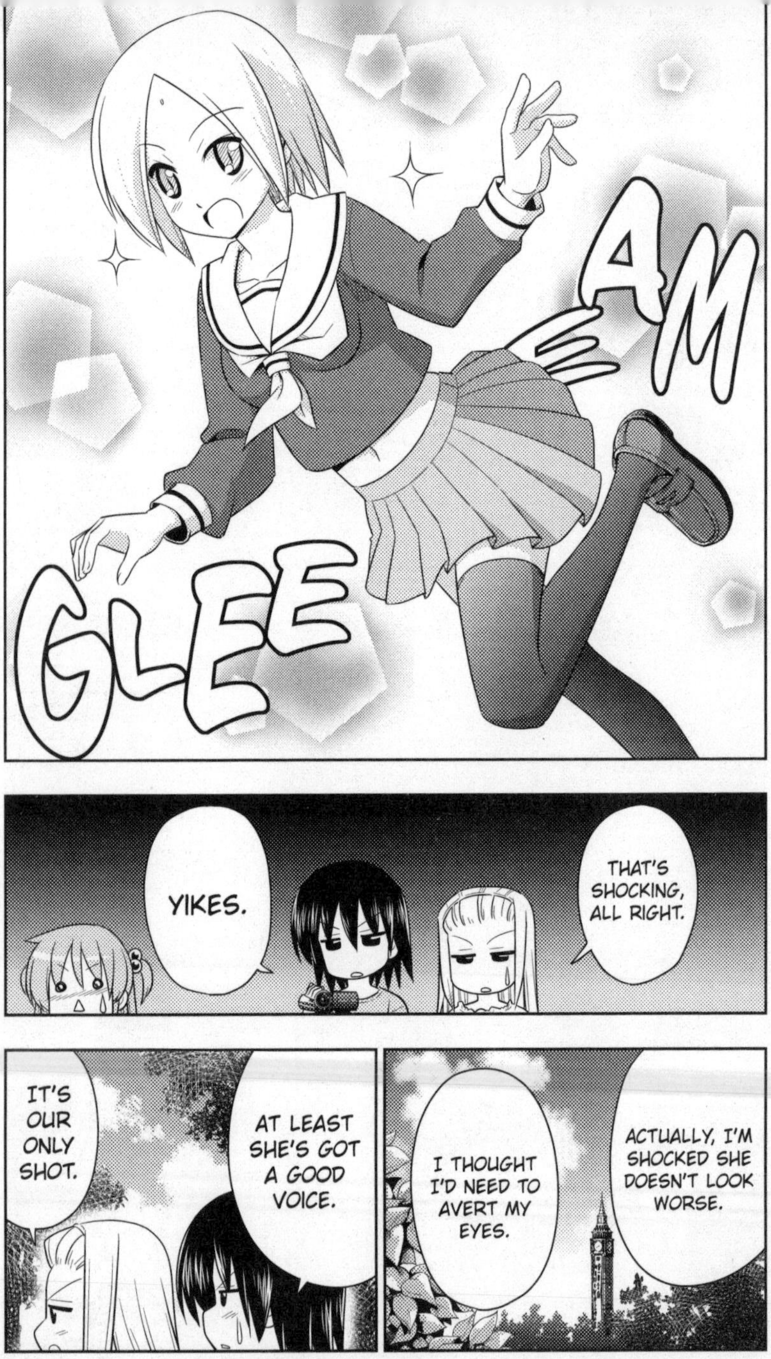
GLEE
AM
THAT'S SHOCKING, ALL RIGHT.
YIKES.
ACTUALLY, I'M SHOCKED SHE DOESN'T LOOK WORSE.
I THOUGHT I'D NEED TO AVERT MY EYES.
AT LEAST SHE'S GOT A GOOD VOICE.
IT'S OUR ONLY SHOT.

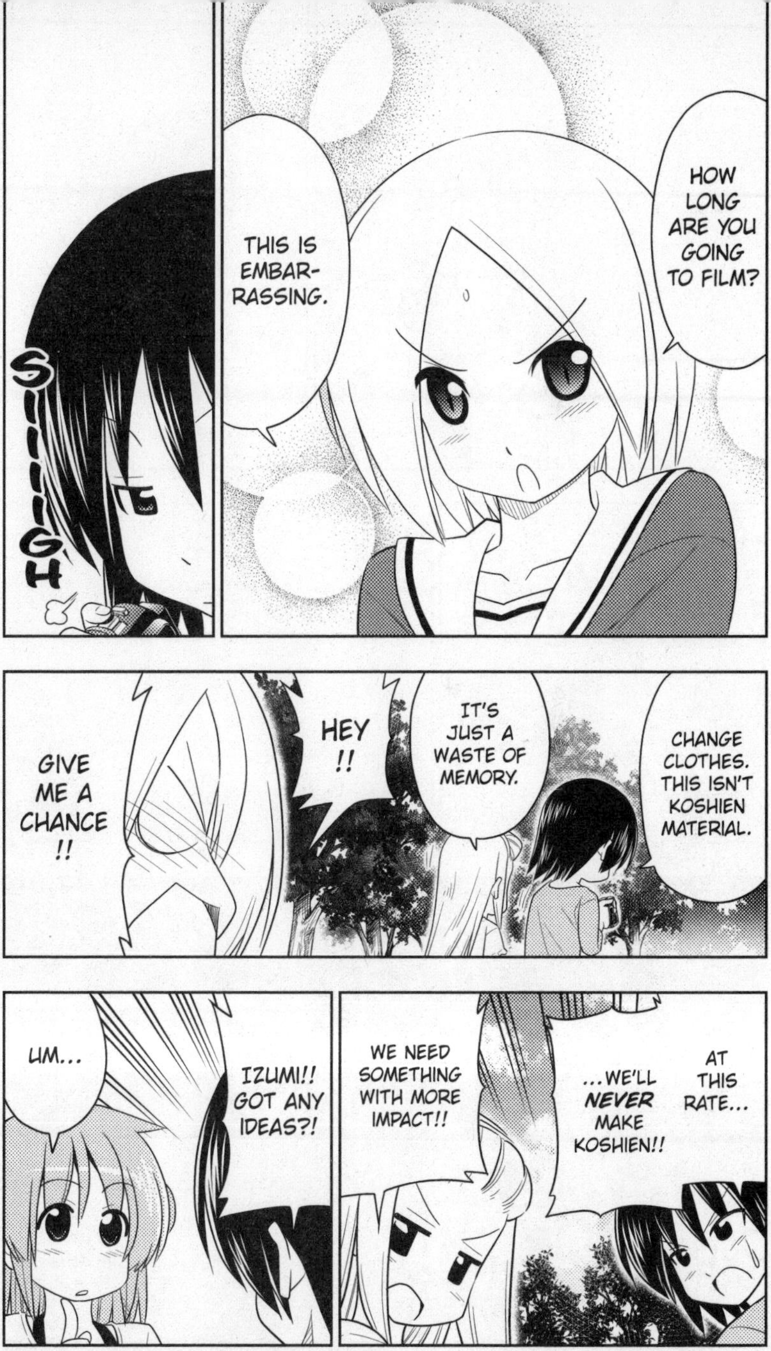
HOW LONG ARE YOU GOING TO FILM?
THIS IS EMBARRASSING.
SIIIIGH
CHANGE CLOTHES. THIS ISN'T KOSHIEN MATERIAL.
IT'S JUST A WASTE OF MEMORY.
HEY!!
GIVE ME A CHANCE!!
AT THIS RATE...
...WE'LL **NEVER** MAKE KOSHIEN!!
WE NEED SOMETHING WITH MORE IMPACT!!
IZUMI!! GOT ANY IDEAS?!
UM...

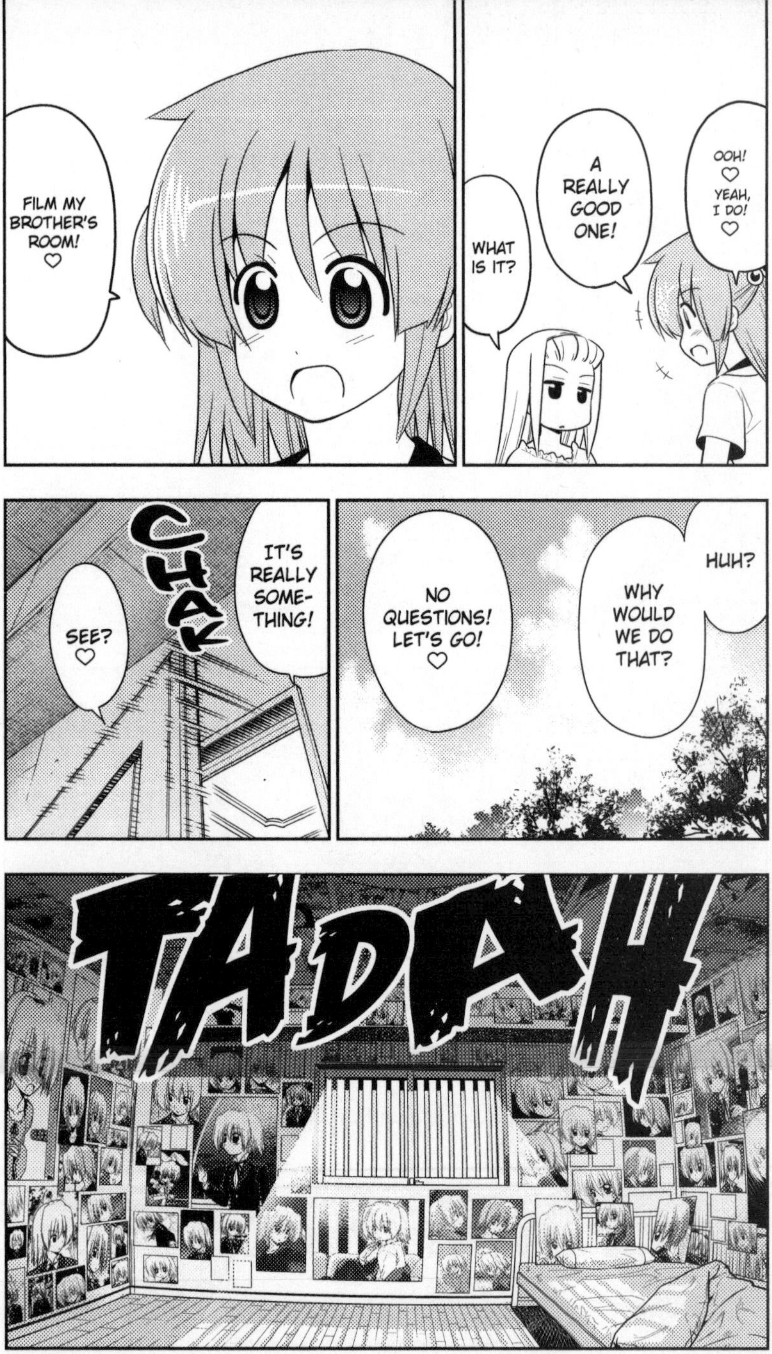
OOH! ♡ YEAH, I DO! ♡
A REALLY GOOD ONE!
WHAT IS IT?
FILM MY BROTHER'S ROOM! ♡
HUH?
WHY WOULD WE DO THAT?
NO QUESTIONS! LET'S GO! ♡
IT'S REALLY SOME-THING!
CHAK
SEE? ♡
TADAH

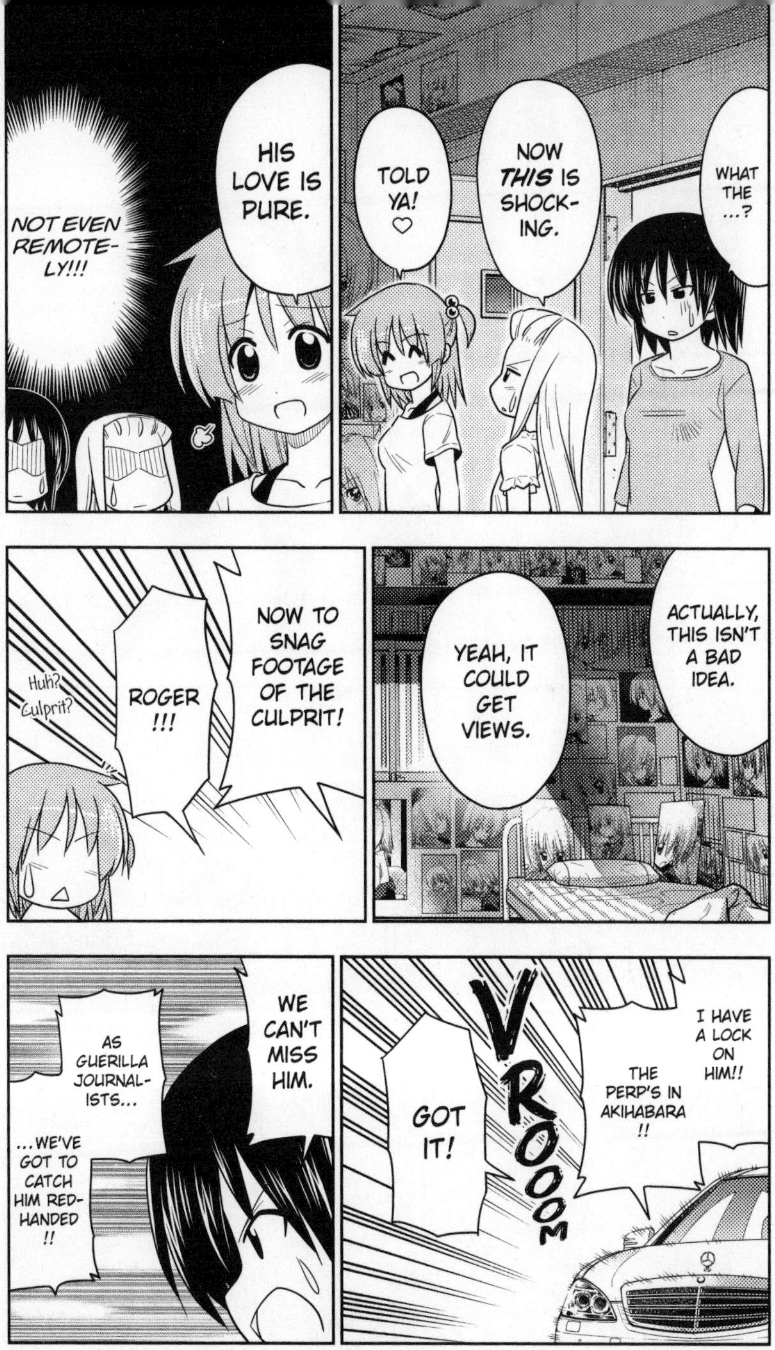
WHAT THE ...?
NOW *THIS* IS SHOCKING.
TOLD YA! ♡
HIS LOVE IS PURE.
NOT EVEN REMOTELY!!!
ACTUALLY, THIS ISN'T A BAD IDEA.
YEAH, IT COULD GET VIEWS.
NOW TO SNAG FOOTAGE OF THE CULPRIT!
ROGER!!!
Huh? Culprit?
I HAVE A LOCK ON HIM!!
THE PERP'S IN AKIHABARA!!
GOT IT!
VROOOOM
WE CAN'T MISS HIM.
AS GUERILLA JOURNALISTS...
...WE'VE GOT TO CATCH HIM RED-HANDED!!

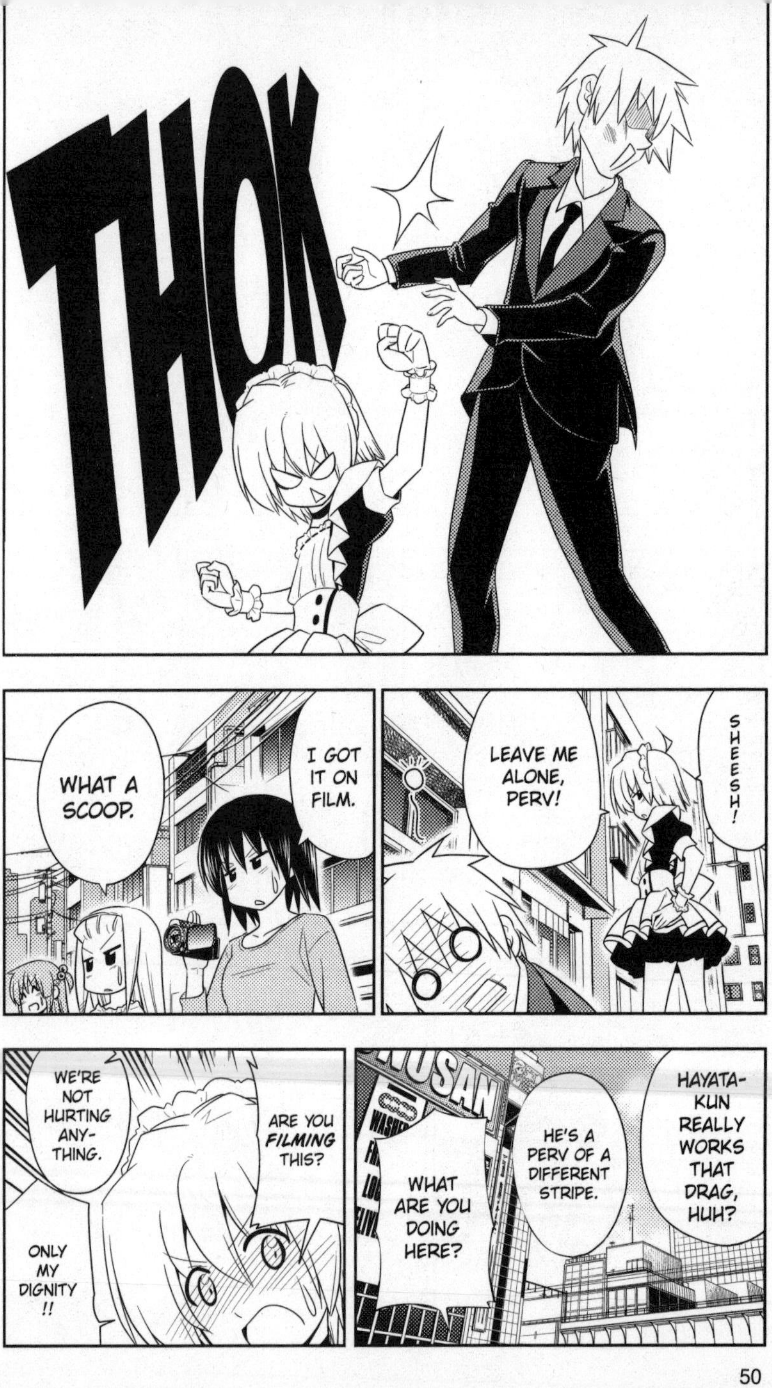
THOK
SHEESH!
LEAVE ME ALONE, PERV!
I GOT IT ON FILM.
WHAT A SCOOP.
HAYATA-KUN REALLY WORKS THAT DRAG, HUH?
HE'S A PERV OF A DIFFERENT STRIPE.
WHAT ARE YOU DOING HERE?
ARE YOU *FILMING* THIS?
WE'RE NOT HURTING ANYTHING.
ONLY MY DIGNITY!!

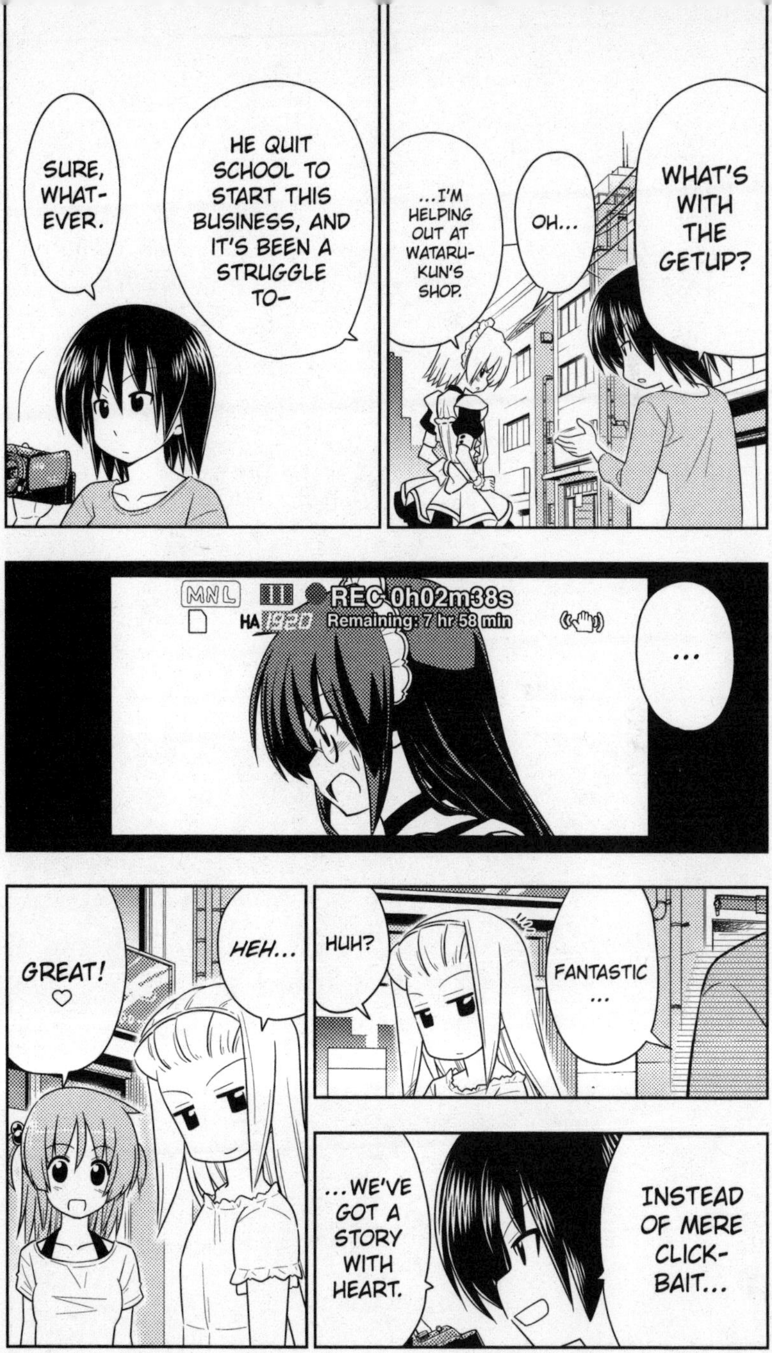
WHAT'S WITH THE GETUP?
OH...
...I'M HELPING OUT AT WATARU-KUN'S SHOP.
HE QUIT SCHOOL TO START THIS BUSINESS, AND IT'S BEEN A STRUGGLE TO-
SURE, WHAT-EVER.
MNL
REC 0h02m38s
HA 1920
Remaining: 7 hr 58 min
...
FANTASTIC...
HUH?
INSTEAD OF MERE CLICK-BAIT...
...WE'VE GOT A STORY WITH HEART.
HEH...
GREAT! ♡

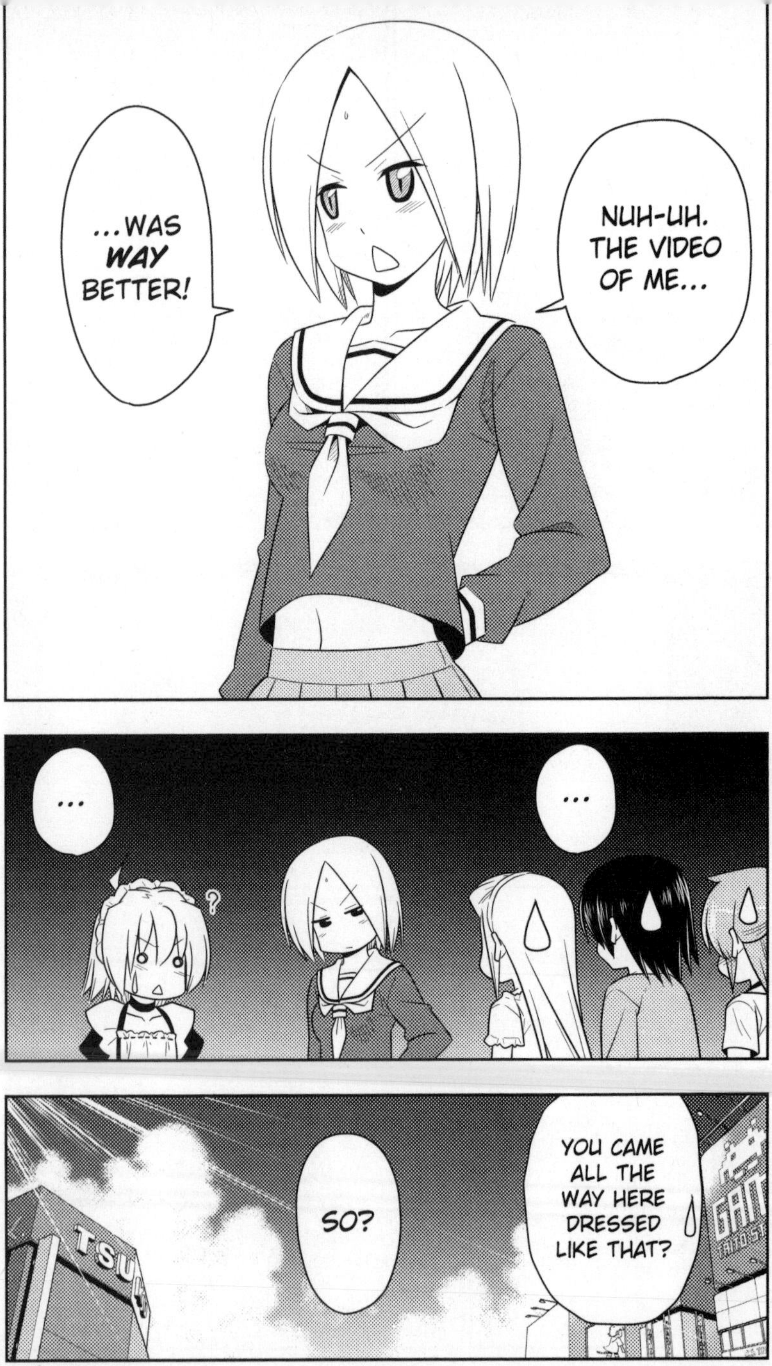
NUH-UH. THE VIDEO OF ME...
...WAS **WAY** BETTER!
...
...
YOU CAME ALL THE WAY HERE DRESSED LIKE THAT?
SO?

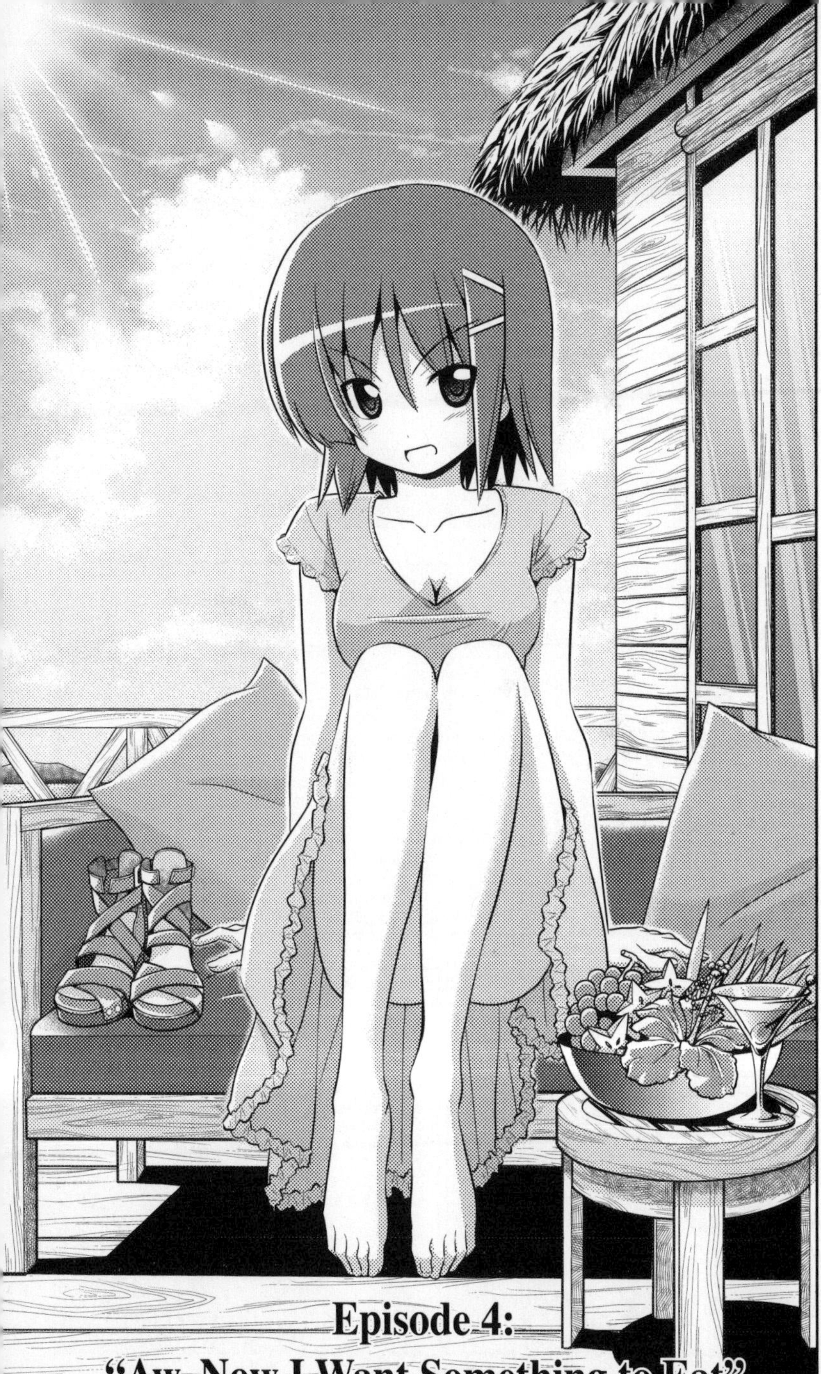

Episode 4:
"Aw, Now I Want Something to Eat"

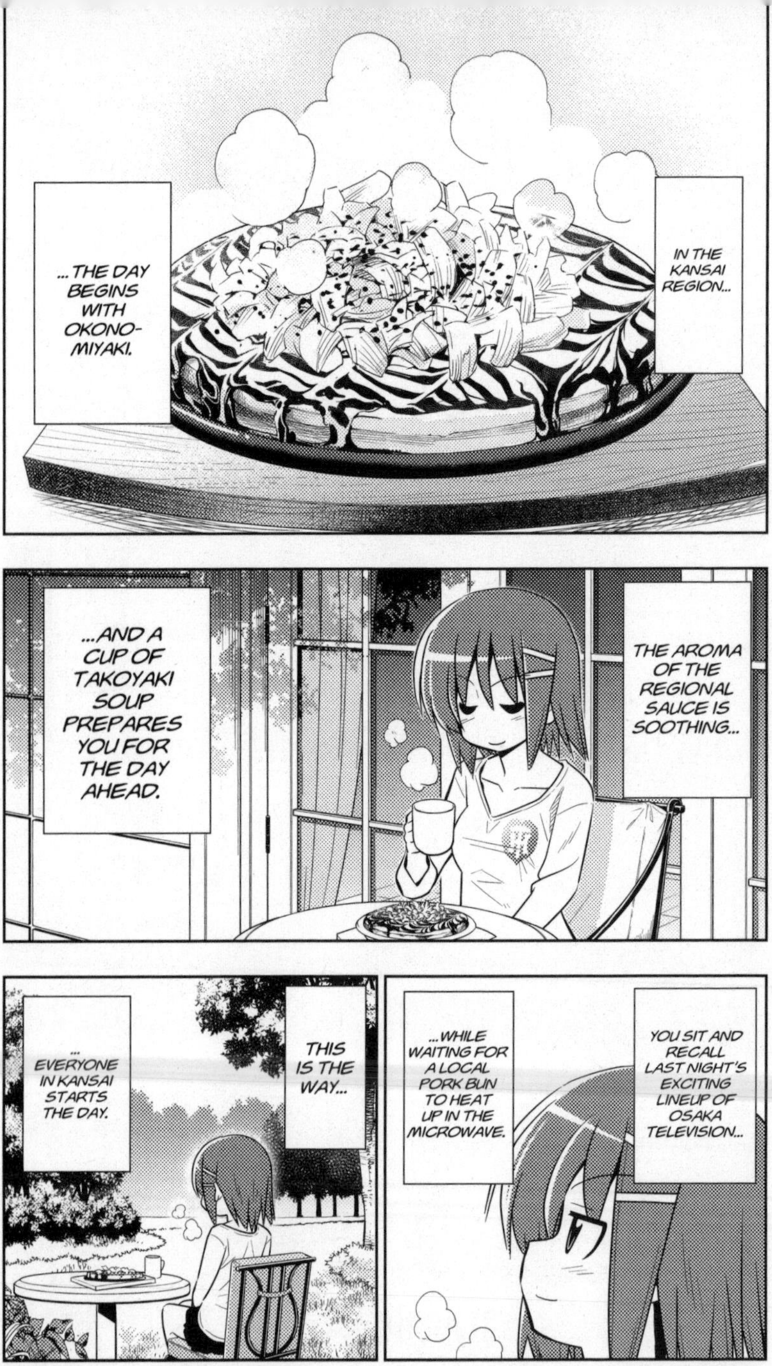
IN THE KANSAI REGION...
...THE DAY BEGINS WITH OKONO-MIYAKI.
THE AROMA OF THE REGIONAL SAUCE IS SOOTHING...
...AND A CUP OF TAKOYAKI SOUP PREPARES YOU FOR THE DAY AHEAD.
YOU SIT AND RECALL LAST NIGHT'S EXCITING LINEUP OF OSAKA TELEVISION...
...WHILE WAITING FOR A LOCAL PORK BUN TO HEAT UP IN THE MICROWAVE.
THIS IS THE WAY...
...EVERYONE IN KANSAI STARTS THE DAY.

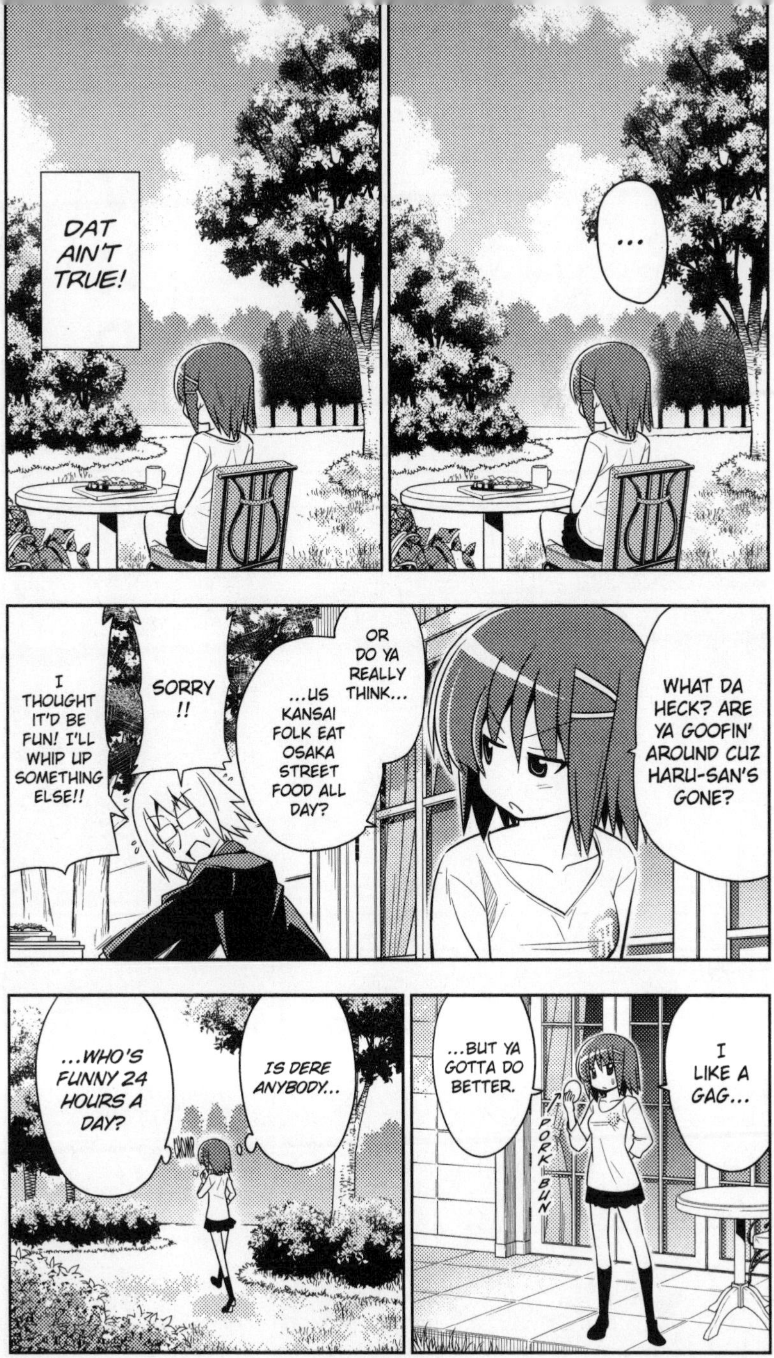
...
DAT AIN'T TRUE!
WHAT DA HECK? ARE YA GOOFIN' AROUND CUZ HARU-SAN'S GONE?
OR DO YA REALLY THINK...
...US KANSAI FOLK EAT OSAKA STREET FOOD ALL DAY?
SORRY!!
I THOUGHT IT'D BE FUN! I'LL WHIP UP SOMETHING ELSE!!
I LIKE A GAG...
...BUT YA GOTTA DO BETTER.
PORK BUN
IS DERE ANYBODY...
...WHO'S FUNNY 24 HOURS A DAY?
CHOMP

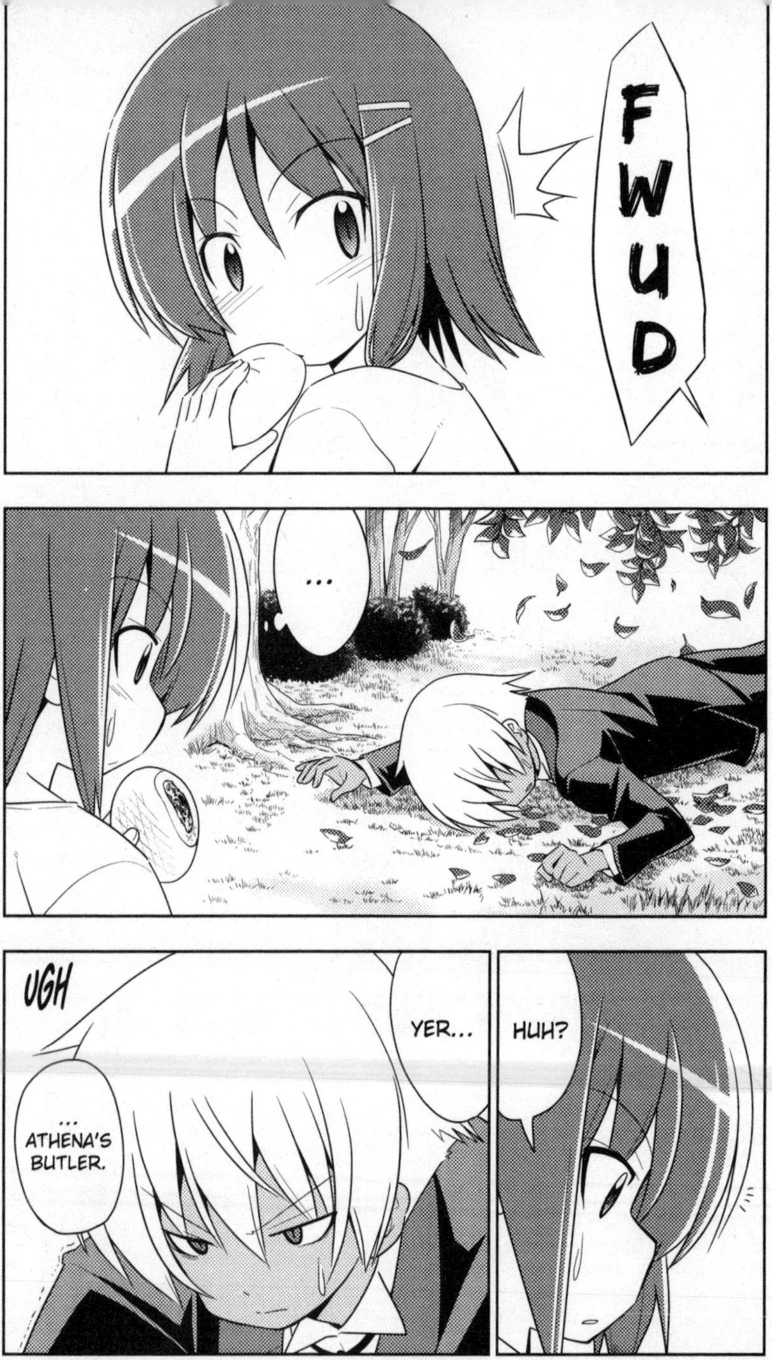
FWUD
...
HUH?
YER...
UGH
... ATHENA'S BUTLER.

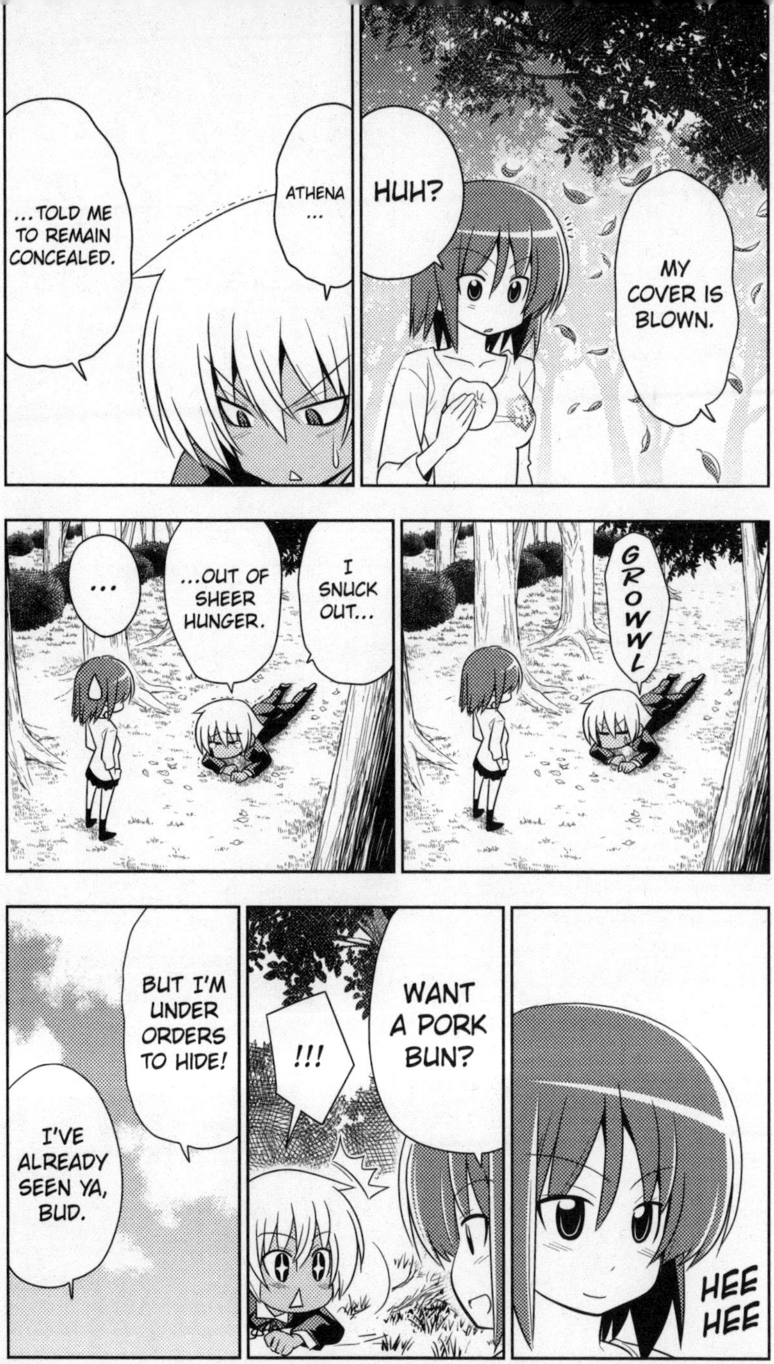
MY COVER IS BLOWN.
HUH?
ATHENA ...
...TOLD ME TO REMAIN CONCEALED.
GROWWL
I SNUCK OUT...
...OUT OF SHEER HUNGER.
...
HEE HEE
WANT A PORK BUN?
!!!
BUT I'M UNDER ORDERS TO HIDE!
I'VE ALREADY SEEN YA, BUD.

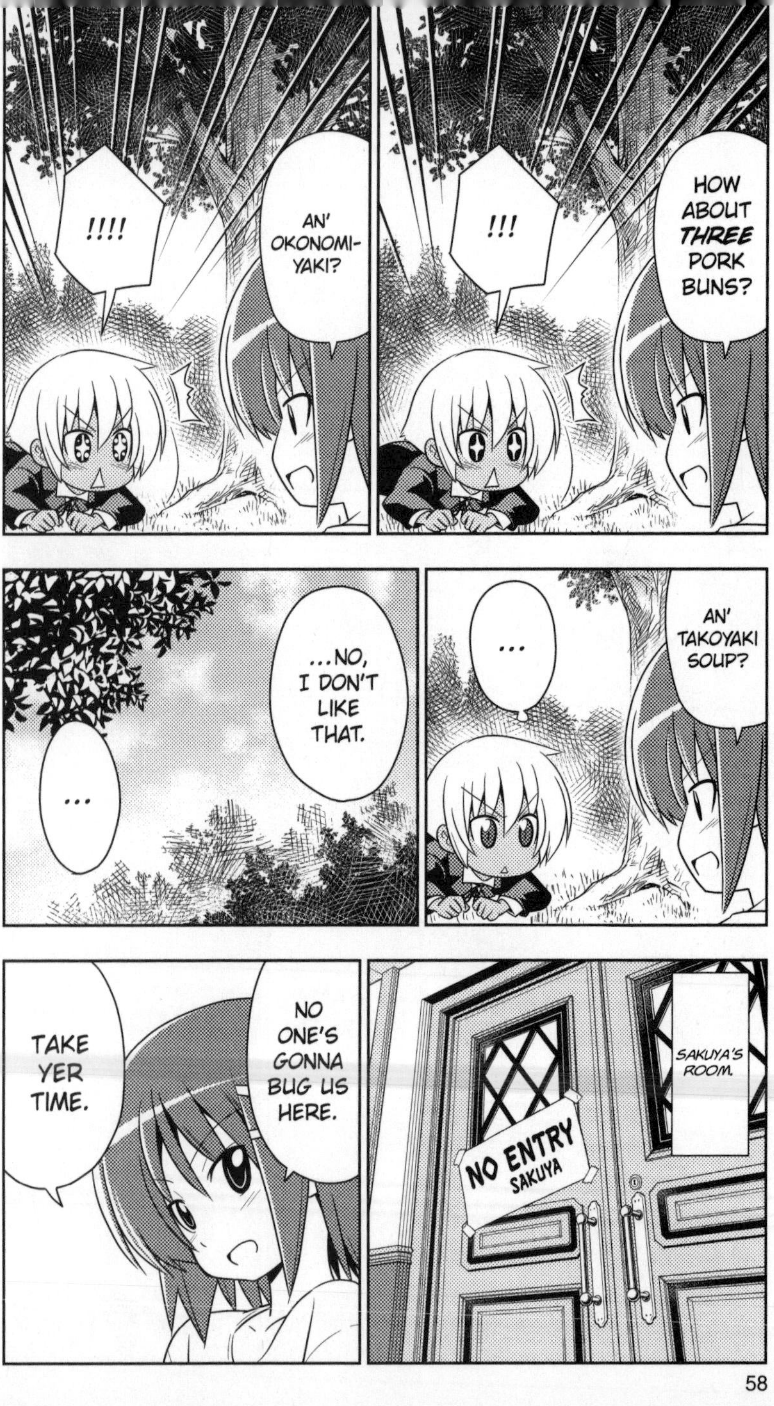
HOW ABOUT *THREE* PORK BUNS?
!!!
AN' OKONOMI-YAKI?
!!!!
AN' TAKOYAKI SOUP?
...
...NO, I DON'T LIKE THAT.
...
SAKUYA'S ROOM.
NO ENTRY
SAKUYA
NO ONE'S GONNA BUG US HERE.
TAKE YER TIME.

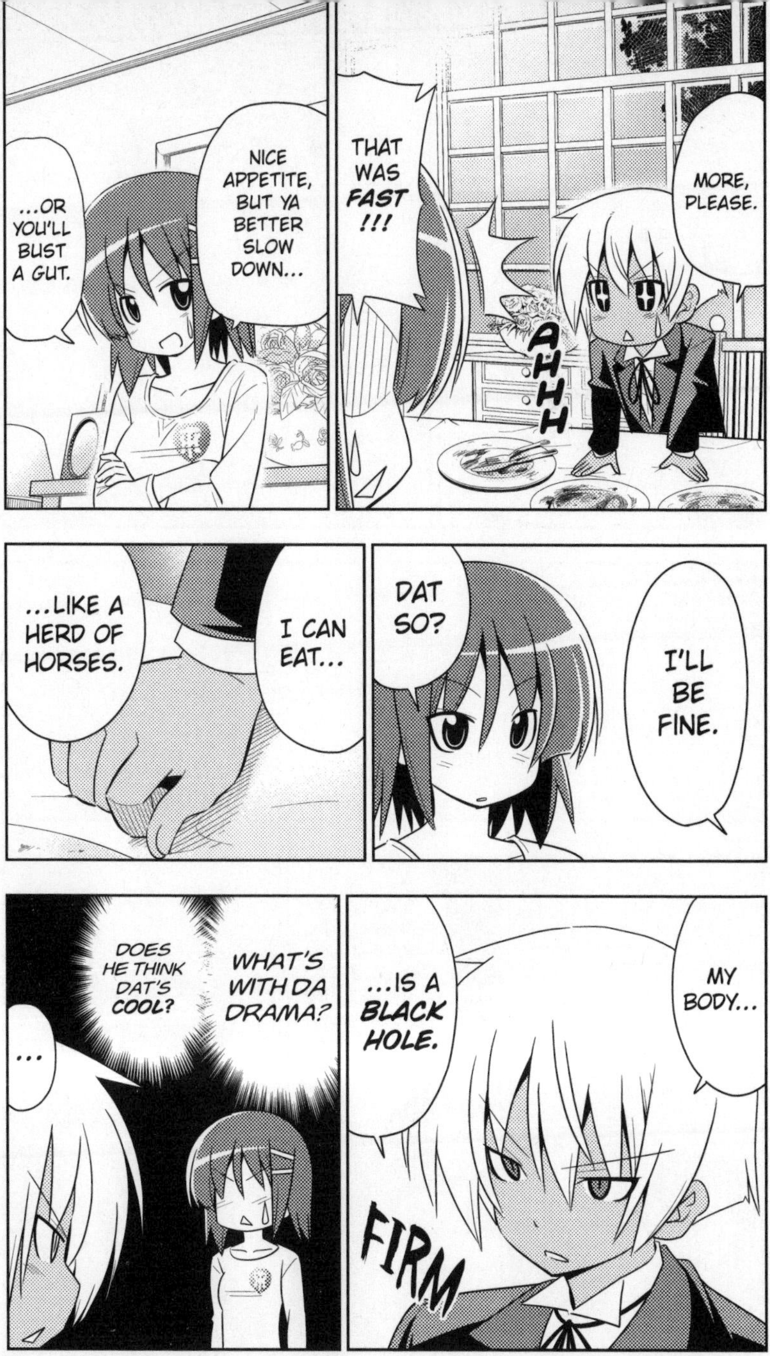
MORE, PLEASE.
THAT WAS FAST!!!
AHHH
NICE APPETITE, BUT YA BETTER SLOW DOWN...
...OR YOU'LL BUST A GUT.
I'LL BE FINE.
DAT SO?
I CAN EAT...
...LIKE A HERD OF HORSES.
MY BODY...
...IS A BLACK HOLE.
FIRM
WHAT'S WITH DA DRAMA?
DOES HE THINK DAT'S COOL?
...

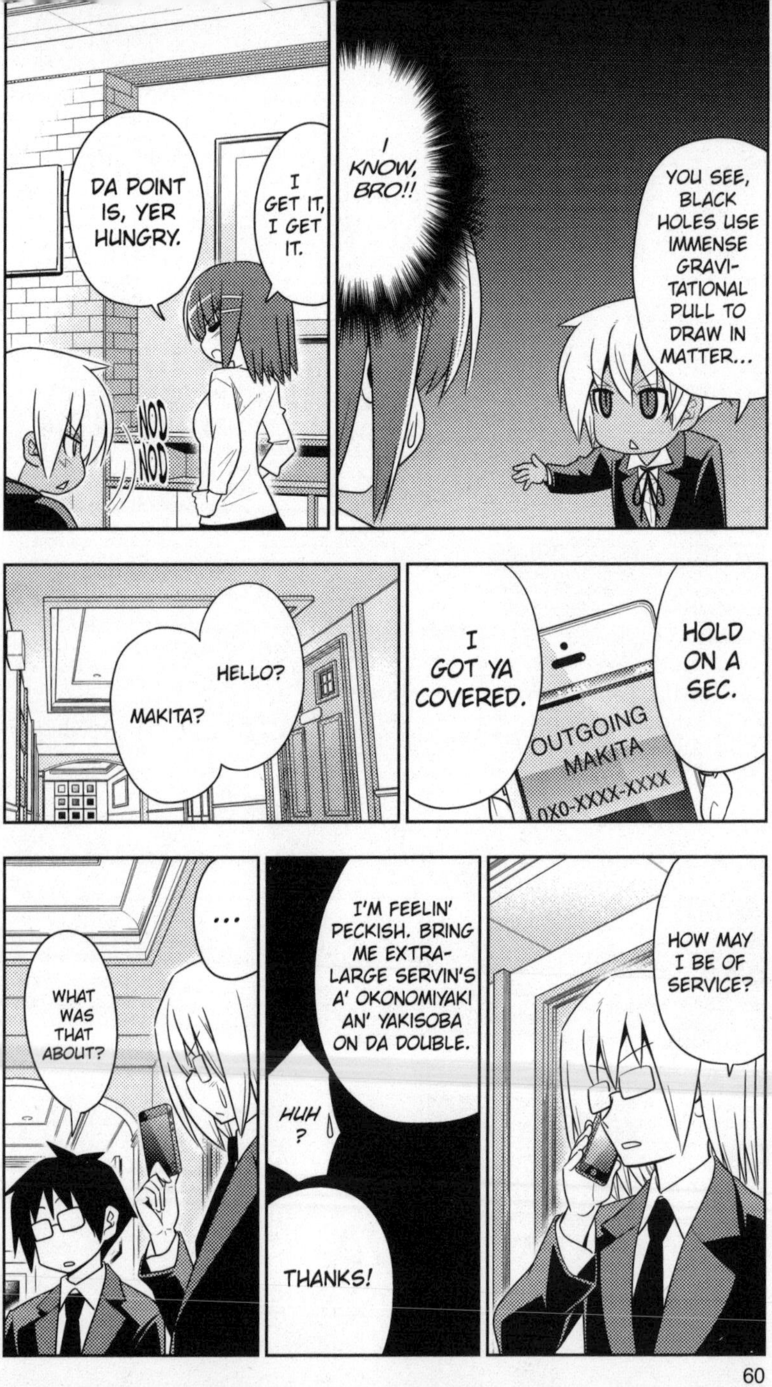
YOU SEE, BLACK HOLES USE IMMENSE GRAVI-TATIONAL PULL TO DRAW IN MATTER...
I KNOW, BRO!!
I GET IT, I GET IT.
DA POINT IS, YER HUNGRY.
NOD NOD
HOLD ON A SEC.
I GOT YA COVERED.
OUTGOING
MAKITA
0X0-XXXX-XXXX
HELLO?
MAKITA?
HOW MAY I BE OF SERVICE?
I'M FEELIN' PECKISH. BRING ME EXTRA-LARGE SERVIN'S A' OKONOMIYAKI AN' YAKISOBA ON DA DOUBLE.
HUH?
THANKS!
...
WHAT WAS THAT ABOUT?

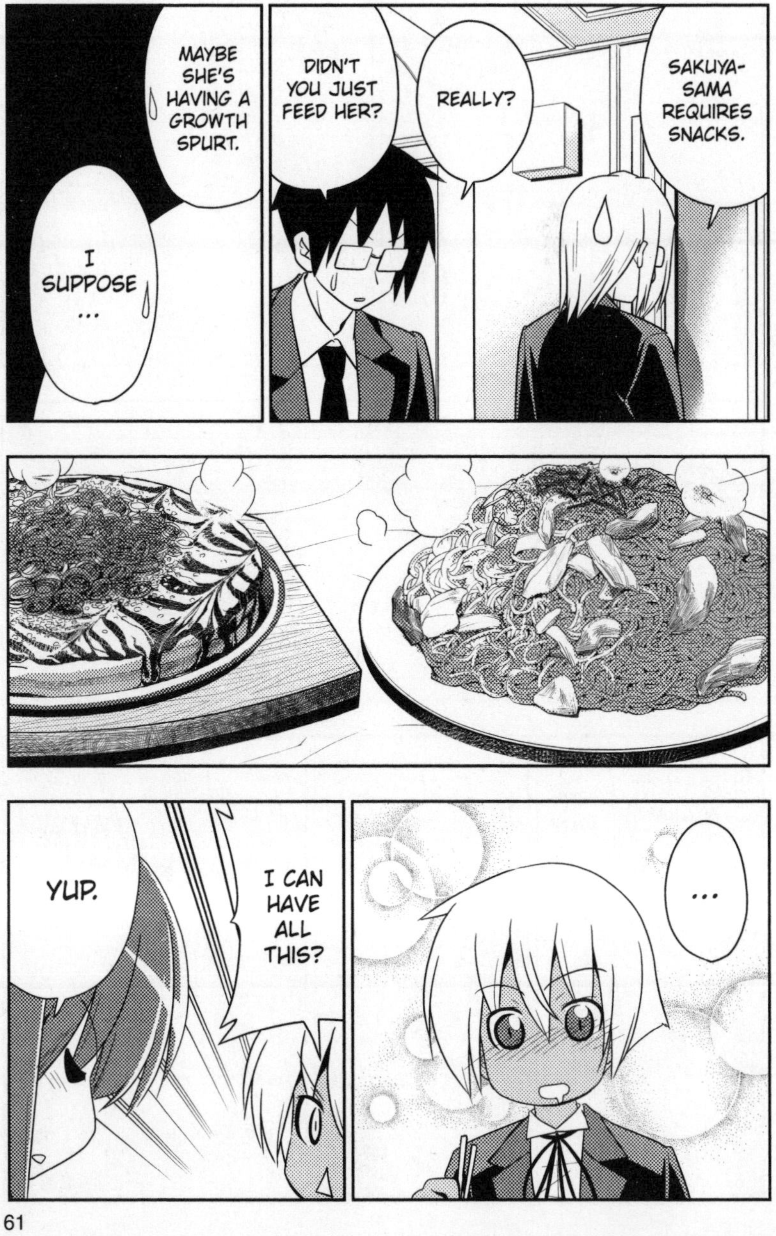
SAKUYA-SAMA REQUIRES SNACKS.
REALLY?
DIDN'T YOU JUST FEED HER?
MAYBE SHE'S HAVING A GROWTH SPURT.
I SUPPOSE...
...
I CAN HAVE ALL THIS?
YUP.

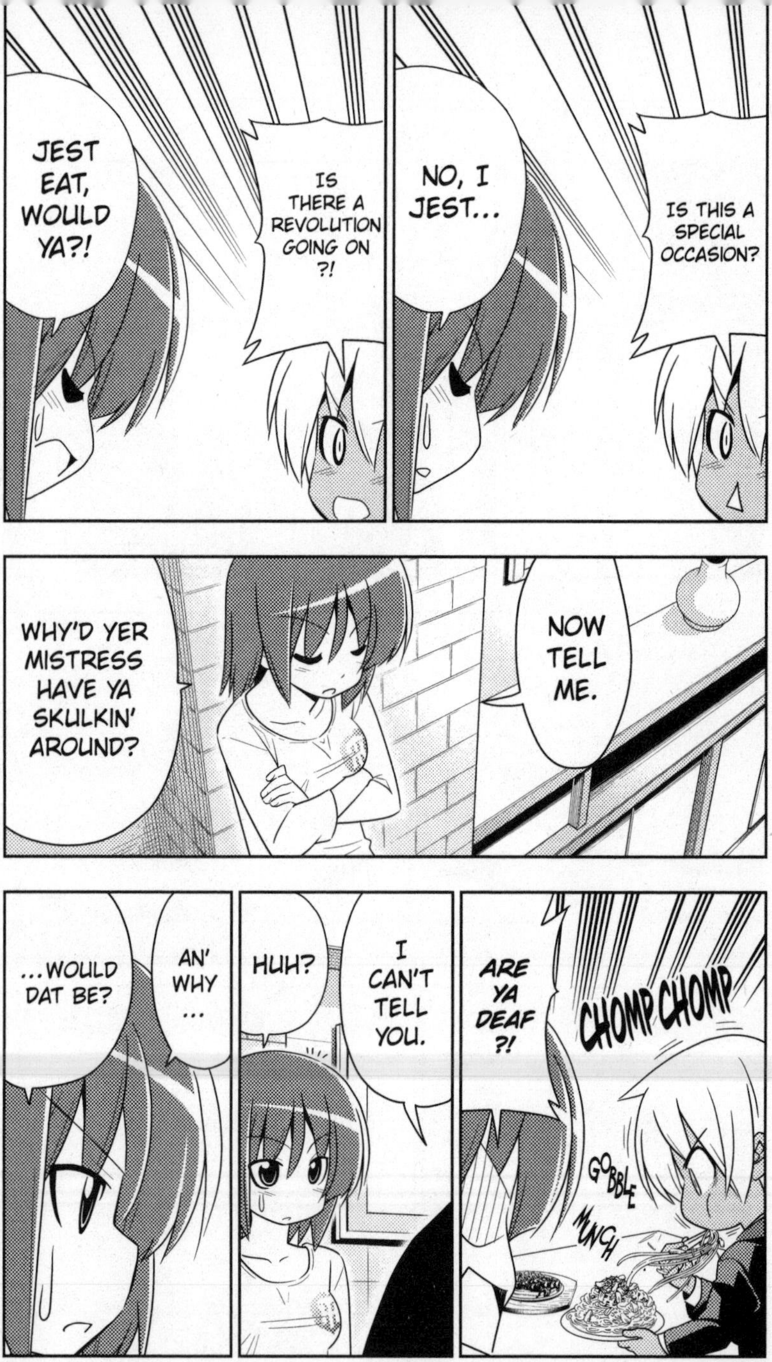
IS THIS A SPECIAL OCCASION?
NO, I JEST...
IS THERE A REVOLUTION GOING ON ?!
JEST EAT, WOULD YA?!
NOW TELL ME.
WHY'D YER MISTRESS HAVE YA SKULKIN' AROUND?
CHOMP CHOMP
ARE YA DEAF ?!
GOBBLE
MUNCH
I CAN'T TELL YOU.
HUH?
AN' WHY ...
...WOULD DAT BE?

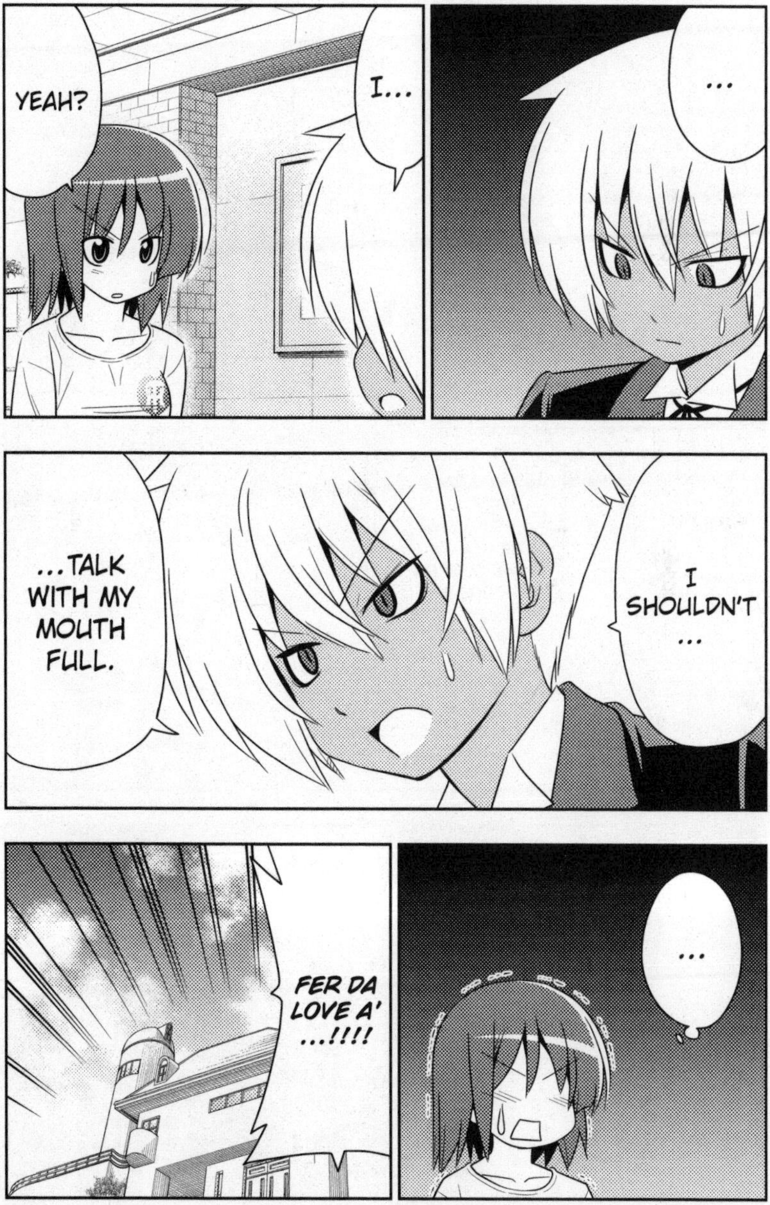
...
I...
YEAH?
I SHOULDN'T ...
...TALK WITH MY MOUTH FULL.
...
FER DA LOVE A' ...!!!!

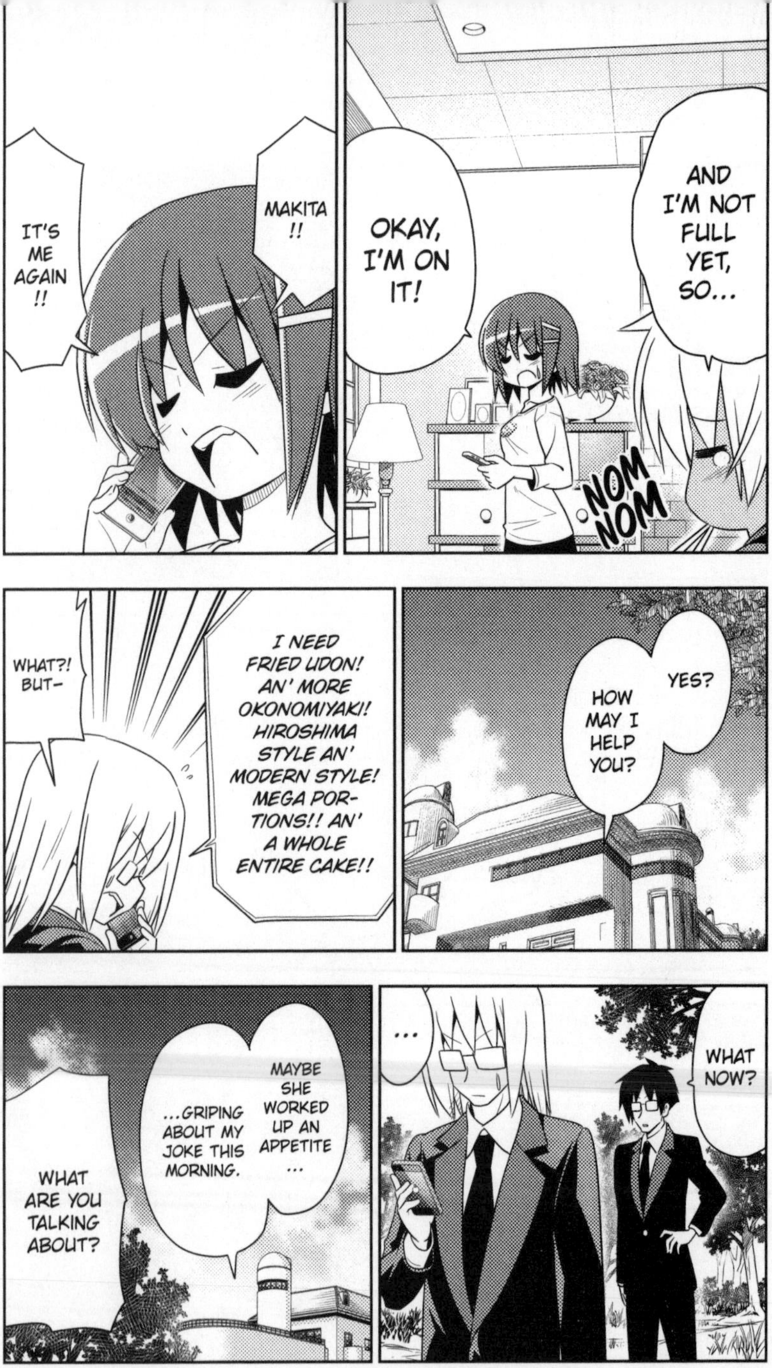
AND I'M NOT FULL YET, SO...
OKAY, I'M ON IT!
NOM NOM
MAKITA!!
IT'S ME AGAIN!!
YES?
HOW MAY I HELP YOU?
I NEED FRIED UDON! AN' MORE OKONOMIYAKI! HIROSHIMA STYLE AN' MODERN STYLE! MEGA PORTIONS!! AN' A WHOLE ENTIRE CAKE!!
WHAT?! BUT-
WHAT NOW?
...
MAYBE SHE WORKED UP AN APPETITE...
...GRIPING ABOUT MY JOKE THIS MORNING.
WHAT ARE YOU TALKING ABOUT?

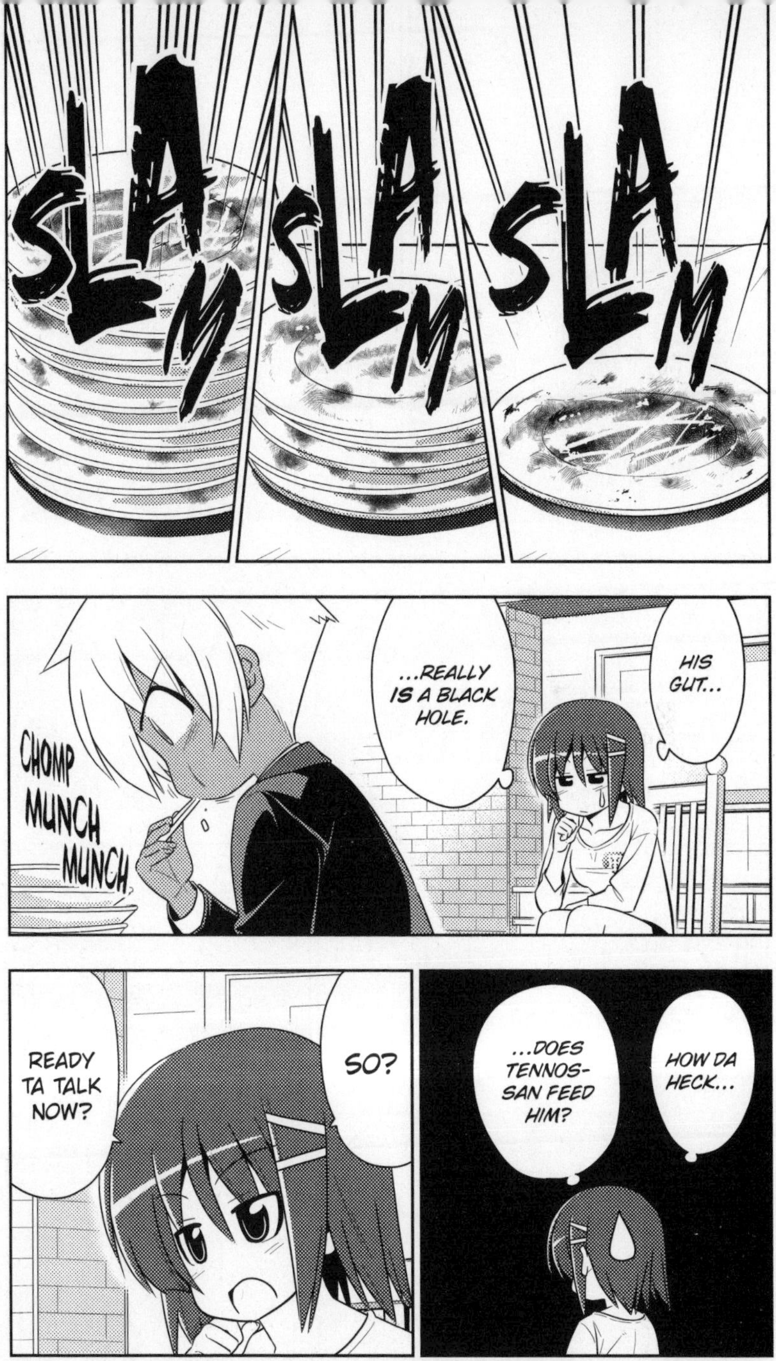
SLAM
SLAM
SLAM
HIS GUT...
...REALLY IS A BLACK HOLE.
CHOMP MUNCH MUNCH
HOW DA HECK...
...DOES TENNOS-SAN FEED HIM?
SO?
READY TA TALK NOW?

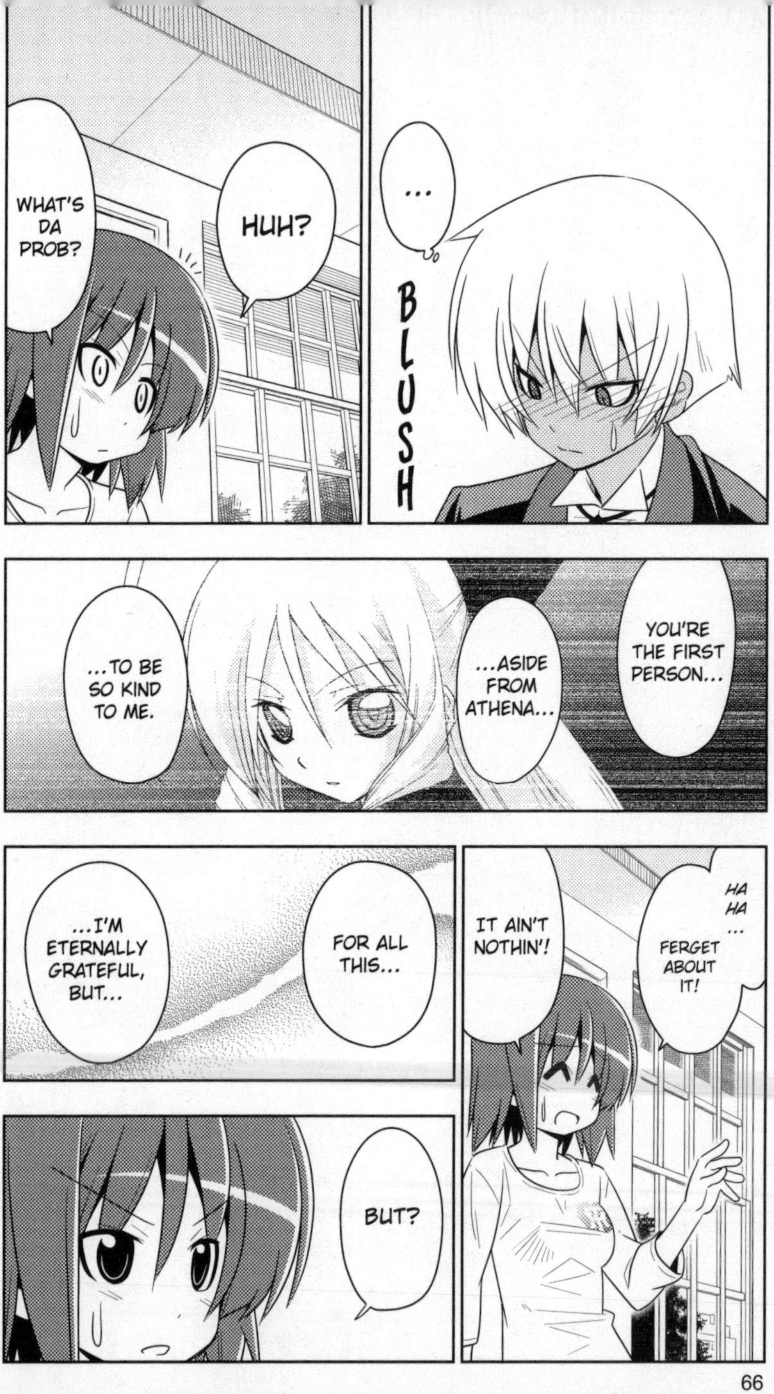
...
BLUSH
HUH?
WHAT'S DA PROB?
YOU'RE THE FIRST PERSON...
...ASIDE FROM ATHENA...
...TO BE SO KIND TO ME.
HA HA...
FERGET ABOUT IT!
IT AIN'T NOTHIN'!
FOR ALL THIS...
...I'M ETERNALLY GRATEFUL, BUT...
BUT?

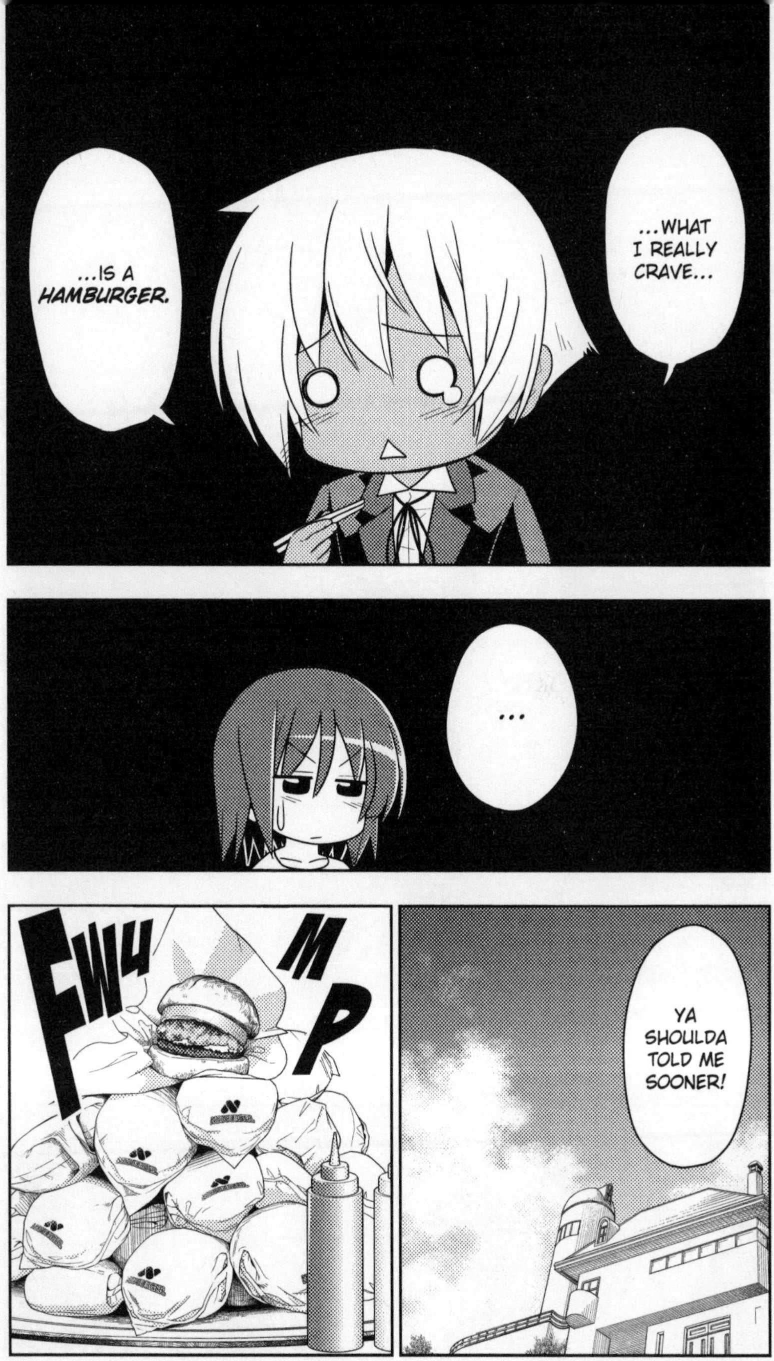
...WHAT I REALLY CRAVE...
...IS A HAMBURGER.
...
YA SHOULDA TOLD ME SOONER!
FWUMP

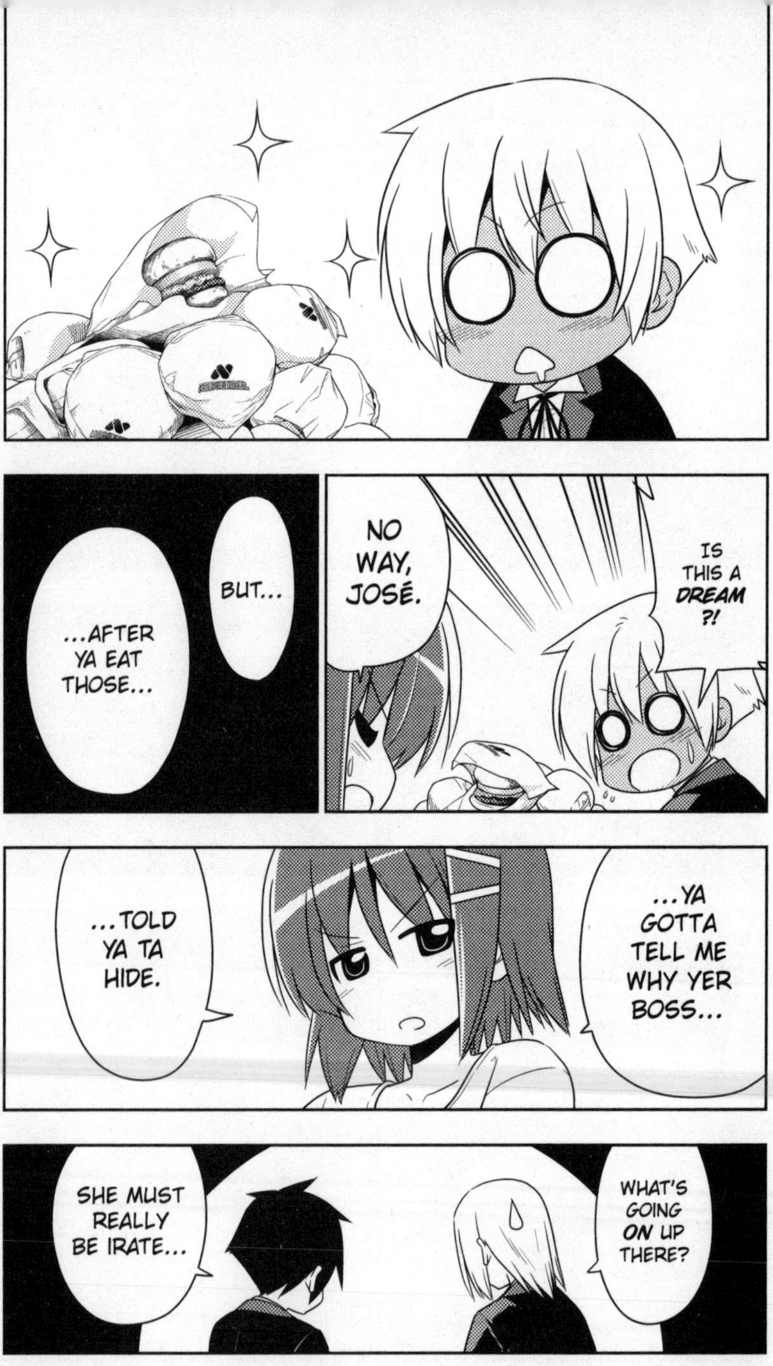
IS THIS A DREAM?!
NO WAY, JOSÉ.
BUT...
...AFTER YA EAT THOSE...
...YA GOTTA TELL ME WHY YER BOSS...
...TOLD YA TA HIDE.
WHAT'S GOING ON UP THERE?
SHE MUST REALLY BE IRATE...

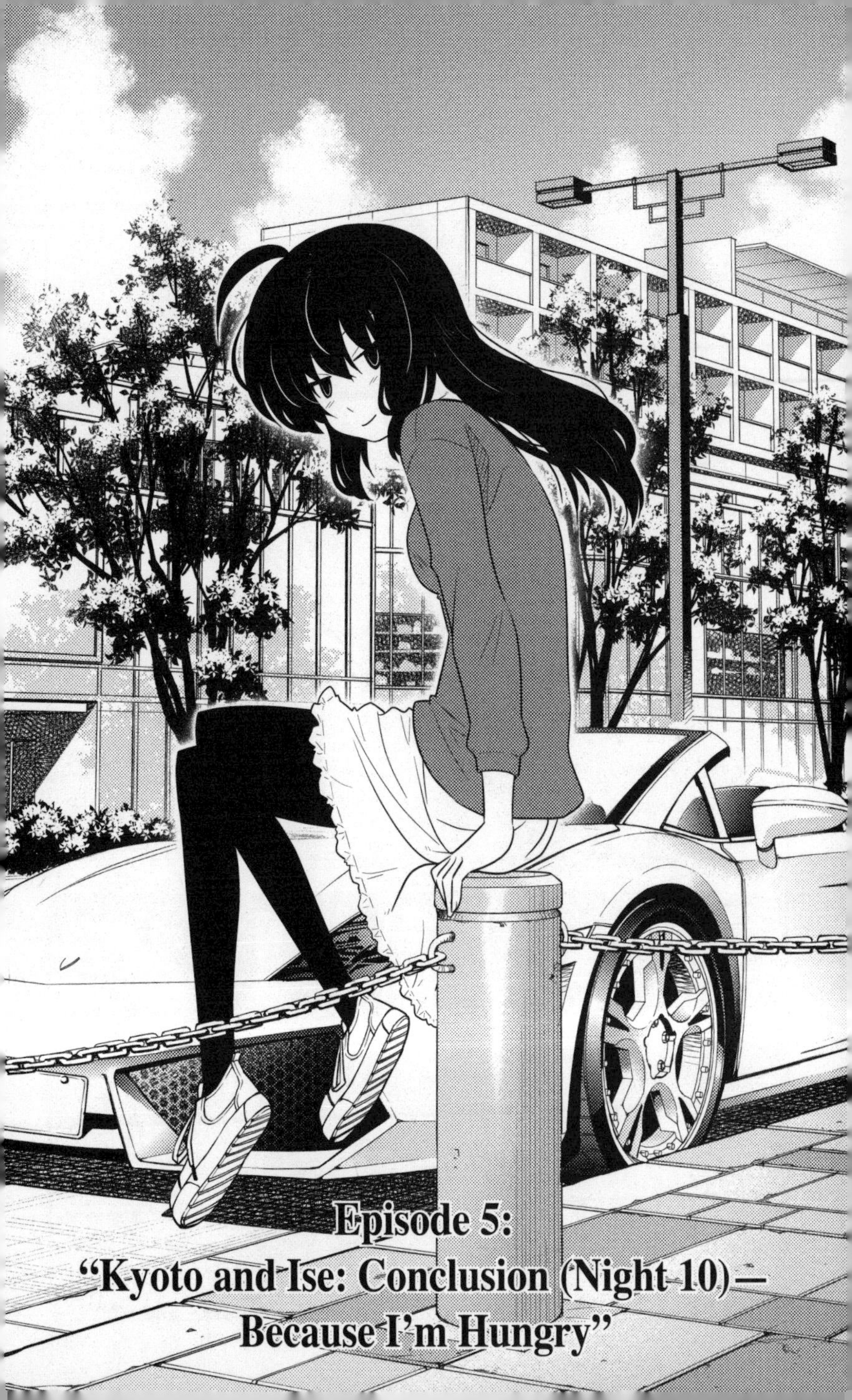

Episode 5: “Kyoto and Ise: Conclusion (Night 10) – Because I’m Hungry”

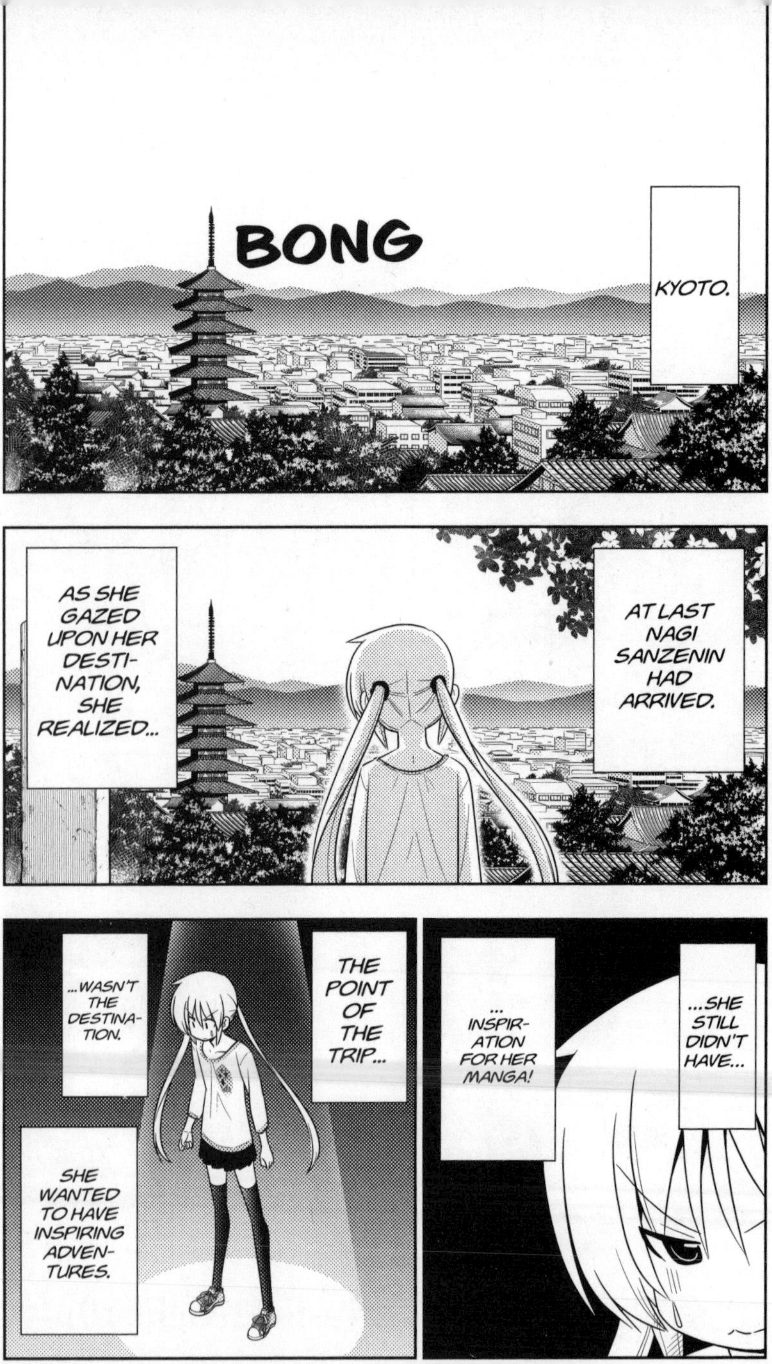
BONG
KYOTO.
AT LAST NAGI SANZENIN HAD ARRIVED.
AS SHE GAZED UPON HER DESTINATION, SHE REALIZED...
...SHE STILL DIDN'T HAVE...
...INSPIRATION FOR HER MANGA!
THE POINT OF THE TRIP...
...WASN'T THE DESTINATION.
SHE WANTED TO HAVE INSPIRING ADVENTURES.

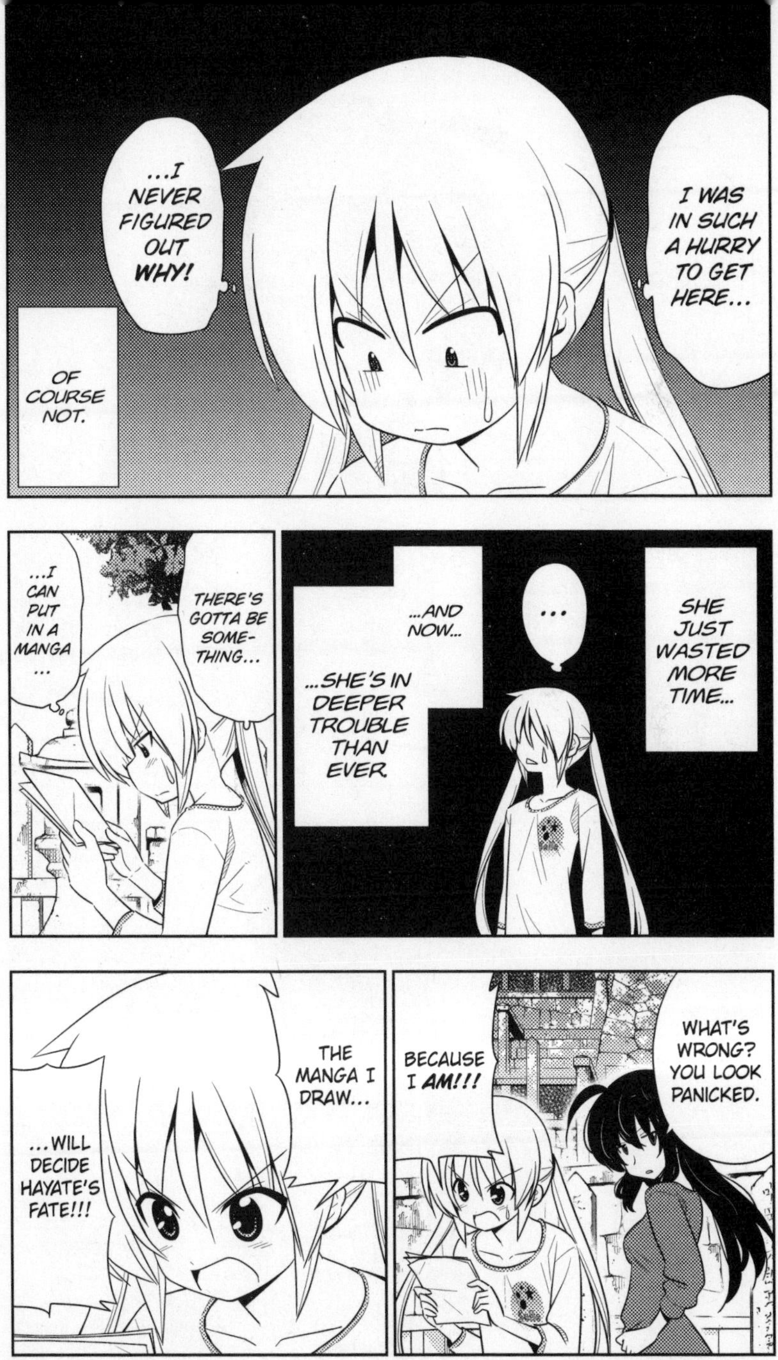
I WAS IN SUCH A HURRY TO GET HERE...
...I NEVER FIGURED OUT WHY!
OF COURSE NOT.
SHE JUST WASTED MORE TIME...
...
...AND NOW...
...SHE'S IN DEEPER TROUBLE THAN EVER.
THERE'S GOTTA BE SOME-THING...
...I CAN PUT IN A MANGA...
WHAT'S WRONG? YOU LOOK PANICKED.
BECAUSE I AM!!!
THE MANGA I DRAW...
...WILL DECIDE HAYATE'S FATE!!!

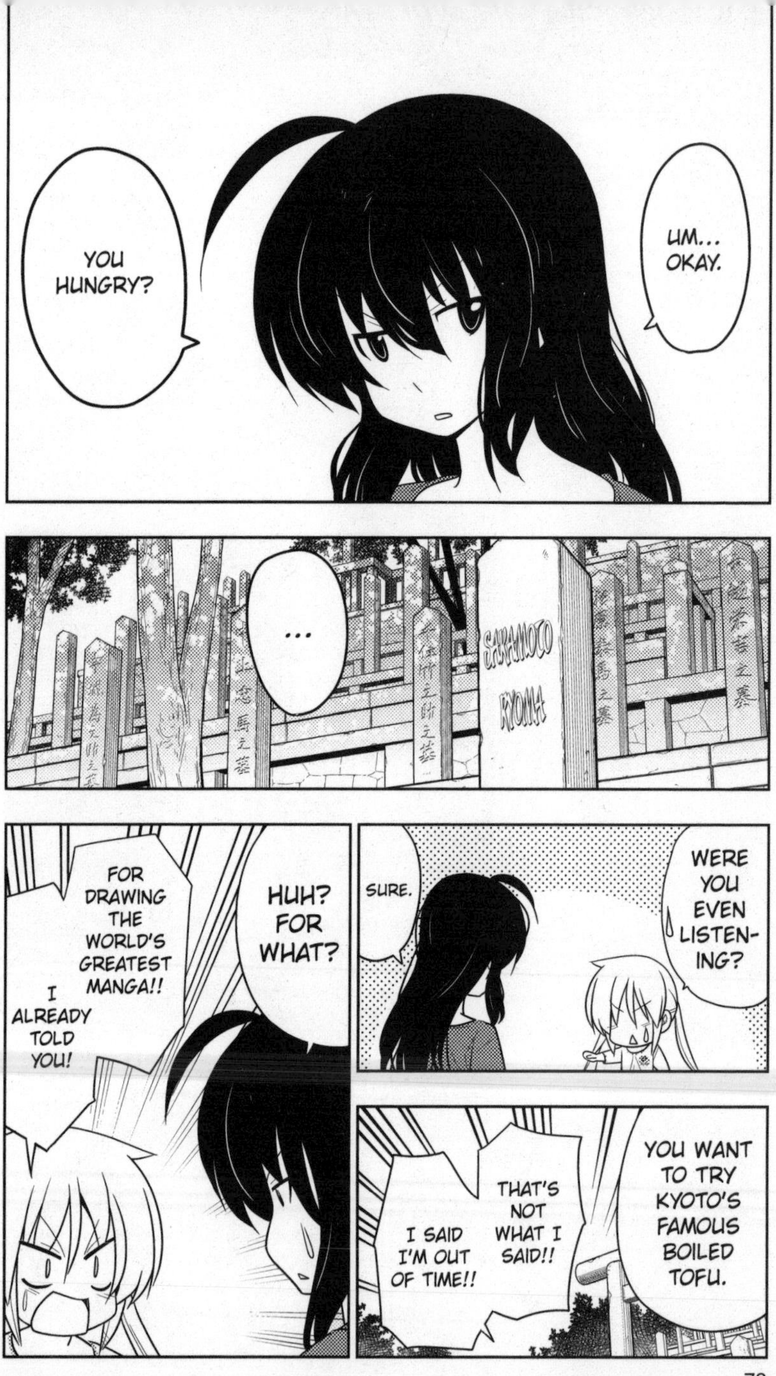
UM... OKAY.
YOU HUNGRY?
...
SAKAMOTO RYOMA
WERE YOU EVEN LISTENING?
SURE.
YOU WANT TO TRY KYOTO'S FAMOUS BOILED TOFU.
THAT'S NOT WHAT I SAID!!
I SAID I'M OUT OF TIME!!
HUH? FOR WHAT?
FOR DRAWING THE WORLD'S GREATEST MANGA!!
I ALREADY TOLD YOU!

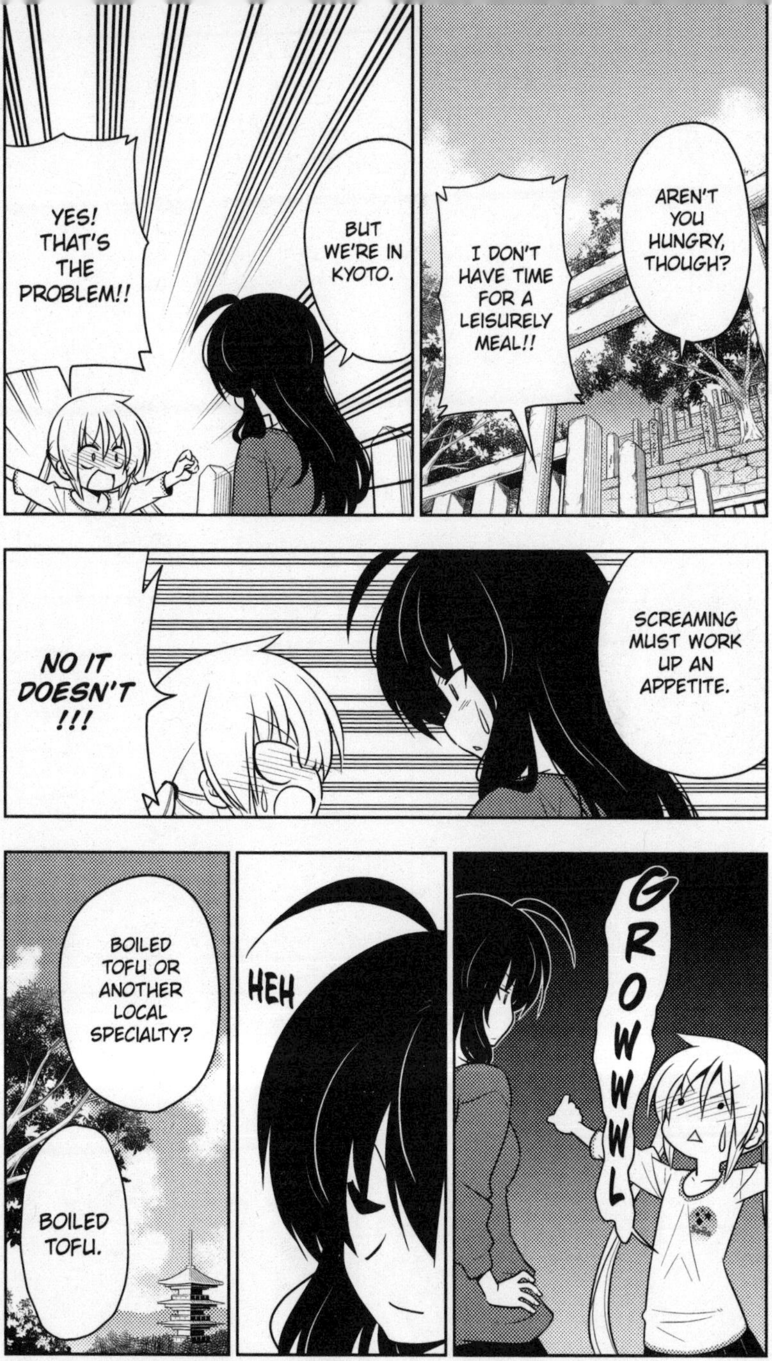
AREN'T YOU HUNGRY, THOUGH?
I DON'T HAVE TIME FOR A LEISURELY MEAL!!
BUT WE'RE IN KYOTO.
YES! THAT'S THE PROBLEM!!
SCREAMING MUST WORK UP AN APPETITE.
NO IT DOESN'T!!!
GROWWWL
HEH
BOILED TOFU OR ANOTHER LOCAL SPECIALTY?
BOILED TOFU.

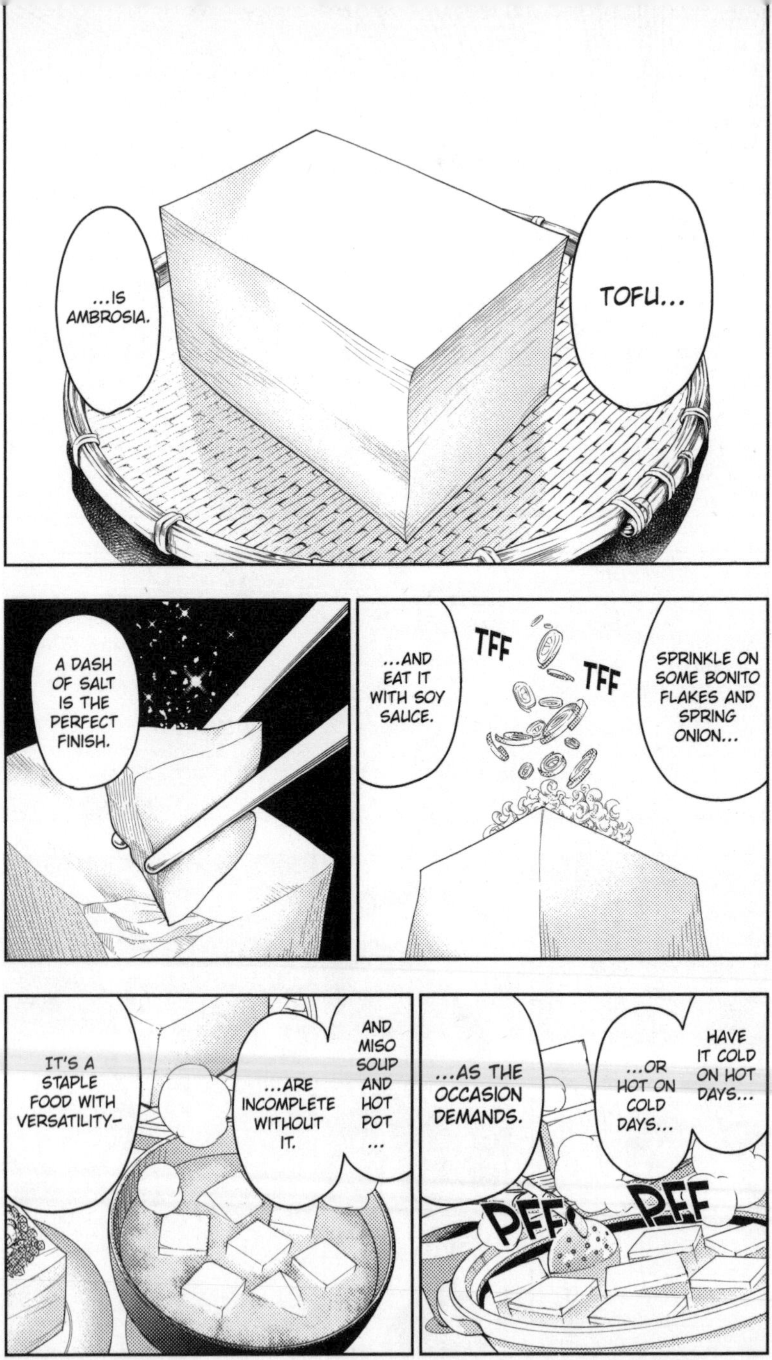
TOFU...
...IS AMBROSIA.
SPRINKLE ON SOME BONITO FLAKES AND SPRING ONION...
TFF
TFF
...AND EAT IT WITH SOY SAUCE.
A DASH OF SALT IS THE PERFECT FINISH.
HAVE IT COLD ON HOT DAYS...
...OR HOT ON COLD DAYS...
PFF
PFF
...AS THE OCCASION DEMANDS.
AND MISO SOUP AND HOT POT...
...ARE INCOMPLETE WITHOUT IT.
IT'S A STAPLE FOOD WITH VERSATILITY-

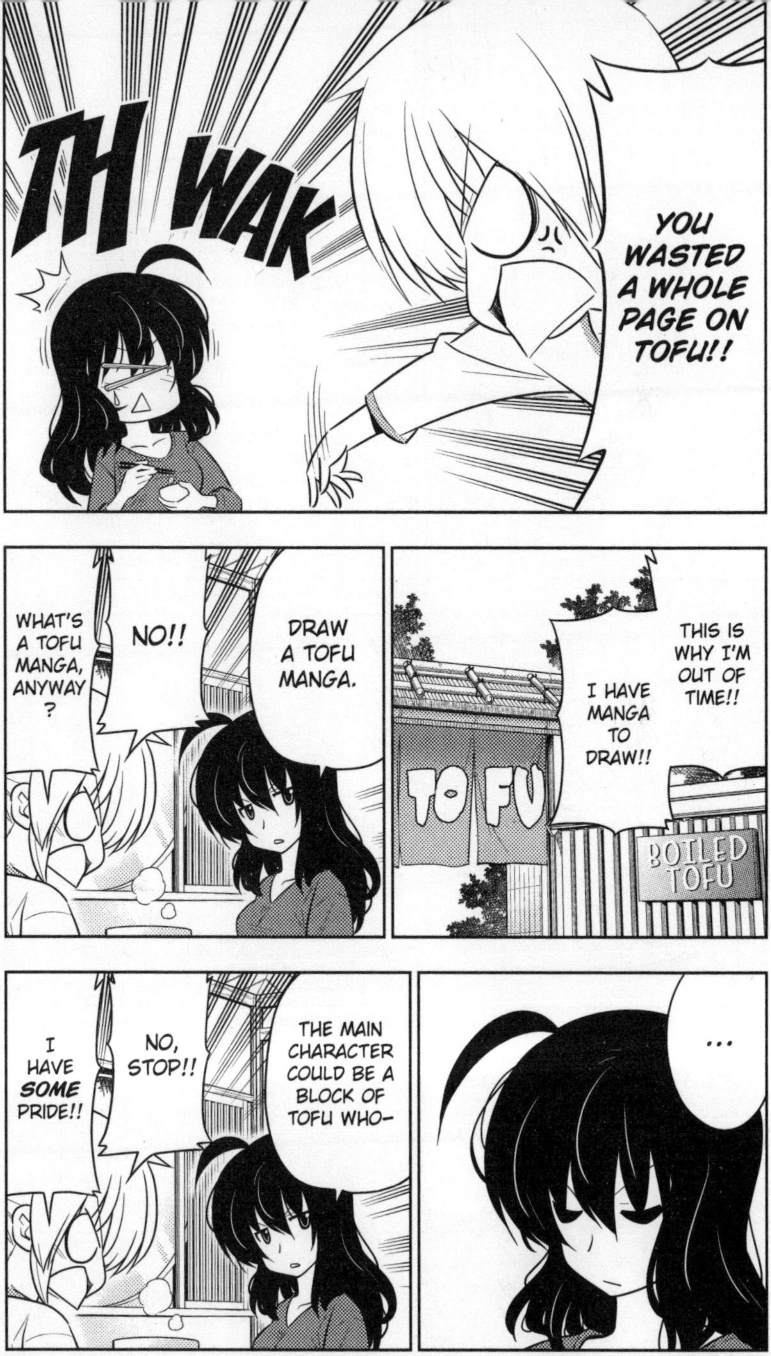
YOU WASTED A WHOLE PAGE ON TOFU!!
TH WAK
THIS IS WHY I'M OUT OF TIME!!
I HAVE MANGA TO DRAW!!
TO FU
BOILED TOFU
DRAW A TOFU MANGA.
NO!!
WHAT'S A TOFU MANGA, ANYWAY?
...
THE MAIN CHARACTER COULD BE A BLOCK OF TOFU WHO-
NO, STOP!!
I HAVE **SOME** PRIDE!!

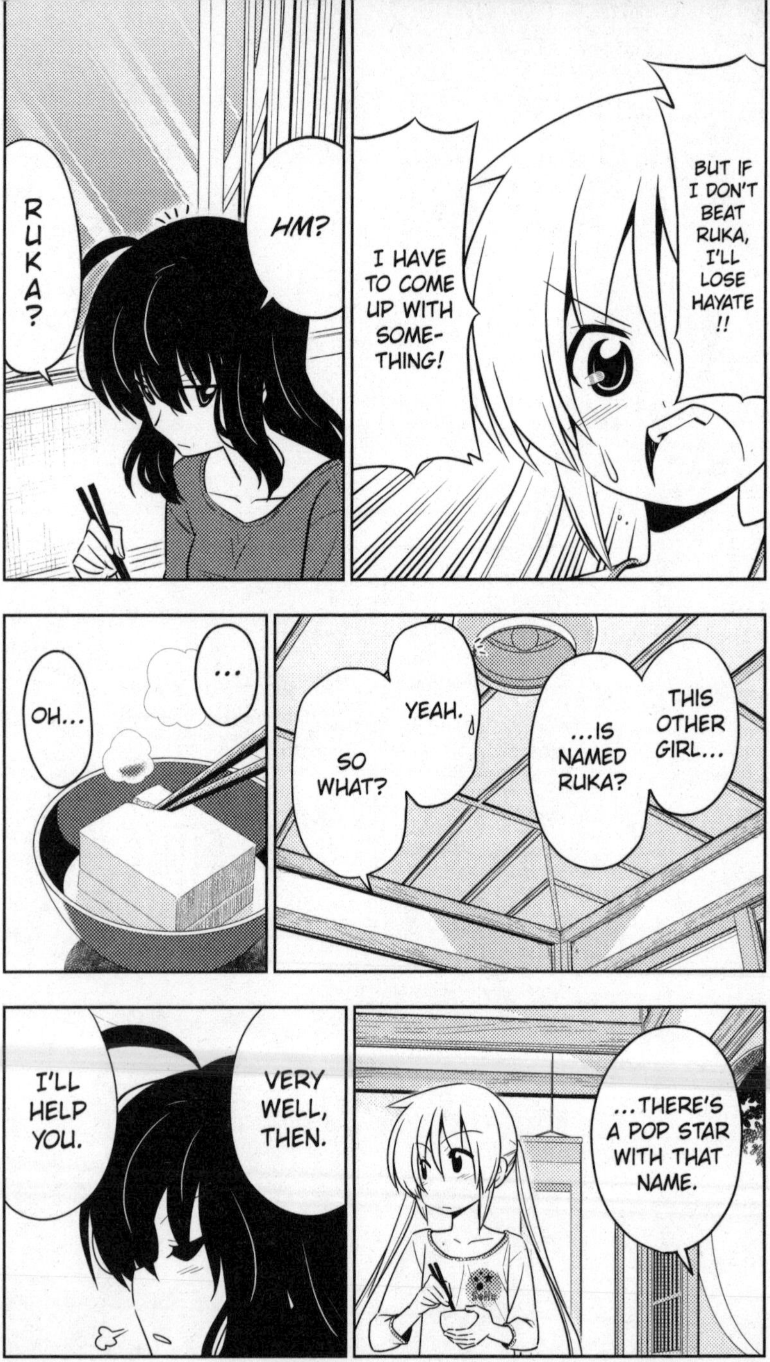
BUT IF I DON'T BEAT RUKA, I'LL LOSE HAYATE!!
I HAVE TO COME UP WITH SOME-THING!
HM?
RUKA?
THIS OTHER GIRL...
...IS NAMED RUKA?
YEAH.
SO WHAT?
...
OH...
...THERE'S A POP STAR WITH THAT NAME.
VERY WELL, THEN.
I'LL HELP YOU.

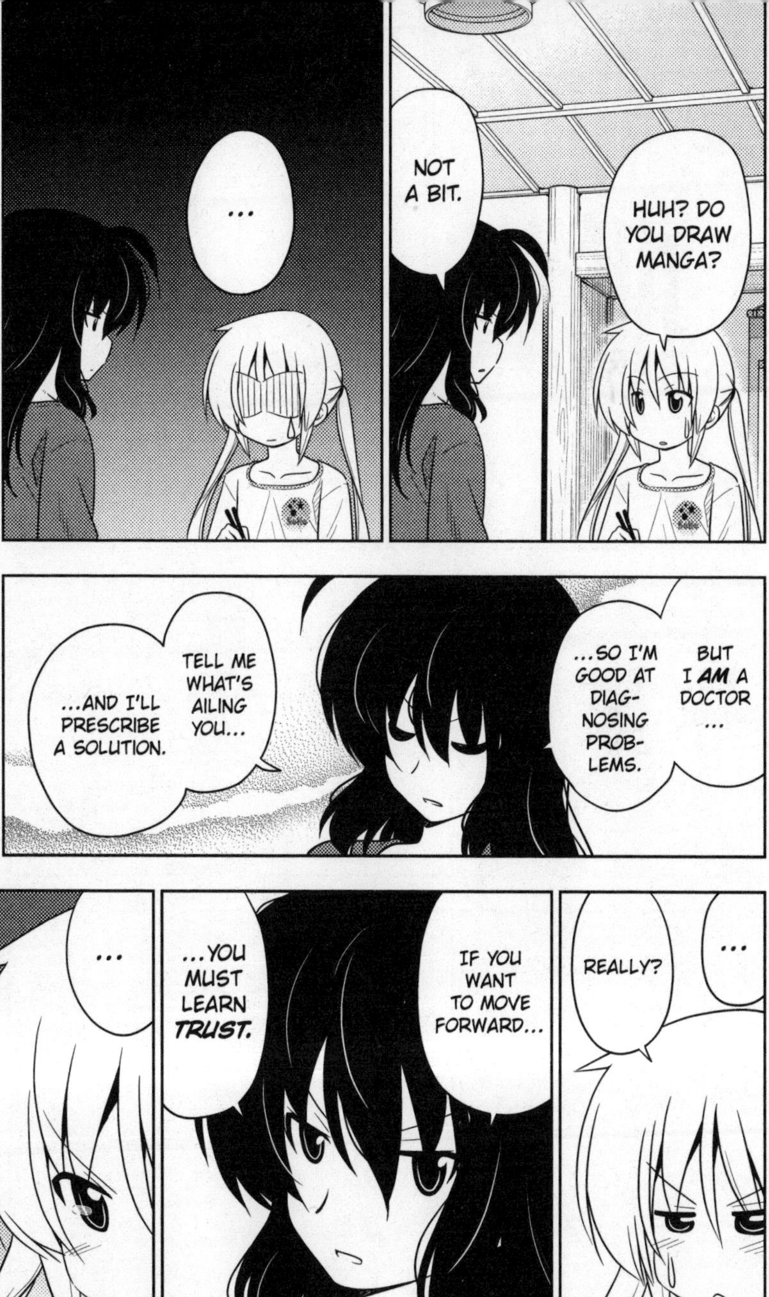
HUH? DO YOU DRAW MANGA?
NOT A BIT.
...
BUT I *AM* A DOCTOR...
...SO I'M GOOD AT DIAG-NOSING PROB-LEMS.
TELL ME WHAT'S AILING YOU...
...AND I'LL PRESCRIBE A SOLUTION.
...
REALLY?
IF YOU WANT TO MOVE FORWARD...
...YOU MUST LEARN *TRUST.*
...

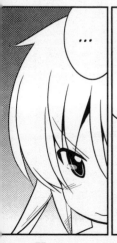

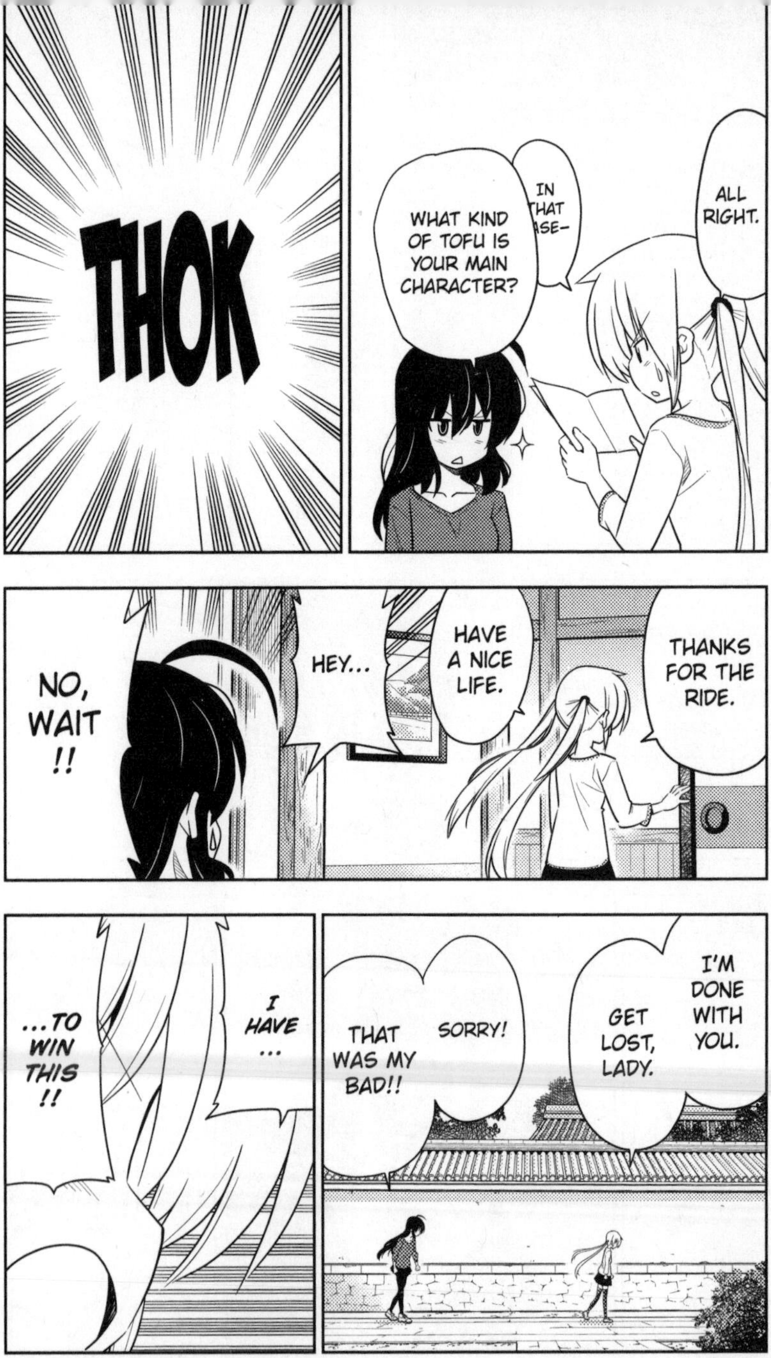
ALL RIGHT.
IN THAT ASE-
WHAT KIND OF TOFU IS YOUR MAIN CHARACTER?
THOK
THANKS FOR THE RIDE.
HAVE A NICE LIFE.
HEY...
NO, WAIT!!
I'M DONE WITH YOU.
GET LOST, LADY.
SORRY!
THAT WAS MY BAD!!
I HAVE...
...TO WIN THIS!!

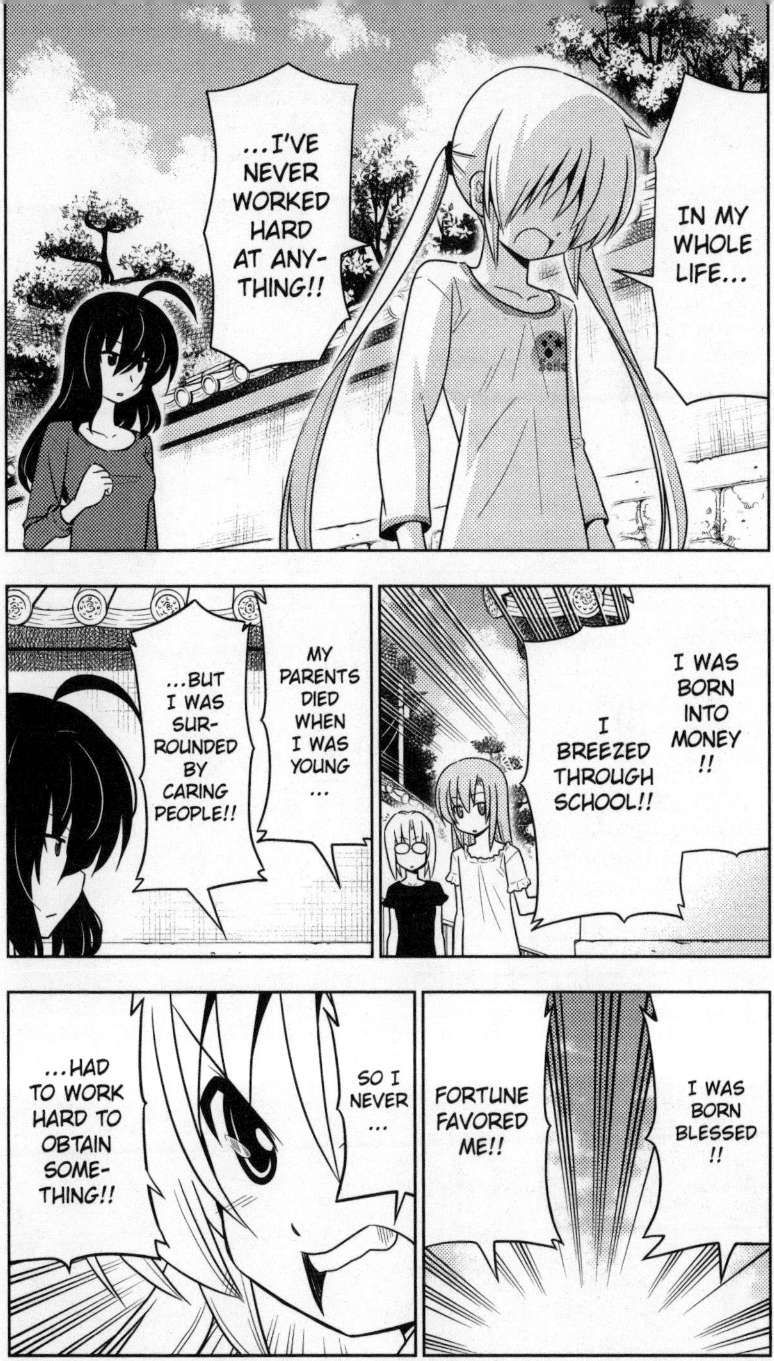
IN MY WHOLE LIFE...
...I'VE NEVER WORKED HARD AT ANYTHING!!
I WAS BORN INTO MONEY!!
I BREEZED THROUGH SCHOOL!!
MY PARENTS DIED WHEN I WAS YOUNG...
...BUT I WAS SURROUNDED BY CARING PEOPLE!!
I WAS BORN BLESSED!!
FORTUNE FAVORED ME!!
SO I NEVER...
...HAD TO WORK HARD TO OBTAIN SOMETHING!!

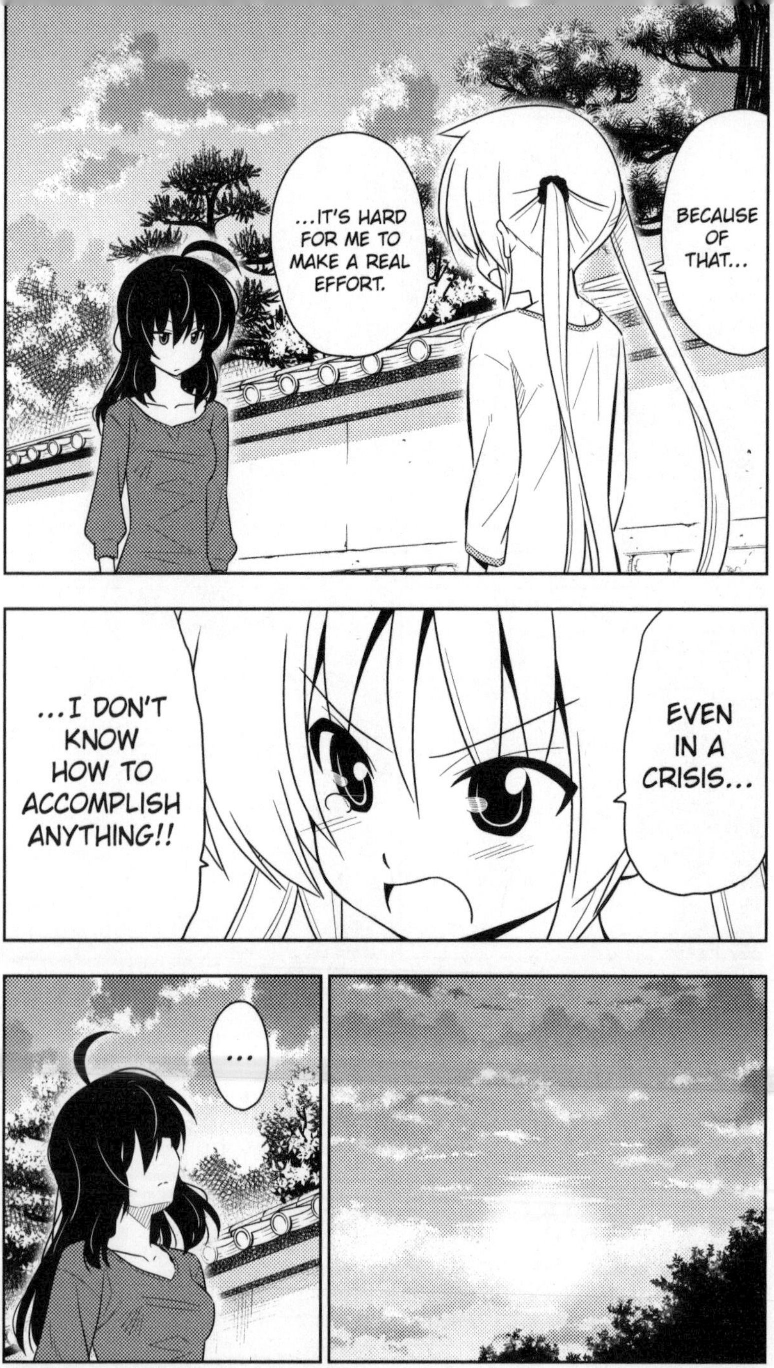
BECAUSE OF THAT...
...IT'S HARD FOR ME TO MAKE A REAL EFFORT.
EVEN IN A CRISIS...
...I DON'T KNOW HOW TO ACCOMPLISH ANYTHING!!
...

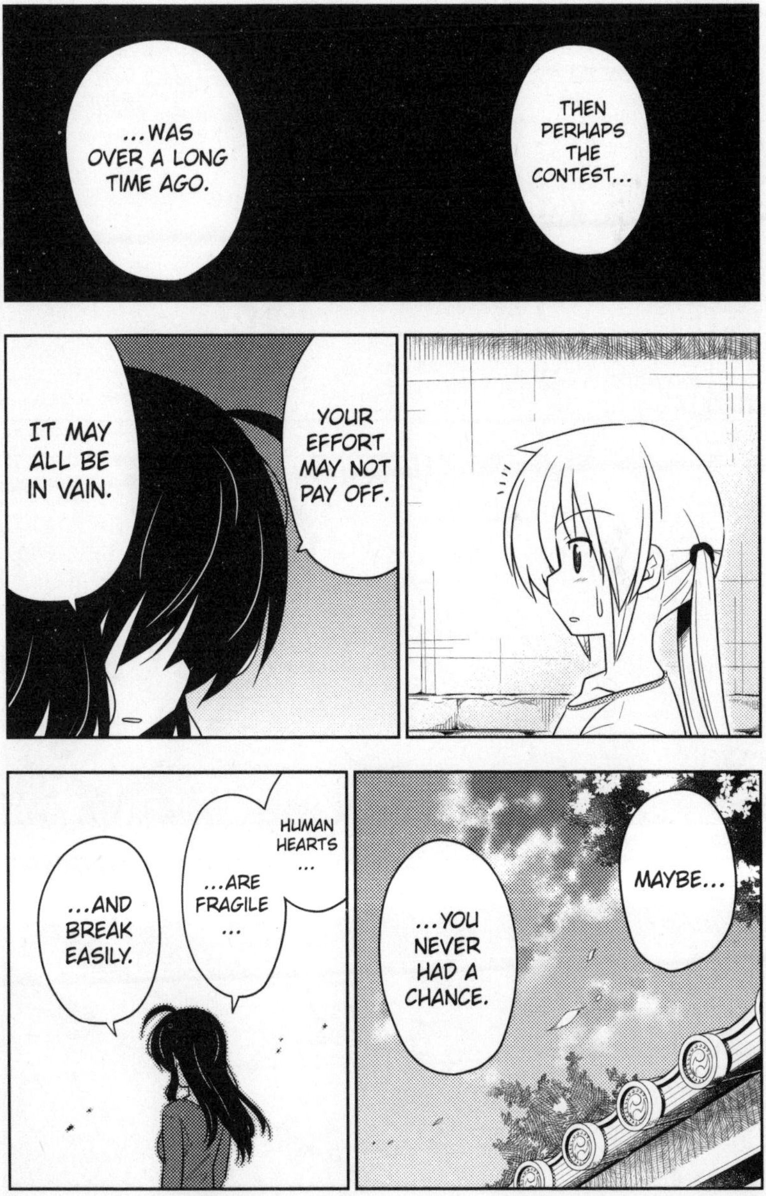
THEN PERHAPS THE CONTEST...
...WAS OVER A LONG TIME AGO.
YOUR EFFORT MAY NOT PAY OFF.
IT MAY ALL BE IN VAIN.
MAYBE...
...YOU NEVER HAD A CHANCE.
HUMAN HEARTS ...
...ARE FRAGILE ...
...AND BREAK EASILY.

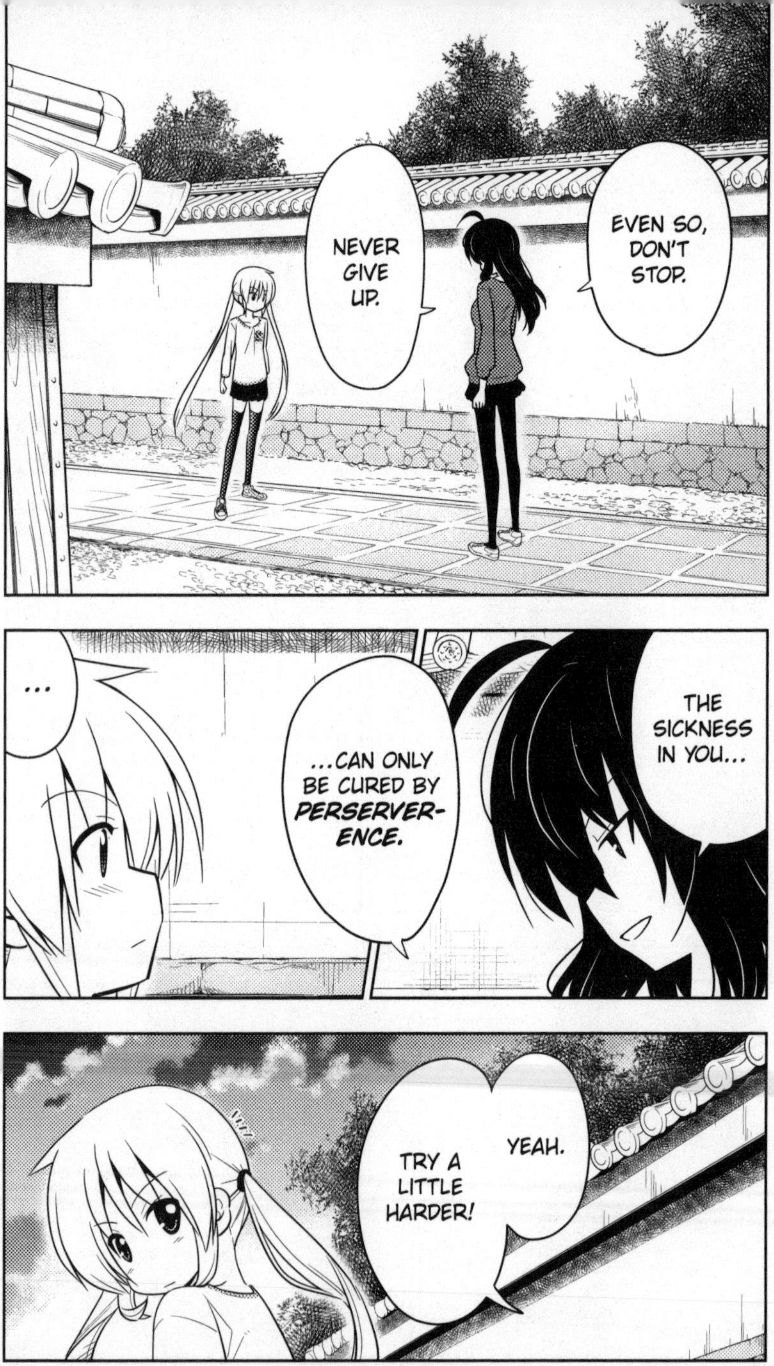
EVEN SO, DON'T STOP.
NEVER GIVE UP.
THE SICKNESS IN YOU...
...CAN ONLY BE CURED BY *PERSERVERENCE.*
...
YEAH.
TRY A LITTLE HARDER!

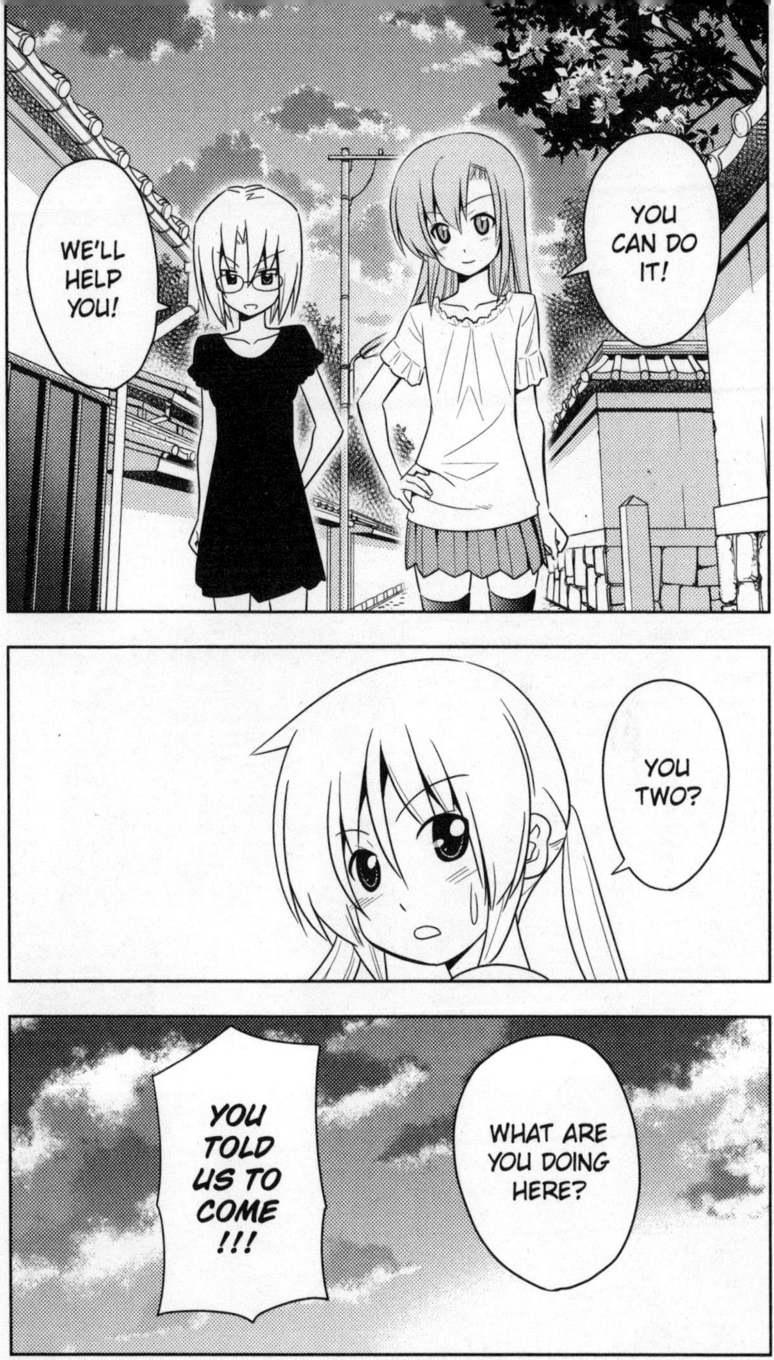
YOU CAN DO IT!
WE'LL HELP YOU!
YOU TWO?
WHAT ARE YOU DOING HERE?
YOU TOLD US TO COME!!!

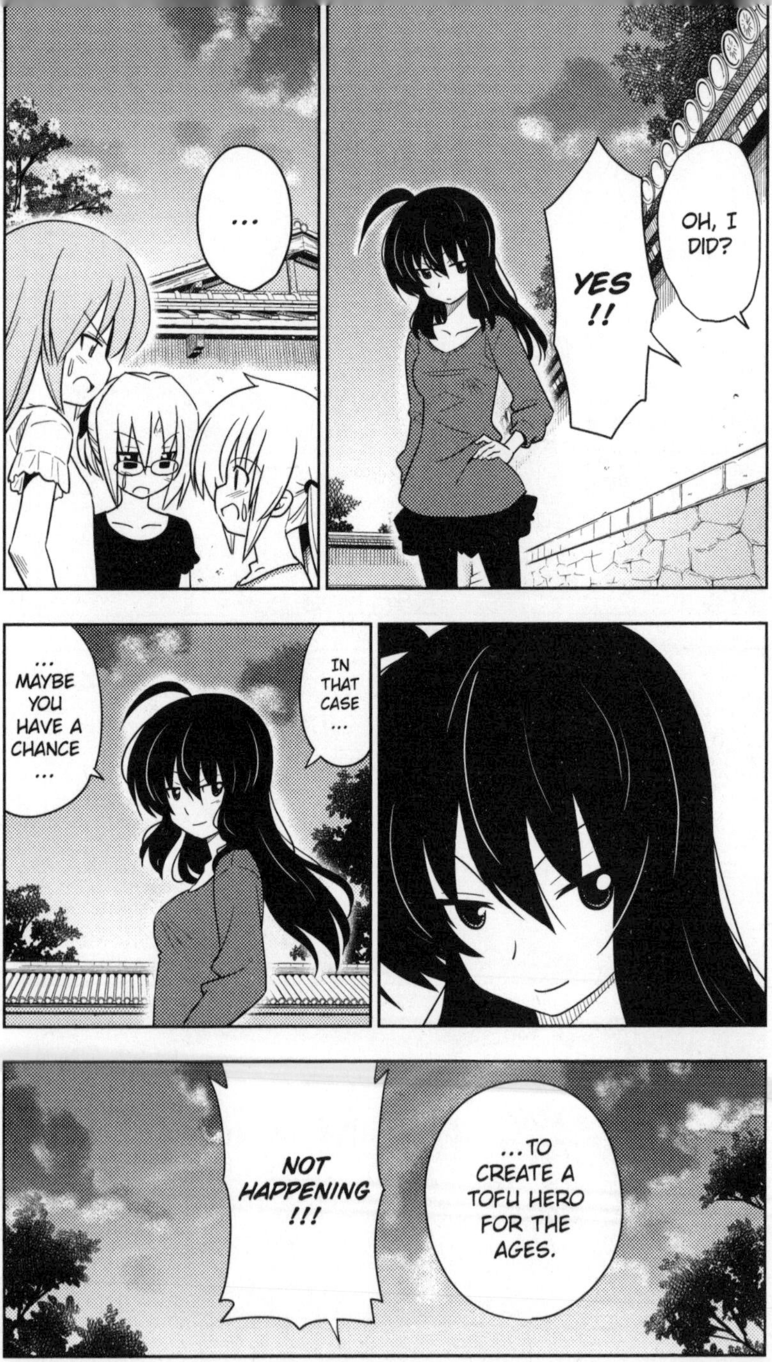
OH, I DID?
YES!!
...
IN THAT CASE...
...MAYBE YOU HAVE A CHANCE...
...TO CREATE A TOFU HERO FOR THE AGES.
NOT HAPPENING!!!

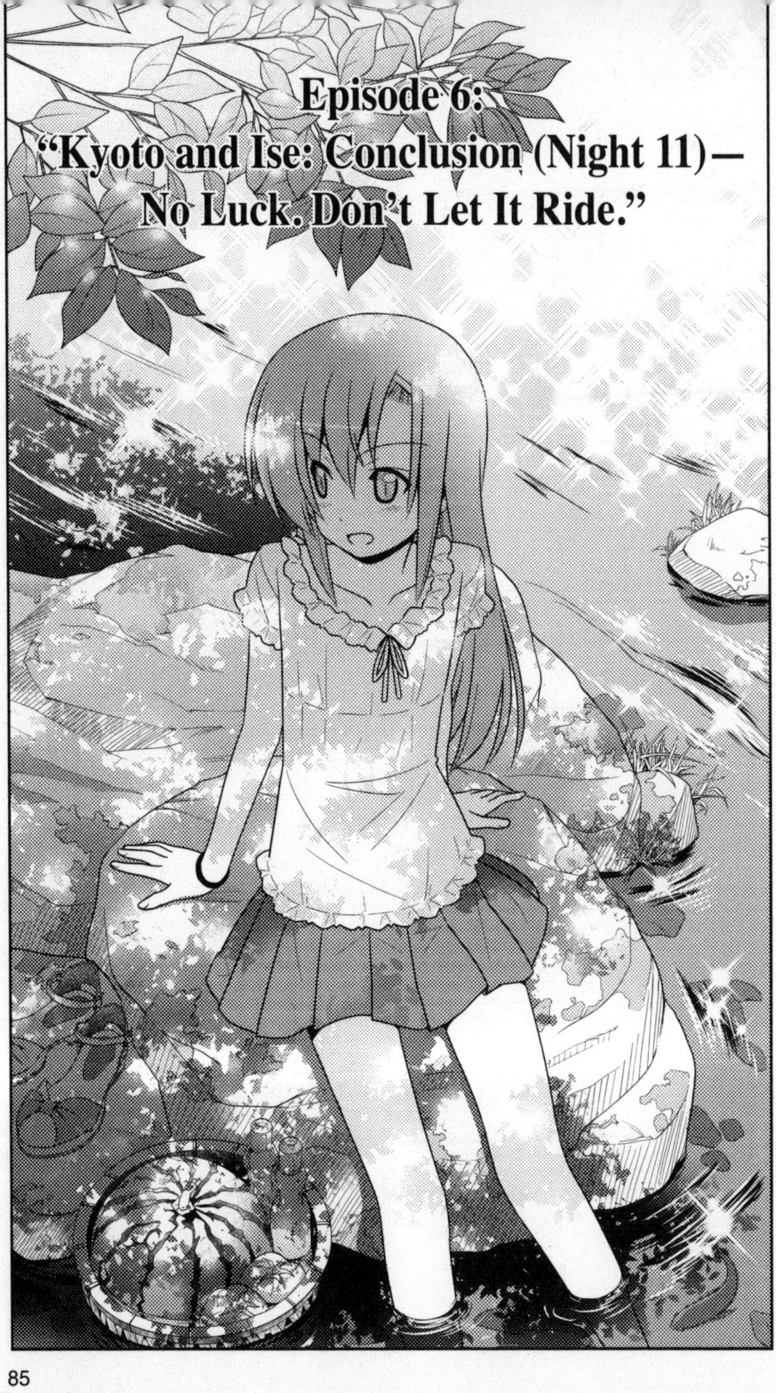
Episode 6:
"Kyoto and Ise: Conclusion (Night 11)—
No Luck. Don't Let It Ride."

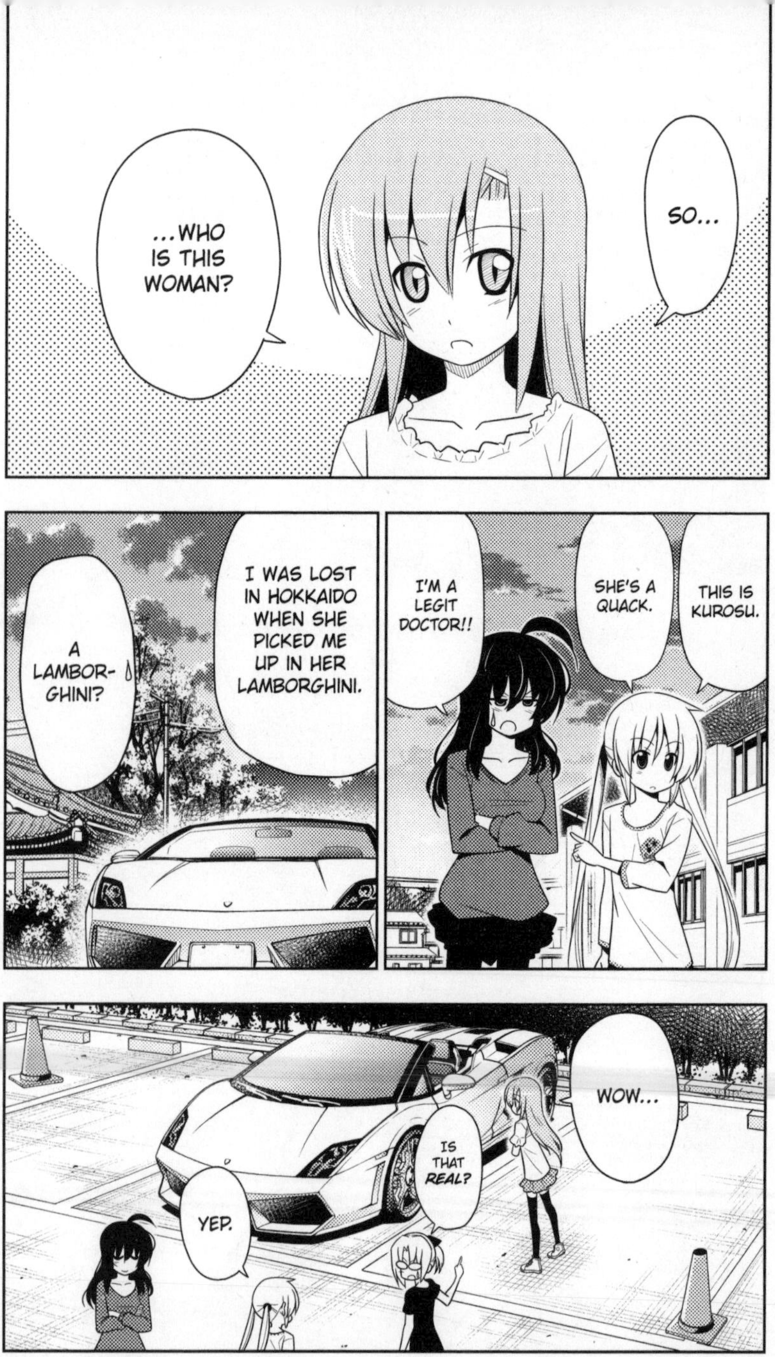
SO...
...WHO IS THIS WOMAN?
THIS IS KUROSU.
SHE'S A QUACK.
I'M A LEGIT DOCTOR!!
I WAS LOST IN HOKKAIDO WHEN SHE PICKED ME UP IN HER LAMBORGHINI.
A LAMBORGHINI?
WOW...
IS THAT *REAL?*
YEP.

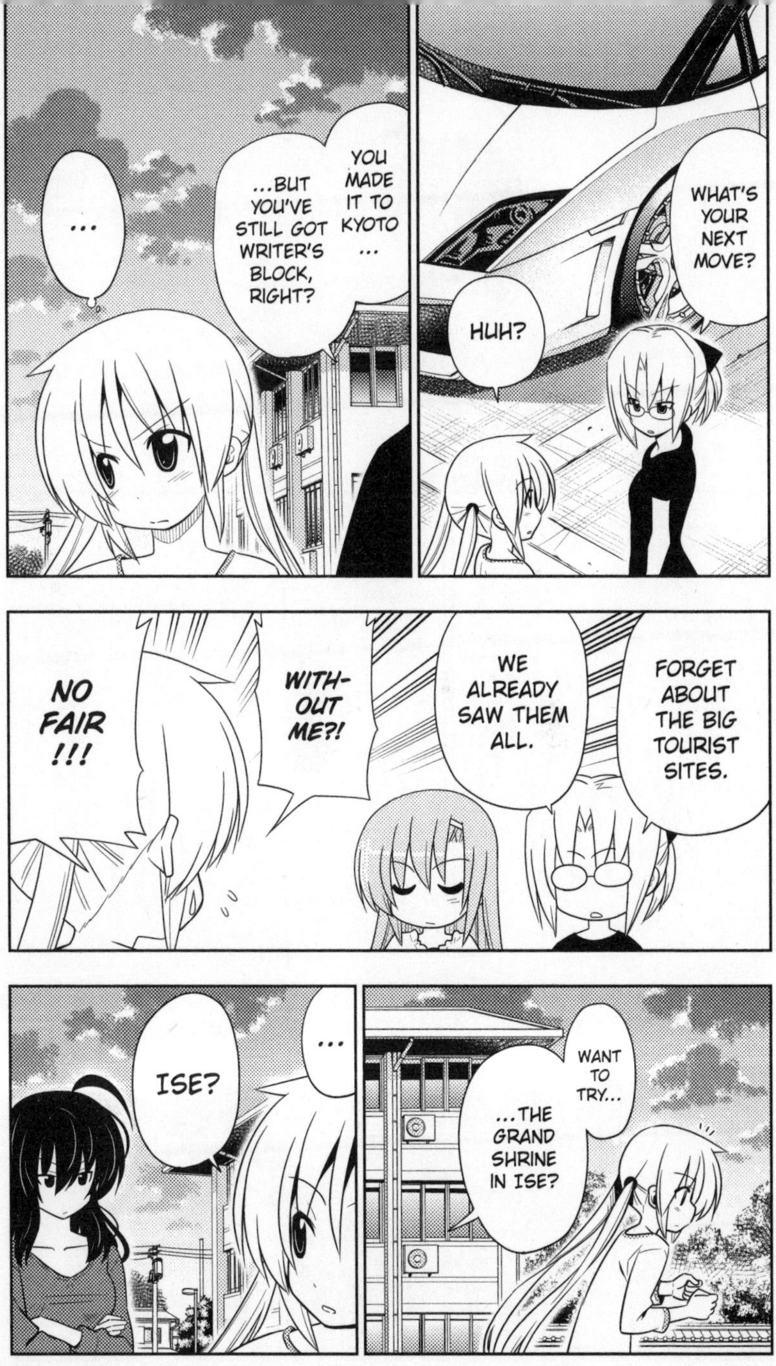
WHAT'S YOUR NEXT MOVE?
HUH?
YOU MADE IT TO KYOTO...
...BUT YOU'VE STILL GOT WRITER'S BLOCK, RIGHT?
...
FORGET ABOUT THE BIG TOURIST SITES.
WE ALREADY SAW THEM ALL.
WITH-OUT ME?!
NO FAIR!!!
WANT TO TRY...
...THE GRAND SHRINE IN ISE?
...
ISE?

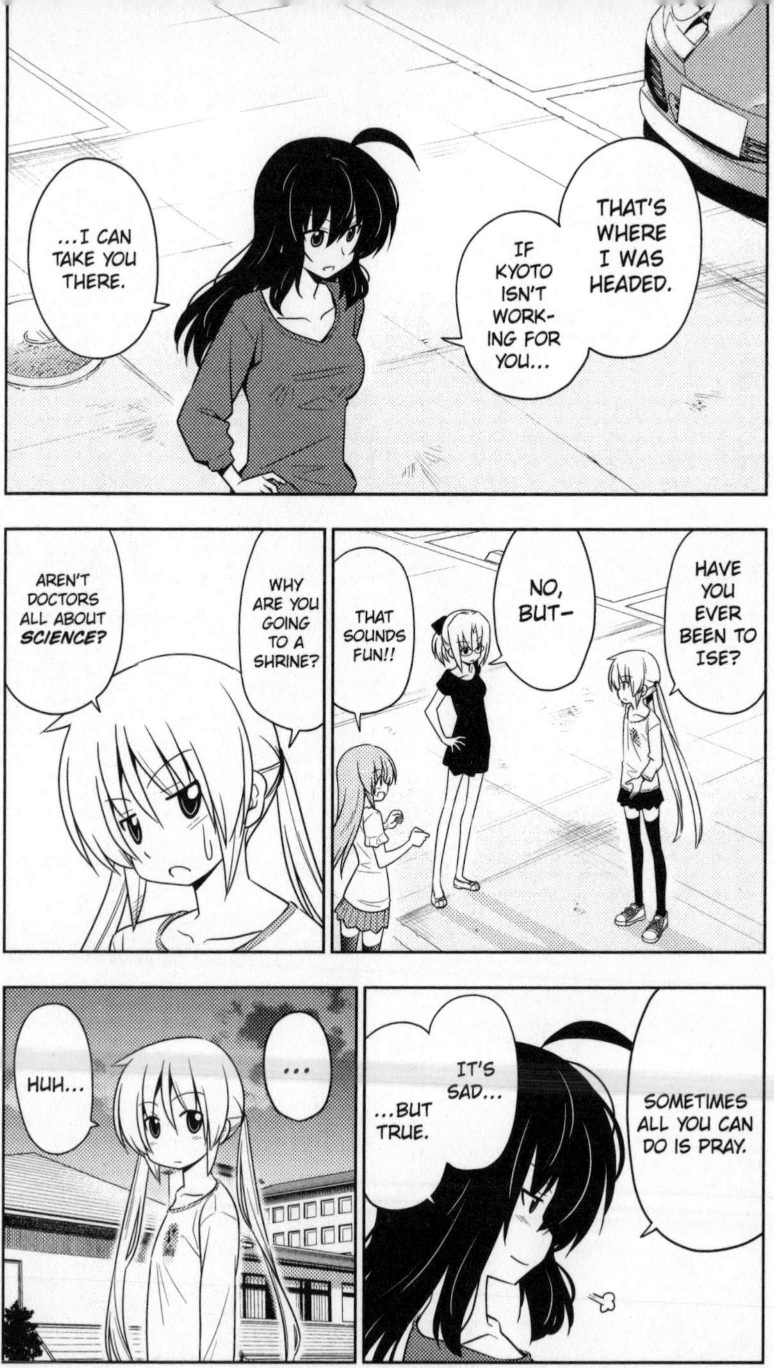
THAT'S WHERE I WAS HEADED.
IF KYOTO ISN'T WORKING FOR YOU...
...I CAN TAKE YOU THERE.
HAVE YOU EVER BEEN TO ISE?
NO, BUT–
THAT SOUNDS FUN!!
WHY ARE YOU GOING TO A SHRINE?
AREN'T DOCTORS ALL ABOUT *SCIENCE?*
SOMETIMES ALL YOU CAN DO IS PRAY.
IT'S SAD...
...BUT TRUE.
...
HUH...

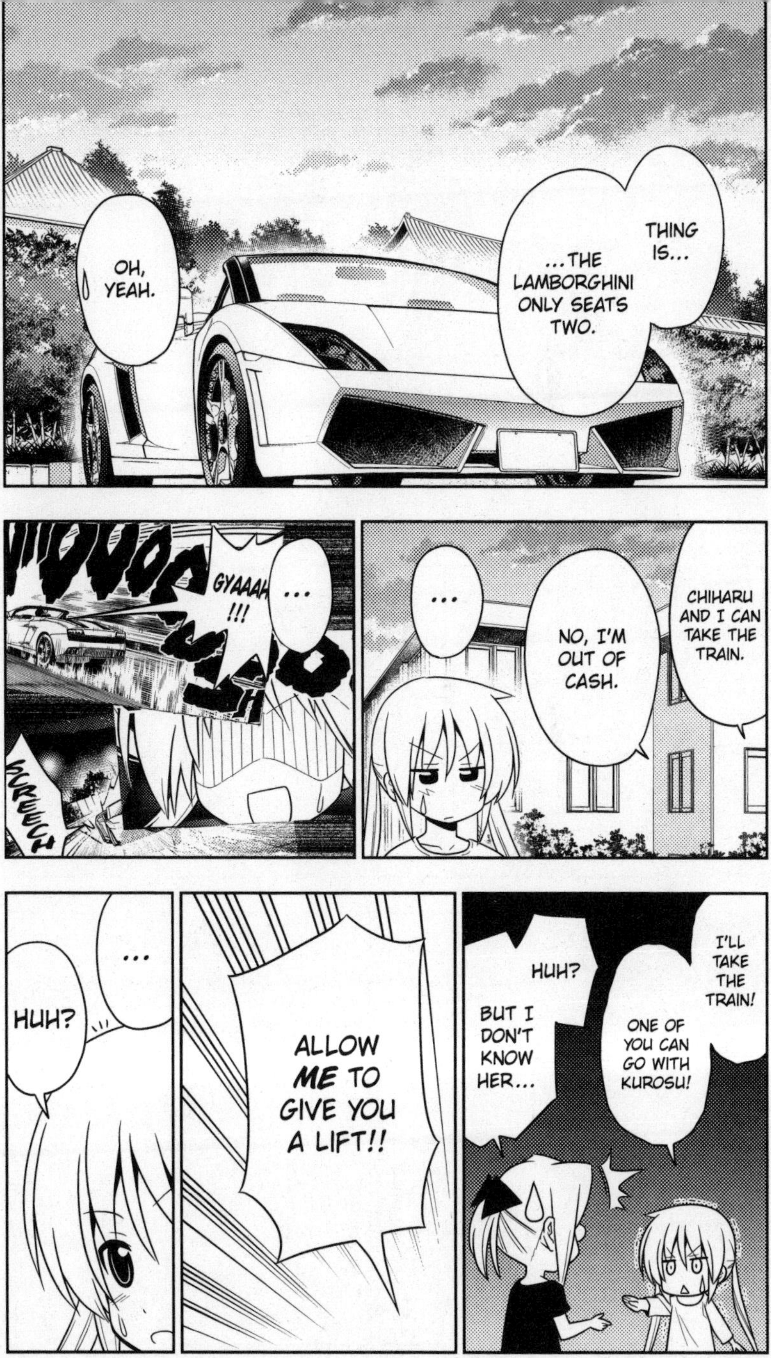
THING IS...
...THE LAMBORGHINI ONLY SEATS TWO.
OH, YEAH.
CHIHARU AND I CAN TAKE THE TRAIN.
NO, I'M OUT OF CASH.
...
...
GYAAAH!!!
SCREECH
I'LL TAKE THE TRAIN!
ONE OF YOU CAN GO WITH KUROSU!
HUH?
BUT I DON'T KNOW HER...
ALLOW ME TO GIVE YOU A LIFT!!
...
HUH?

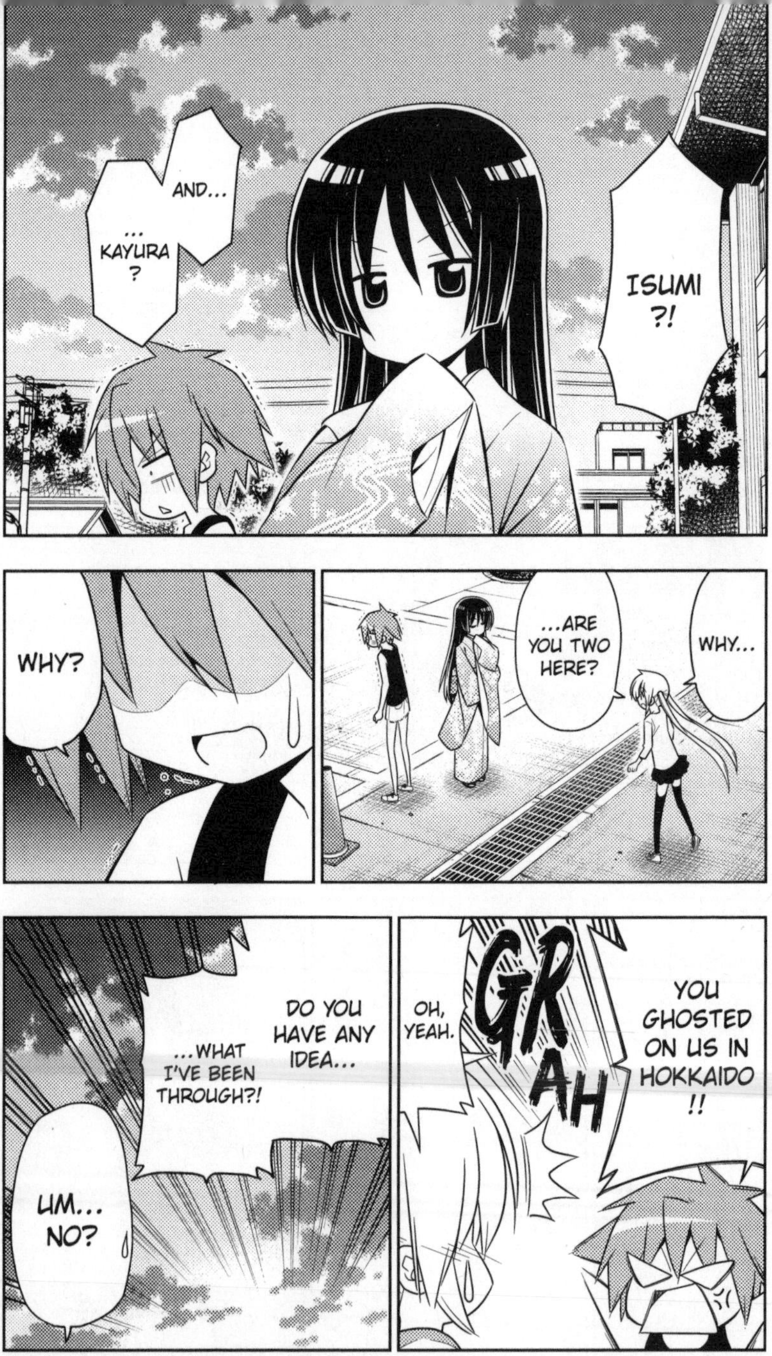
ISUMI ?!
AND...
... KAYURA ?
WHY...
...ARE YOU TWO HERE?
WHY?
YOU GHOSTED ON US IN HOKKAIDO !!
GRAH
OH, YEAH.
DO YOU HAVE ANY IDEA...
...WHAT I'VE BEEN THROUGH?!
UM... NO?

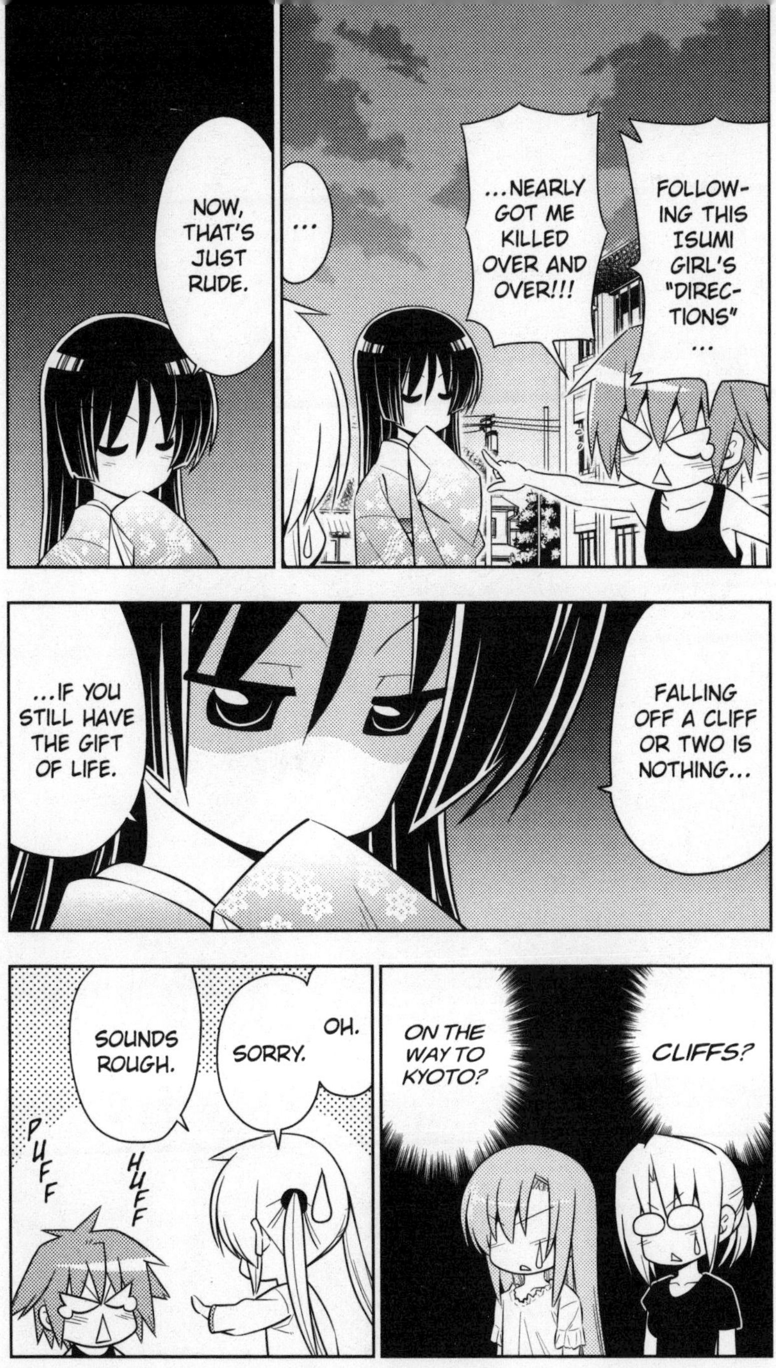
FOLLOWING THIS ISUMI GIRL'S "DIRECTIONS"...
...NEARLY GOT ME KILLED OVER AND OVER!!!
...
NOW, THAT'S JUST RUDE.
FALLING OFF A CLIFF OR TWO IS NOTHING...
...IF YOU STILL HAVE THE GIFT OF LIFE.
CLIFFS?
ON THE WAY TO KYOTO?
OH.
SORRY.
SOUNDS ROUGH.
HUFF
PUFF

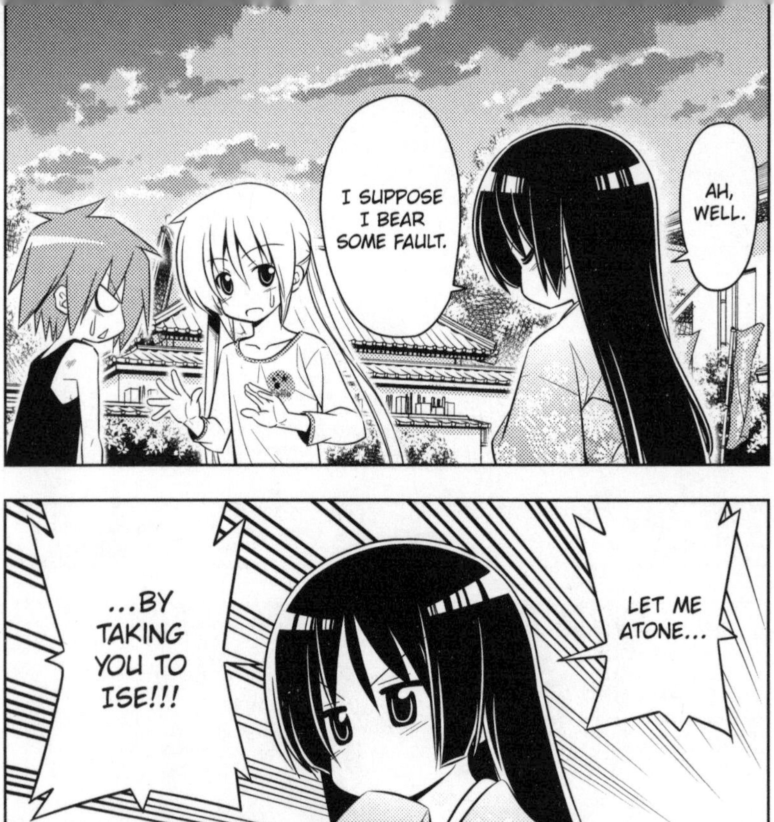

AH, WELL.
I SUPPOSE I BEAR SOME FAULT.
LET ME ATONE...
...BY TAKING YOU TO ISE!!!
I HAVE...
...A BAD FEELING ABOUT THIS!
...
All will end in flames...
MUTTER

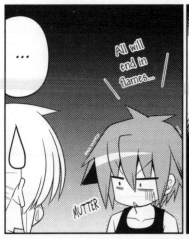

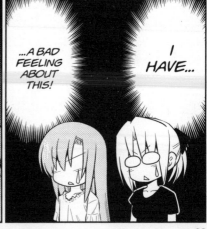

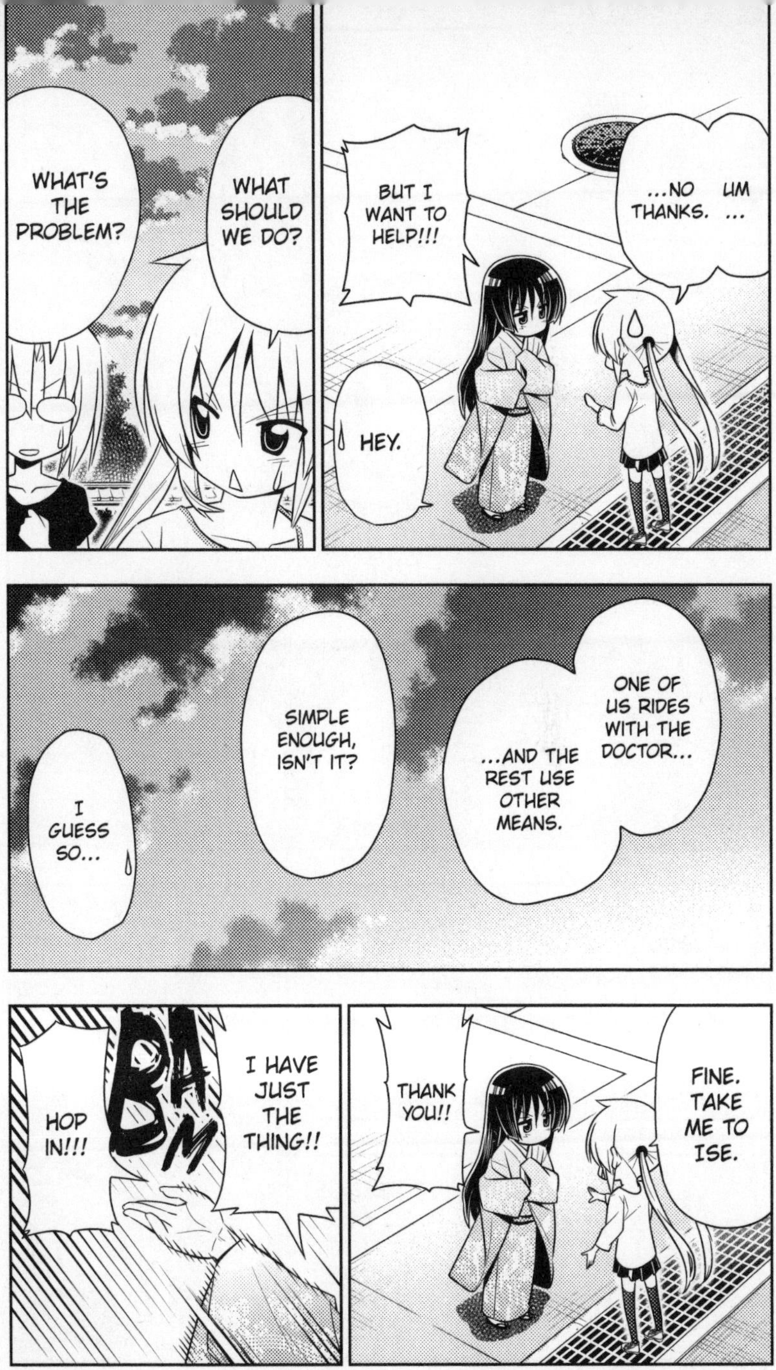
UM ...
...NO THANKS.
BUT I WANT TO HELP!!!
HEY.
WHAT SHOULD WE DO?
WHAT'S THE PROBLEM?
ONE OF US RIDES WITH THE DOCTOR...
...AND THE REST USE OTHER MEANS.
SIMPLE ENOUGH, ISN'T IT?
I GUESS SO...
FINE. TAKE ME TO ISE.
THANK YOU!!
I HAVE JUST THE THING!!
BAM
HOP IN!!!

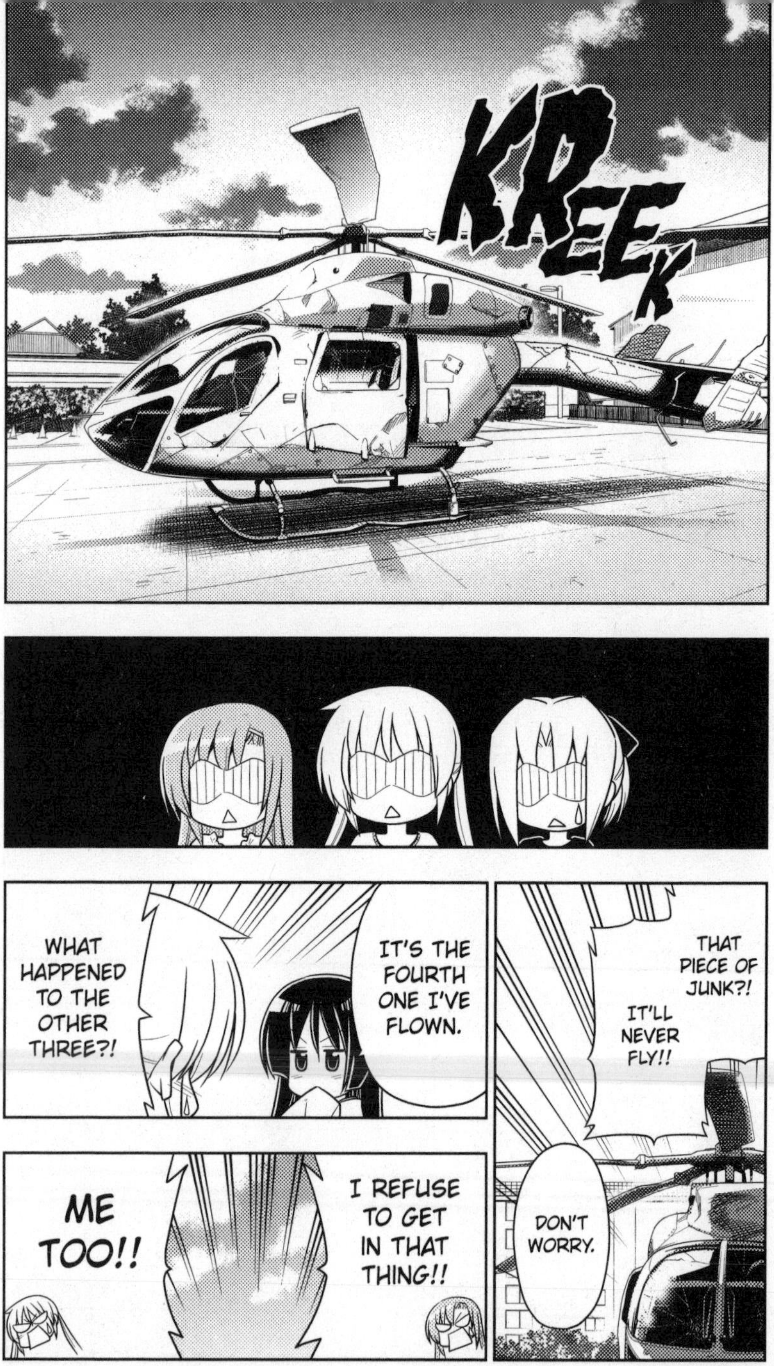
KREEK
THAT PIECE OF JUNK?!
IT'LL NEVER FLY!!
DON'T WORRY.
IT'S THE FOURTH ONE I'VE FLOWN.
WHAT HAPPENED TO THE OTHER THREE?!
I REFUSE TO GET IN THAT THING!!
ME TOO!!

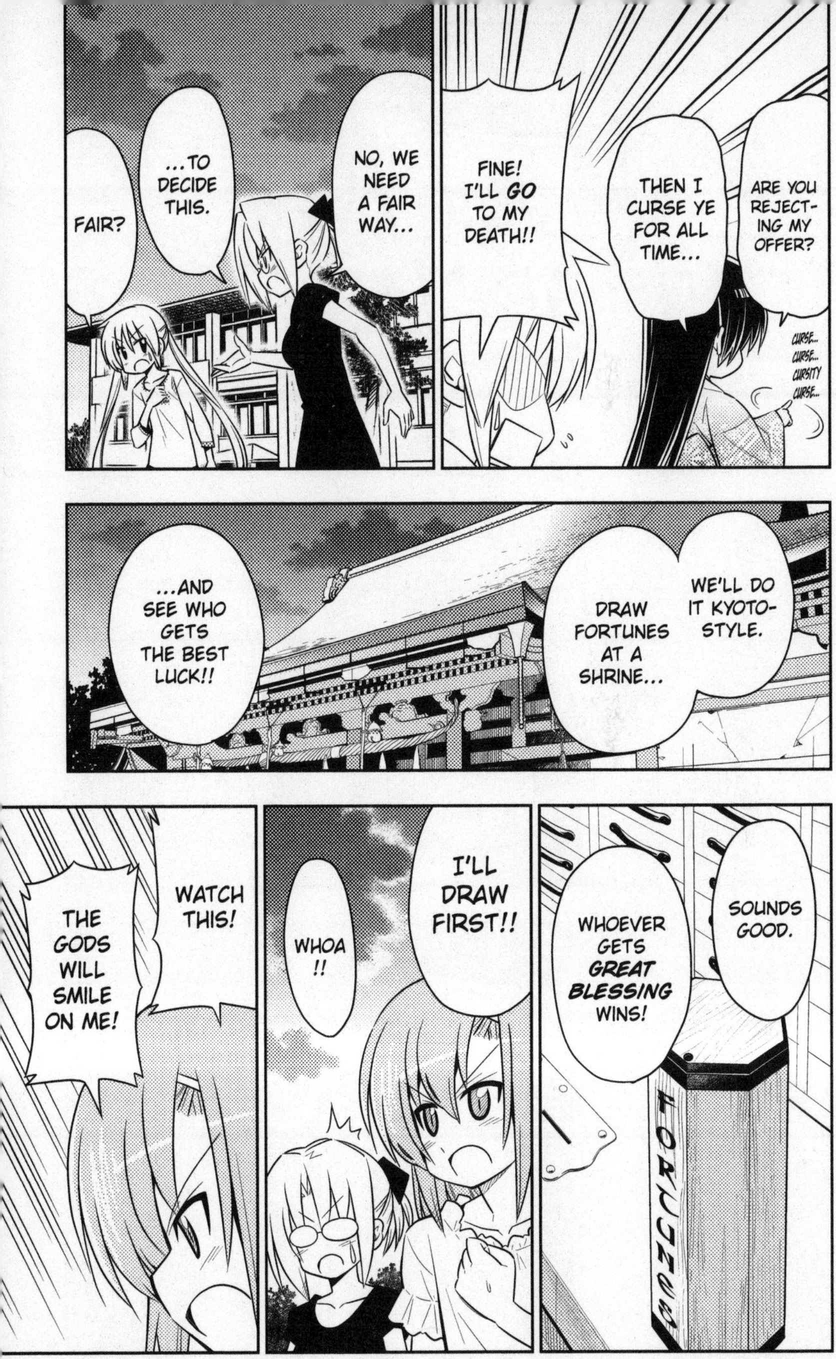
ARE YOU REJECTING MY OFFER?
THEN I CURSE YE FOR ALL TIME...
FINE! I'LL GO TO MY DEATH!!
CURSE... CURSE... CURSITY CURSE...
NO, WE NEED A FAIR WAY...
...TO DECIDE THIS.
FAIR?
WE'LL DO IT KYOTO-STYLE.
DRAW FORTUNES AT A SHRINE...
...AND SEE WHO GETS THE BEST LUCK!!
SOUNDS GOOD.
WHOEVER GETS GREAT BLESSING WINS!
FORTUNES
I'LL DRAW FIRST!!
WHOA!!
WATCH THIS!
THE GODS WILL SMILE ON ME!

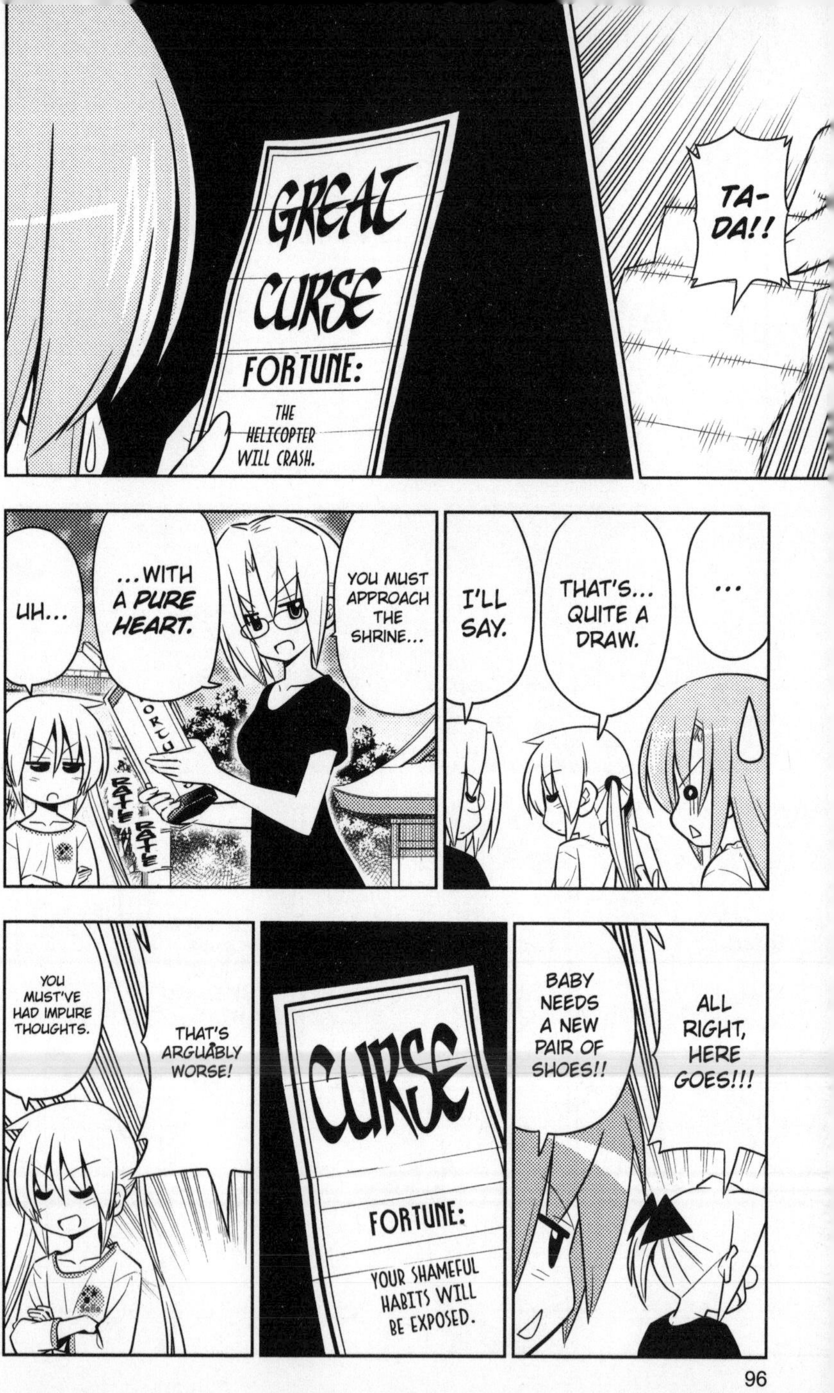

TA-DA!!
GREAT CURSE
FORTUNE:
THE HELICOPTER WILL CRASH.
...
THAT'S... QUITE A DRAW.
I'LL SAY.
YOU MUST APPROACH THE SHRINE...
...WITH A *PURE HEART.*
UH...
RATTLE RATTLE
ALL RIGHT, HERE GOES!!!
BABY NEEDS A NEW PAIR OF SHOES!!
CURSE
FORTUNE:
YOUR SHAMEFUL HABITS WILL BE EXPOSED.
THAT'S ARGUABLY WORSE!
YOU MUST'VE HAD IMPURE THOUGHTS.

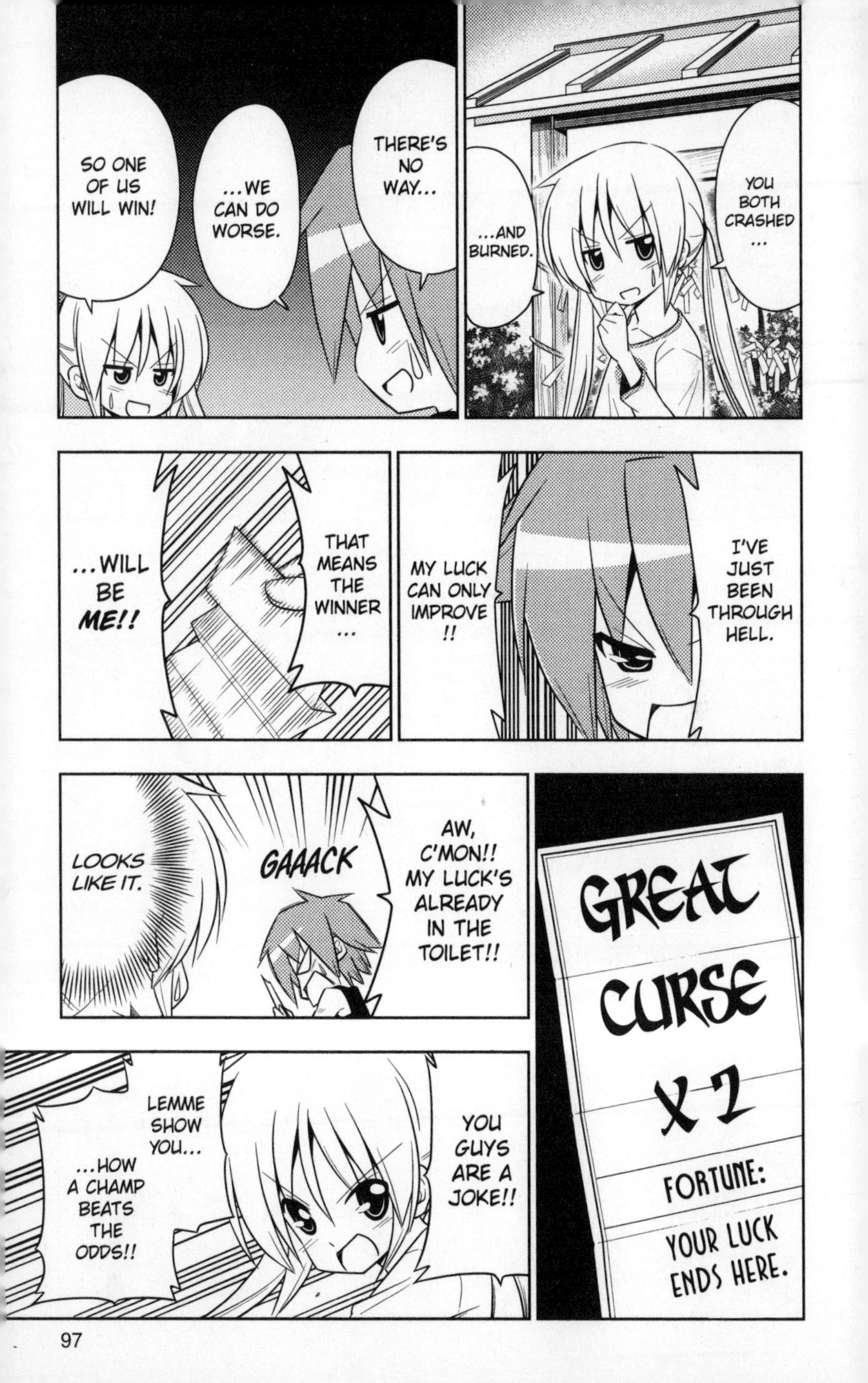
YOU BOTH CRASHED...
...AND BURNED.
THERE'S NO WAY...
...WE CAN DO WORSE.
SO ONE OF US WILL WIN!
I'VE JUST BEEN THROUGH HELL.
MY LUCK CAN ONLY IMPROVE!!
THAT MEANS THE WINNER...
...WILL BE ME!!
GREAT CURSE X 2
FORTUNE:
YOUR LUCK ENDS HERE.
AW, C'MON!! MY LUCK'S ALREADY IN THE TOILET!!
GAAACK
LOOKS LIKE IT.
YOU GUYS ARE A JOKE!!
LEMME SHOW YOU...
...HOW A CHAMP BEATS THE ODDS!!

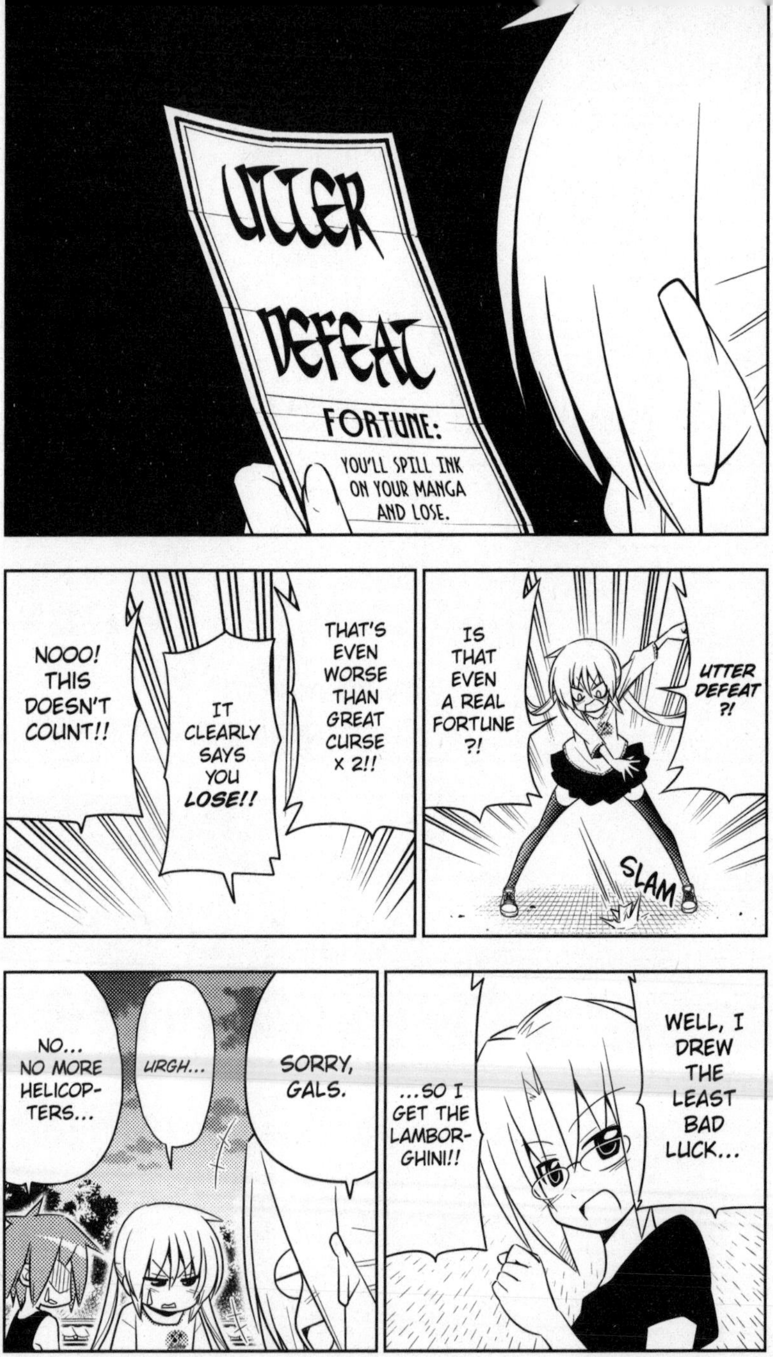
UTTER DEFEAT
FORTUNE:
YOU'LL SPILL INK ON YOUR MANGA AND LOSE.
UTTER DEFEAT ?!
IS THAT EVEN A REAL FORTUNE ?!
SLAM
THAT'S EVEN WORSE THAN GREAT CURSE x 2!!
IT CLEARLY SAYS YOU *LOSE!!*
NOOO! THIS DOESN'T COUNT!!
WELL, I DREW THE LEAST BAD LUCK...
...SO I GET THE LAMBORGHINI!!
SORRY, GALS.
URGH...
NO... NO MORE HELICOPTERS...

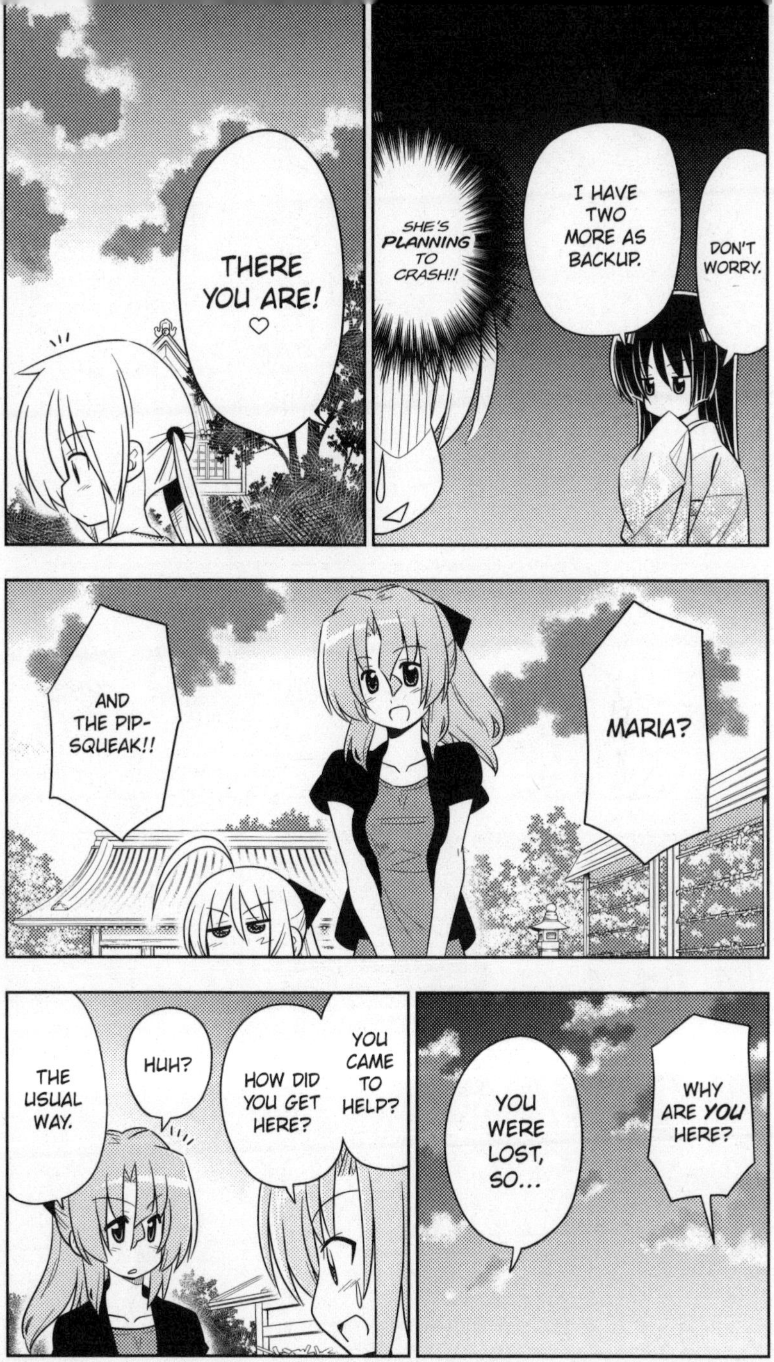
DON'T WORRY.
I HAVE TWO MORE AS BACKUP.
SHE'S PLANNING TO CRASH!!
THERE YOU ARE! ♡
MARIA?
AND THE PIP-SQUEAK!!
WHY ARE YOU HERE?
YOU WERE LOST, SO...
YOU CAME TO HELP?
HOW DID YOU GET HERE?
HUH?
THE USUAL WAY.

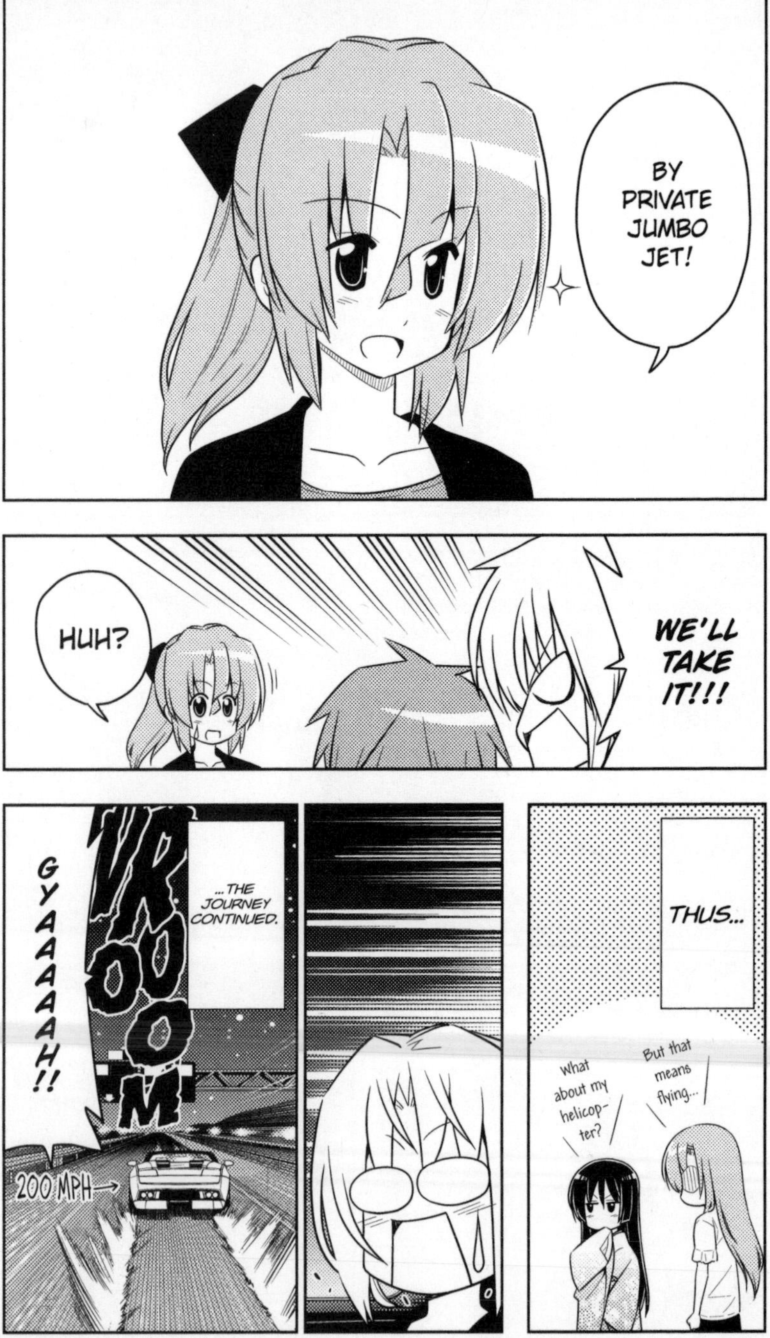

BY PRIVATE JUMBO JET!
WE'LL TAKE IT!!!
HUH?
THUS...
But that means flying...
What about my helicop-ter?
...THE JOURNEY CONTINUED.
VROOOOM
GYAAAAAAH!!
200 MPH→

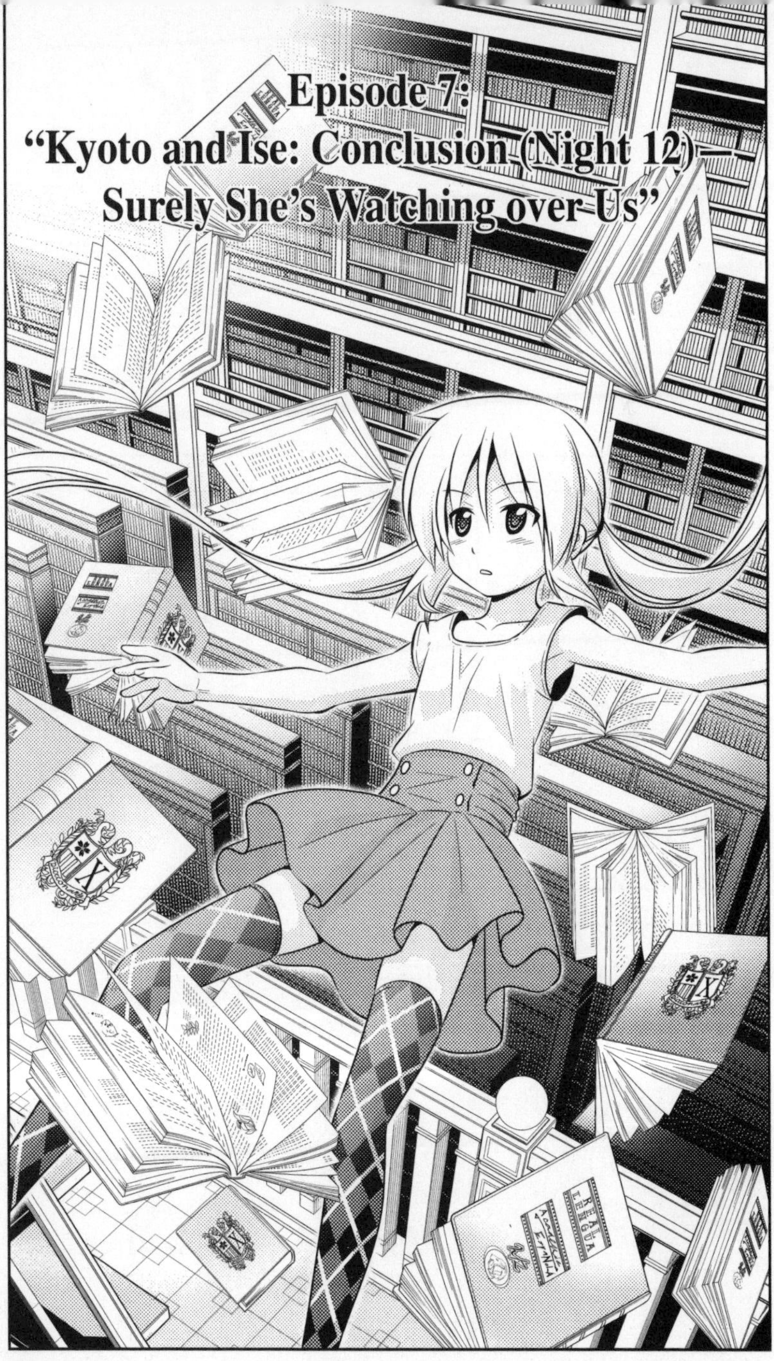
Episode 7:
"Kyoto and Ise: Conclusion (Night 12)—
Surely She's Watching over Us"

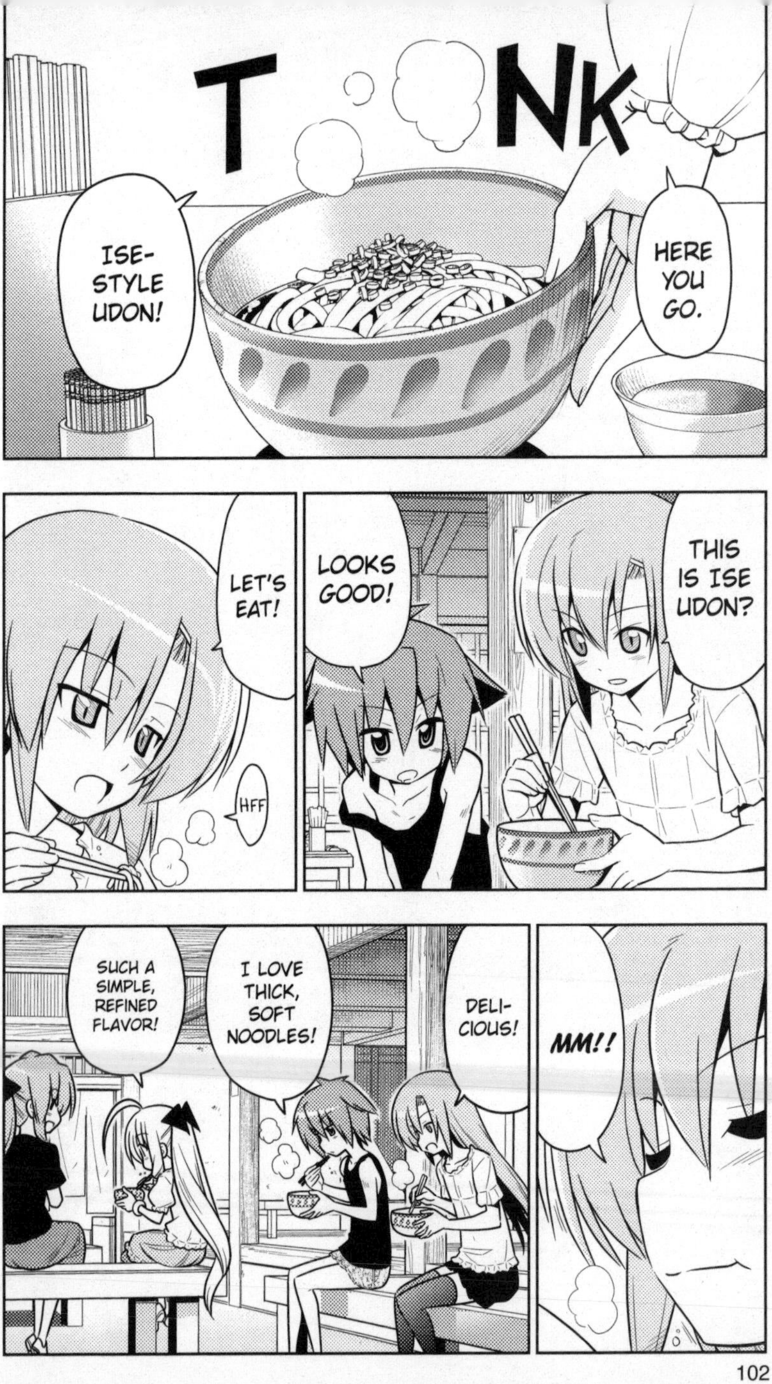
T NK
HERE YOU GO.
ISE-STYLE UDON!
THIS IS ISE UDON?
LOOKS GOOD!
LET'S EAT!
HFF
MM!!
DELI-CIOUS!
I LOVE THICK, SOFT NOODLES!
SUCH A SIMPLE, REFINED FLAVOR!

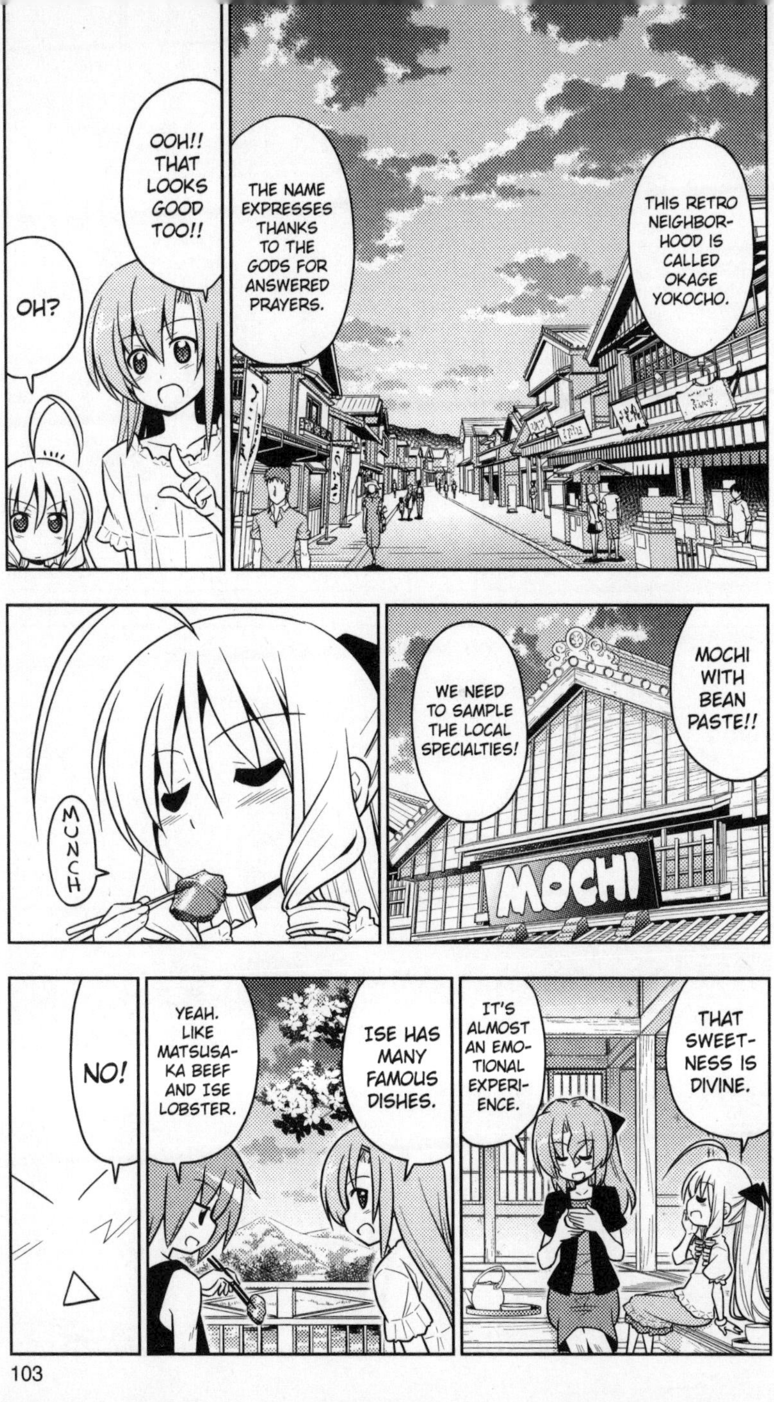
THIS RETRO NEIGHBORHOOD IS CALLED OKAGE YOKOCHO.
THE NAME EXPRESSES THANKS TO THE GODS FOR ANSWERED PRAYERS.
OOH!! THAT LOOKS GOOD TOO!!
OH?
MOCHI WITH BEAN PASTE!!
WE NEED TO SAMPLE THE LOCAL SPECIALTIES!
MOCHI
MUNCH
THAT SWEETNESS IS DIVINE.
IT'S ALMOST AN EMOTIONAL EXPERIENCE.
ISE HAS MANY FAMOUS DISHES.
YEAH. LIKE MATSUSAKA BEEF AND ISE LOBSTER.
NO!

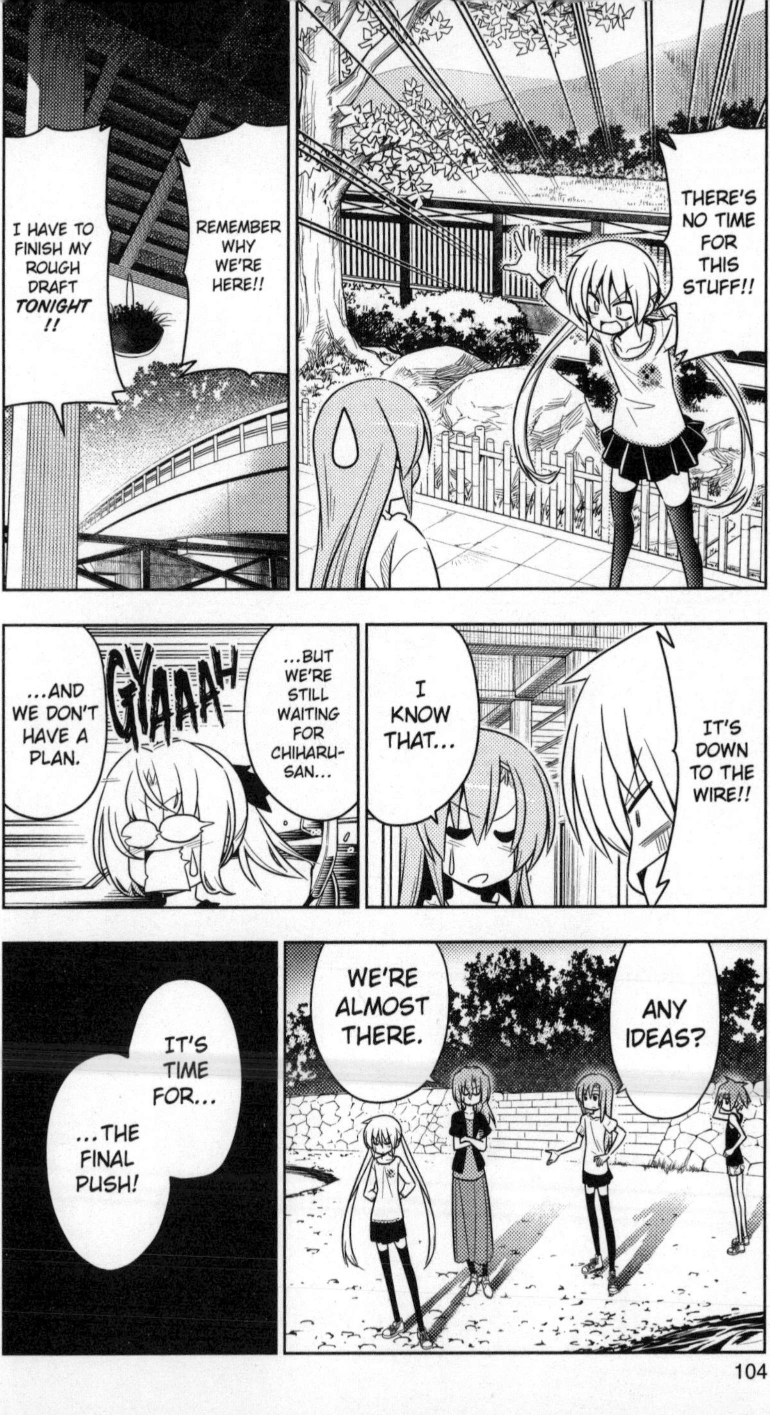
THERE'S NO TIME FOR THIS STUFF!!
REMEMBER WHY WE'RE HERE!!
I HAVE TO FINISH MY ROUGH DRAFT *TONIGHT*!!
IT'S DOWN TO THE WIRE!!
I KNOW THAT...
...BUT WE'RE STILL WAITING FOR CHIHARU-SAN...
GYAAAH
...AND WE DON'T HAVE A PLAN.
ANY IDEAS?
WE'RE ALMOST THERE.
IT'S TIME FOR...
...THE FINAL PUSH!

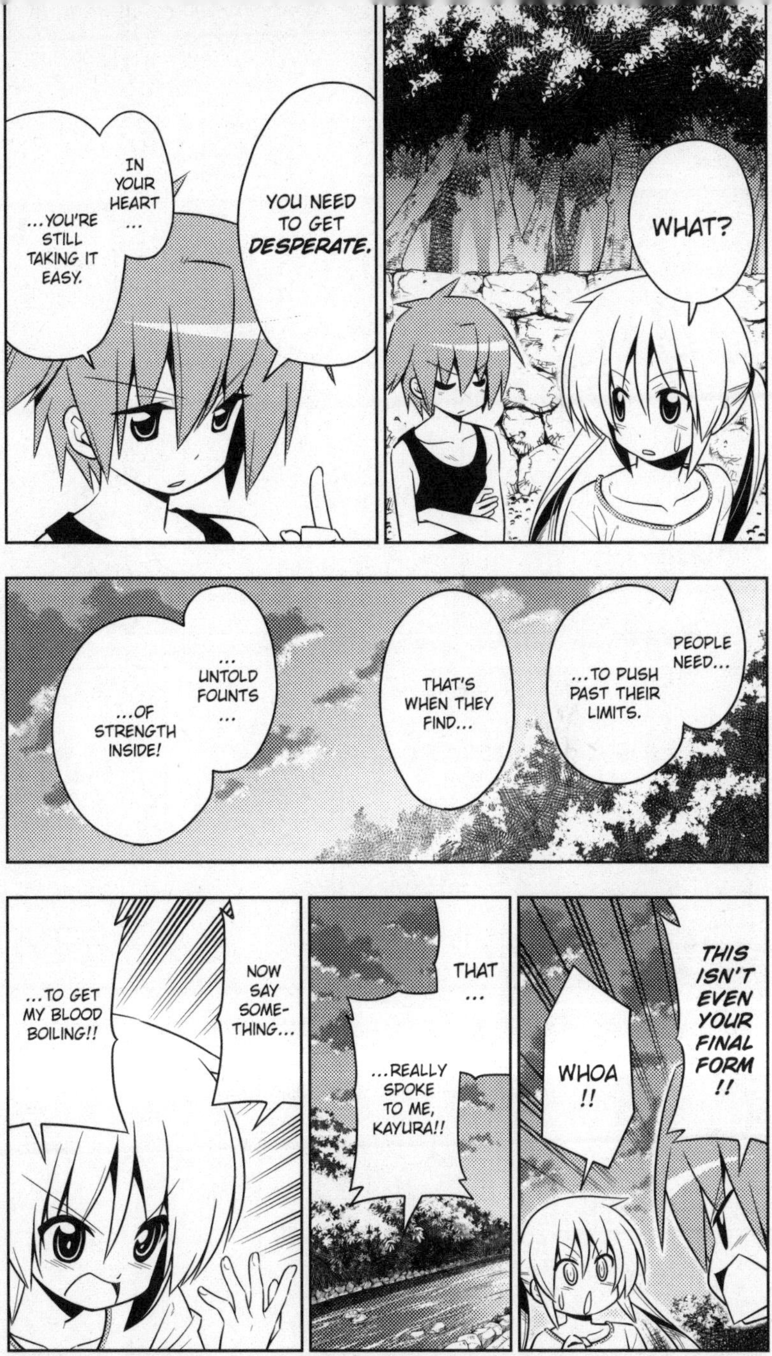
WHAT?
YOU NEED TO GET DESPERATE.
IN YOUR HEART...
...YOU'RE STILL TAKING IT EASY.
PEOPLE NEED...
...TO PUSH PAST THEIR LIMITS.
THAT'S WHEN THEY FIND...
...UNTOLD FOUNTS...
...OF STRENGTH INSIDE!
THIS ISN'T EVEN YOUR FINAL FORM!!
WHOA!!
THAT...
...REALLY SPOKE TO ME, KAYURA!!
NOW SAY SOMETHING...
...TO GET MY BLOOD BOILING!!

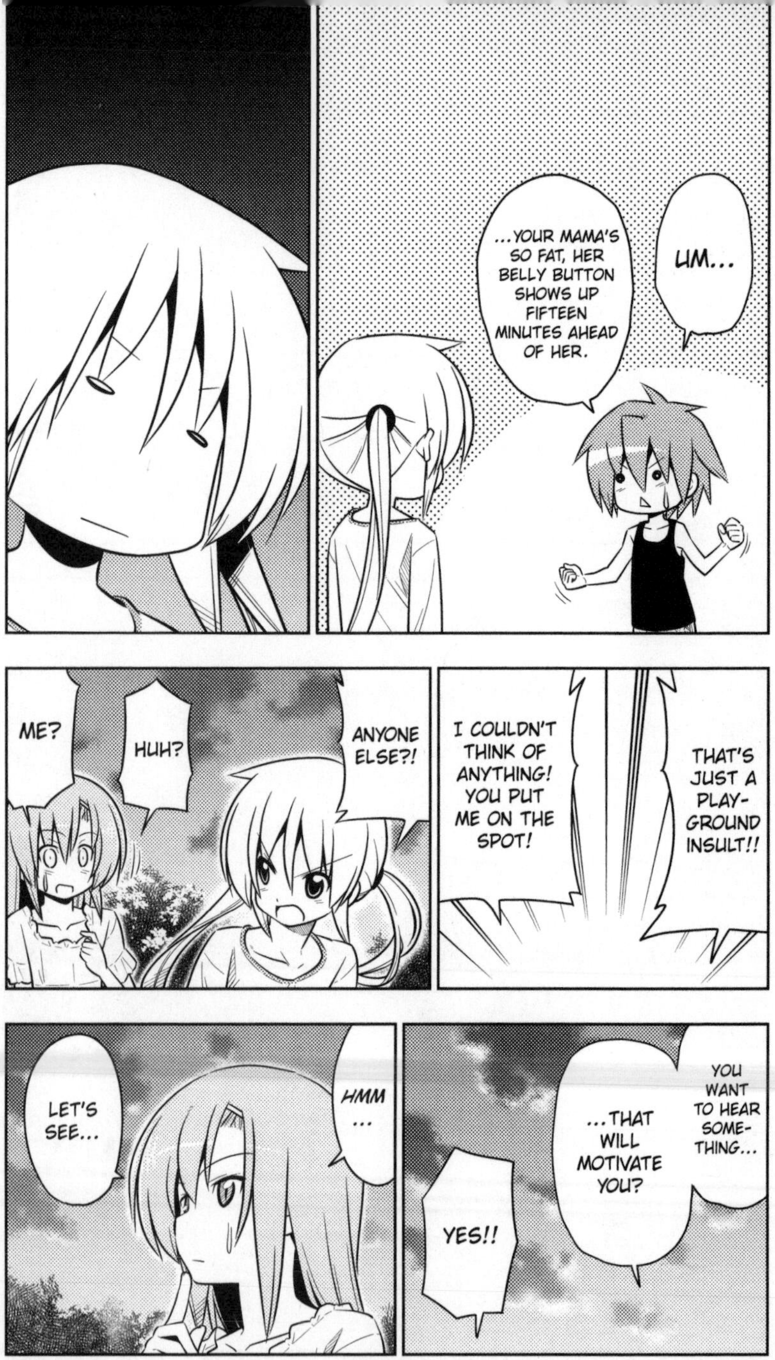
UM...
...YOUR MAMA'S SO FAT, HER BELLY BUTTON SHOWS UP FIFTEEN MINUTES AHEAD OF HER.
THAT'S JUST A PLAY-GROUND INSULT!!
I COULDN'T THINK OF ANYTHING! YOU PUT ME ON THE SPOT!
ANYONE ELSE?!
HUH?
ME?
YOU WANT TO HEAR SOME-THING...
...THAT WILL MOTIVATE YOU?
YES!!
HMM...
LET'S SEE...

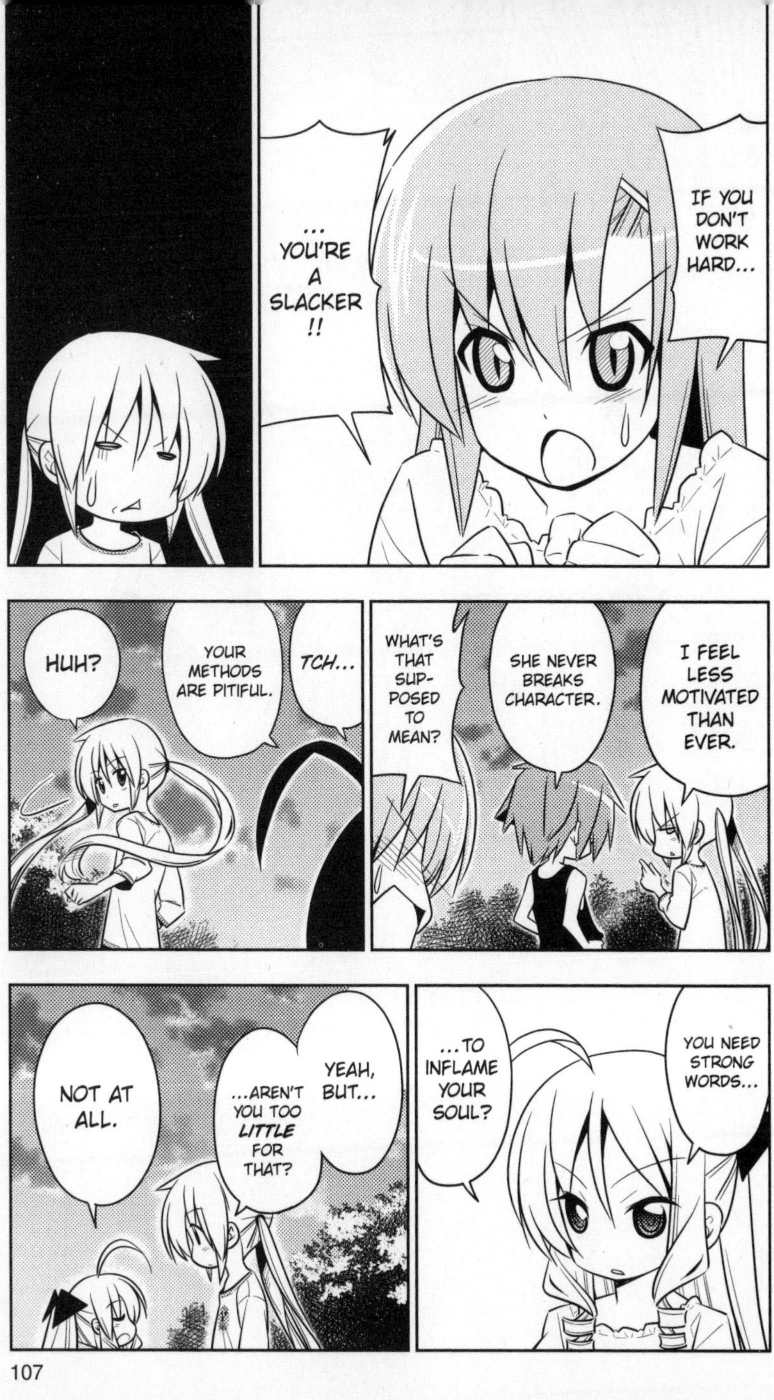
IF YOU DON'T WORK HARD...
...YOU'RE A SLACKER!!
I FEEL LESS MOTIVATED THAN EVER.
SHE NEVER BREAKS CHARACTER.
WHAT'S THAT SUP-POSED TO MEAN?
TCH...
YOUR METHODS ARE PITIFUL.
HUH?
YOU NEED STRONG WORDS...
...TO INFLAME YOUR SOUL?
YEAH, BUT...
...AREN'T YOU TOO *LITTLE* FOR THAT?
NOT AT ALL.

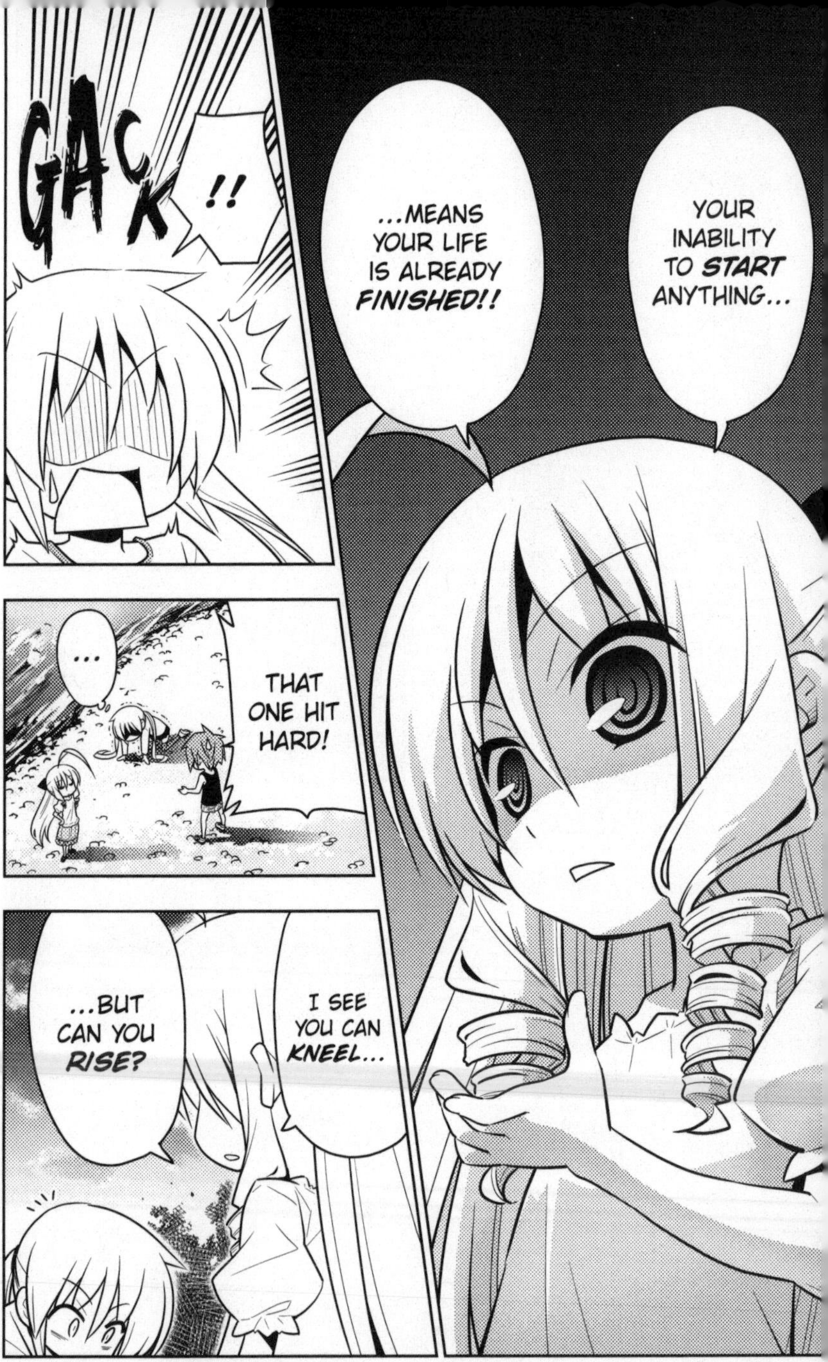
YOUR INABILITY TO START ANYTHING...
...MEANS YOUR LIFE IS ALREADY FINISHED!!
GACK
!!
THAT ONE HIT HARD!
...
I SEE YOU CAN KNEEL...
...BUT CAN YOU RISE?

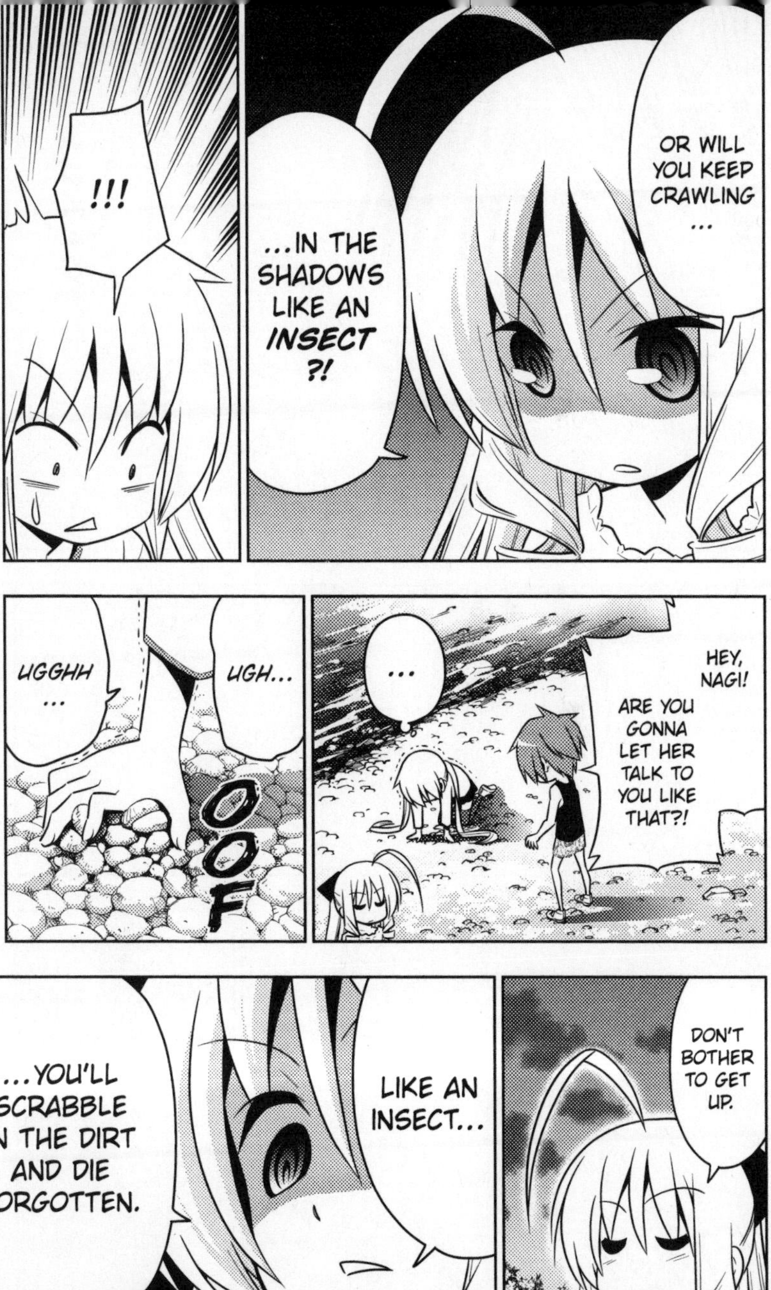
OR WILL YOU KEEP CRAWLING ...
...IN THE SHADOWS LIKE AN INSECT ?!
!!!
HEY, NAGI! ARE YOU GONNA LET HER TALK TO YOU LIKE THAT?!
...
UGH...
UGGHH ...
OOF
DON'T BOTHER TO GET UP.
LIKE AN INSECT...
...YOU'LL SCRABBLE IN THE DIRT AND DIE FORGOTTEN.

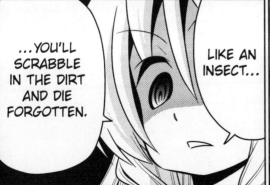

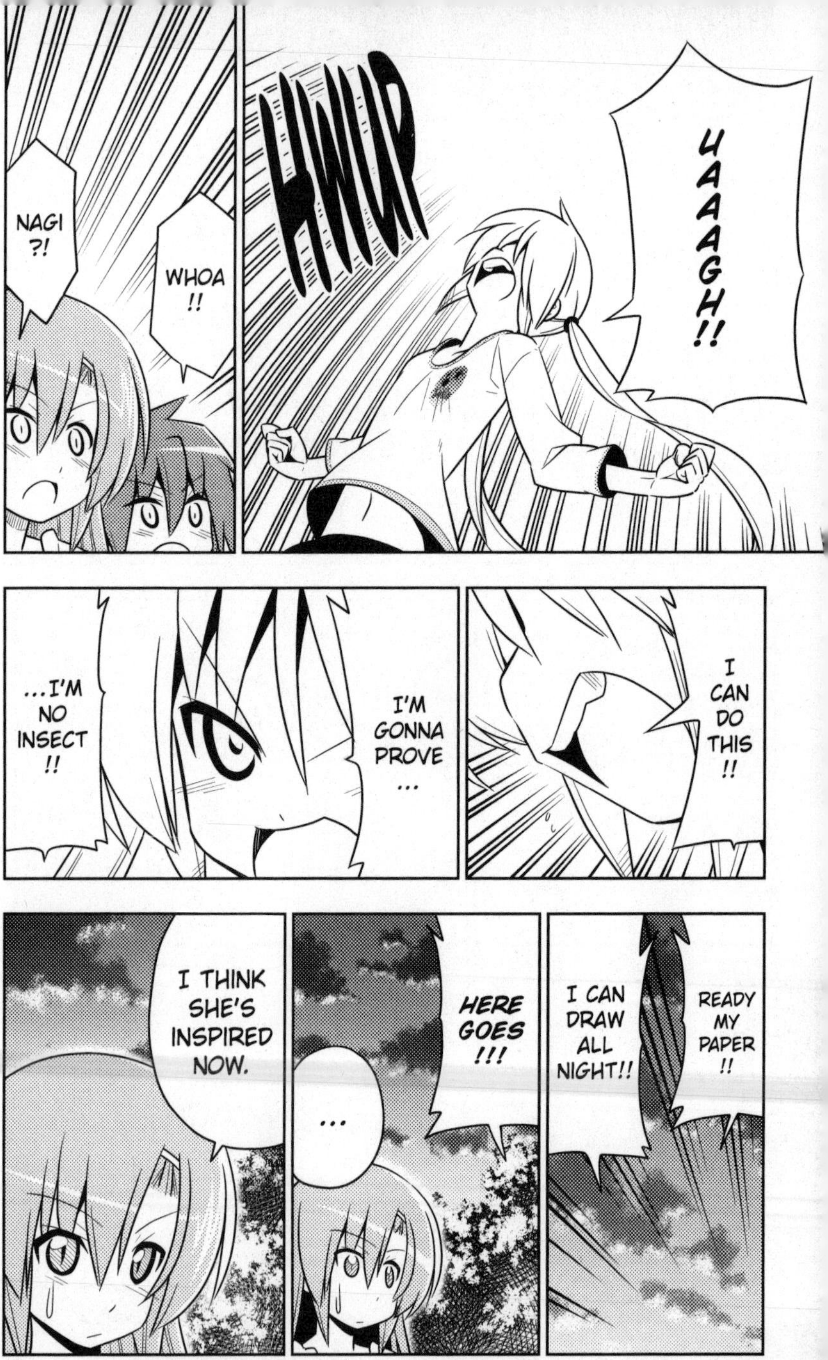
UAAAAGH!!
HWUP
WHOA !!
NAGI ?!
I CAN DO THIS !!
I'M GONNA PROVE ...
...I'M NO INSECT !!
READY MY PAPER !!
I CAN DRAW ALL NIGHT!!
HERE GOES !!!
...
I THINK SHE'S INSPIRED NOW.

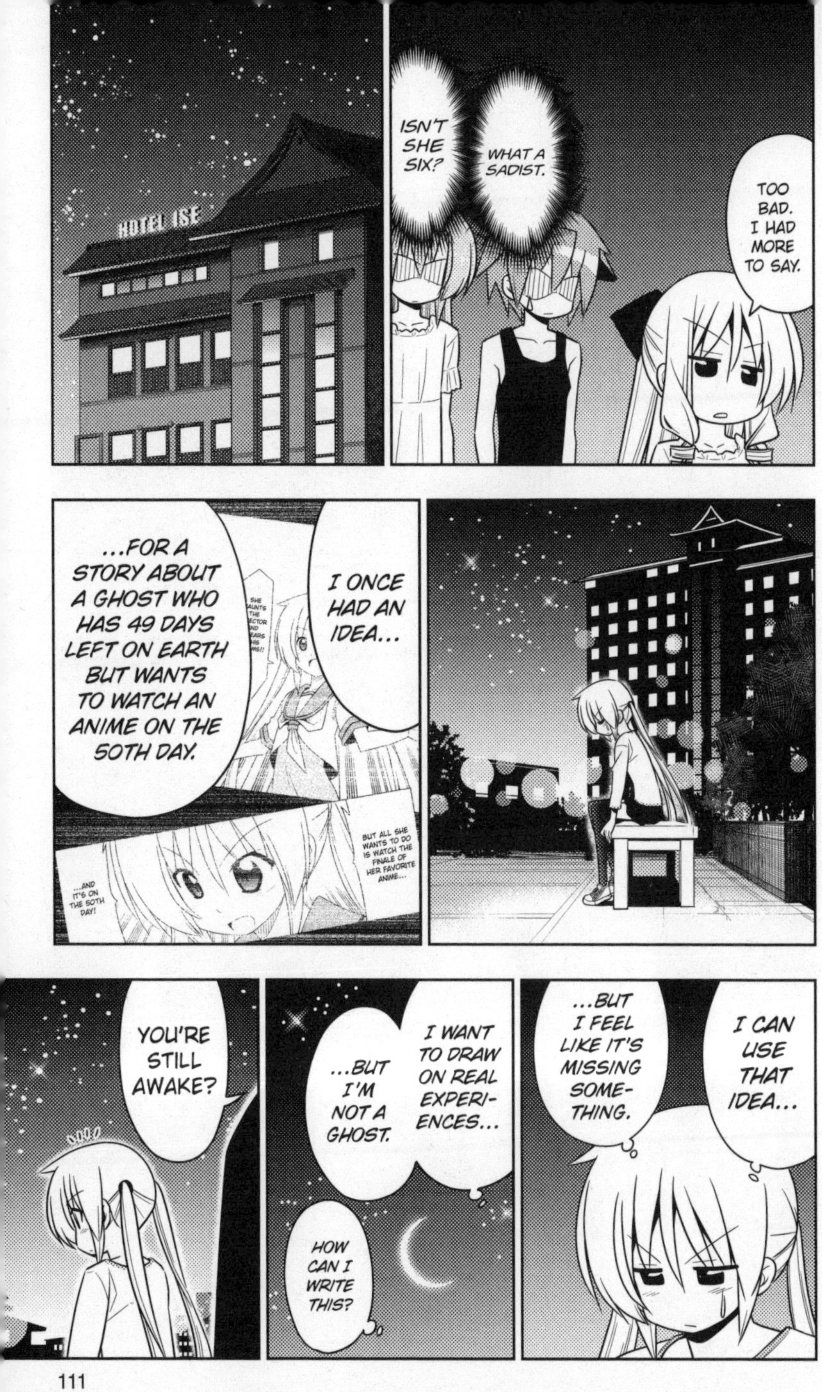
TOO BAD. I HAD MORE TO SAY.
WHAT A SADIST.
ISN'T SHE SIX?
HOTEL ISE
I ONCE HAD AN IDEA...
...FOR A STORY ABOUT A GHOST WHO HAS 49 DAYS LEFT ON EARTH BUT WANTS TO WATCH AN ANIME ON THE 50TH DAY.
BUT ALL SHE WANTS TO DO IS WATCH THE FINALE OF HER FAVORITE ANIME...
...AND IT'S ON THE 50TH DAY!
I CAN USE THAT IDEA...
...BUT I FEEL LIKE IT'S MISSING SOME-THING.
I WANT TO DRAW ON REAL EXPERI-ENCES...
...BUT I'M NOT A GHOST.
HOW CAN I WRITE THIS?
YOU'RE STILL AWAKE?

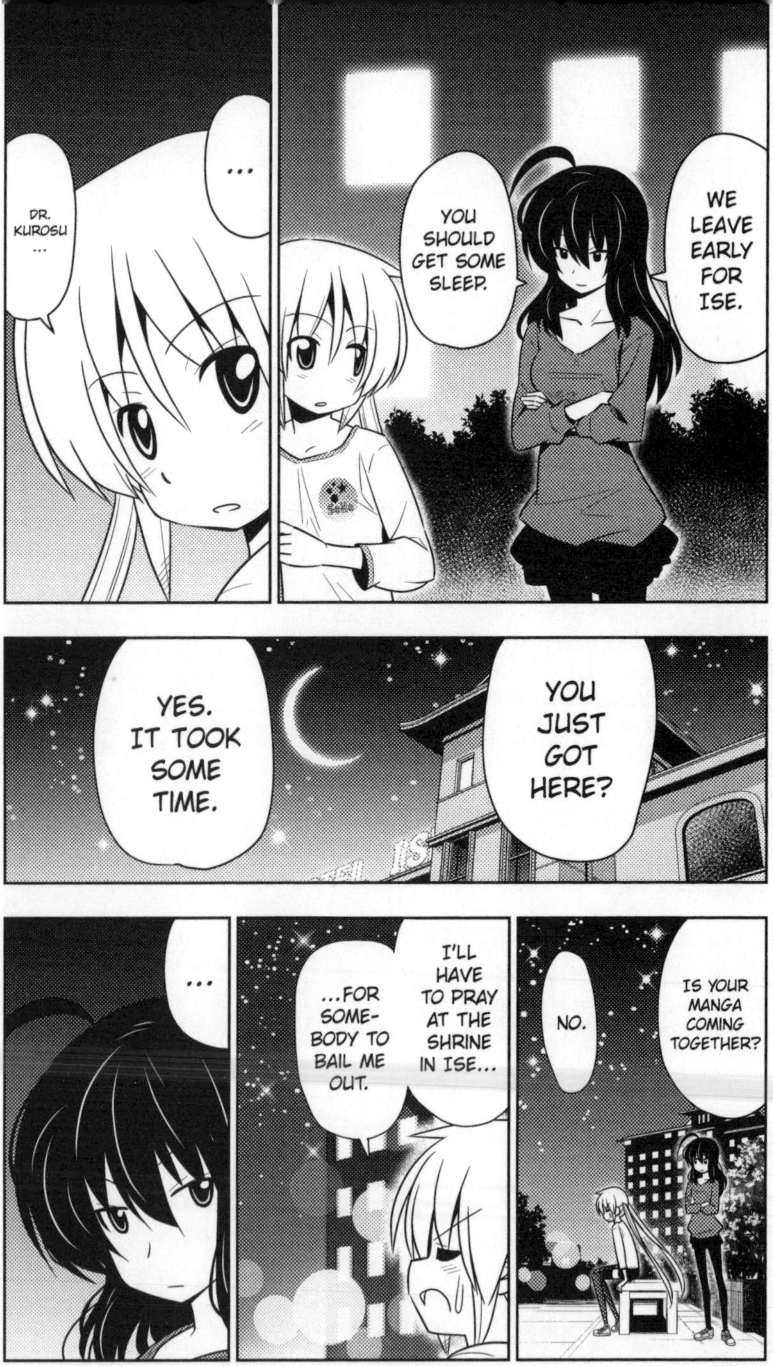
WE LEAVE EARLY FOR ISE.
YOU SHOULD GET SOME SLEEP.
...
DR. KUROSU ...
YOU JUST GOT HERE?
YES. IT TOOK SOME TIME.
IS YOUR MANGA COMING TOGETHER?
NO.
I'LL HAVE TO PRAY AT THE SHRINE IN ISE...
...FOR SOME-BODY TO BAIL ME OUT.
...

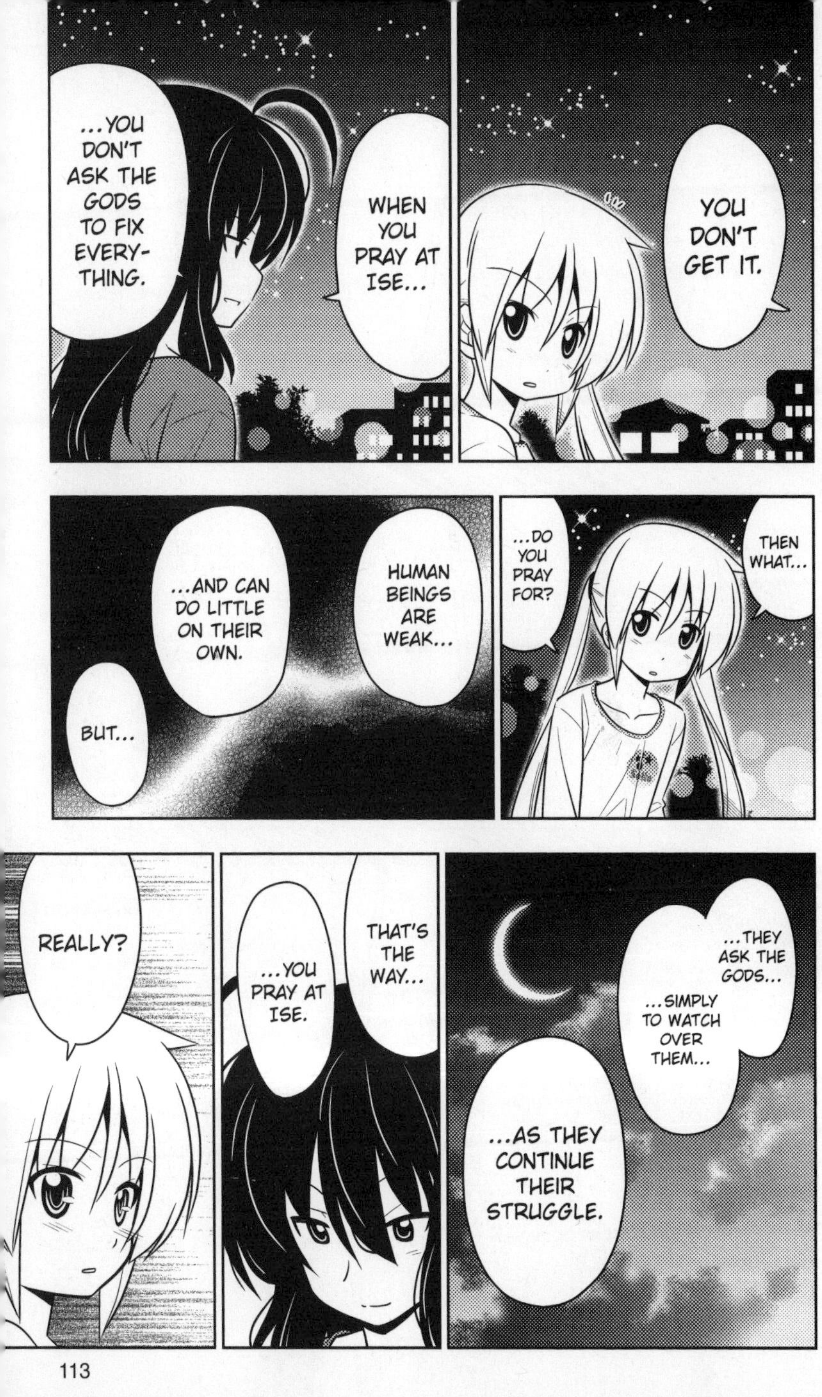
YOU DON'T GET IT.
WHEN YOU PRAY AT ISE...
...YOU DON'T ASK THE GODS TO FIX EVERY-THING.
THEN WHAT...
...DO YOU PRAY FOR?
HUMAN BEINGS ARE WEAK...
...AND CAN DO LITTLE ON THEIR OWN.
BUT...
...THEY ASK THE GODS...
...SIMPLY TO WATCH OVER THEM...
...AS THEY CONTINUE THEIR STRUGGLE.
THAT'S THE WAY...
...YOU PRAY AT ISE.
REALLY?

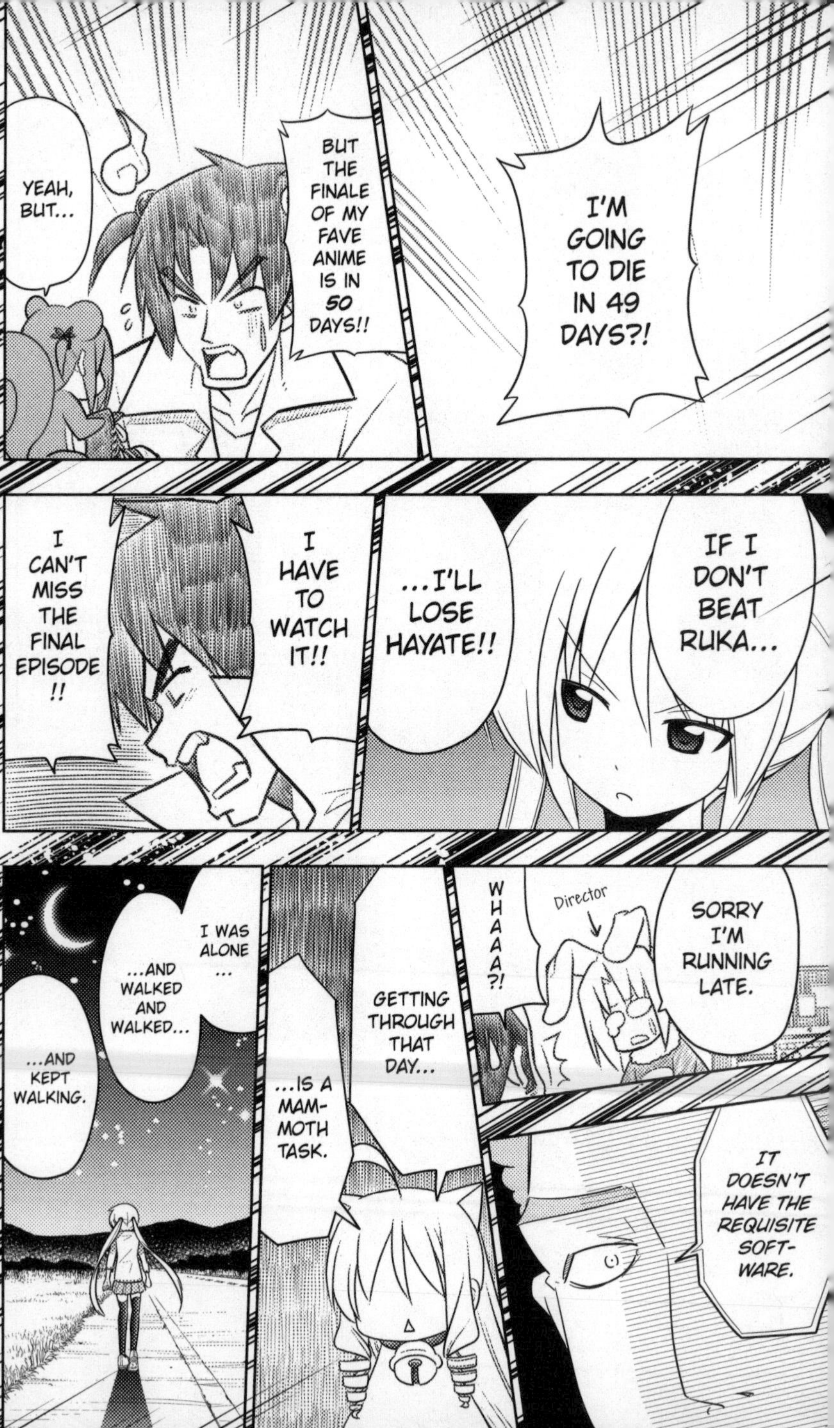
I'M GOING TO DIE IN 49 DAYS?!
BUT THE FINALE OF MY FAVE ANIME IS IN 50 DAYS!!
YEAH, BUT...
IF I DON'T BEAT RUKA...
...I'LL LOSE HAYATE!!
I HAVE TO WATCH IT!!
I CAN'T MISS THE FINAL EPISODE!!
SORRY I'M RUNNING LATE.
Director
WHAAAA?!
IT DOESN'T HAVE THE REQUISITE SOFT-WARE.
GETTING THROUGH THAT DAY...
...IS A MAMMOTH TASK.
I WAS ALONE...
...AND WALKED AND WALKED...
...AND KEPT WALKING.

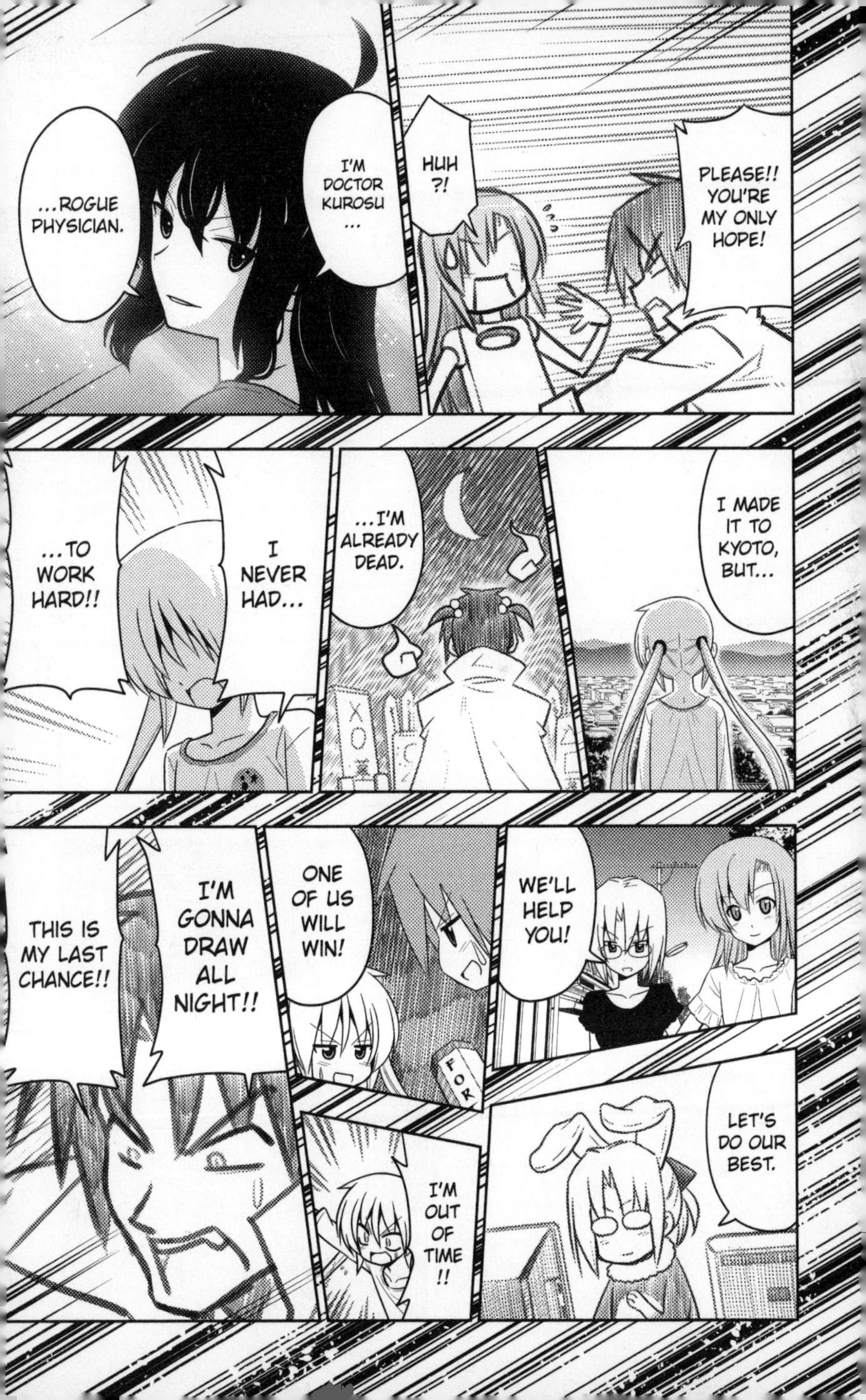
PLEASE!! YOU'RE MY ONLY HOPE!
HUH ?!
I'M DOCTOR KUROSU ...
...ROGUE PHYSICIAN.
I MADE IT TO KYOTO, BUT...
...I'M ALREADY DEAD.
I NEVER HAD...
...TO WORK HARD!!
WE'LL HELP YOU!
ONE OF US WILL WIN!
FOR
LET'S DO OUR BEST.
I'M OUT OF TIME !!
I'M GONNA DRAW ALL NIGHT!!
THIS IS MY LAST CHANCE!!

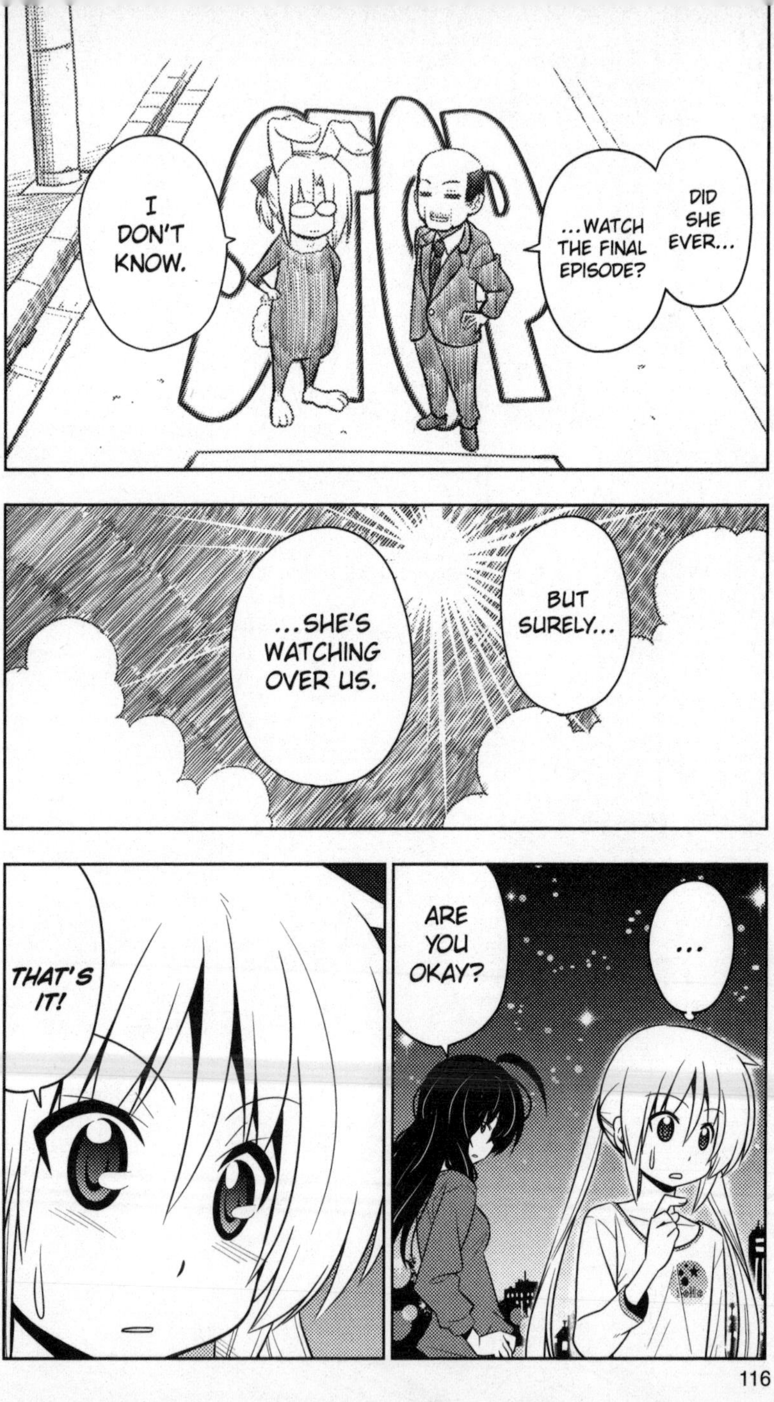
DID SHE EVER...
...WATCH THE FINAL EPISODE?
I DON'T KNOW.
BUT SURELY...
...SHE'S WATCHING OVER US.
...
ARE YOU OKAY?
THAT'S IT!

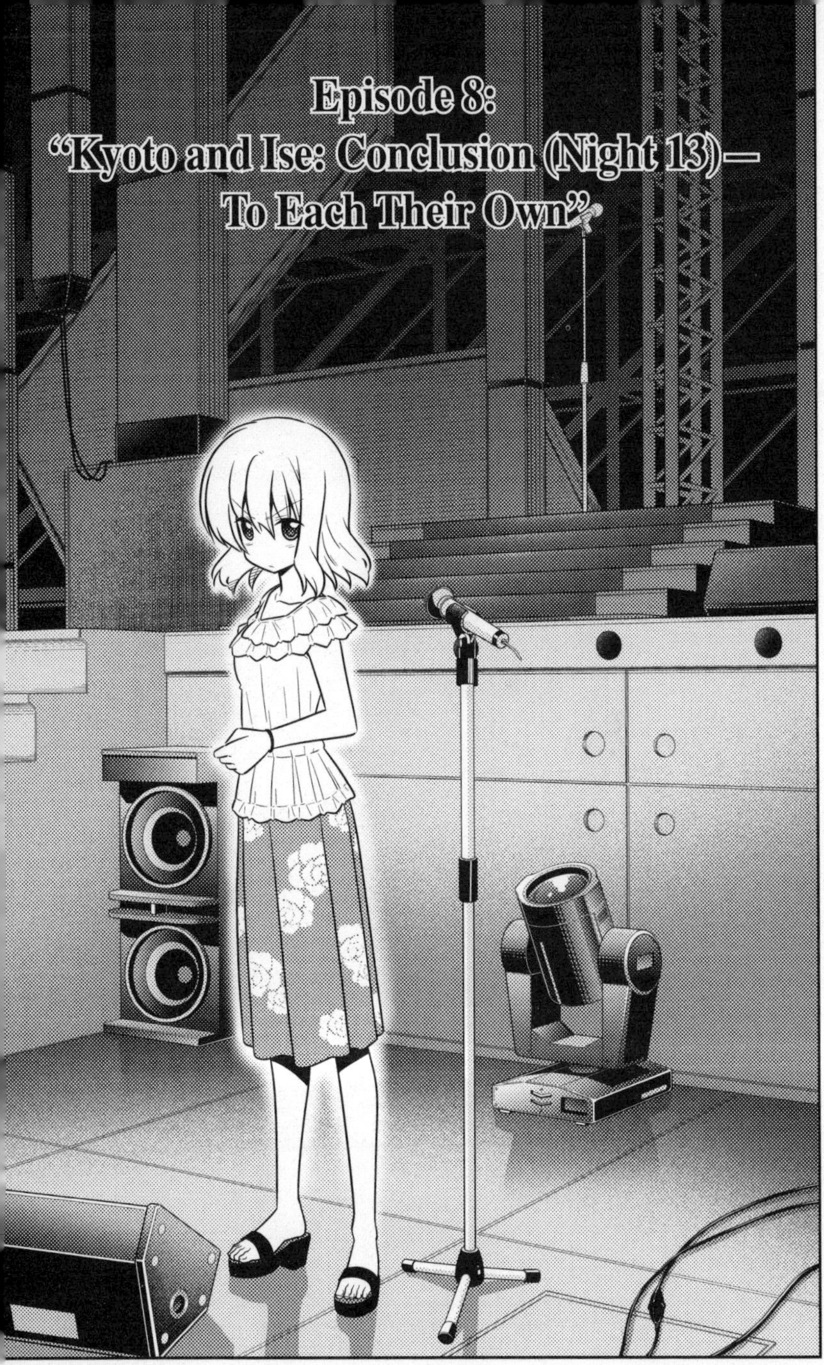
Episode 8:
"Kyoto and Ise: Conclusion (Night 13)—
To Each Their Own"

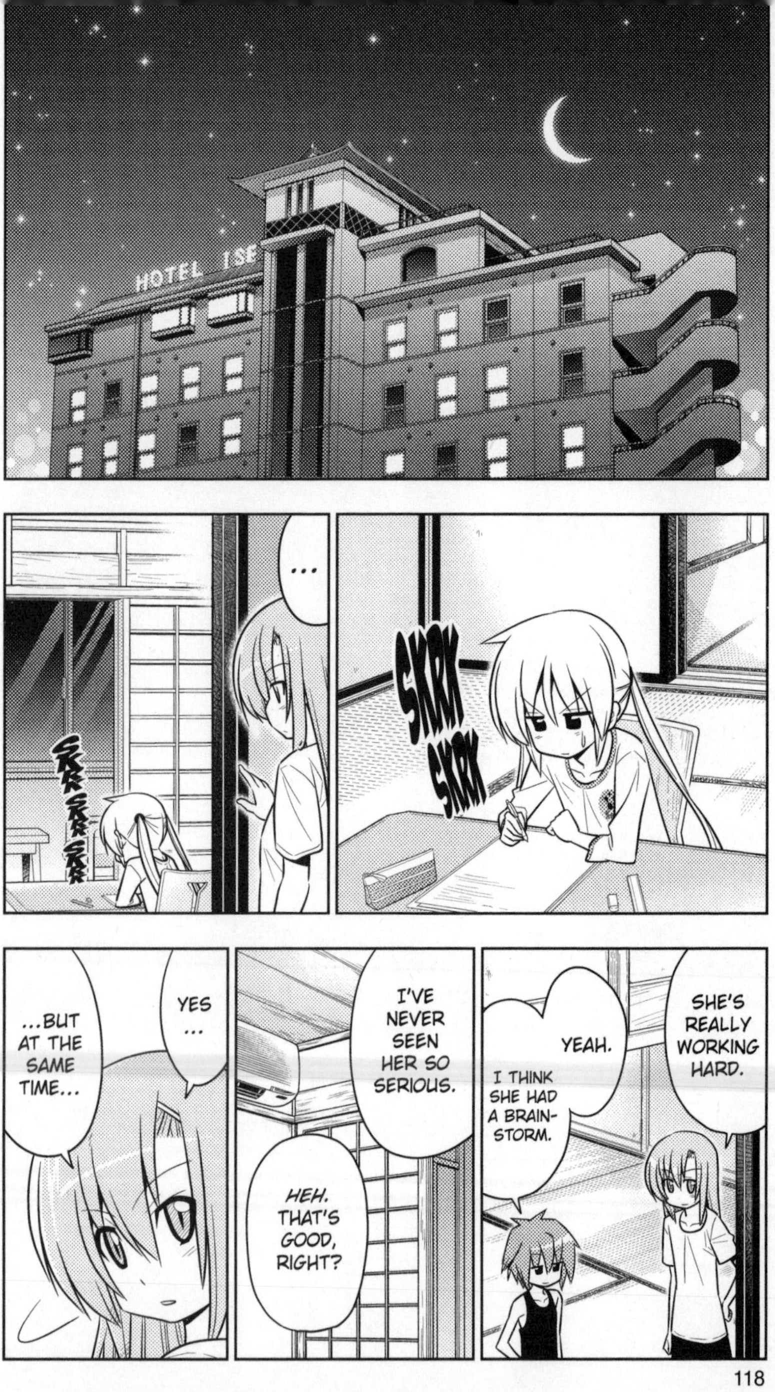
HOTEL ISE
SKRK SKRK
...
SKRK SKRK SKRK
SHE'S REALLY WORKING HARD.
YEAH.
I THINK SHE HAD A BRAIN-STORM.
I'VE NEVER SEEN HER SO SERIOUS.
HEH. THAT'S GOOD, RIGHT?
YES...
...BUT AT THE SAME TIME...

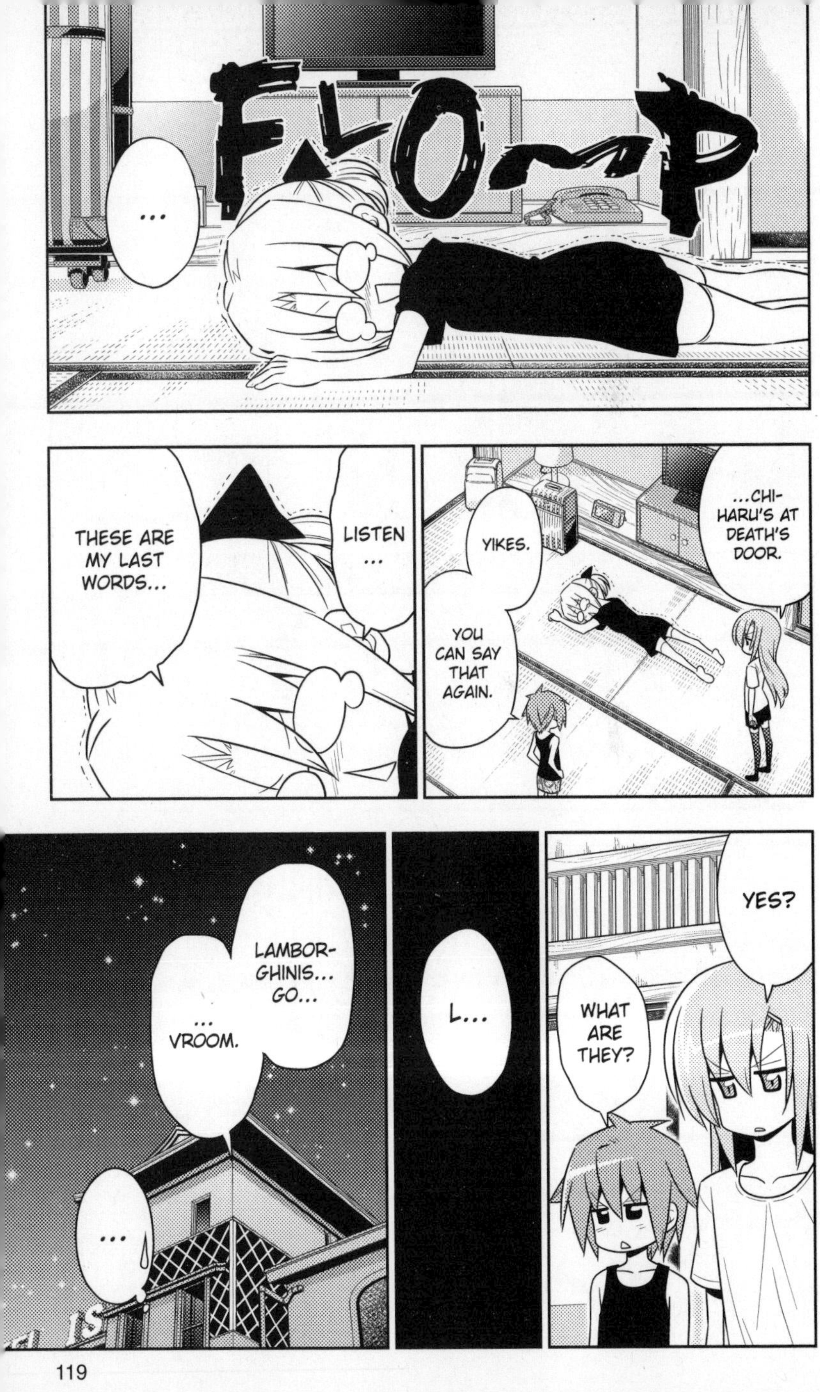
FLOP
...
...CHI-HARU'S AT DEATH'S DOOR.
YIKES.
YOU CAN SAY THAT AGAIN.
LISTEN...
THESE ARE MY LAST WORDS...
YES?
WHAT ARE THEY?
L...
LAMBOR-GHINIS... GO...
... VROOM.
...

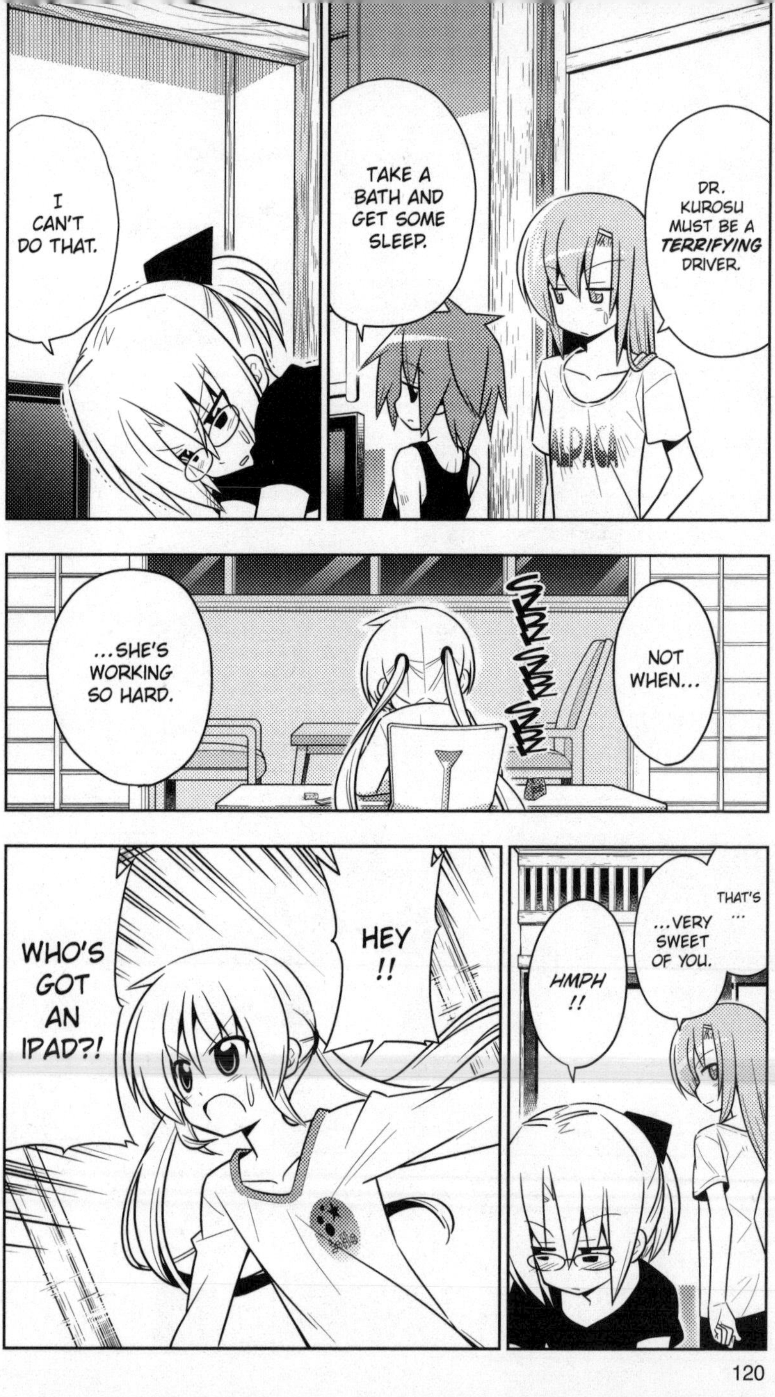
DR. KUROSU MUST BE A *TERRIFYING* DRIVER.
TAKE A BATH AND GET SOME SLEEP.
I CAN'T DO THAT.
NOT WHEN...
...SHE'S WORKING SO HARD.
THAT'S ...
...VERY SWEET OF YOU.
HMPH !!
HEY !!
WHO'S GOT AN IPAD?!

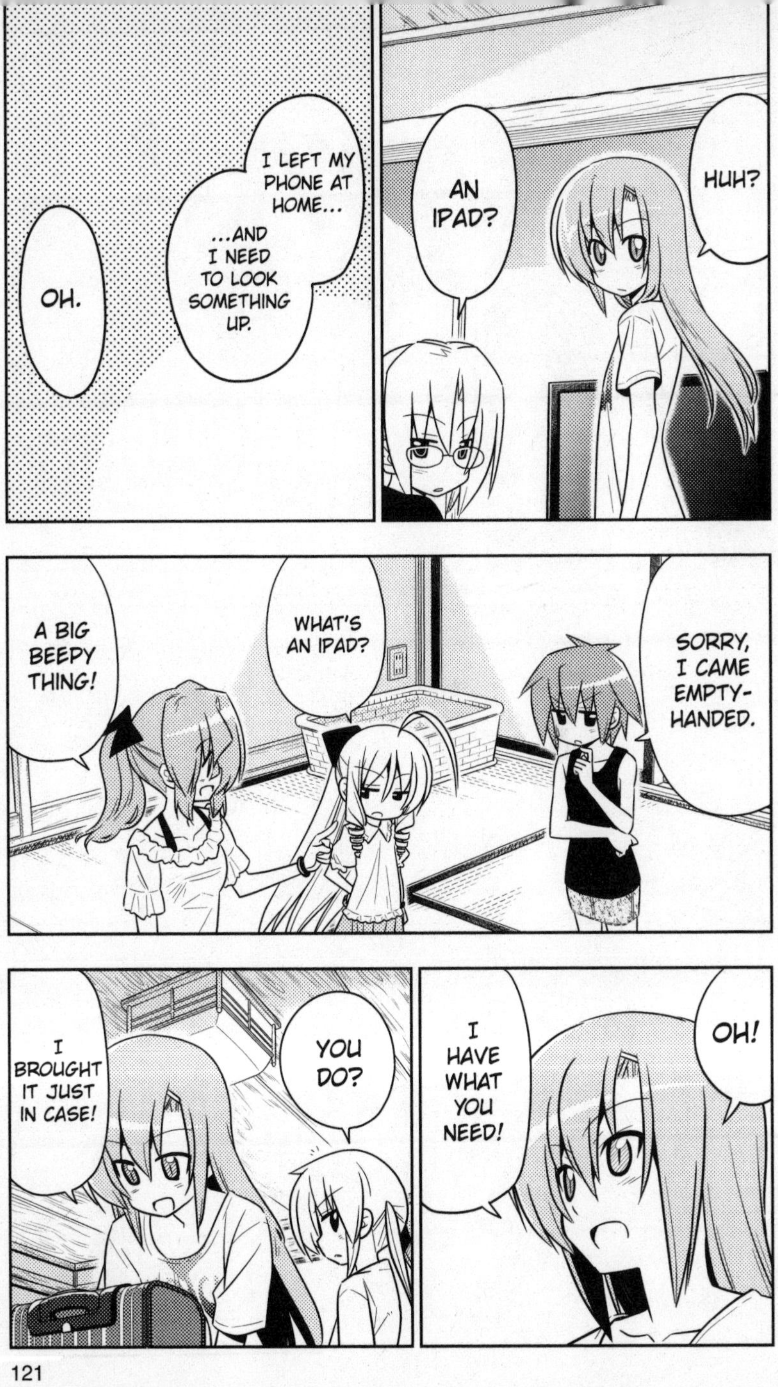
HUH?
AN IPAD?
I LEFT MY PHONE AT HOME...
...AND I NEED TO LOOK SOMETHING UP.
OH.
SORRY, I CAME EMPTY-HANDED.
WHAT'S AN IPAD?
A BIG BEEPY THING!
OH!
I HAVE WHAT YOU NEED!
YOU DO?
I BROUGHT IT JUST IN CASE!

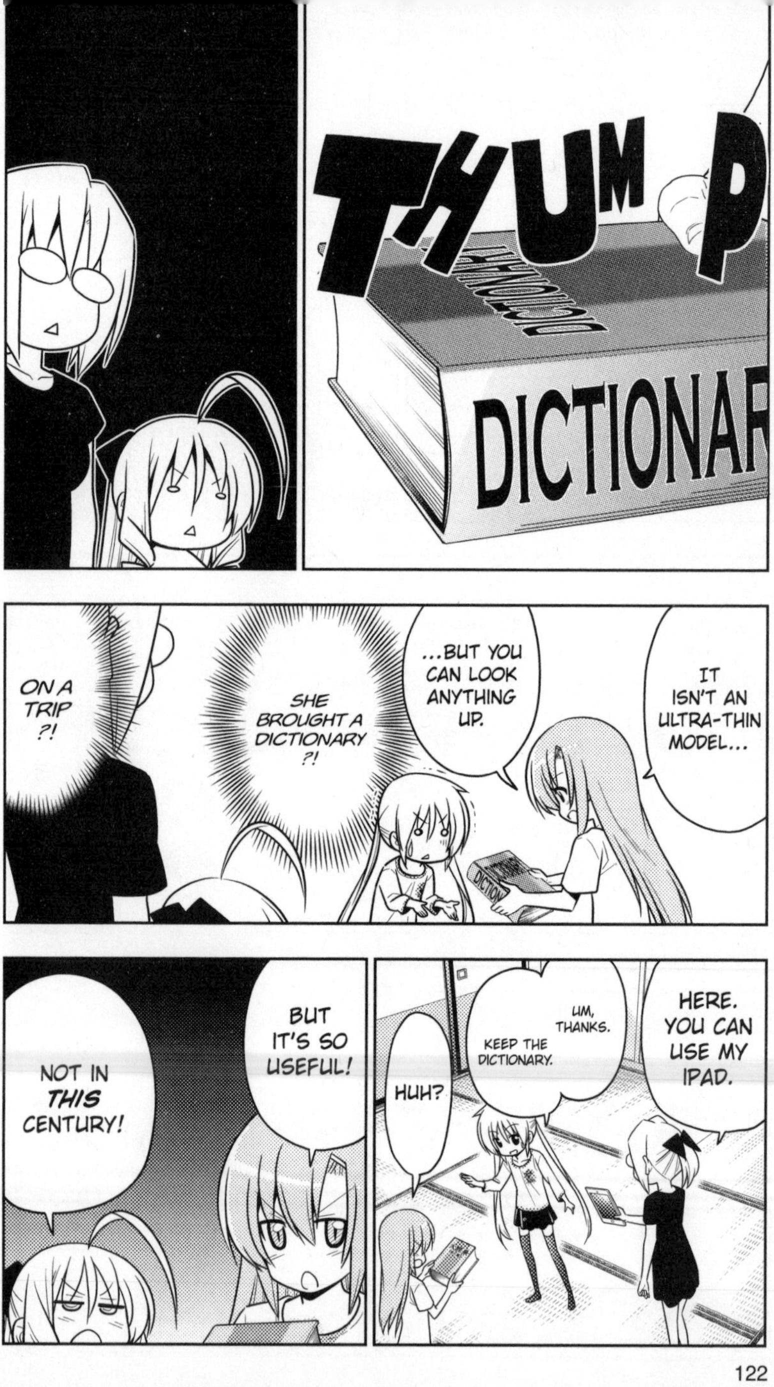
THUMP
DICTIONAR
IT ISN'T AN ULTRA-THIN MODEL...
...BUT YOU CAN LOOK ANYTHING UP.
SHE BROUGHT A DICTIONARY ?!
ON A TRIP ?!
HERE. YOU CAN USE MY IPAD.
UM, THANKS.
KEEP THE DICTIONARY.
HUH?
BUT IT'S SO USEFUL!
NOT IN *THIS* CENTURY!

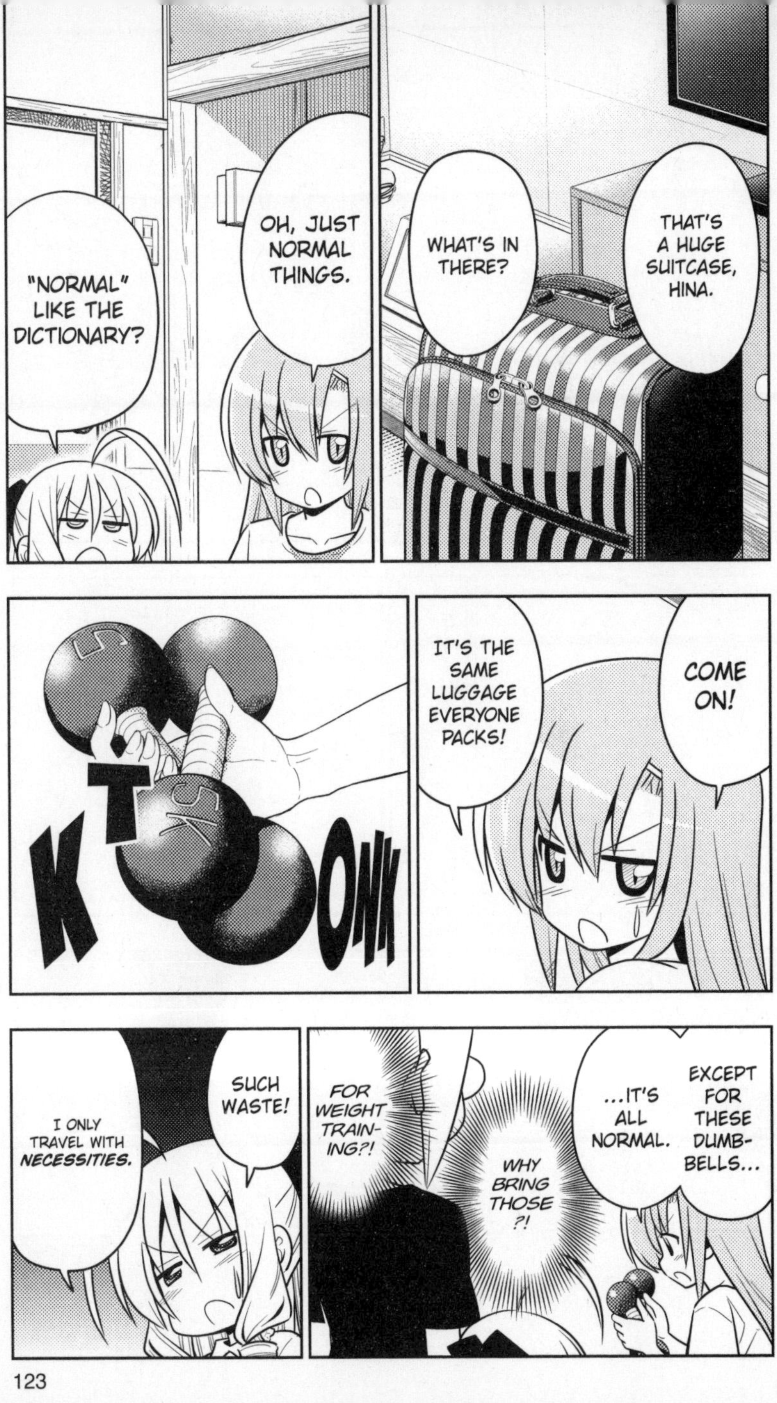
THAT'S A HUGE SUITCASE, HINA.
WHAT'S IN THERE?
OH, JUST NORMAL THINGS.
"NORMAL" LIKE THE DICTIONARY?
COME ON!
IT'S THE SAME LUGGAGE EVERYONE PACKS!
KTONK
EXCEPT FOR THESE DUMB-BELLS...
...IT'S ALL NORMAL.
WHY BRING THOSE?!
FOR WEIGHT TRAIN-ING?!
SUCH WASTE!
I ONLY TRAVEL WITH *NECESSITIES.*

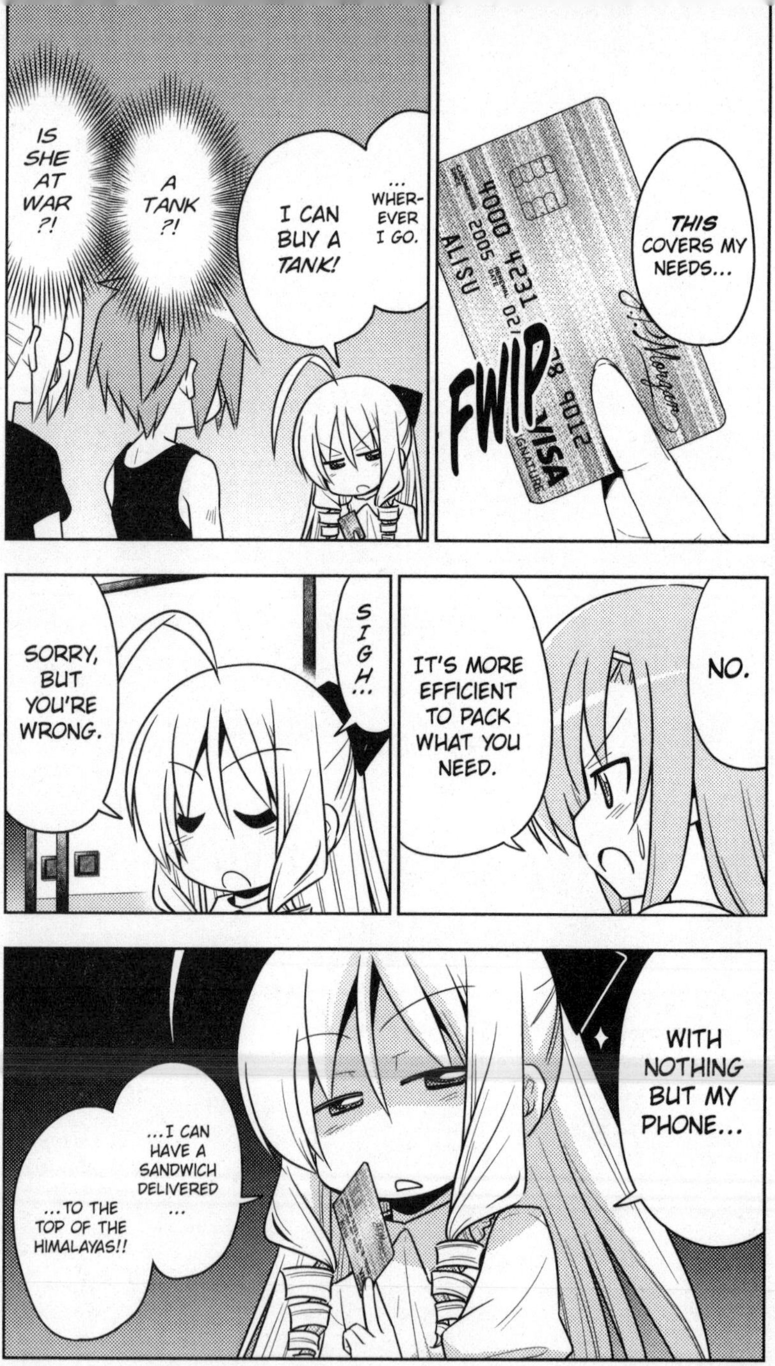
THIS COVERS MY NEEDS...
FWIP
... WHEREVER I GO.
I CAN BUY A TANK!
A TANK ?!
IS SHE AT WAR ?!
NO.
IT'S MORE EFFICIENT TO PACK WHAT YOU NEED.
SIGH...
SORRY, BUT YOU'RE WRONG.
WITH NOTHING BUT MY PHONE...
...I CAN HAVE A SANDWICH DELIVERED...
...TO THE TOP OF THE HIMALAYAS!!

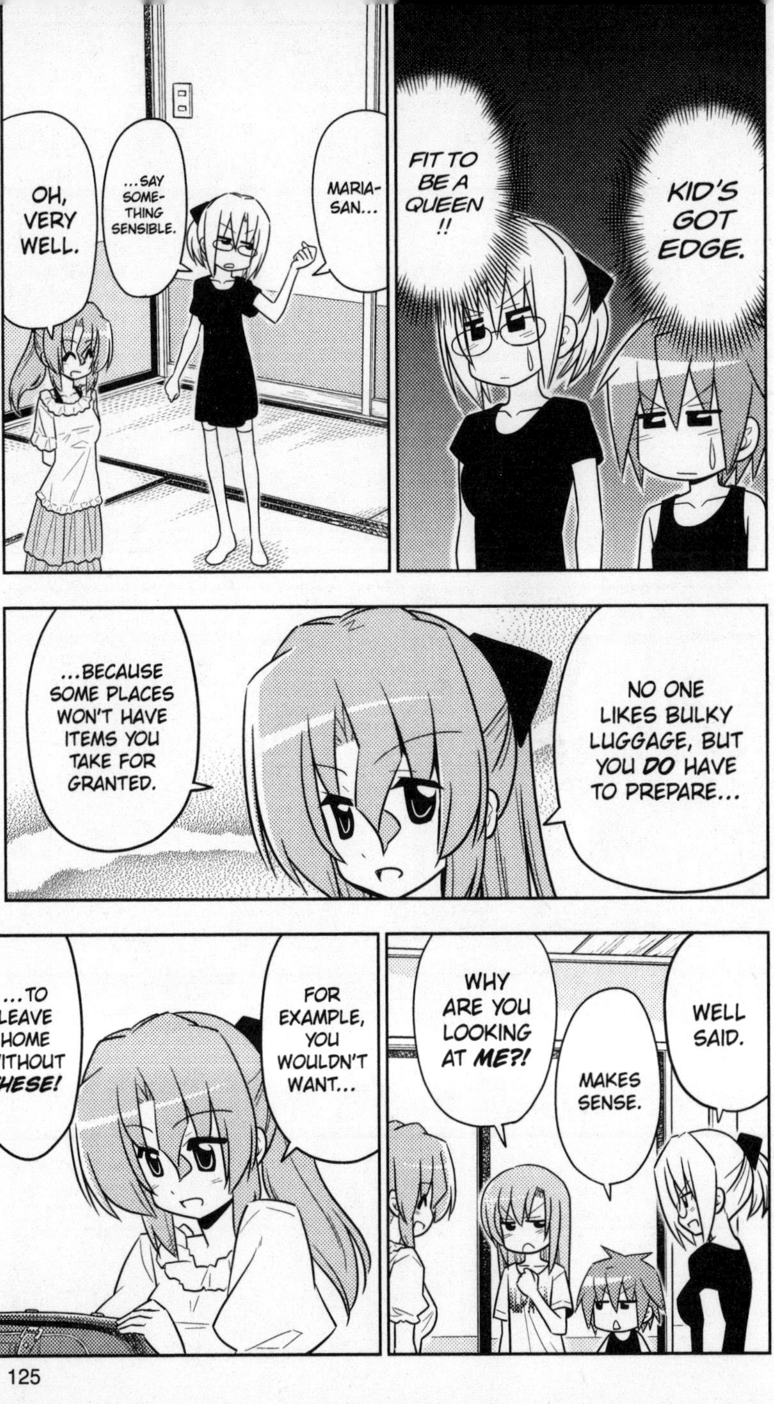
KID'S GOT EDGE.
FIT TO BE A QUEEN !!
MARIA-SAN...
...SAY SOME-THING SENSIBLE.
OH, VERY WELL.
NO ONE LIKES BULKY LUGGAGE, BUT YOU ***DO*** HAVE TO PREPARE...
...BECAUSE SOME PLACES WON'T HAVE ITEMS YOU TAKE FOR GRANTED.
WELL SAID.
MAKES SENSE.
WHY ARE YOU LOOKING AT ***ME?!***
FOR EXAMPLE, YOU WOULDN'T WANT...
...TO LEAVE HOME WITHOUT ***THESE!***

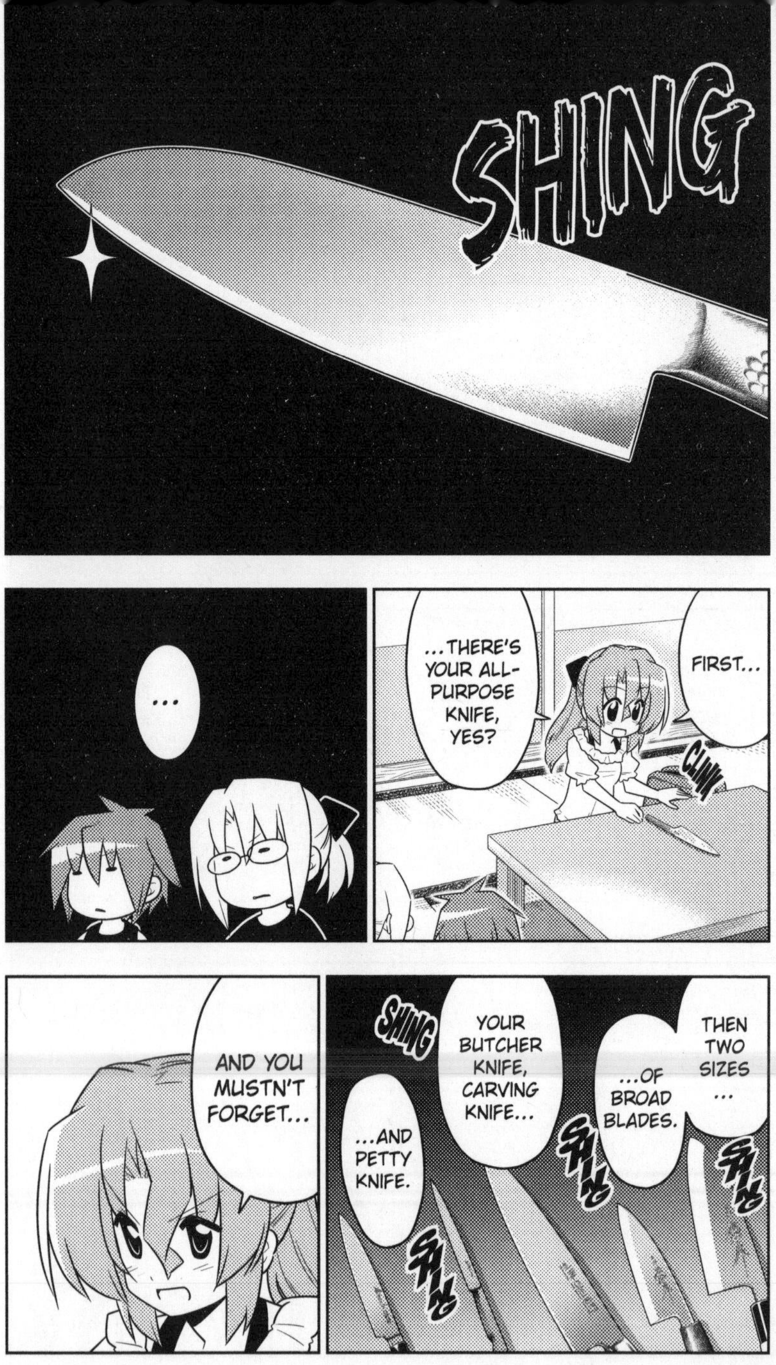
SHING
FIRST...
CLINK
...THERE'S YOUR ALL-PURPOSE KNIFE, YES?
...
THEN TWO SIZES...
...OF BROAD BLADES.
SHING
SHING
YOUR BUTCHER KNIFE, CARVING KNIFE...
SHING
...AND PETTY KNIFE.
SHING
AND YOU MUSTN'T FORGET...

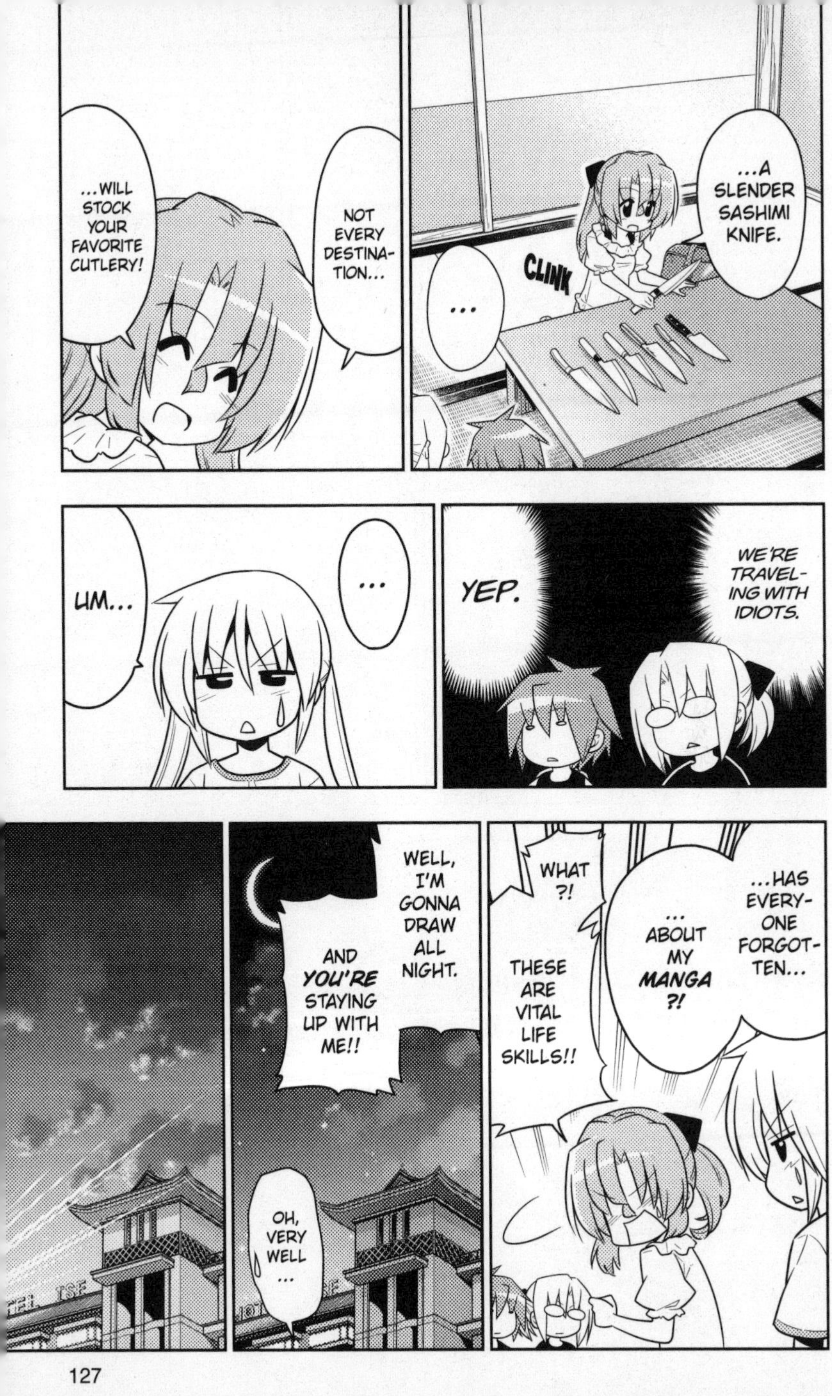
...A SLENDER SASHIMI KNIFE.
CLINK
...
NOT EVERY DESTINATION...
...WILL STOCK YOUR FAVORITE CUTLERY!
WE'RE TRAVELING WITH IDIOTS.
YEP.
...
UM...
...HAS EVERYONE FORGOTTEN...
...ABOUT MY *MANGA*?!
WHAT?!
THESE ARE VITAL LIFE SKILLS!!
WELL, I'M GONNA DRAW ALL NIGHT.
AND *YOU'RE* STAYING UP WITH ME!!
OH, VERY WELL...

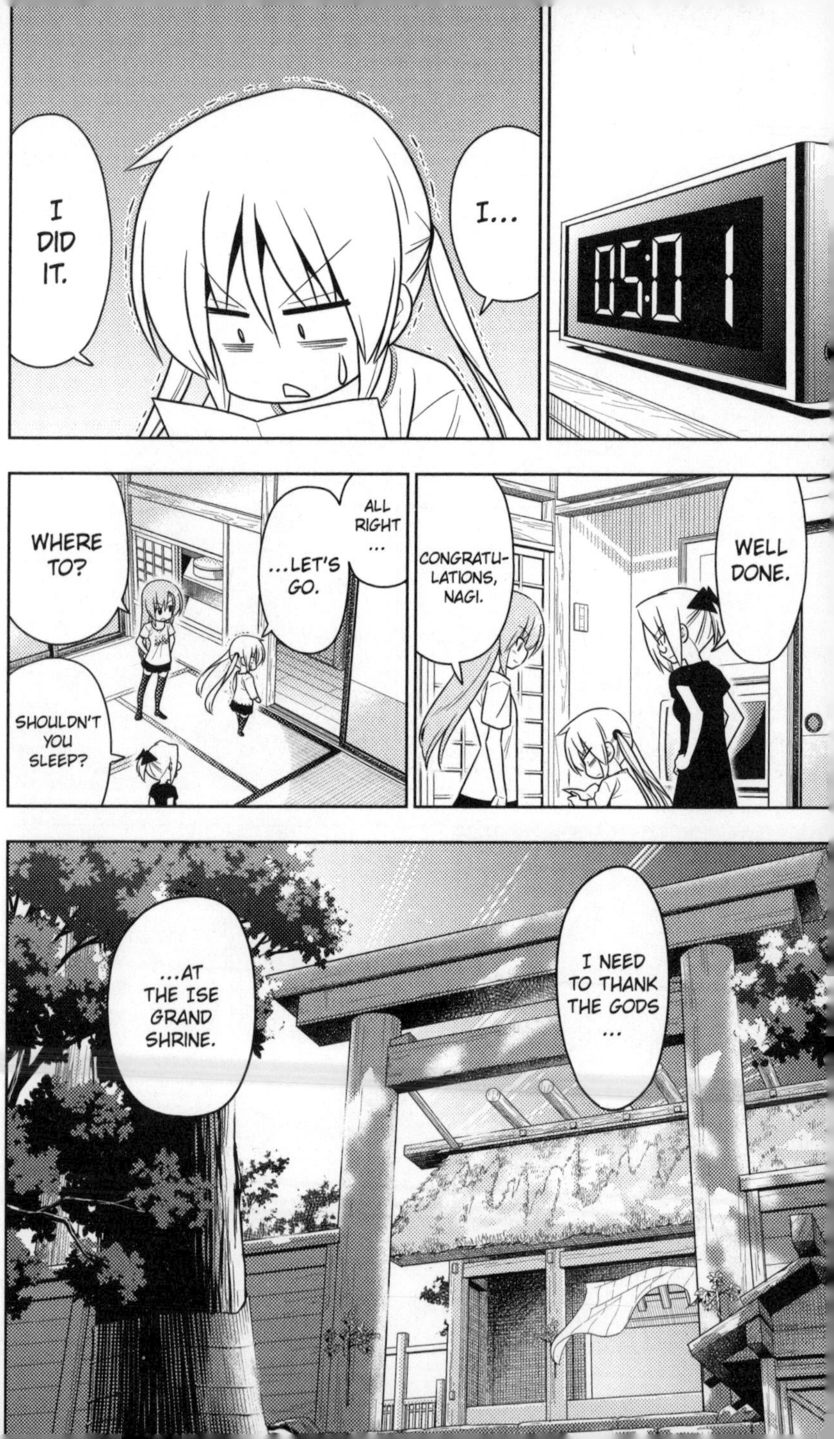
05:01
I...
I DID IT.
WELL DONE.
CONGRATULATIONS, NAGI.
ALL RIGHT ...
...LET'S GO.
WHERE TO?
SHOULDN'T YOU SLEEP?
I NEED TO THANK THE GODS ...
...AT THE ISE GRAND SHRINE.

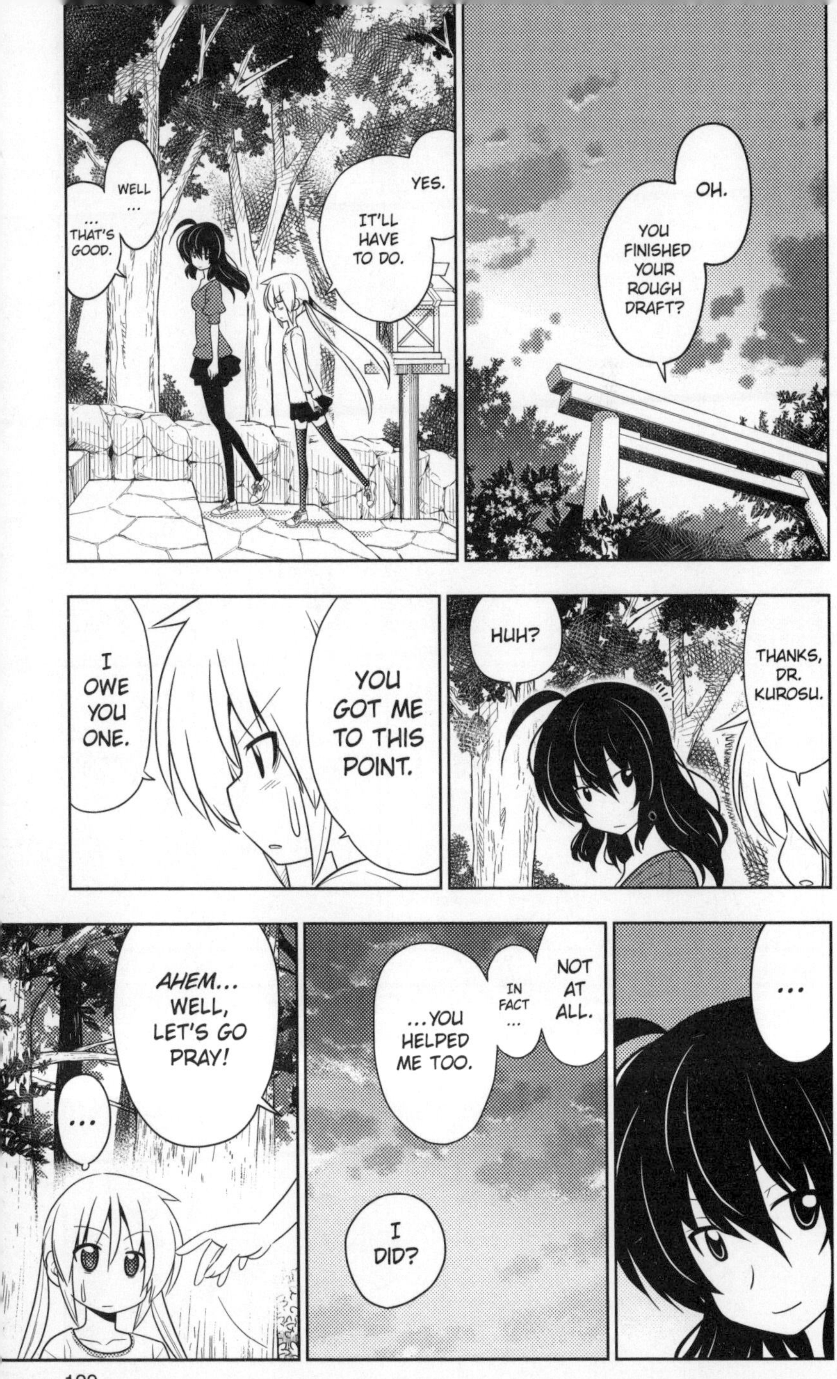
OH.
YOU FINISHED YOUR ROUGH DRAFT?
YES.
IT'LL HAVE TO DO.
WELL ...
... THAT'S GOOD.
THANKS, DR. KUROSU.
HUH?
YOU GOT ME TO THIS POINT.
I OWE YOU ONE.
...
NOT AT ALL.
IN FACT ...
...YOU HELPED ME TOO.
I DID?
AHEM... WELL, LET'S GO PRAY!
...

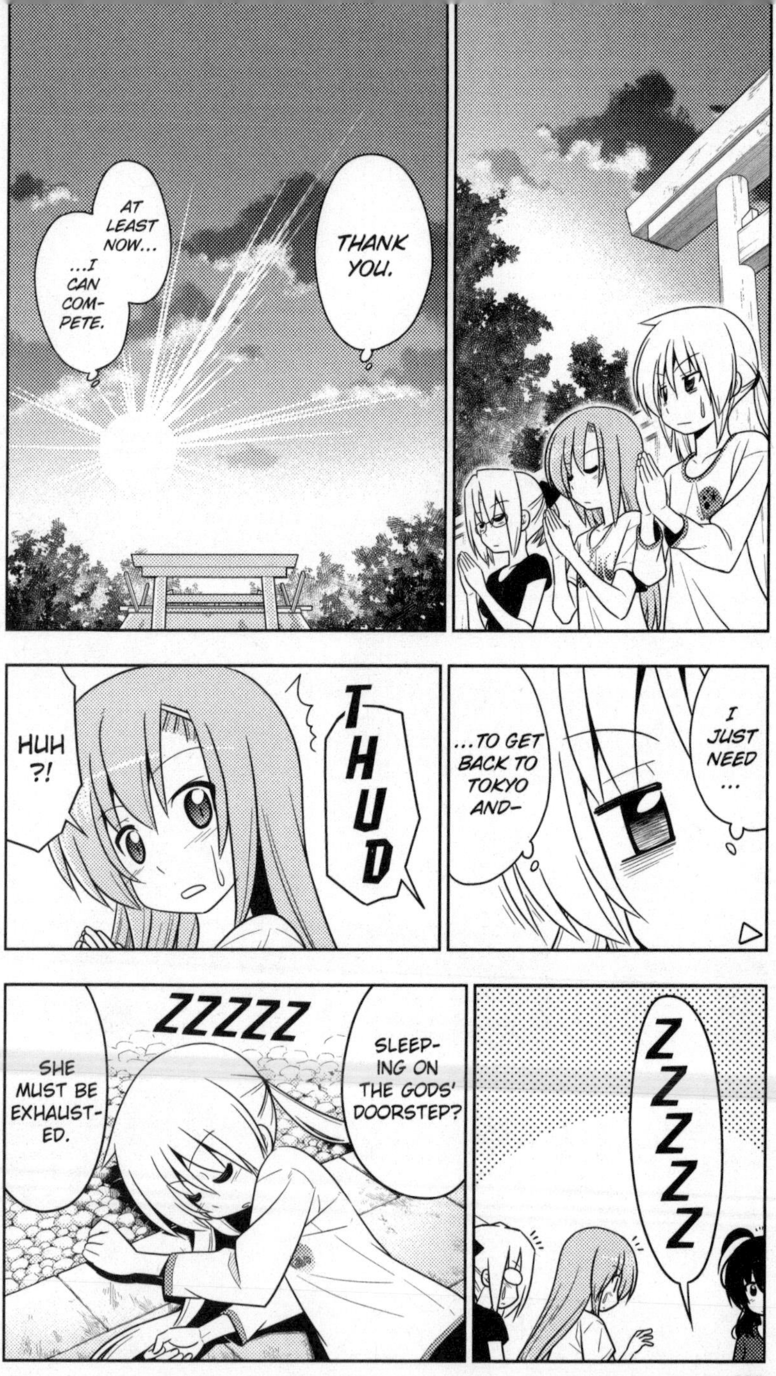
THANK YOU.
AT LEAST NOW... ...I CAN COMPETE.
I JUST NEED...
...TO GET BACK TO TOKYO AND-
THUD
HUH ?!
ZZZZZ
SLEEPING ON THE GODS' DOORSTEP?
ZZZZZ
SHE MUST BE EXHAUSTED.

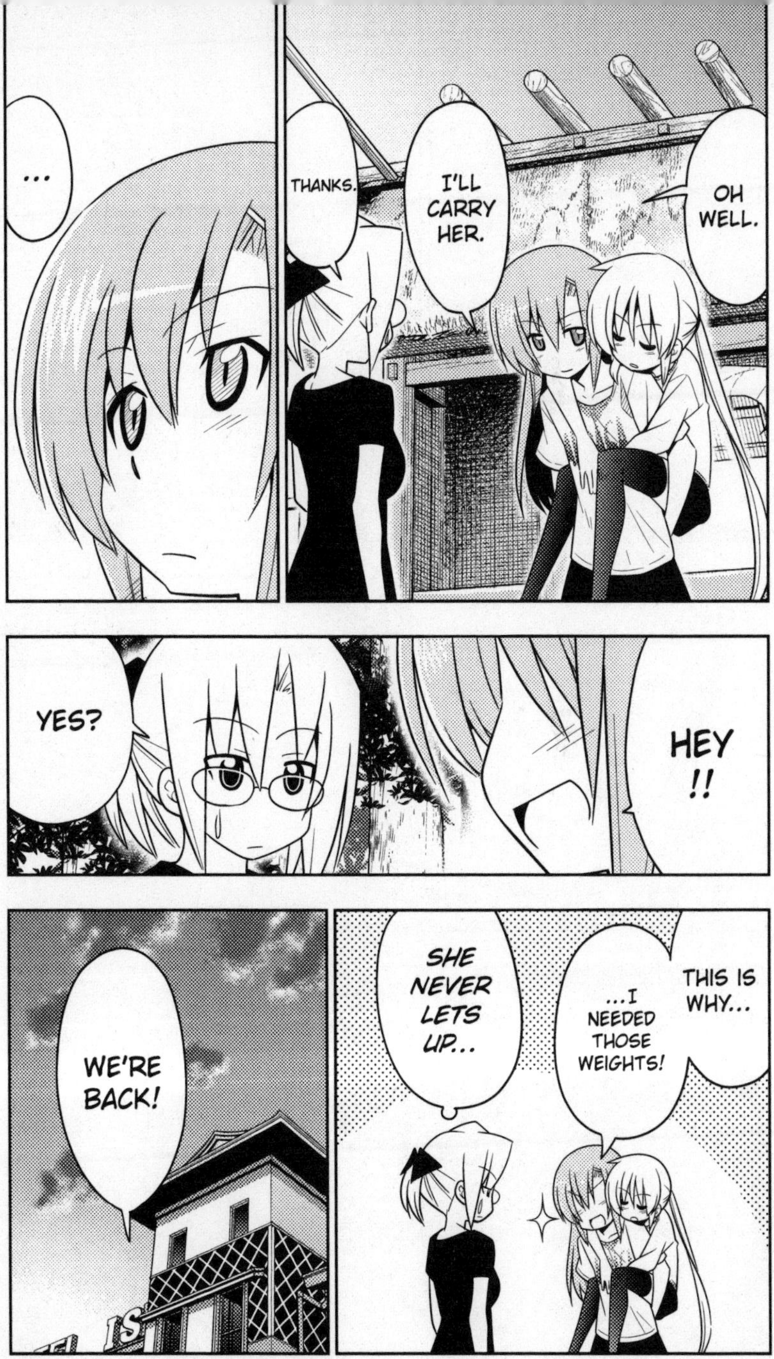
OH WELL.
I'LL CARRY HER.
THANKS.
...
HEY!!
YES?
THIS IS WHY...
...I NEEDED THOSE WEIGHTS!
SHE NEVER LETS UP...
WE'RE BACK!

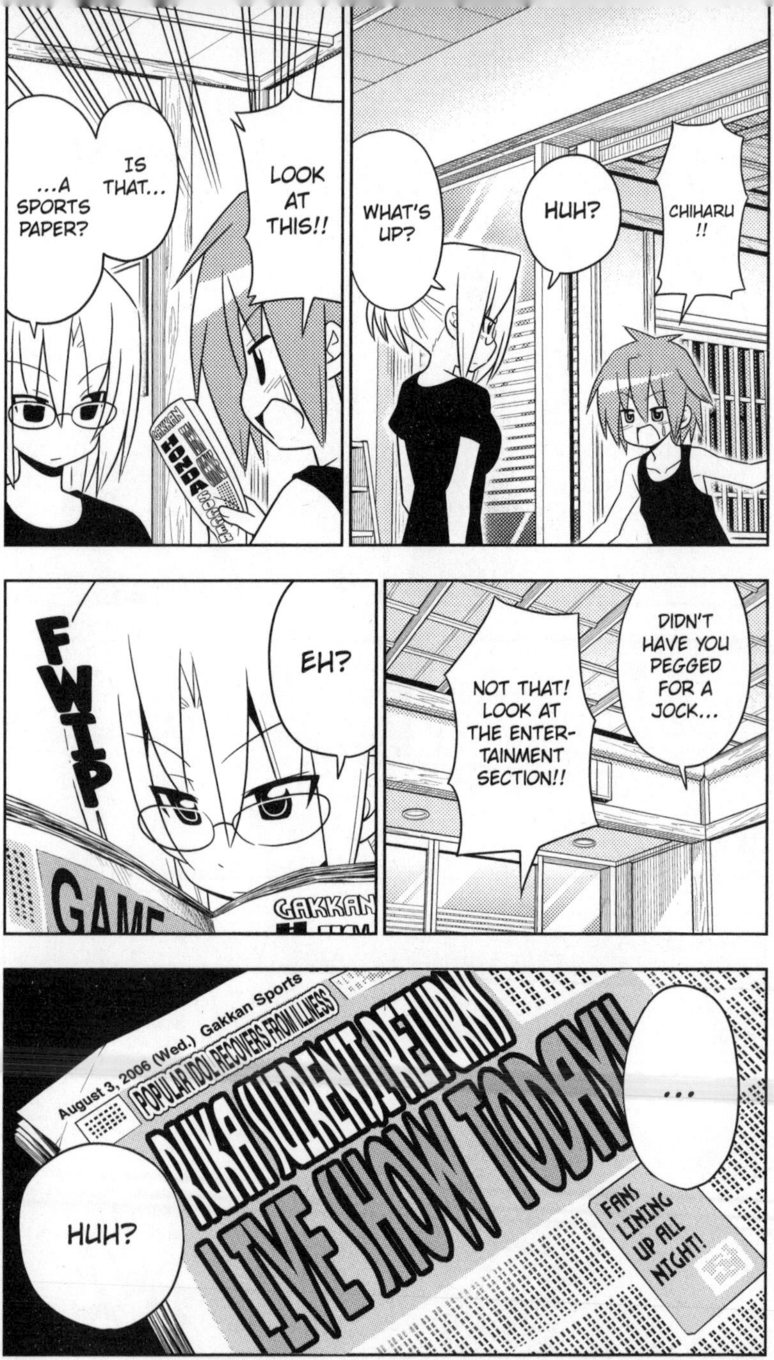

CHIHARU!!
HUH?
WHAT'S UP?
LOOK AT THIS!!
IS THAT...
...A SPORTS PAPER?
DIDN'T HAVE YOU PEGGED FOR A JOCK...
NOT THAT! LOOK AT THE ENTER-TAINMENT SECTION!!
EH?
FWIP
GAME
GAKKAN
...
August 3, 2006 (Wed.) Gakkan Sports
POPULAR IDOL RECOVERS FROM ILLNESS
RUKA (STUDENT) RETURNS
LIVE SHOW TODAY!
FANS LINING UP ALL NIGHT!
HUH?

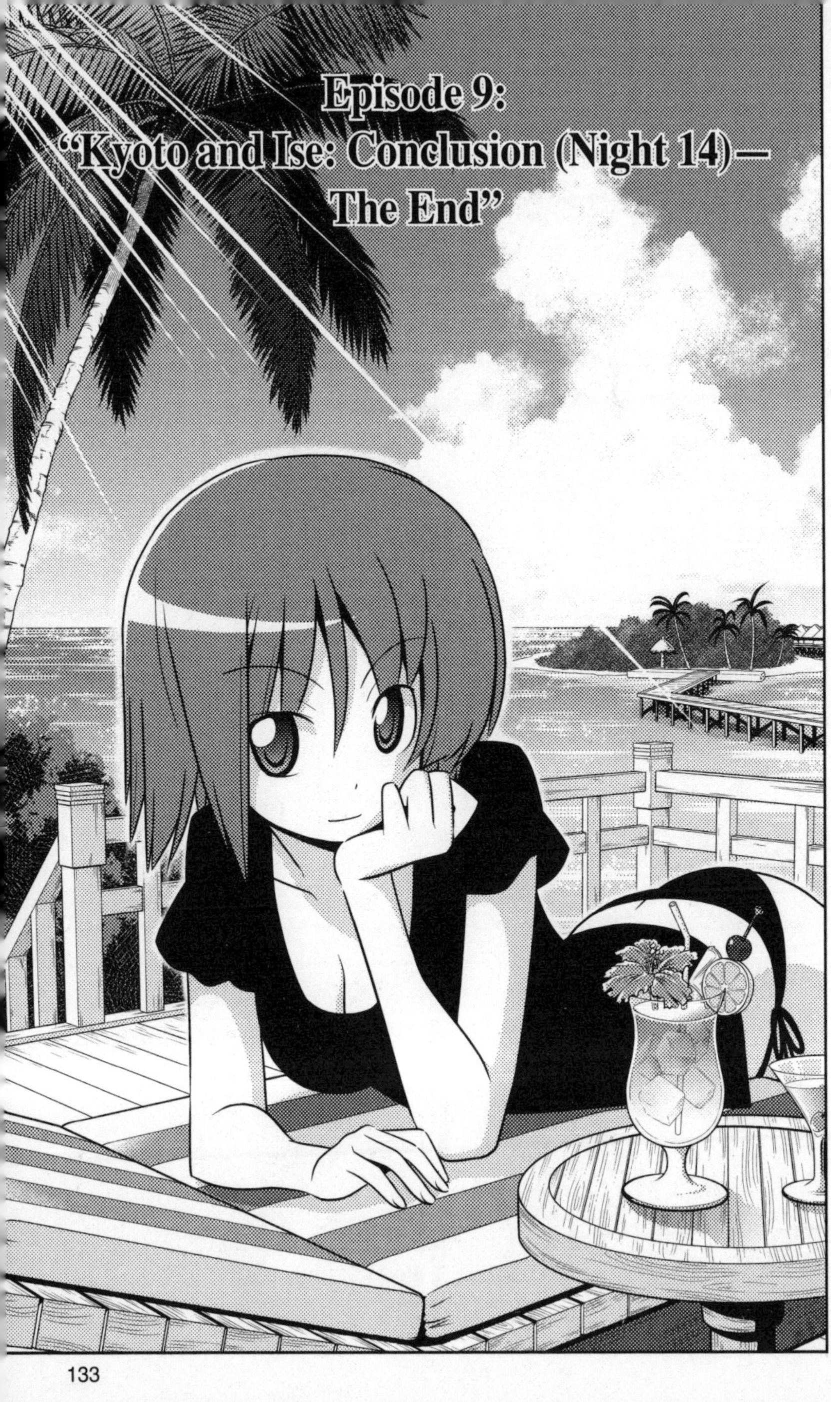
Episode 9:
"Kyoto and Ise: Conclusion (Night 14) – The End"

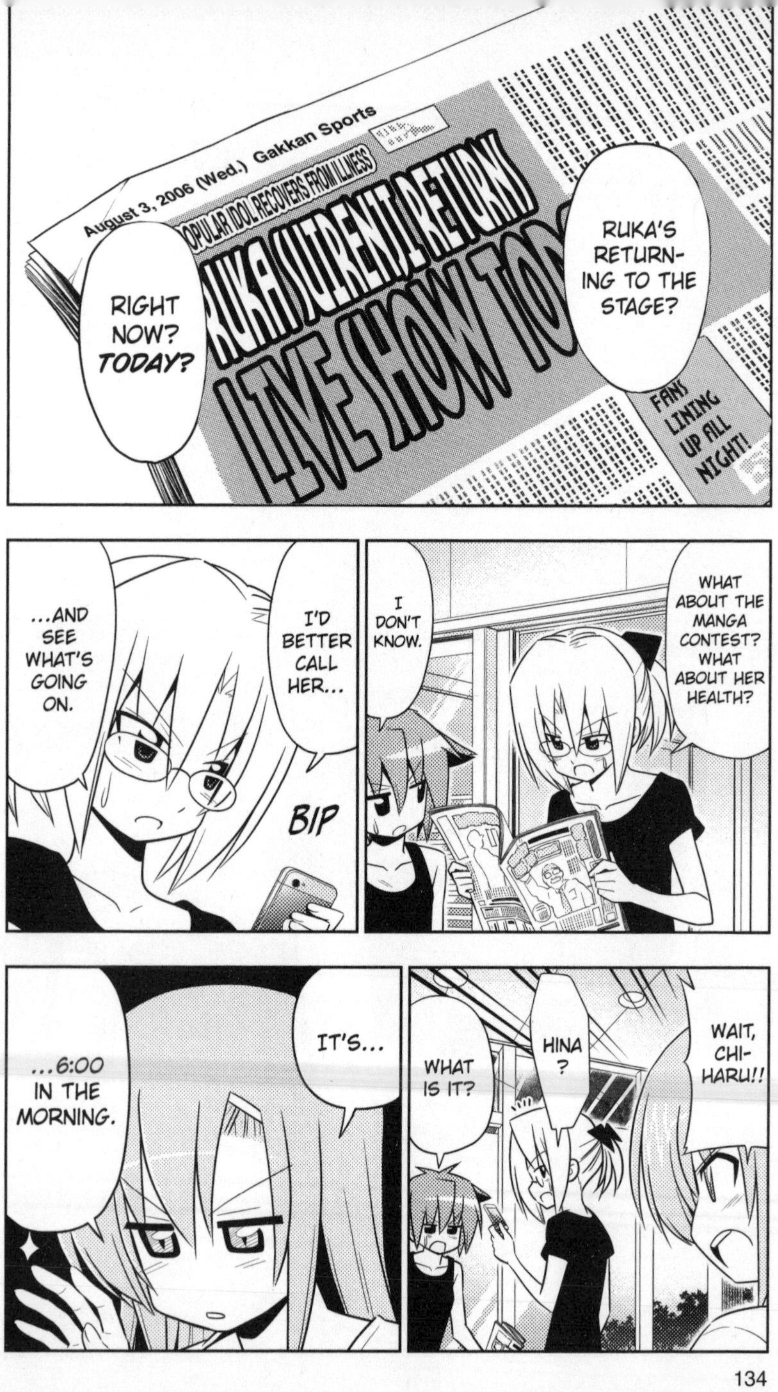
August 3, 2006 (Wed.) Gakkan Sports
OPULAR IDOL RECOVERS FROM ILLNESS
RUKA'S RETURNING TO THE STAGE?
RIGHT NOW? *TODAY?*
FANS LINING UP ALL NIGHT!
WHAT ABOUT THE MANGA CONTEST? WHAT ABOUT HER HEALTH?
I DON'T KNOW.
I'D BETTER CALL HER...
...AND SEE WHAT'S GOING ON.
BIP
WAIT, CHI-HARU!!
HINA ?
WHAT IS IT?
IT'S...
...6:00 IN THE MORNING.

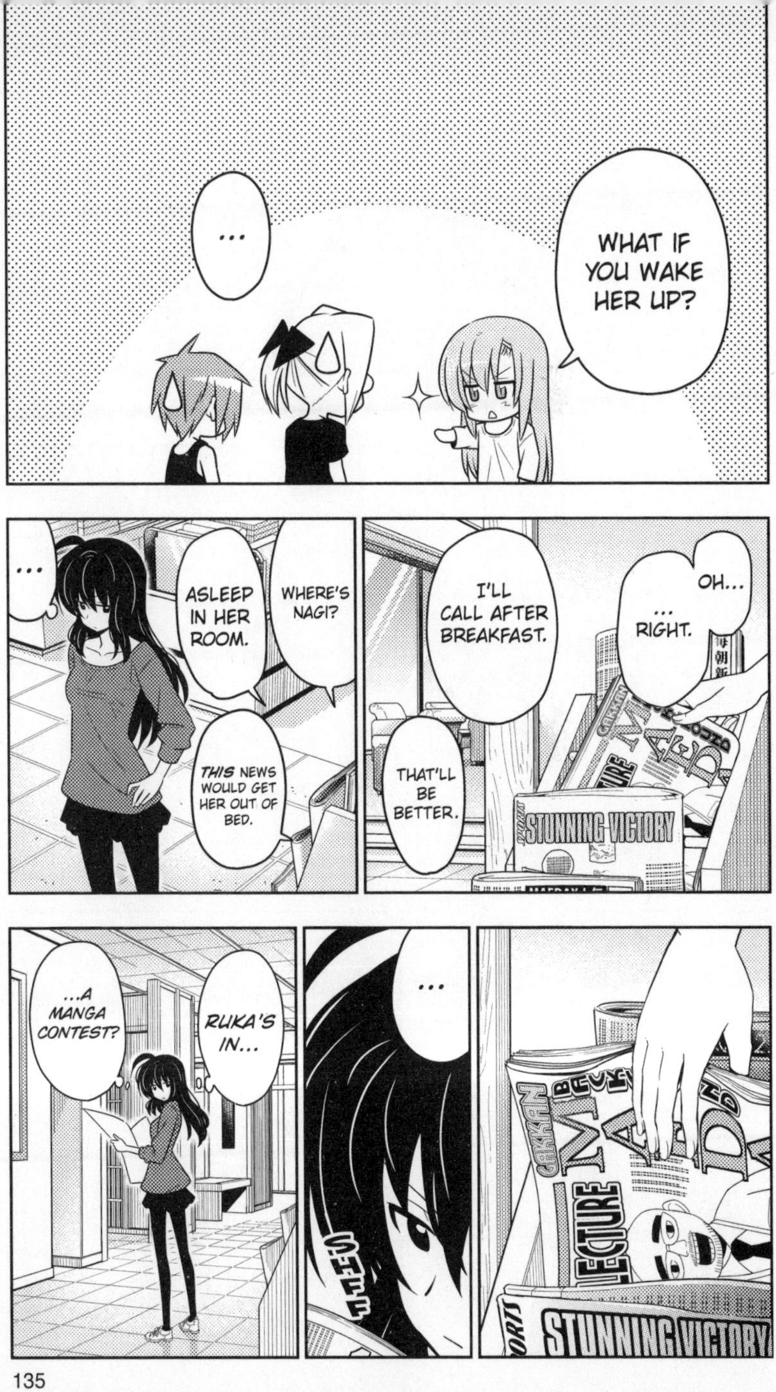
WHAT IF YOU WAKE HER UP?
...
OH...
... RIGHT.
I'LL CALL AFTER BREAKFAST.
THAT'LL BE BETTER.
STUNNING VICTORY
WHERE'S NAGI?
ASLEEP IN HER ROOM.
THIS NEWS WOULD GET HER OUT OF BED.
...
STUNNING VICTORY
...
RUKA'S IN...
...A MANGA CONTEST?

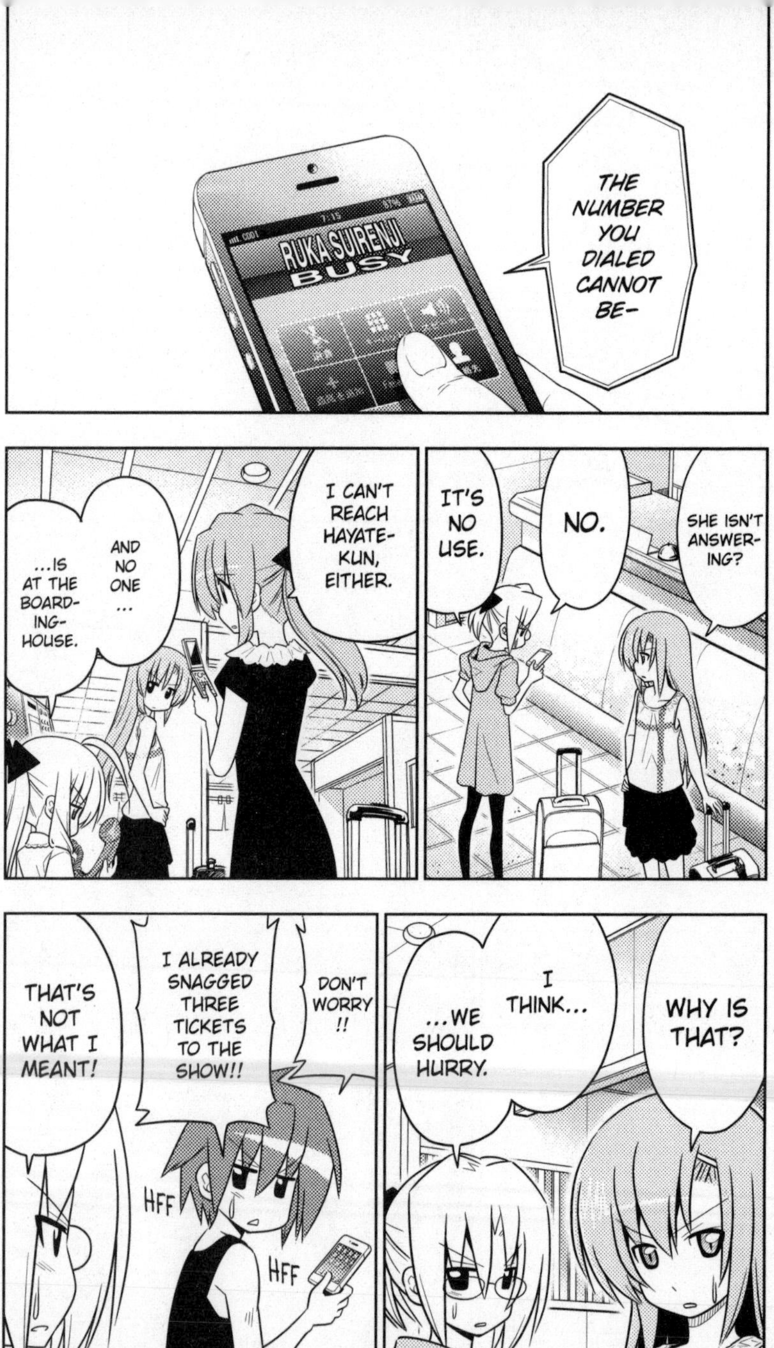
RUKA SUIRENJI
BUSY
THE NUMBER YOU DIALED CANNOT BE-
SHE ISN'T ANSWERING?
NO.
IT'S NO USE.
I CAN'T REACH HAYATE-KUN, EITHER.
AND NO ONE...
...IS AT THE BOARDING-HOUSE.
WHY IS THAT?
I THINK...
...WE SHOULD HURRY.
DON'T WORRY!!
I ALREADY SNAGGED THREE TICKETS TO THE SHOW!!
HFF
HFF
THAT'S NOT WHAT I MEANT!

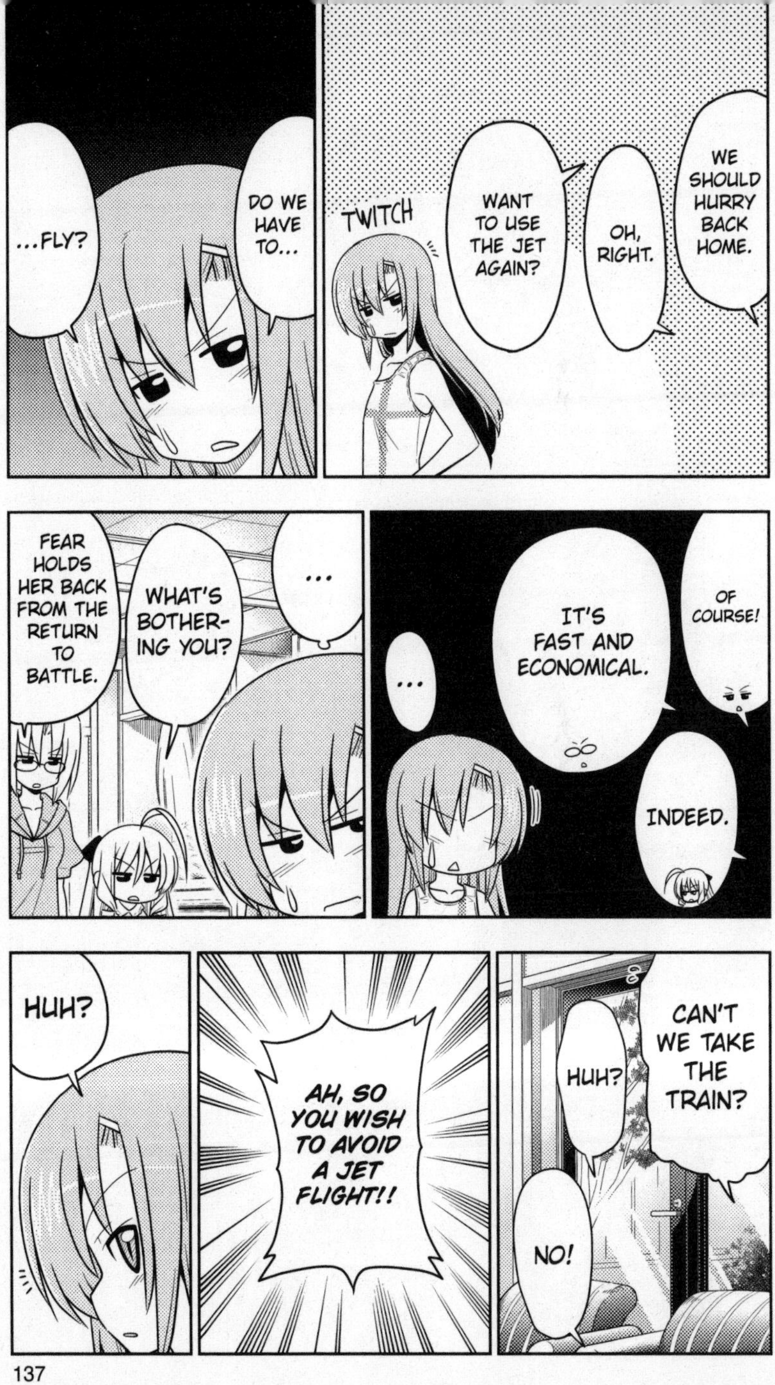
WE SHOULD HURRY BACK HOME.
OH, RIGHT.
WANT TO USE THE JET AGAIN?
TWITCH
DO WE HAVE TO...
...FLY?
OF COURSE!
IT'S FAST AND ECONOMICAL.
...
INDEED.
...
WHAT'S BOTHERING YOU?
FEAR HOLDS HER BACK FROM THE RETURN TO BATTLE.
CAN'T WE TAKE THE TRAIN?
HUH?
NO!
AH, SO YOU WISH TO AVOID A JET FLIGHT!!
HUH?

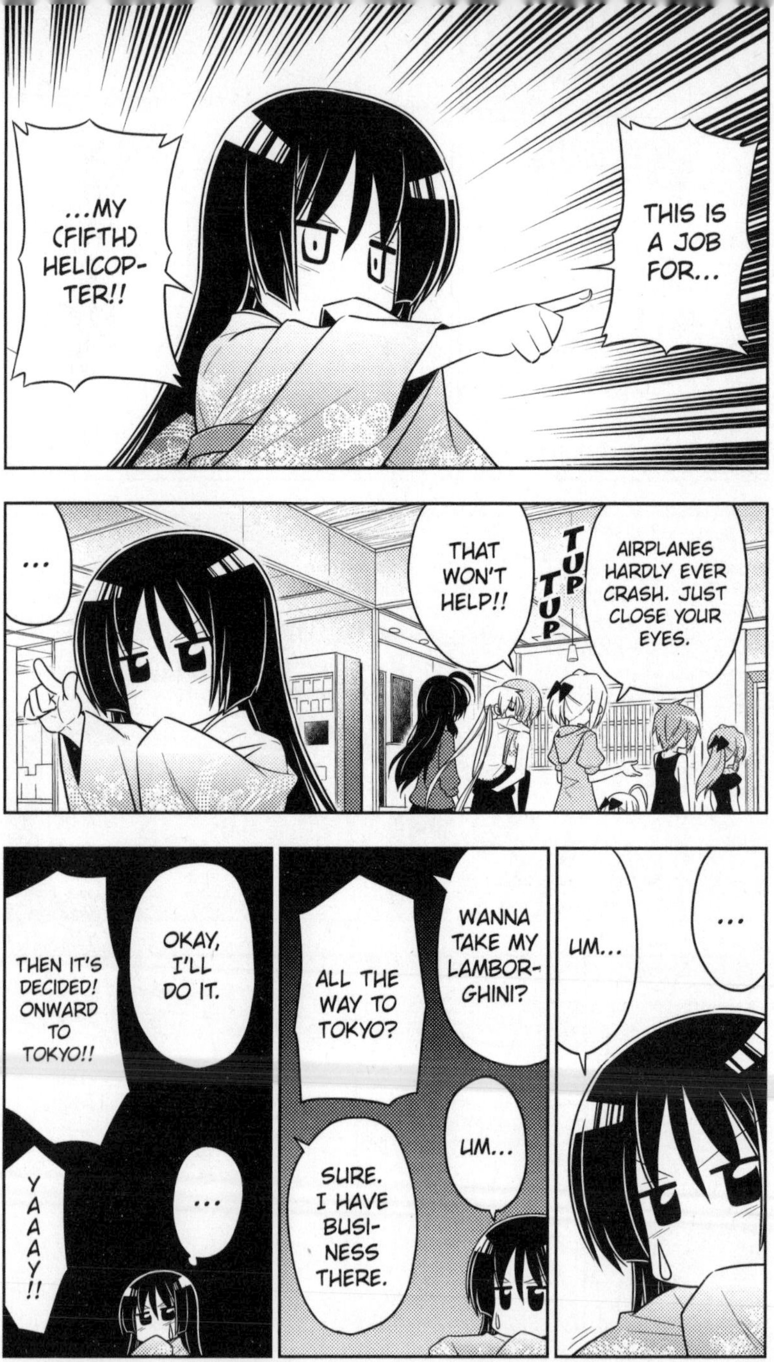
THIS IS A JOB FOR...
...MY (FIFTH) HELICOPTER!!
AIRPLANES HARDLY EVER CRASH. JUST CLOSE YOUR EYES.
TUP TUP
THAT WON'T HELP!!
...
...
UM...
WANNA TAKE MY LAMBORGHINI?
ALL THE WAY TO TOKYO?
UM...
SURE. I HAVE BUSINESS THERE.
OKAY, I'LL DO IT.
THEN IT'S DECIDED! ONWARD TO TOKYO!!
...
YAAAAY!!

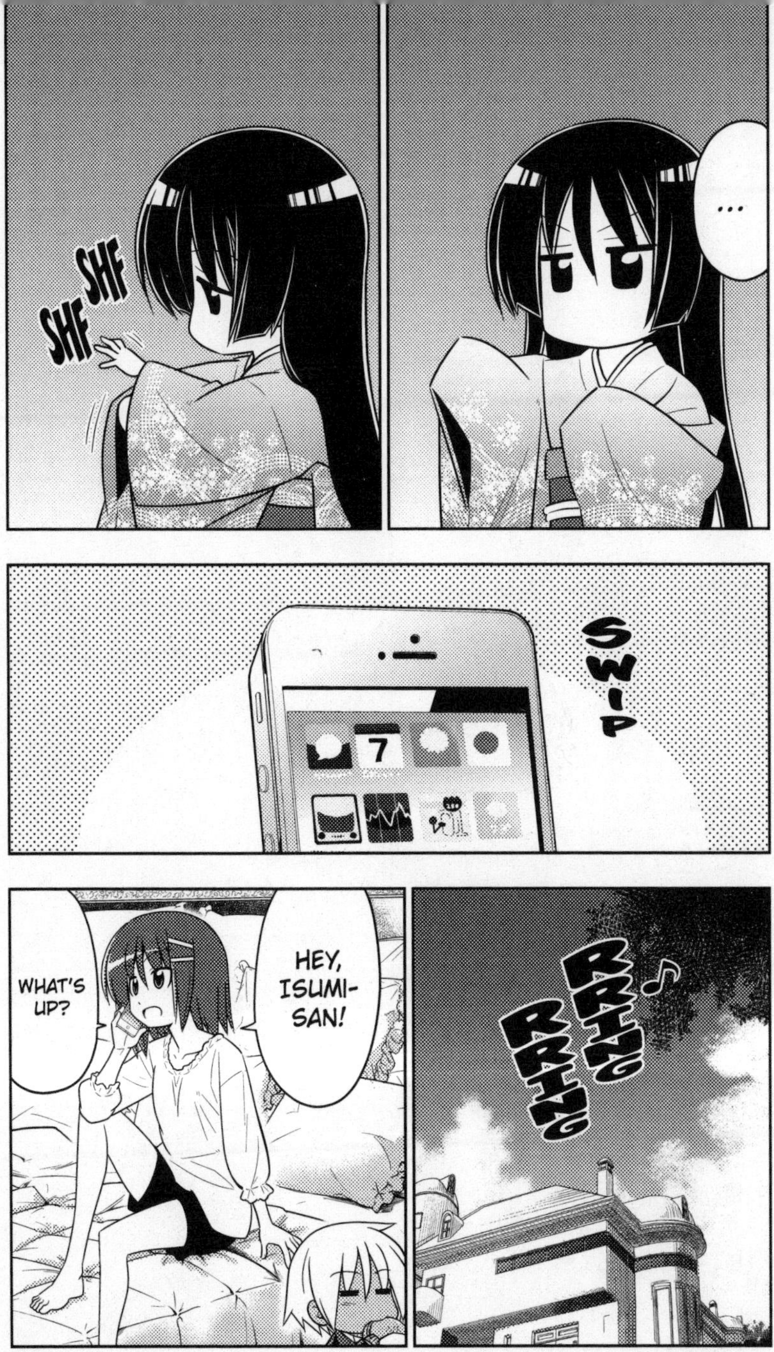
...
SHF SHF
SWIP
RRING RRING ♪
HEY, ISUMI-SAN!
WHAT'S UP?

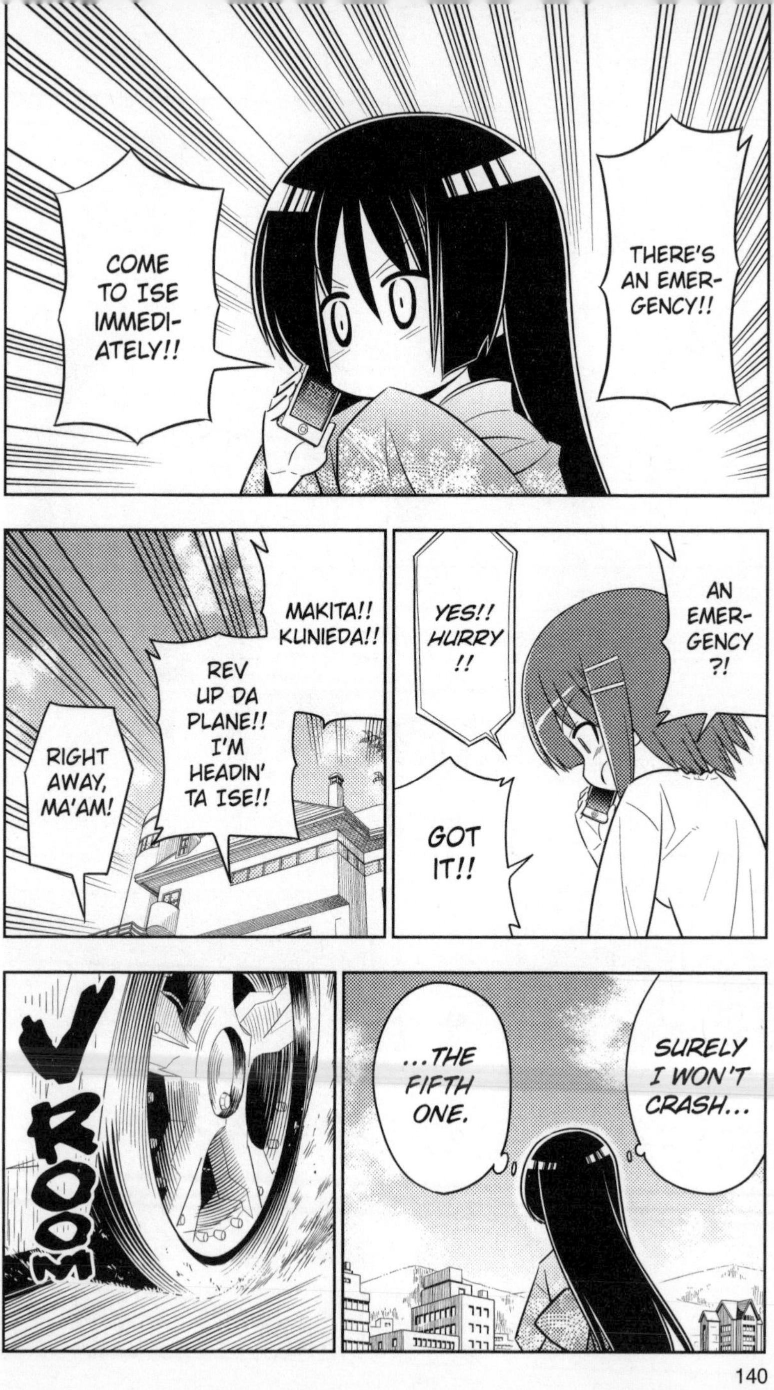
THERE'S AN EMER-GENCY!!
COME TO ISE IMMEDI-ATELY!!
AN EMER-GENCY?!
YES!! HURRY!!
GOT IT!!
MAKITA!! KUNIEDA!!
REV UP DA PLANE!! I'M HEADIN' TA ISE!!
RIGHT AWAY, MA'AM!
SURELY I WON'T CRASH...
...THE FIFTH ONE.
VROOOM

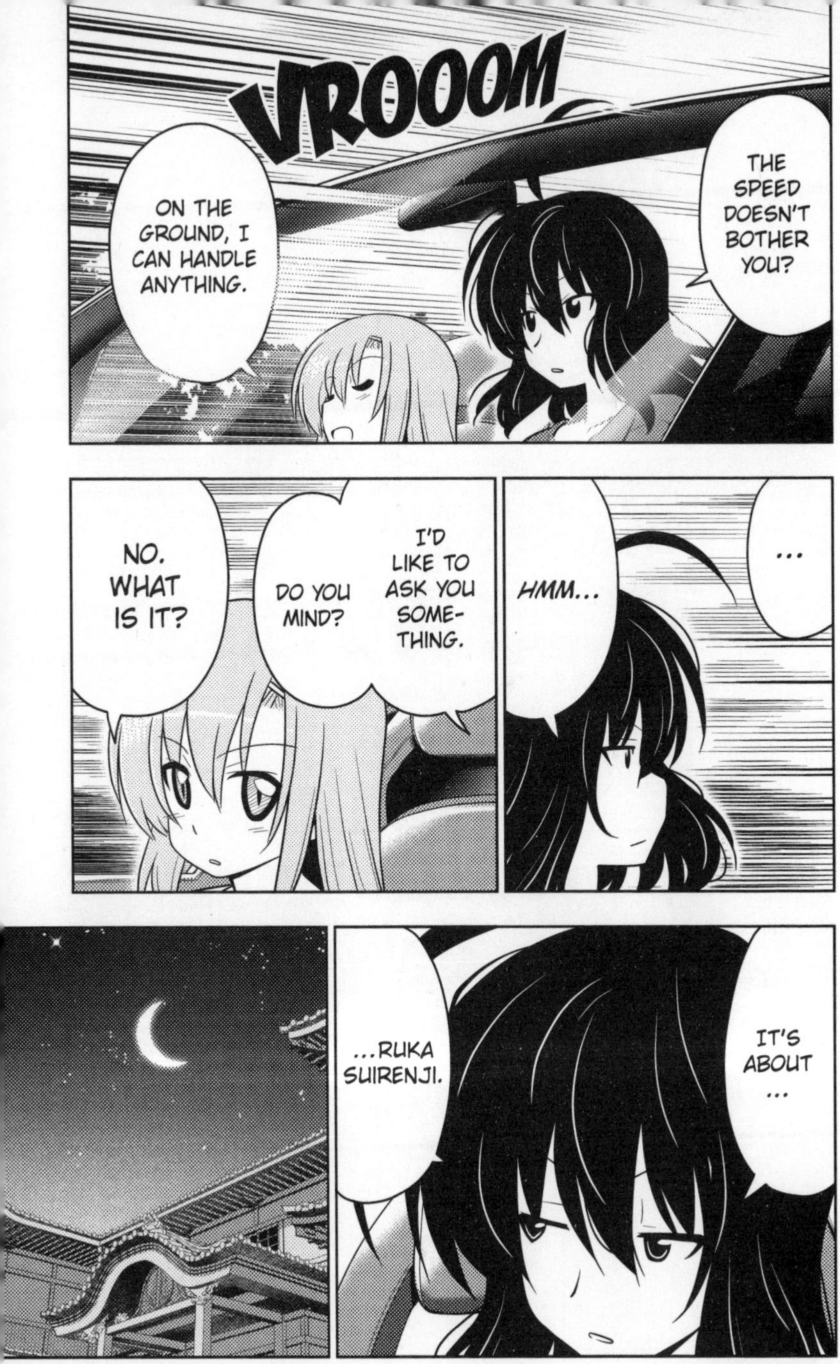
THE SPEED DOESN'T BOTHER YOU?
VROOOM
ON THE GROUND, I CAN HANDLE ANYTHING.
...
HMM...
I'D LIKE TO ASK YOU SOME-THING.
DO YOU MIND?
NO. WHAT IS IT?
IT'S ABOUT...
...RUKA SUIRENJI.

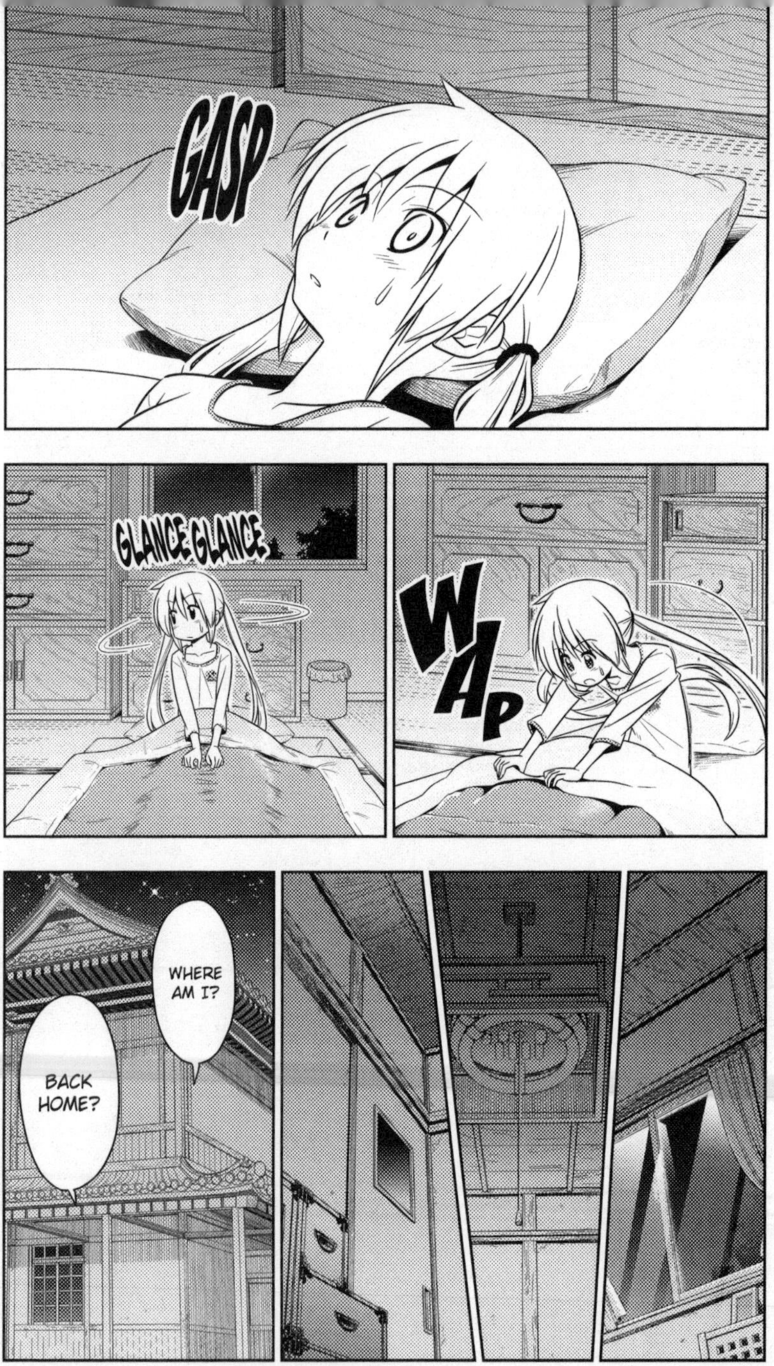
GASP
WAP
GLANCE GLANCE
WHERE AM I?
BACK HOME?

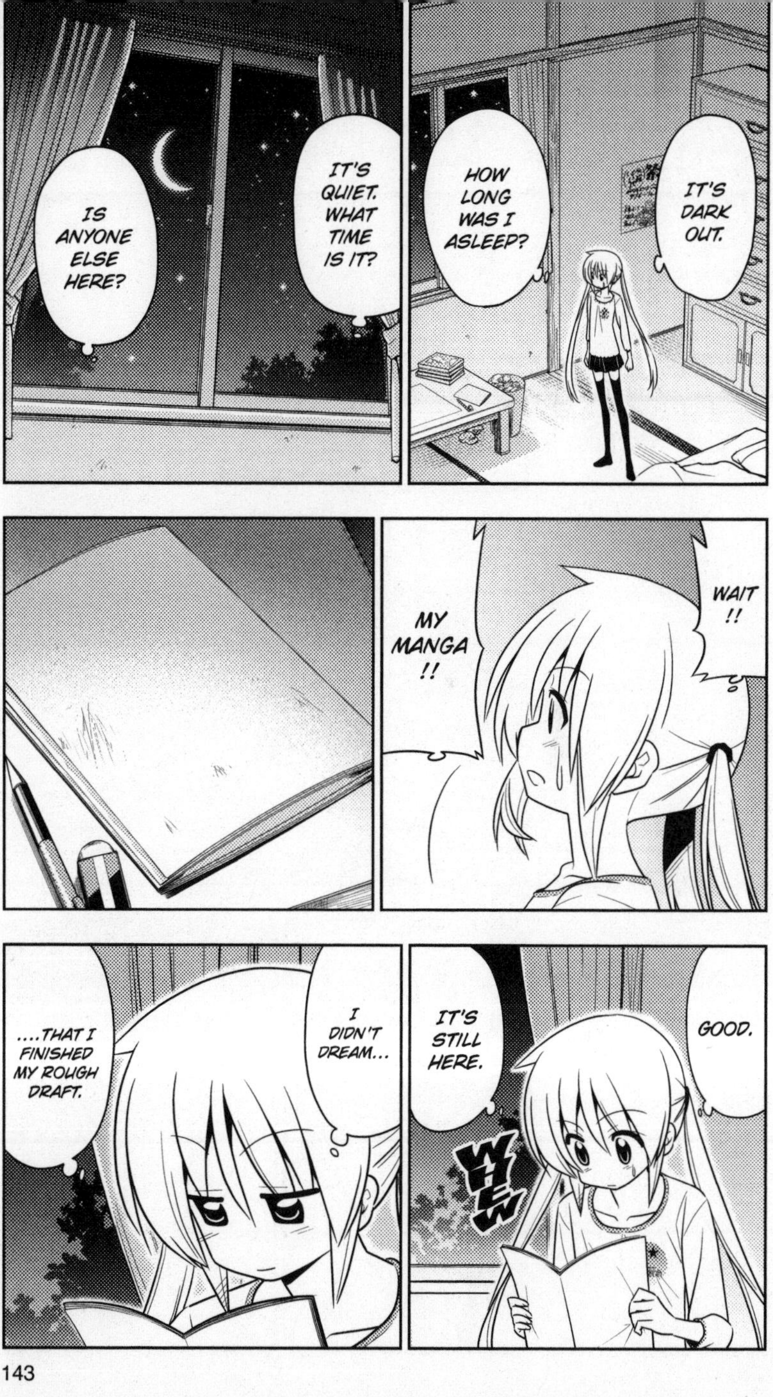
IT'S DARK OUT.
HOW LONG WAS I ASLEEP?
IT'S QUIET. WHAT TIME IS IT?
IS ANYONE ELSE HERE?
WAIT!!
MY MANGA!!
GOOD.
IT'S STILL HERE.
WHEW
I DIDN'T DREAM...
....THAT I FINISHED MY ROUGH DRAFT.

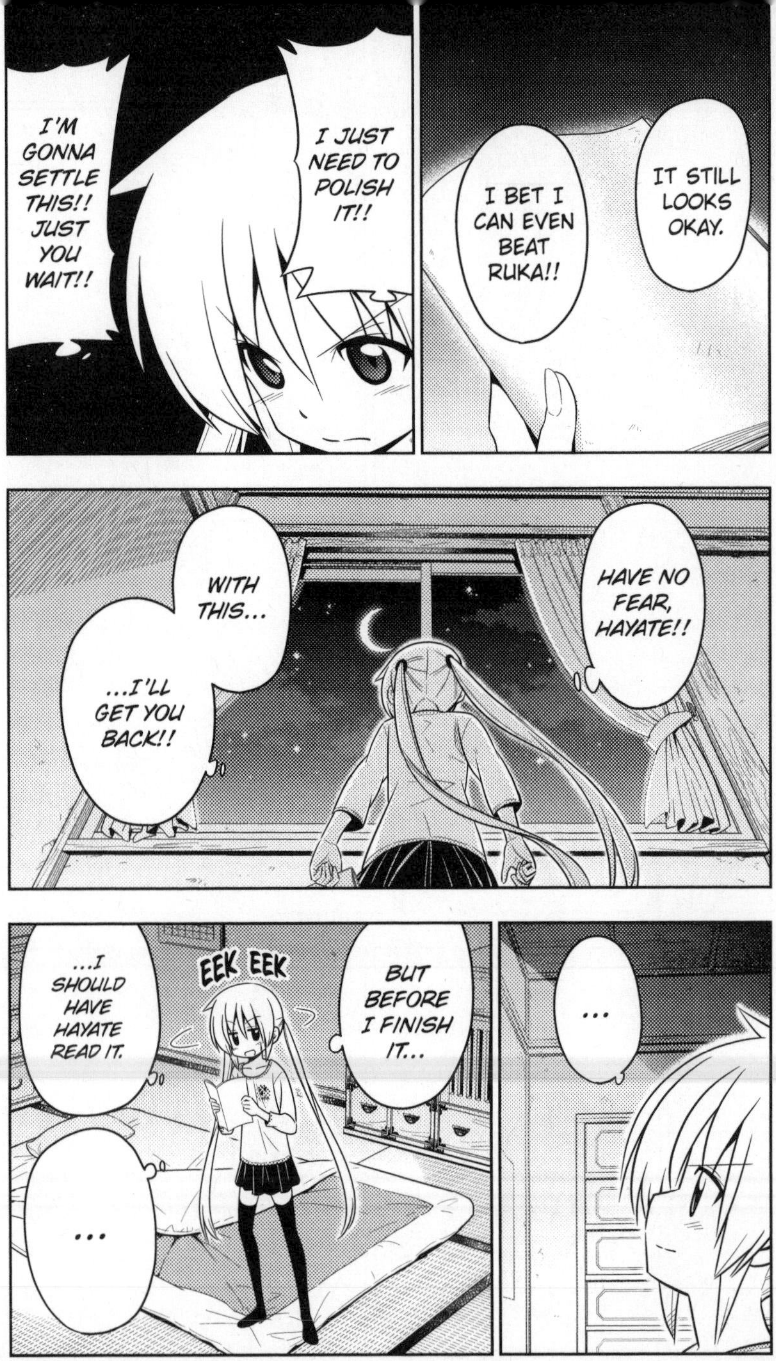
IT STILL LOOKS OKAY.
I BET I CAN EVEN BEAT RUKA!!
I JUST NEED TO POLISH IT!!
I'M GONNA SETTLE THIS!! JUST YOU WAIT!!
HAVE NO FEAR, HAYATE!!
WITH THIS...
...I'LL GET YOU BACK!!
...
BUT BEFORE I FINISH IT...
EEK EEK
...I SHOULD HAVE HAYATE READ IT.
...

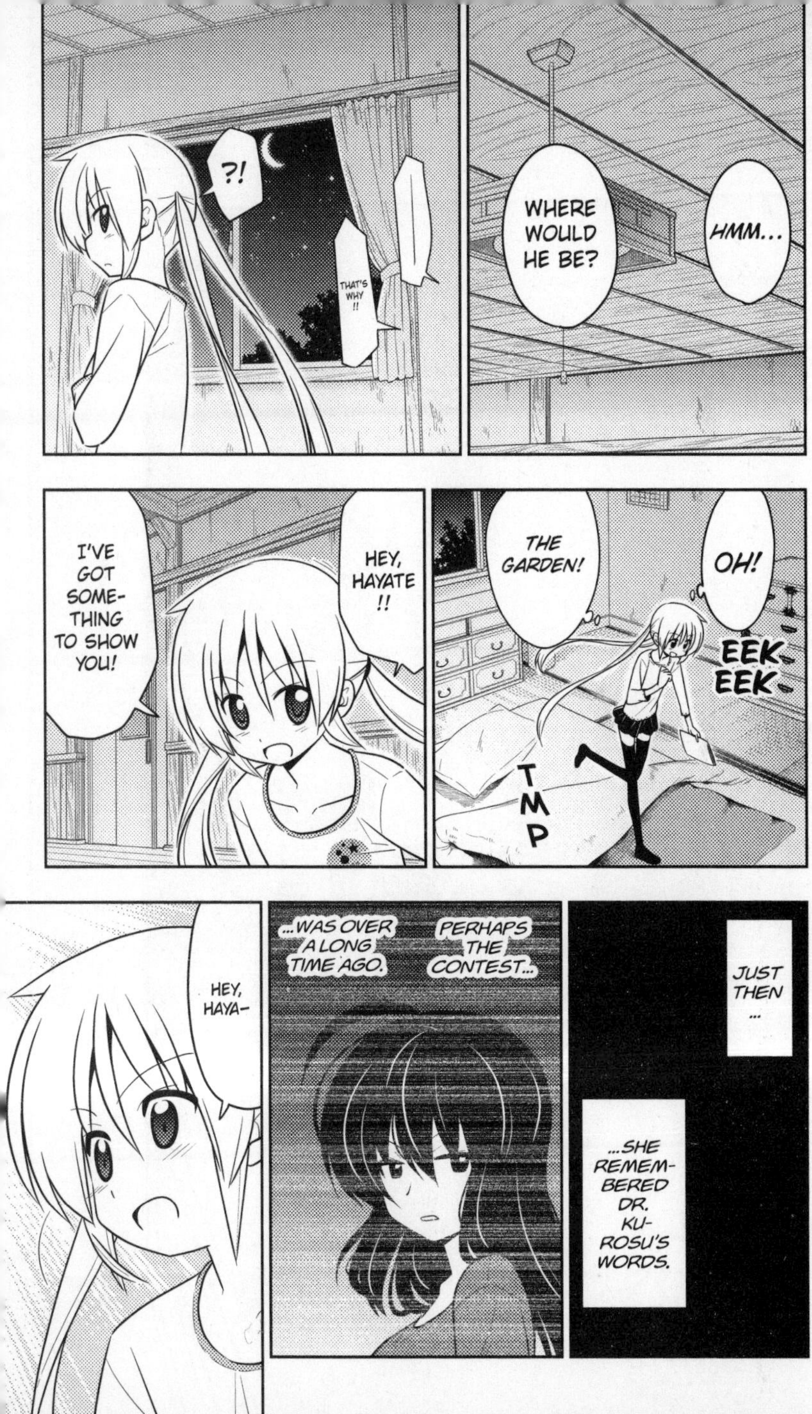
HMM...
WHERE WOULD HE BE?
THAT'S WHY !!
?!
OH!
THE GARDEN!
EEK EEK
TMP
HEY, HAYATE !!
I'VE GOT SOME-THING TO SHOW YOU!
JUST THEN ...
...SHE REMEM-BERED DR. KU-ROSU'S WORDS.
PERHAPS THE CONTEST...
...WAS OVER A LONG TIME AGO.
HEY, HAYA-

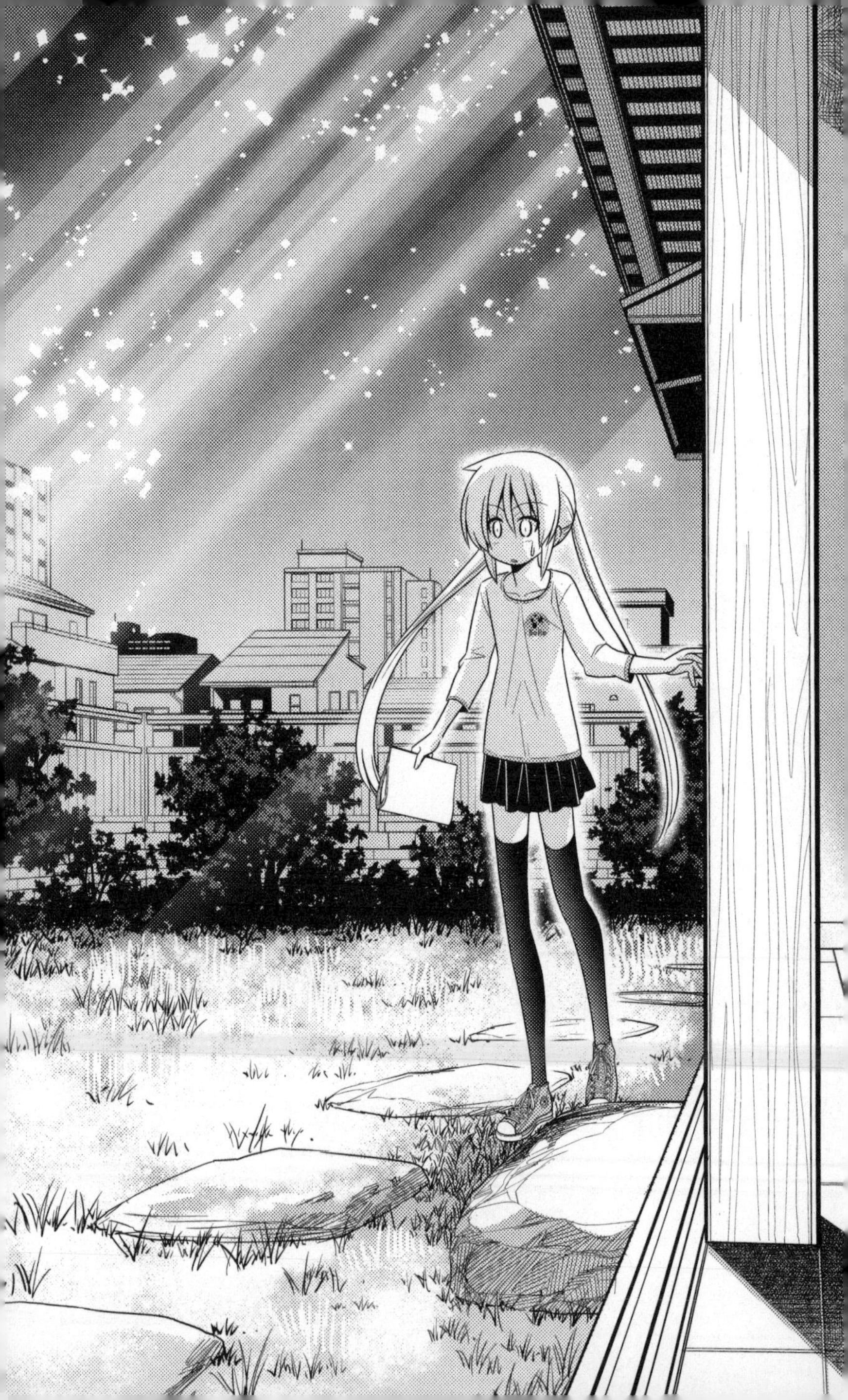

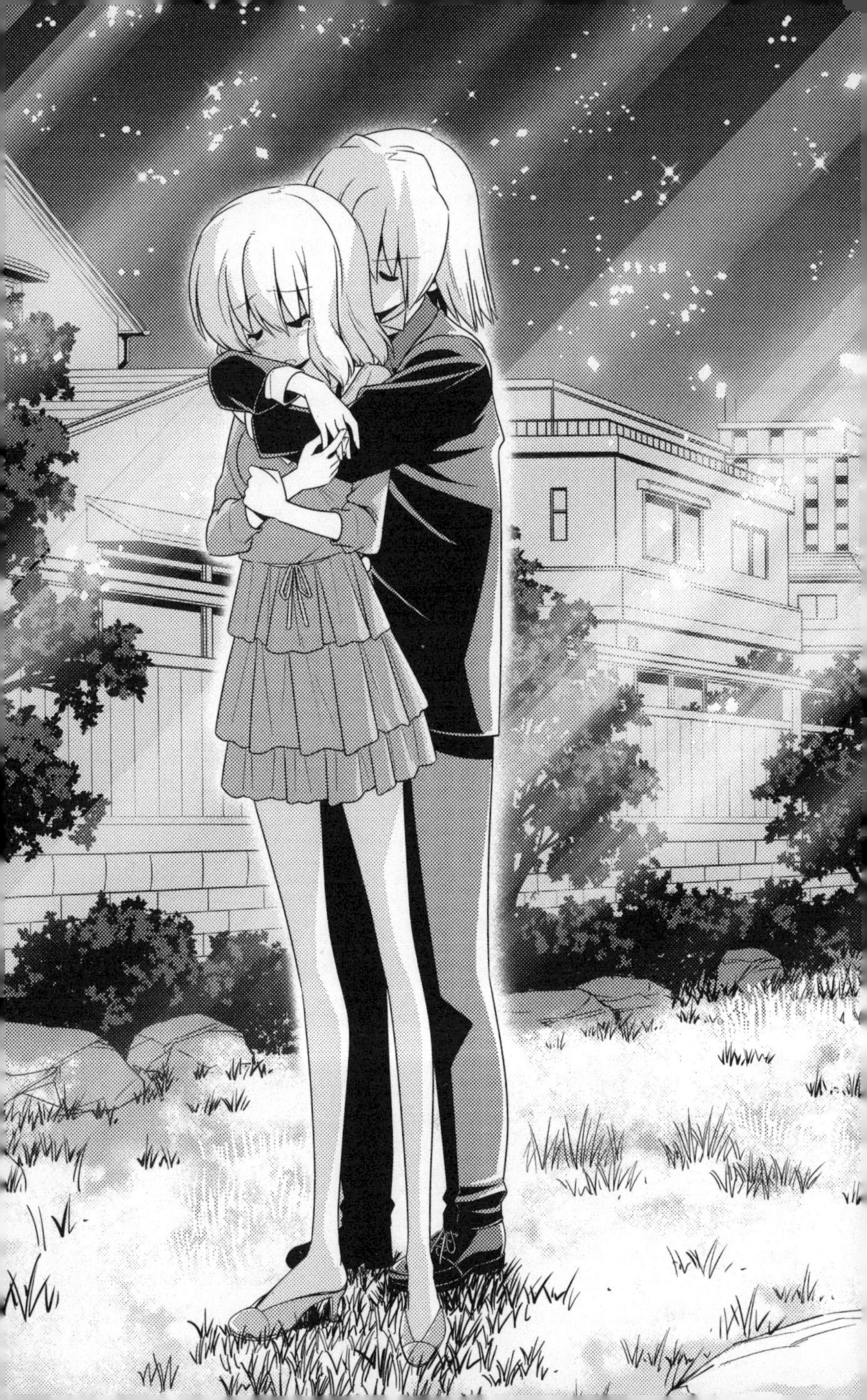

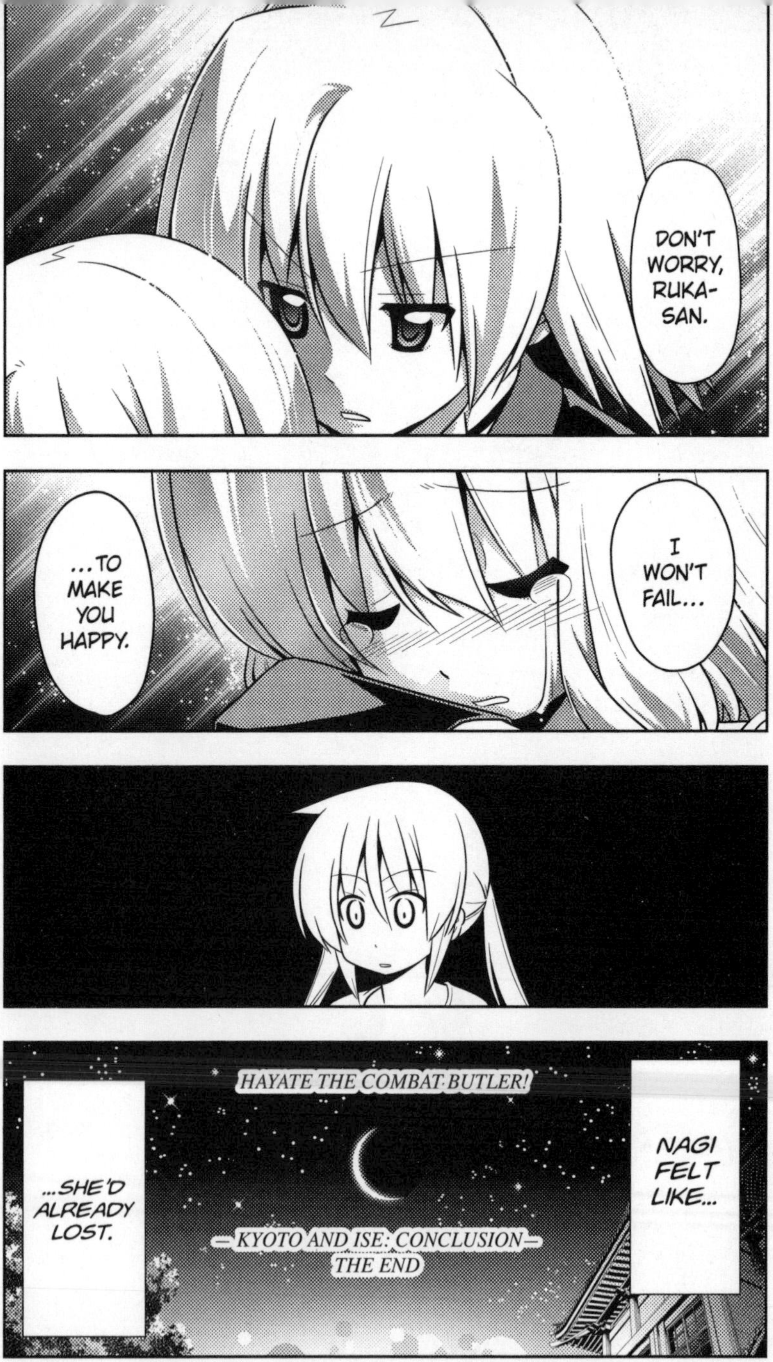
DON'T WORRY, RUKA-SAN.
I WON'T FAIL...
...TO MAKE YOU HAPPY.
NAGI FELT LIKE...
...SHE'D ALREADY LOST.
HAYATE THE COMBAT BUTLER!
—KYOTO AND ISE: CONCLUSION—
THE END

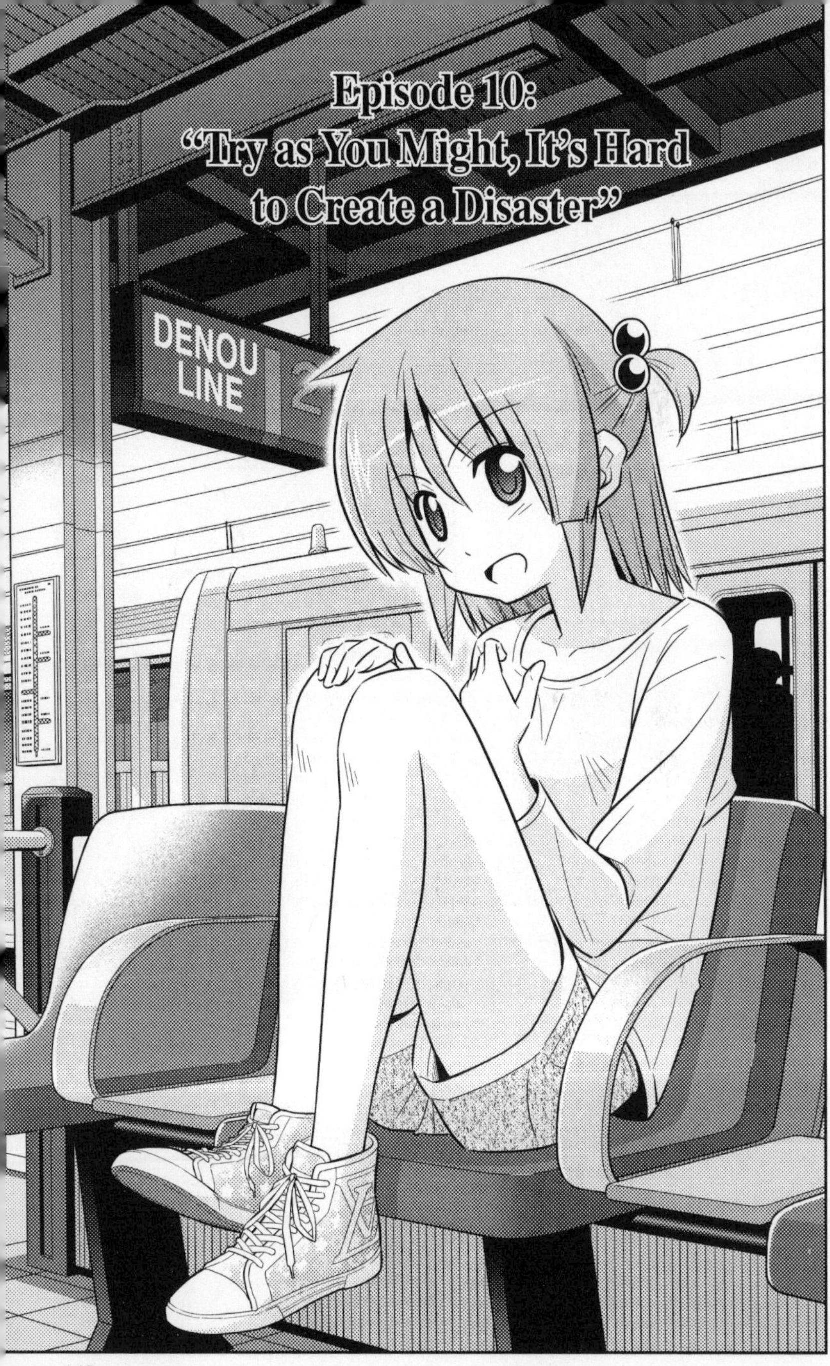
Episode 10:
"Try as You Might, It's Hard to Create a Disaster"
DENOU LINE
2

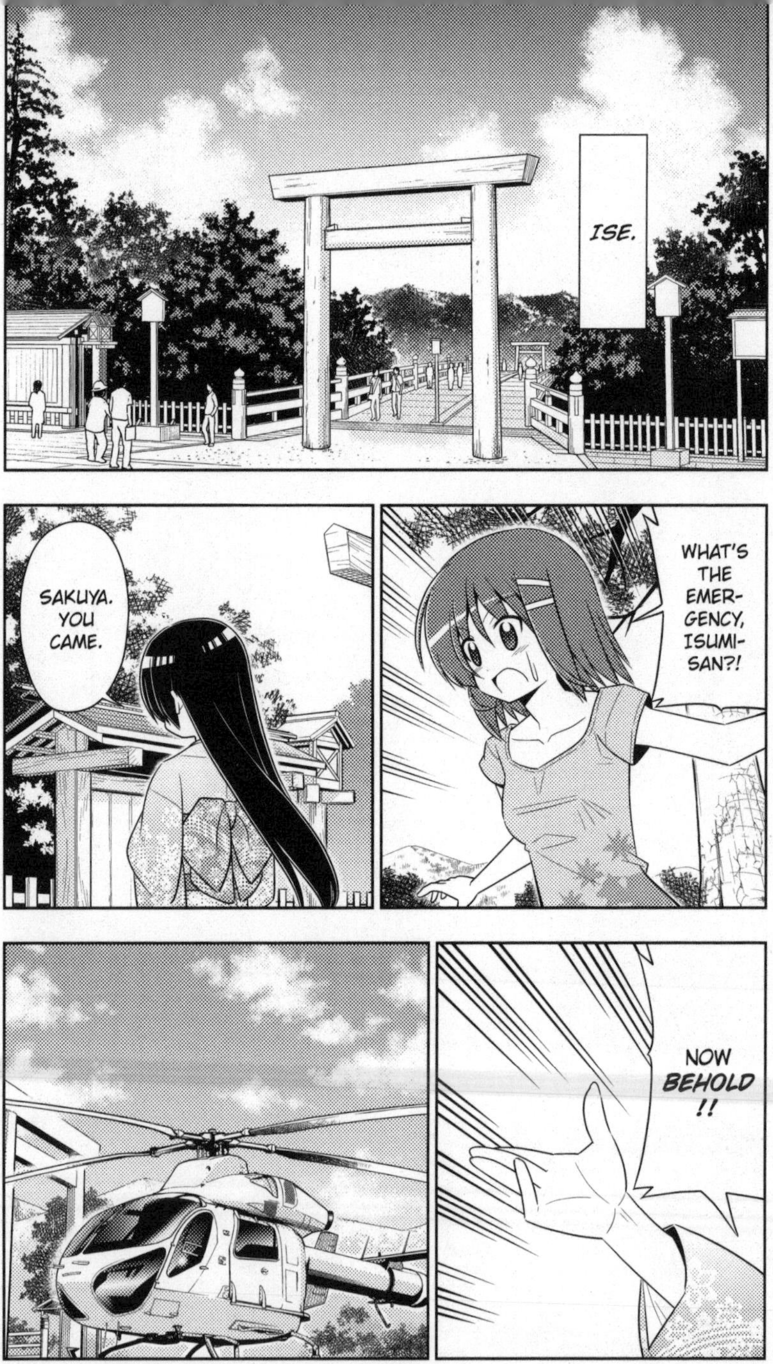
ISE.
WHAT'S THE EMERGENCY, ISUMI-SAN?!
SAKUYA. YOU CAME.
NOW BEHOLD!!

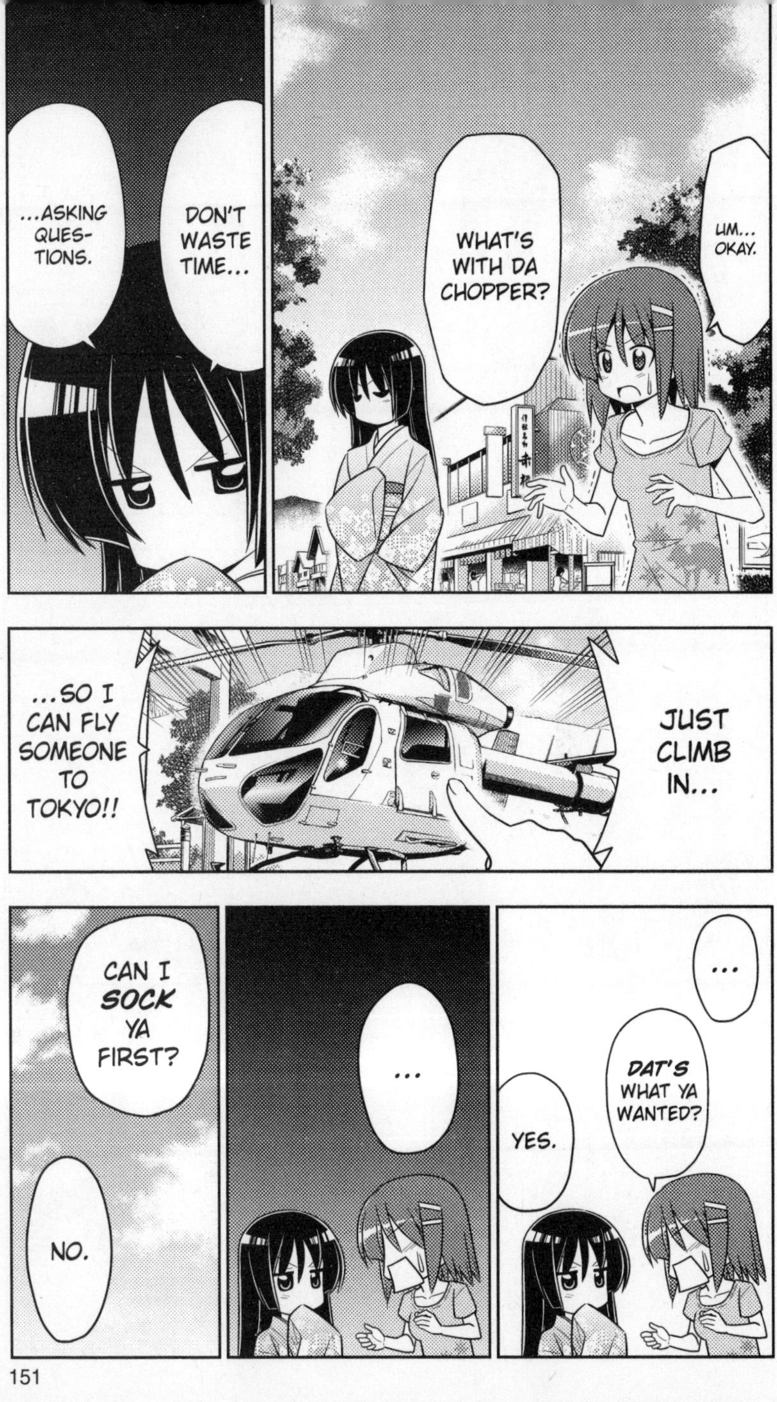
UM... OKAY.
WHAT'S WITH DA CHOPPER?
DON'T WASTE TIME...
...ASKING QUES-TIONS.
JUST CLIMB IN...
...SO I CAN FLY SOMEONE TO TOKYO!!
...
DAT'S WHAT YA WANTED?
YES.
...
CAN I SOCK YA FIRST?
NO.

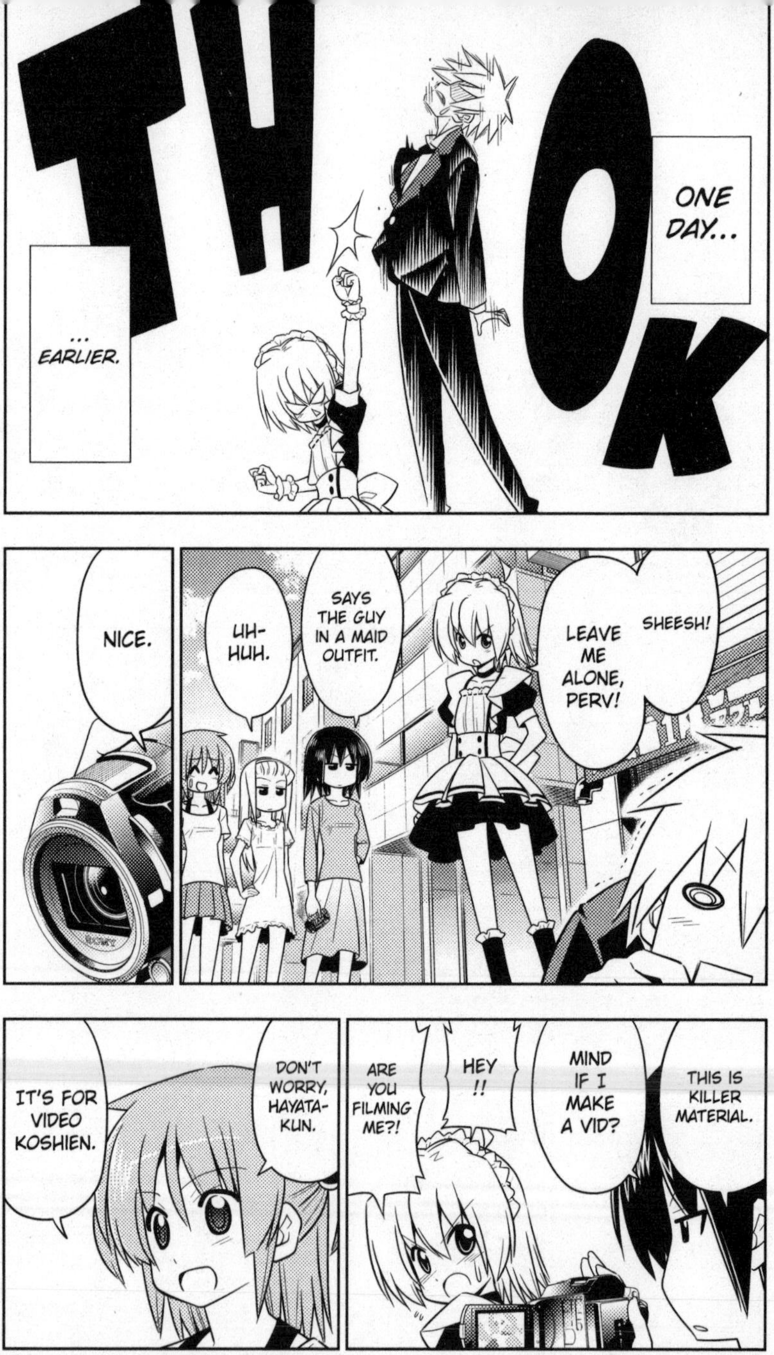
ONE DAY...
THOK
... EARLIER.
SHEESH!
LEAVE ME ALONE, PERV!
SAYS THE GUY IN A MAID OUTFIT.
UH-HUH.
NICE.
THIS IS KILLER MATERIAL.
MIND IF I MAKE A VID?
HEY!!
ARE YOU FILMING ME?!
DON'T WORRY, HAYATA-KUN.
IT'S FOR VIDEO KOSHIEN.

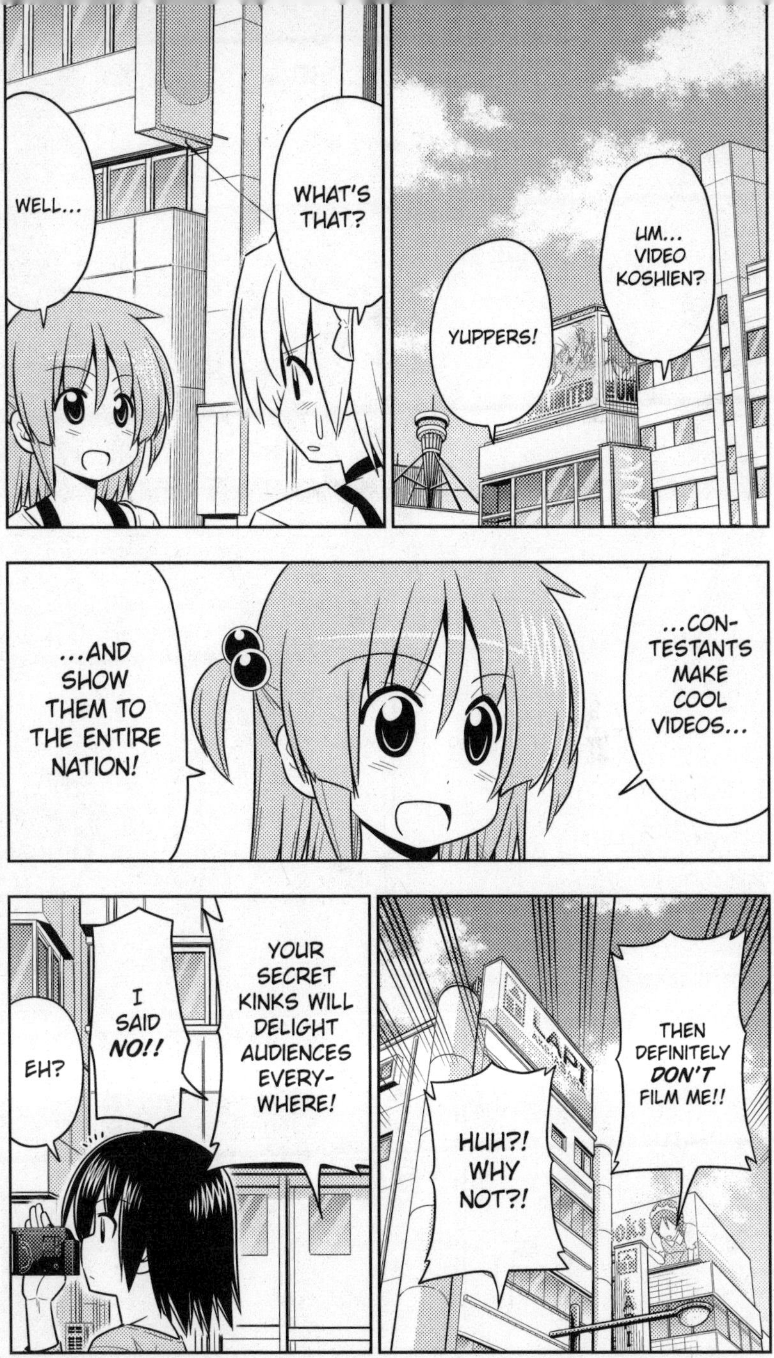
UM... VIDEO KOSHIEN?
YUPPERS!
WHAT'S THAT?
WELL...
...CON-TESTANTS MAKE COOL VIDEOS...
...AND SHOW THEM TO THE ENTIRE NATION!
THEN DEFINITELY *DON'T* FILM ME!!
HUH?! WHY NOT?!
YOUR SECRET KINKS WILL DELIGHT AUDIENCES EVERY-WHERE!
I SAID *NO!!*
EH?

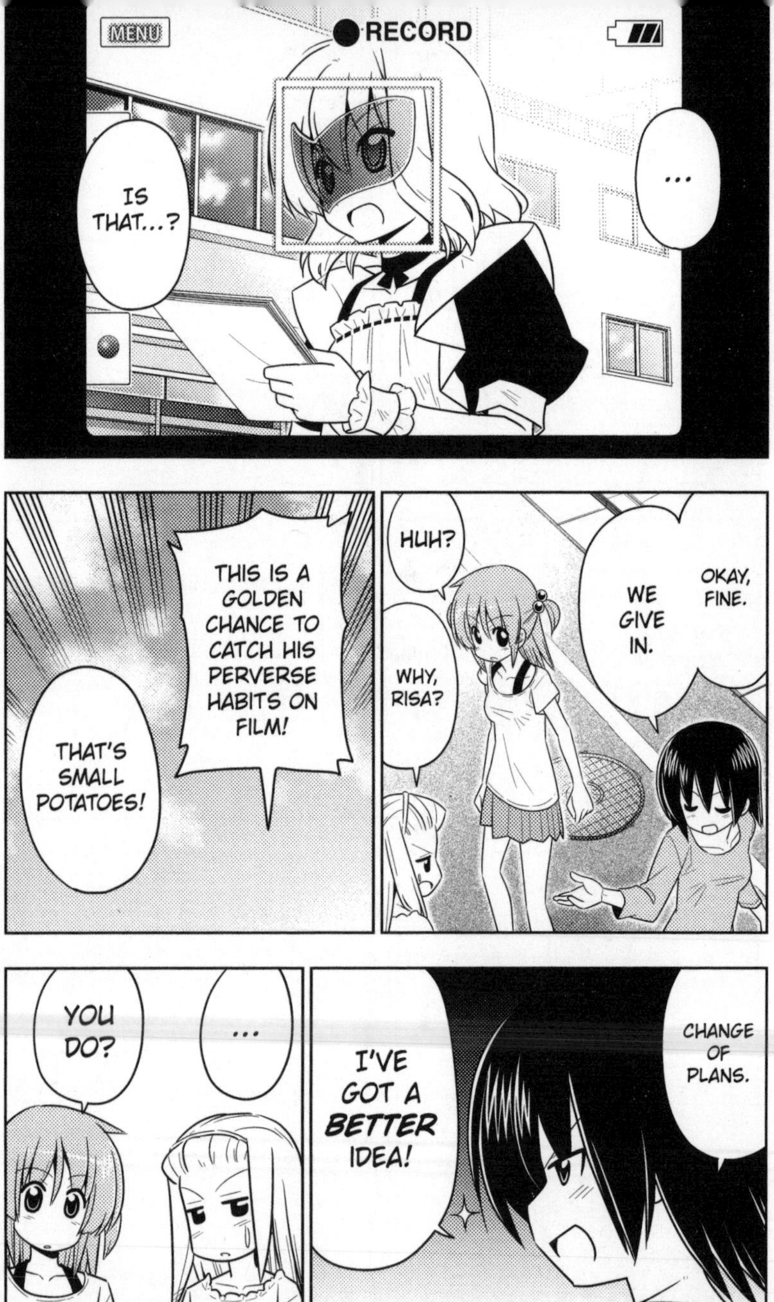
MENU
RECORD
...
IS THAT...?
OKAY, FINE. WE GIVE IN.
HUH?
WHY, RISA?
THIS IS A GOLDEN CHANCE TO CATCH HIS PERVERSE HABITS ON FILM!
THAT'S SMALL POTATOES!
CHANGE OF PLANS.
I'VE GOT A *BETTER* IDEA!
...
YOU DO?

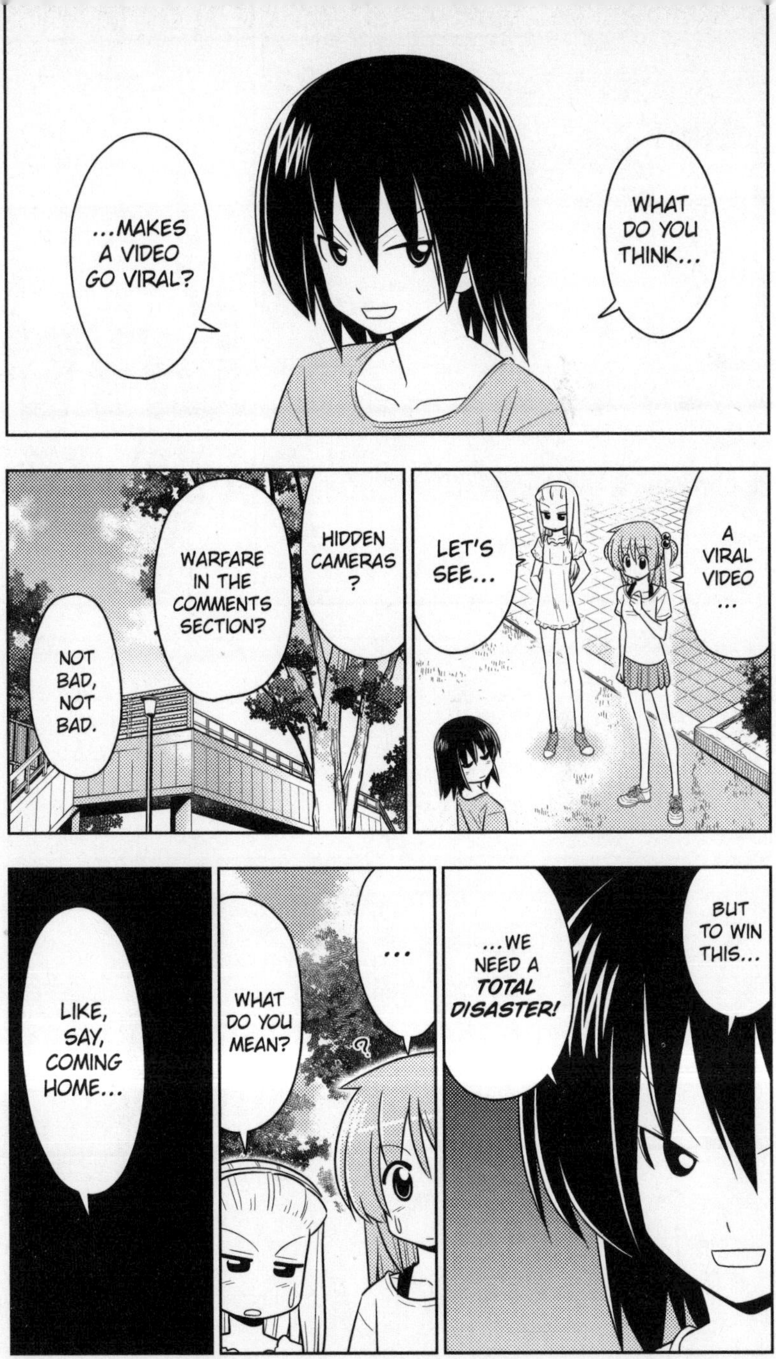
WHAT DO YOU THINK...
...MAKES A VIDEO GO VIRAL?
A VIRAL VIDEO ...
LET'S SEE...
HIDDEN CAMERAS ?
WARFARE IN THE COMMENTS SECTION?
NOT BAD, NOT BAD.
BUT TO WIN THIS...
...WE NEED A *TOTAL DISASTER!*
...
WHAT DO YOU MEAN?
LIKE, SAY, COMING HOME...

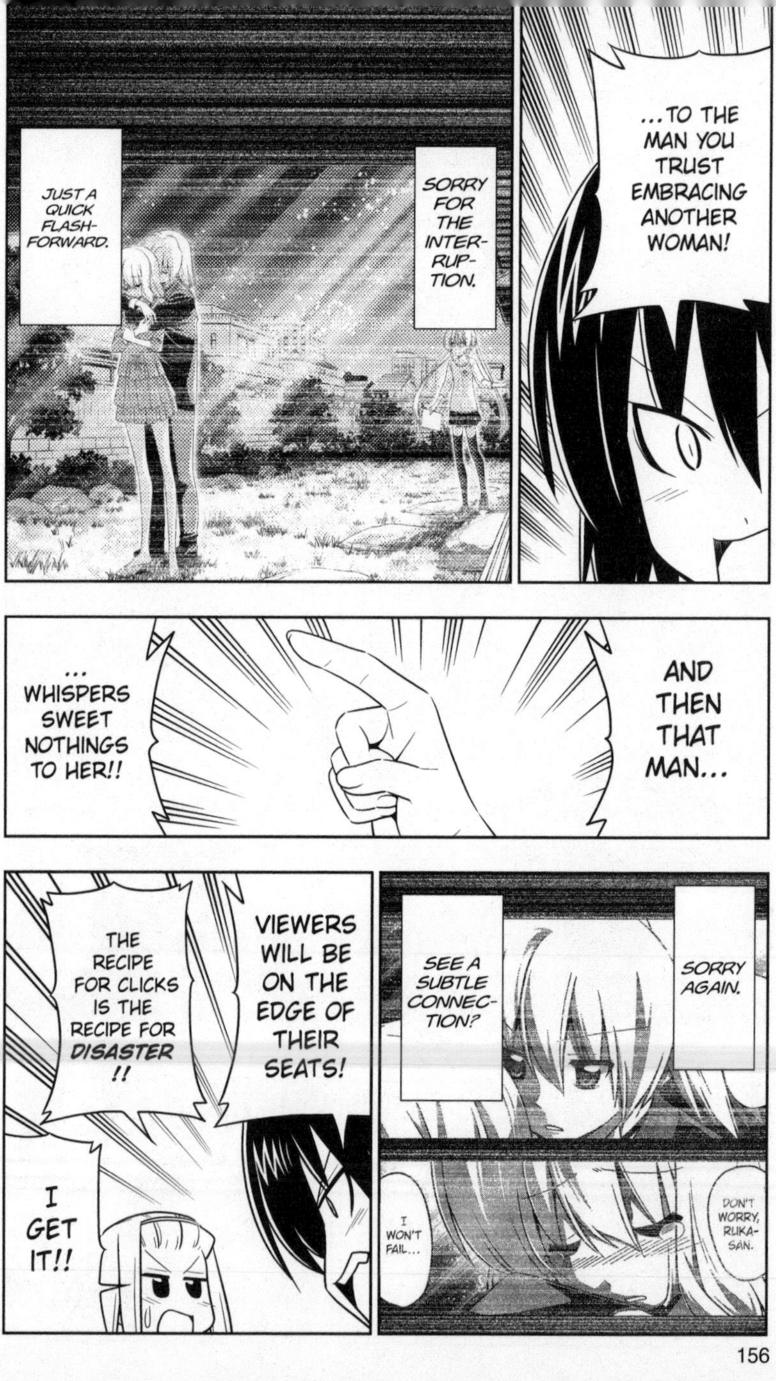

...TO THE MAN YOU TRUST EMBRACING ANOTHER WOMAN!
SORRY FOR THE INTER-RUP-TION.
JUST A QUICK FLASH-FORWARD.
AND THEN THAT MAN...
...WHISPERS SWEET NOTHINGS TO HER!!
SORRY AGAIN.
SEE A SUBTLE CONNEC-TION?
DON'T WORRY, RUKA-SAN.
I WON'T FAIL...
VIEWERS WILL BE ON THE EDGE OF THEIR SEATS!
THE RECIPE FOR CLICKS IS THE RECIPE FOR DISASTER!!
I GET IT!!

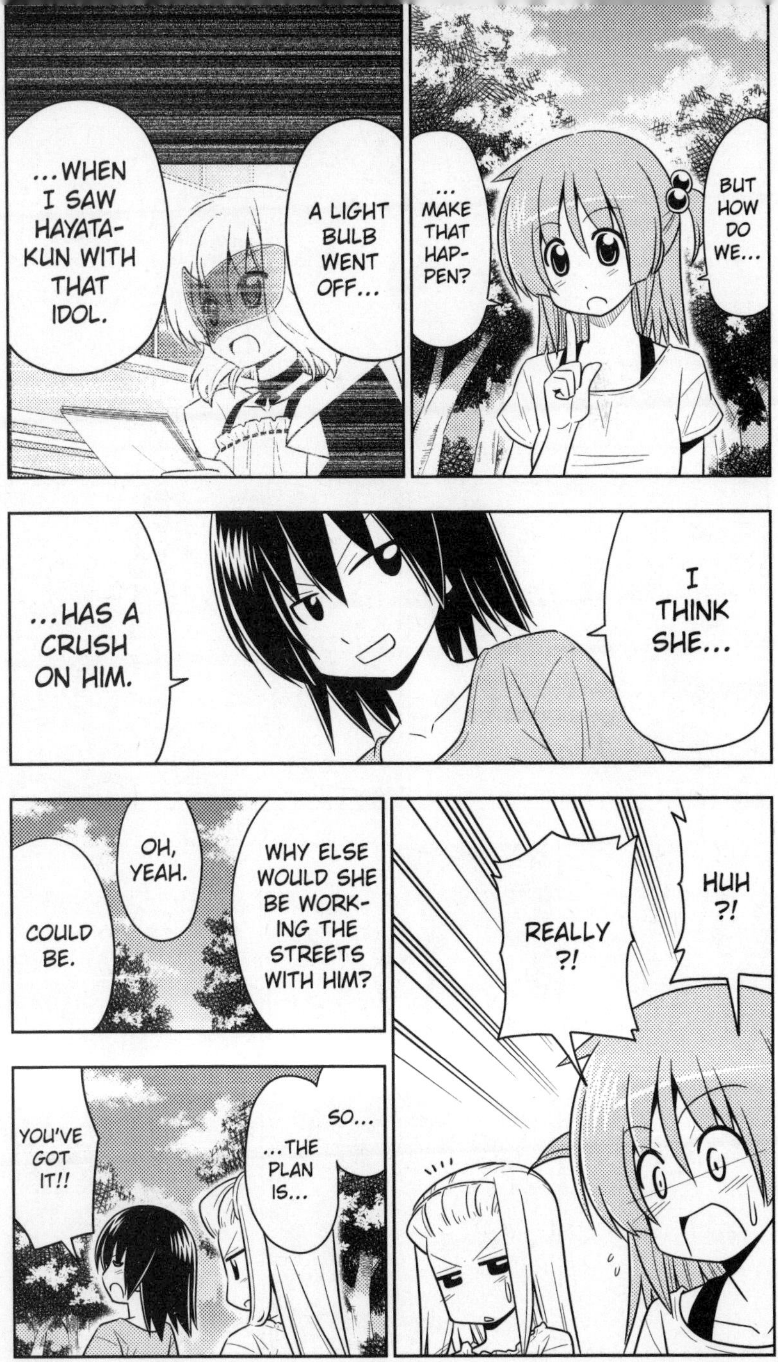
BUT HOW DO WE...
...MAKE THAT HAPPEN?
A LIGHT BULB WENT OFF...
...WHEN I SAW HAYATA-KUN WITH THAT IDOL.
I THINK SHE...
...HAS A CRUSH ON HIM.
HUH?!
REALLY?!
WHY ELSE WOULD SHE BE WORKING THE STREETS WITH HIM?
OH, YEAH.
COULD BE.
SO...
...THE PLAN IS...
YOU'VE GOT IT!!

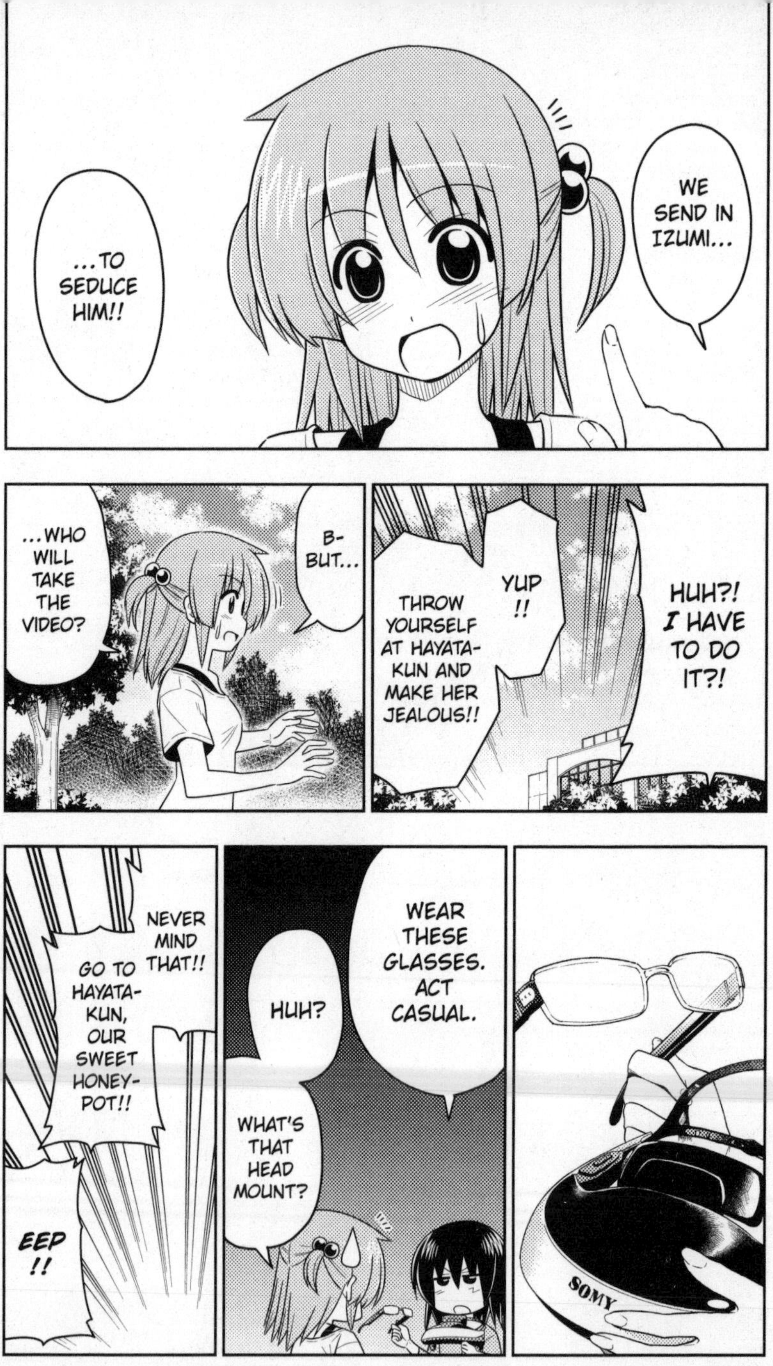
WE SEND IN IZUMI...
...TO SEDUCE HIM!!
HUH?! I HAVE TO DO IT?!
YUP!!
THROW YOURSELF AT HAYATA-KUN AND MAKE HER JEALOUS!!
B-BUT...
...WHO WILL TAKE THE VIDEO?
SOMY
WEAR THESE GLASSES. ACT CASUAL.
HUH?
WHAT'S THAT HEAD MOUNT?
NEVER MIND THAT!!
GO TO HAYATA-KUN, OUR SWEET HONEY-POT!!
EEP!!

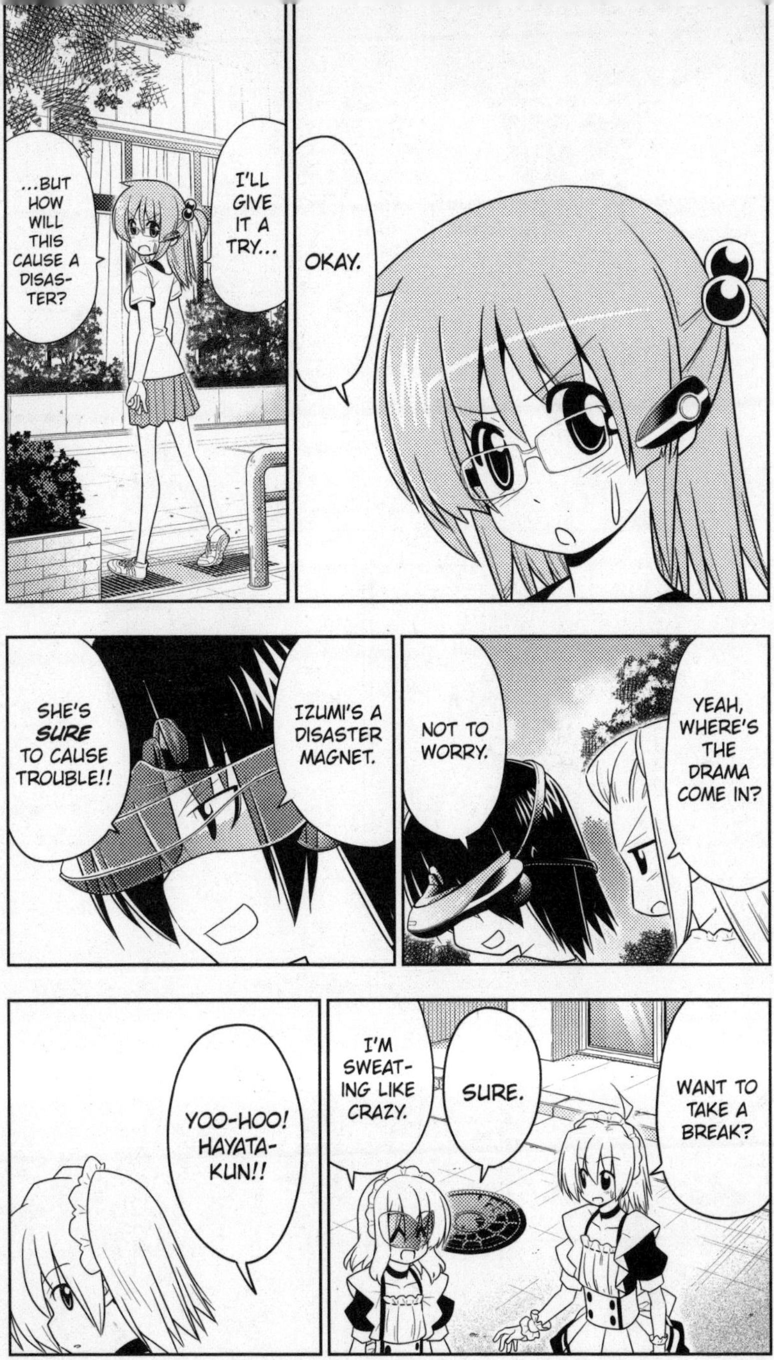
OKAY.
I'LL GIVE IT A TRY...
...BUT HOW WILL THIS CAUSE A DISASTER?
YEAH, WHERE'S THE DRAMA COME IN?
NOT TO WORRY.
IZUMI'S A DISASTER MAGNET.
SHE'S *SURE* TO CAUSE TROUBLE!!
WANT TO TAKE A BREAK?
SURE.
I'M SWEATING LIKE CRAZY.
YOO-HOO! HAYATA-KUN!!

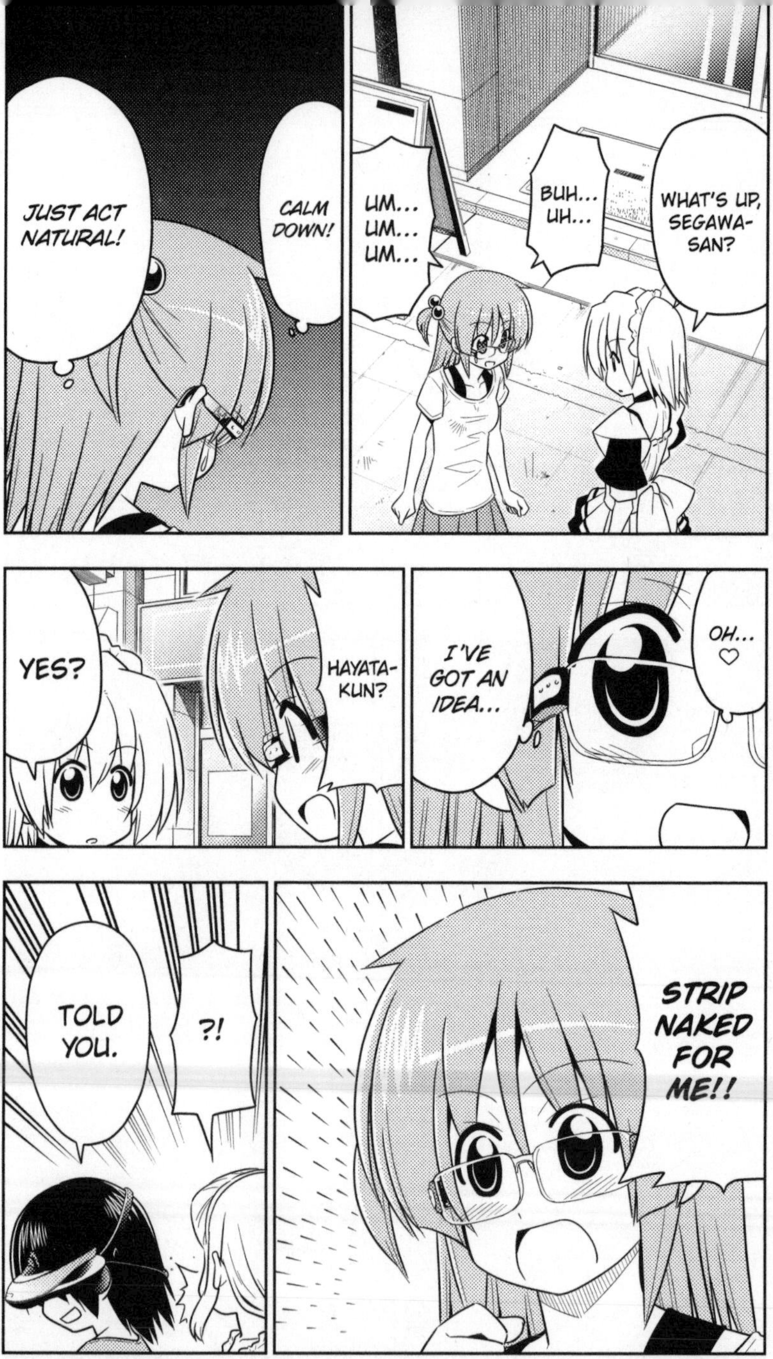
WHAT'S UP, SEGAWA-SAN?
BUH... UH...
UM... UM... UM...
CALM DOWN!
JUST ACT NATURAL!
OH... ♡
I'VE GOT AN IDEA...
HAYATA-KUN?
YES?
STRIP NAKED FOR ME!!
?!
TOLD YOU.

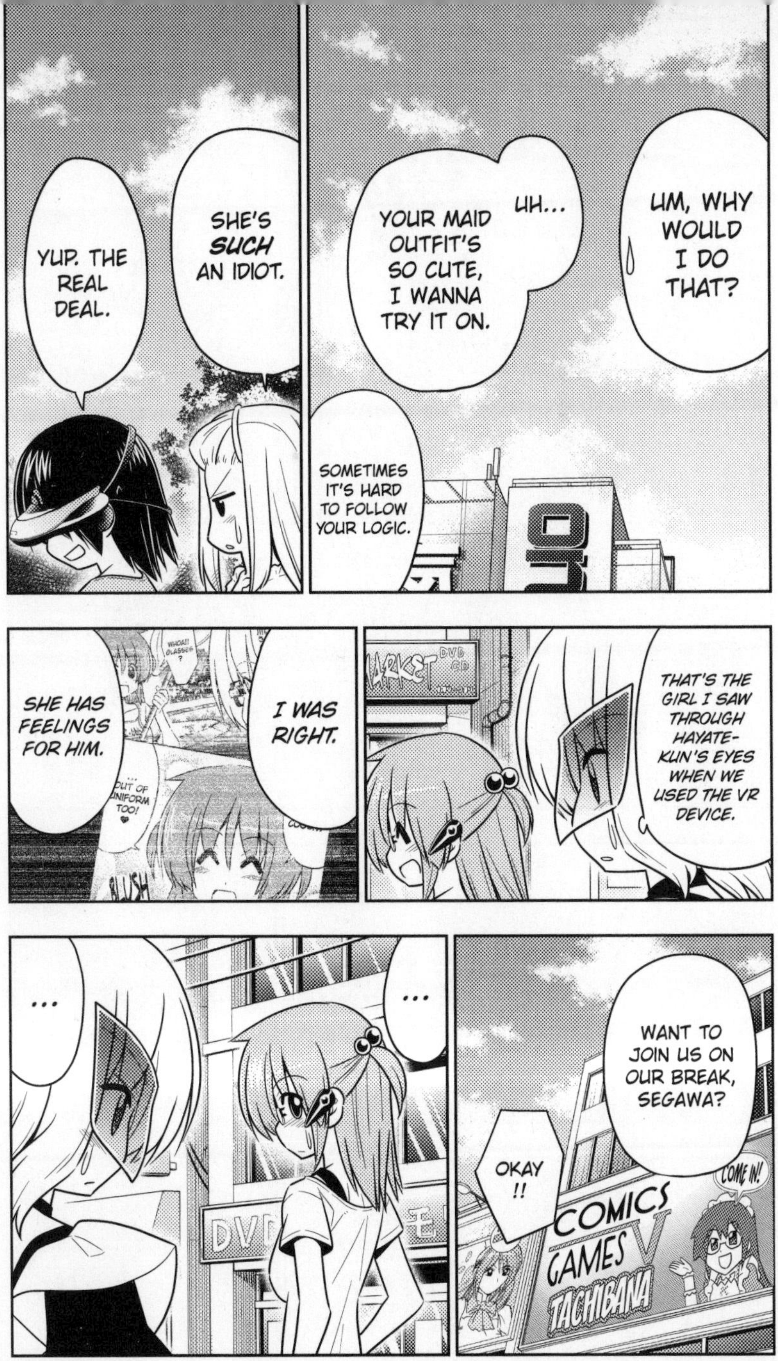
UM, WHY WOULD I DO THAT?
UH...
YOUR MAID OUTFIT'S SO CUTE, I WANNA TRY IT ON.
SOMETIMES IT'S HARD TO FOLLOW YOUR LOGIC.
SHE'S *SUCH* AN IDIOT.
YUP. THE REAL DEAL.
MARKET
DVD CD
THAT'S THE GIRL I SAW THROUGH HAYATE-KUN'S EYES WHEN WE USED THE VR DEVICE.
I WAS RIGHT.
WHOA!! GLASSES?
...OUT OF UNIFORM TOO! ♥
BLUSH
SHE HAS FEELINGS FOR HIM.
WANT TO JOIN US ON OUR BREAK, SEGAWA?
OKAY !!
COME IN!
COMICS
GAMES
V
TACHIBANA
...
...
DVD

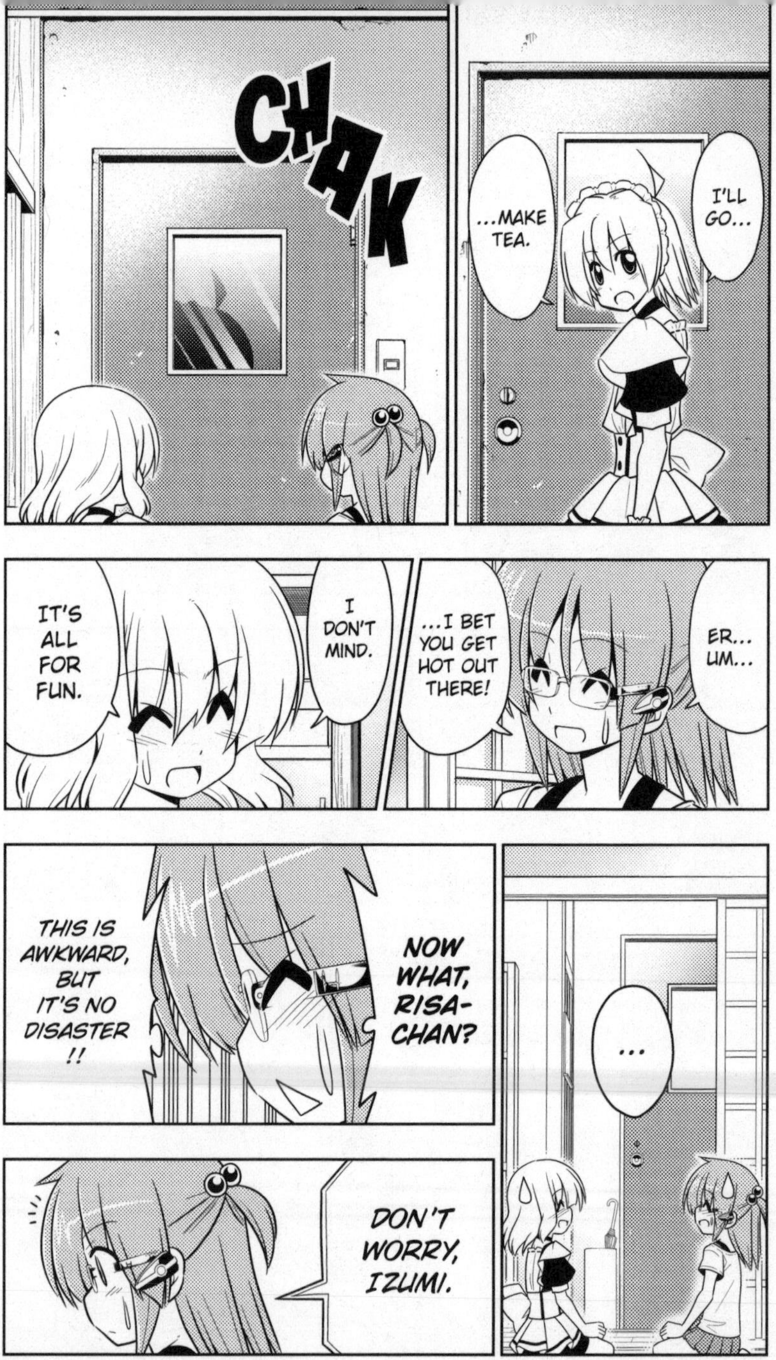
I'LL GO...
...MAKE TEA.
CHAK
ER... UM...
...I BET YOU GET HOT OUT THERE!
I DON'T MIND.
IT'S ALL FOR FUN.
...
NOW WHAT, RISA-CHAN?
THIS IS AWKWARD, BUT IT'S NO DISASTER!!
DON'T WORRY, IZUMI.

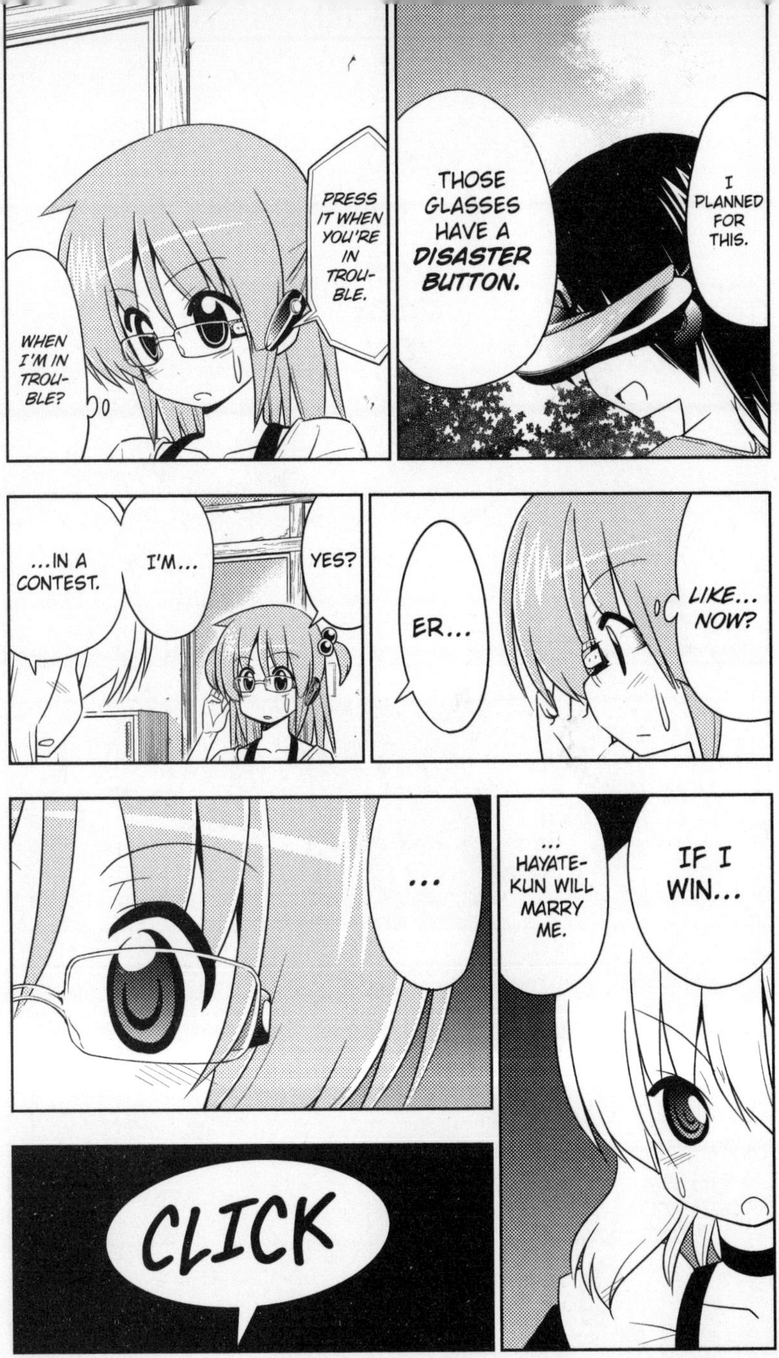
I PLANNED FOR THIS.
THOSE GLASSES HAVE A DISASTER BUTTON.
PRESS IT WHEN YOU'RE IN TROUBLE.
WHEN I'M IN TROUBLE?
LIKE... NOW?
ER...
YES?
I'M...
...IN A CONTEST.
IF I WIN...
...HAYATE-KUN WILL MARRY ME.
...
CLICK

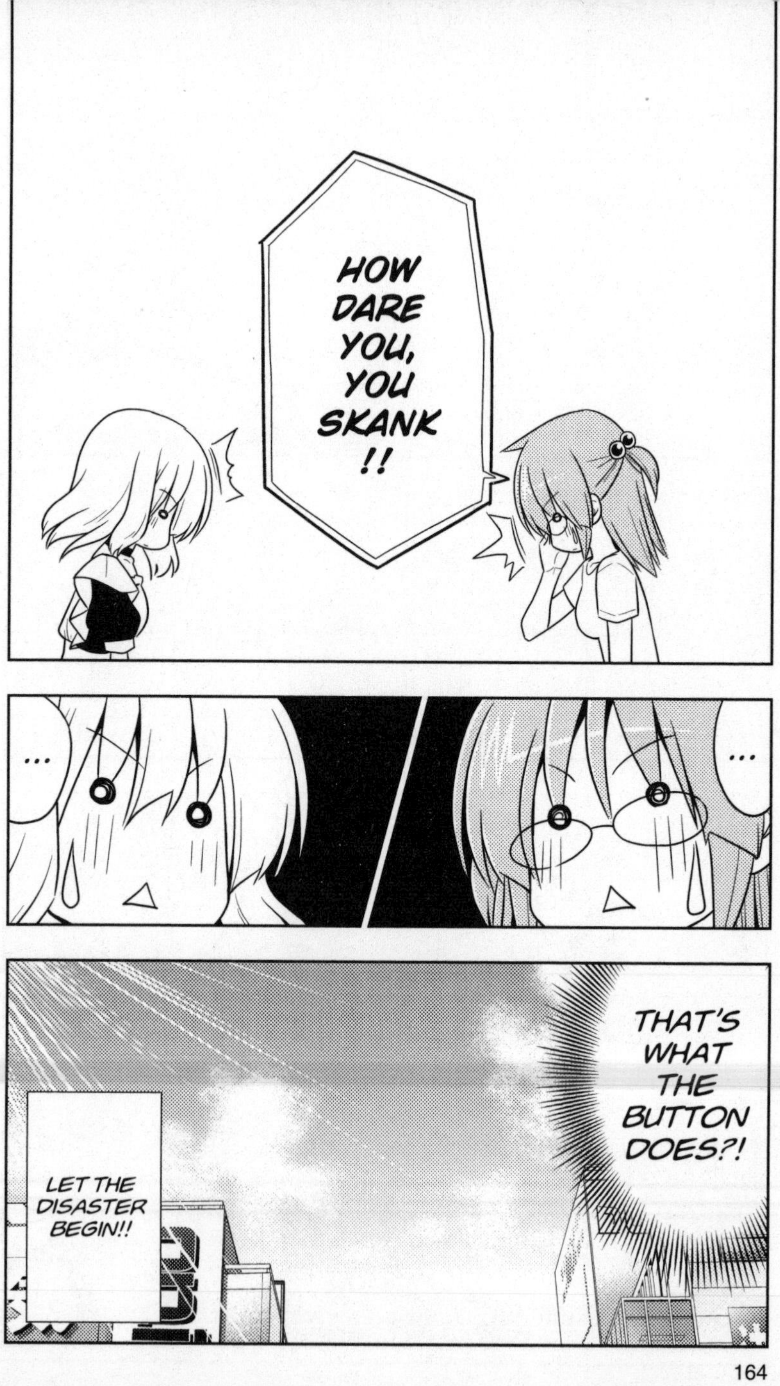
HOW DARE YOU, YOU SKANK!!
...
...
THAT'S WHAT THE BUTTON DOES?!
LET THE DISASTER BEGIN!!

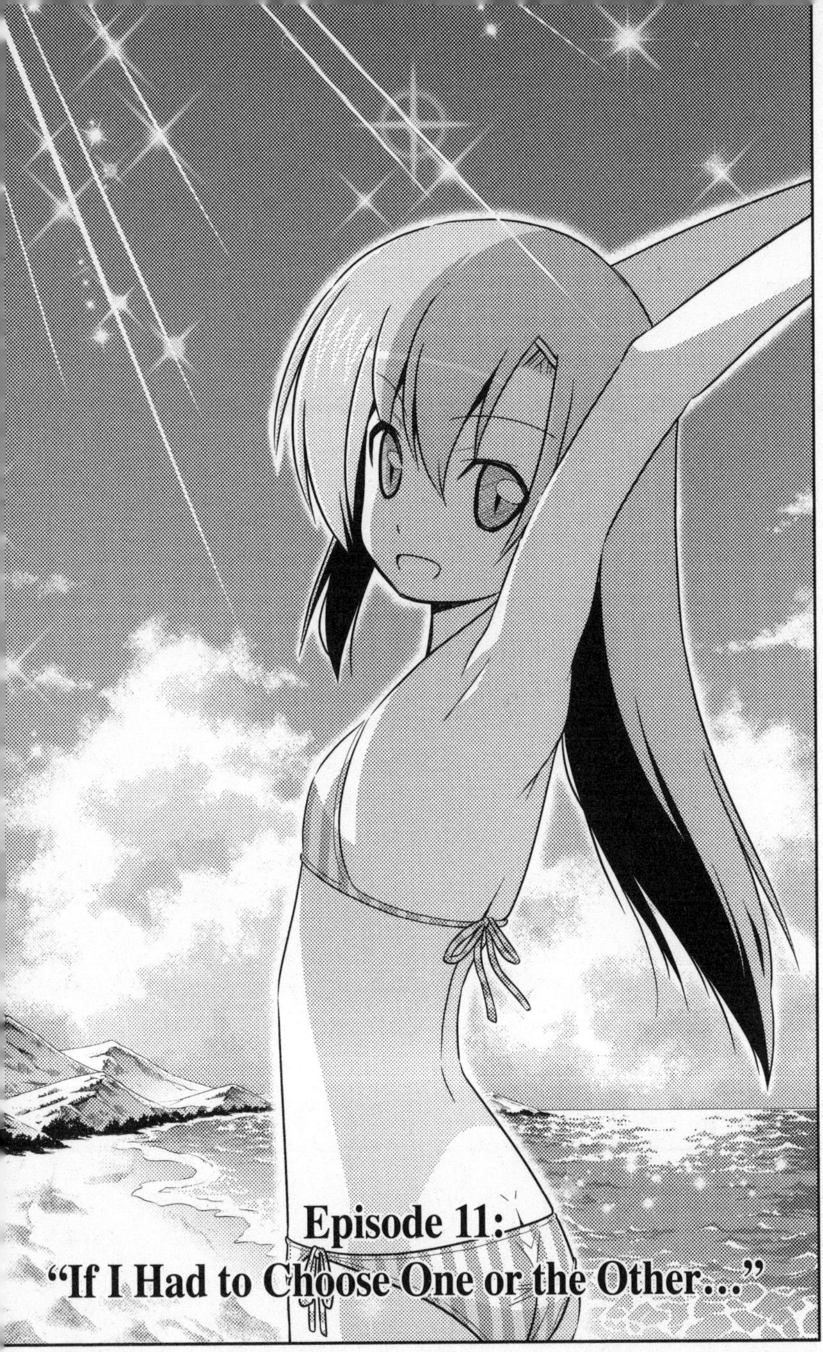
Episode 11:
“If I Had to Choose One or the Other...”

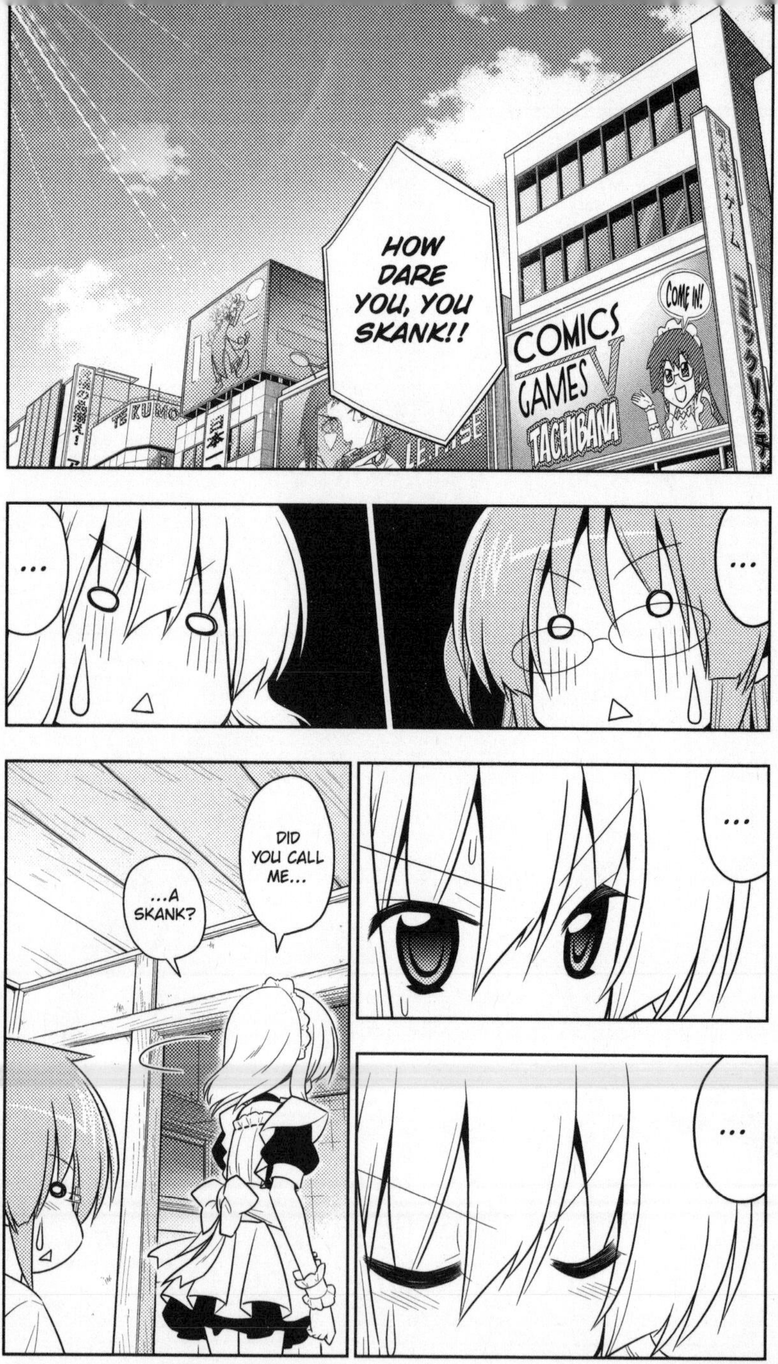
COME IN!
COMICS GAMES V TACHIBANA
HOW DARE YOU, YOU SKANK!!
TEKUMO
...
...
...
...
DID YOU CALL ME...
...A SKANK?

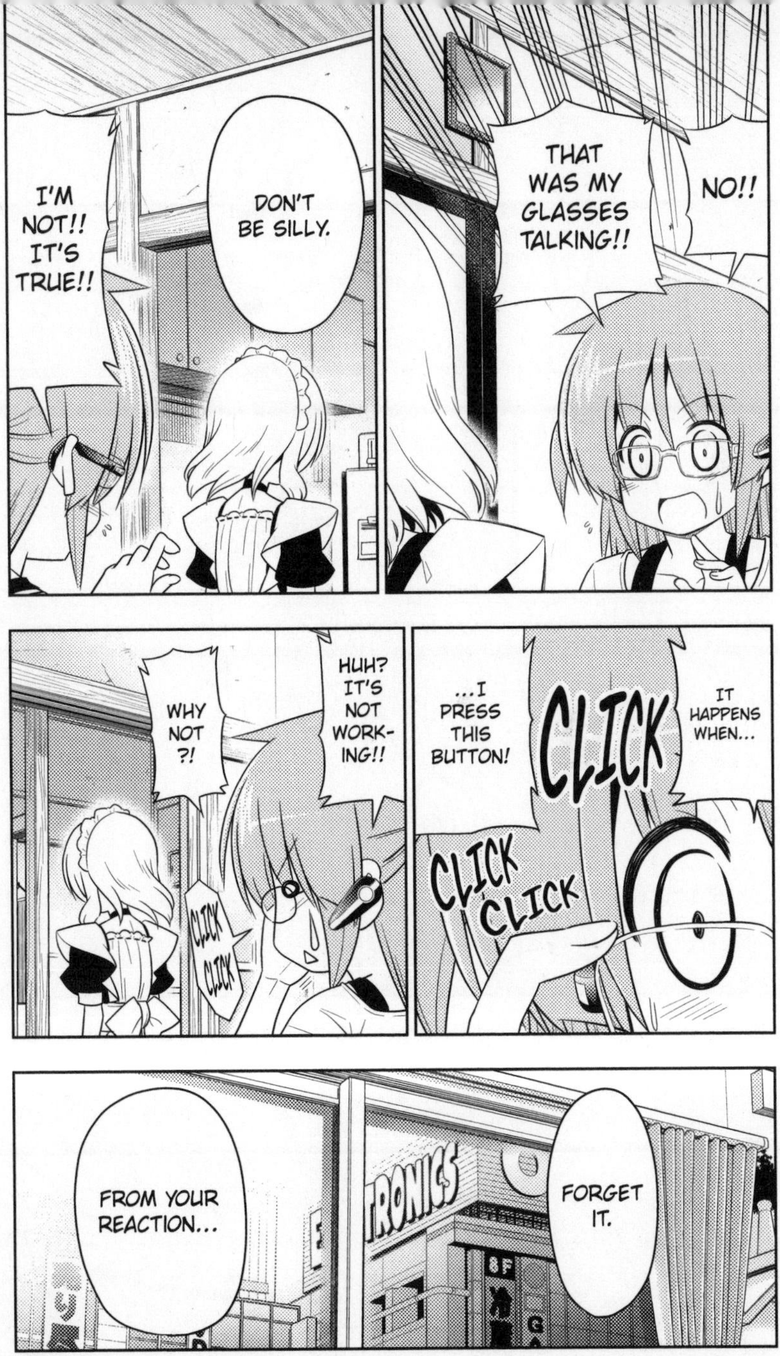
NO!!
THAT WAS MY GLASSES TALKING!!
DON'T BE SILLY.
I'M NOT!! IT'S TRUE!!
IT HAPPENS WHEN...
CLICK
...I PRESS THIS BUTTON!
CLICK CLICK
HUH? IT'S NOT WORKING!!
WHY NOT?!
CLICK CLICK
FORGET IT.
FROM YOUR REACTION...
TRONICS

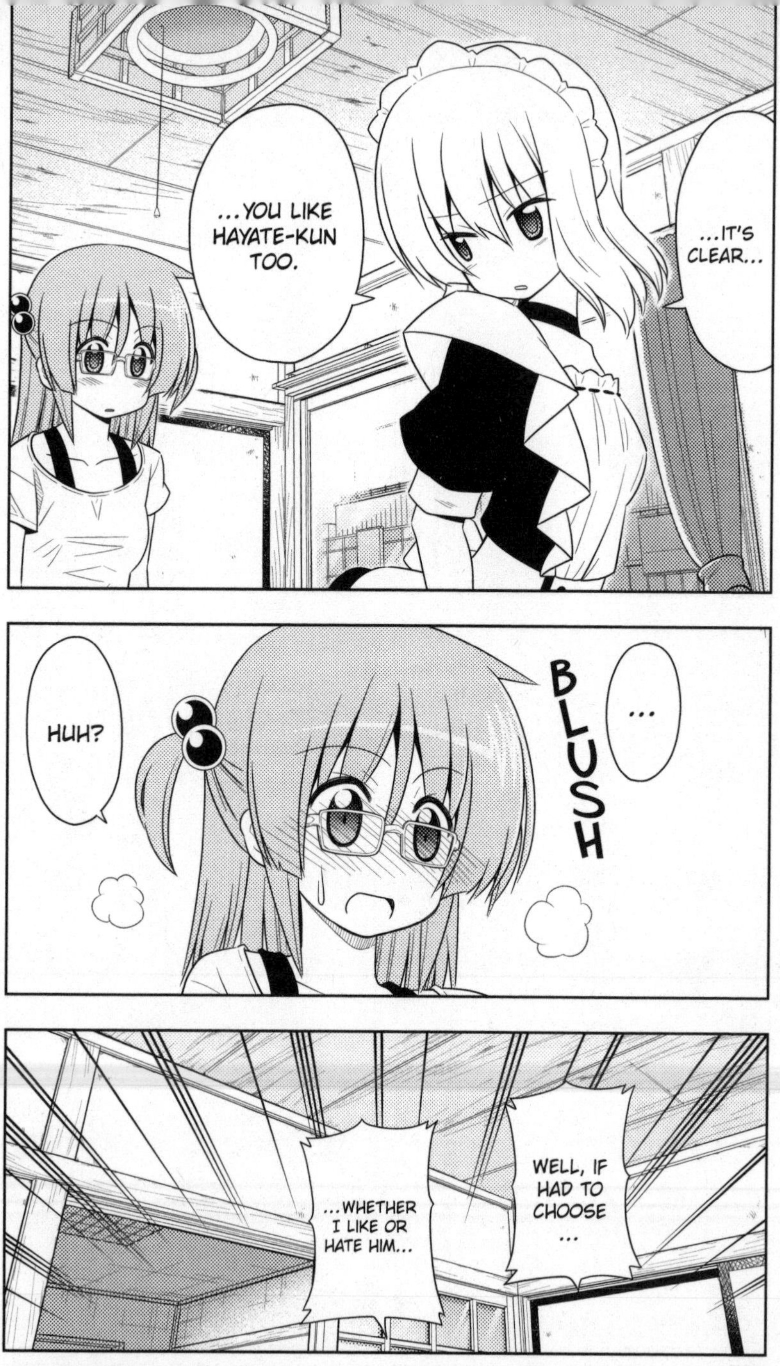
...IT'S CLEAR...
...YOU LIKE HAYATE-KUN TOO.
...
BLUSH
HUH?
WELL, IF HAD TO CHOOSE ...
...WHETHER I LIKE OR HATE HIM...

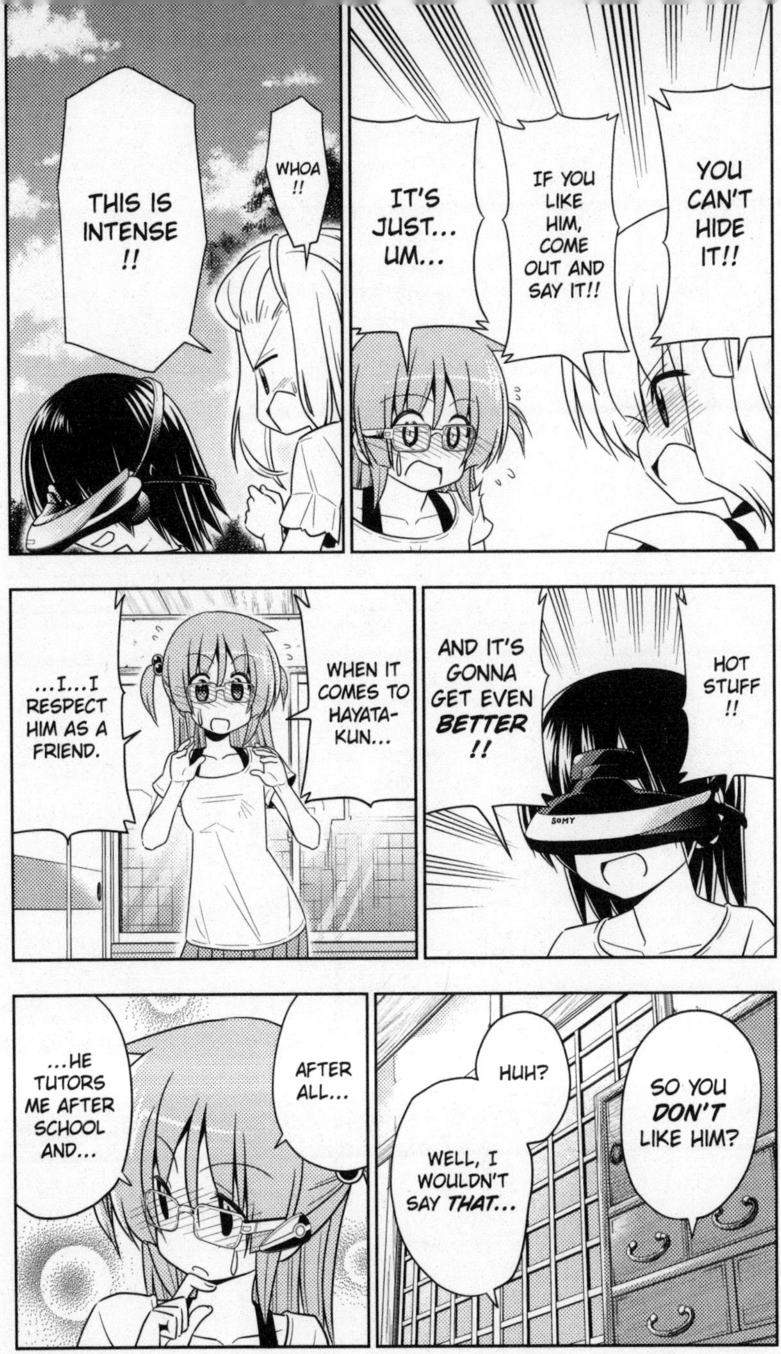
YOU CAN'T HIDE IT!!
IF YOU LIKE HIM, COME OUT AND SAY IT!!
IT'S JUST... UM...
WHOA!!
THIS IS INTENSE!!
HOT STUFF!!
AND IT'S GONNA GET EVEN *BETTER*!!
SOMY
WHEN IT COMES TO HAYATA-KUN...
...I...I RESPECT HIM AS A FRIEND.
SO YOU *DON'T* LIKE HIM?
HUH?
WELL, I WOULDN'T SAY *THAT*...
AFTER ALL...
...HE TUTORS ME AFTER SCHOOL AND...

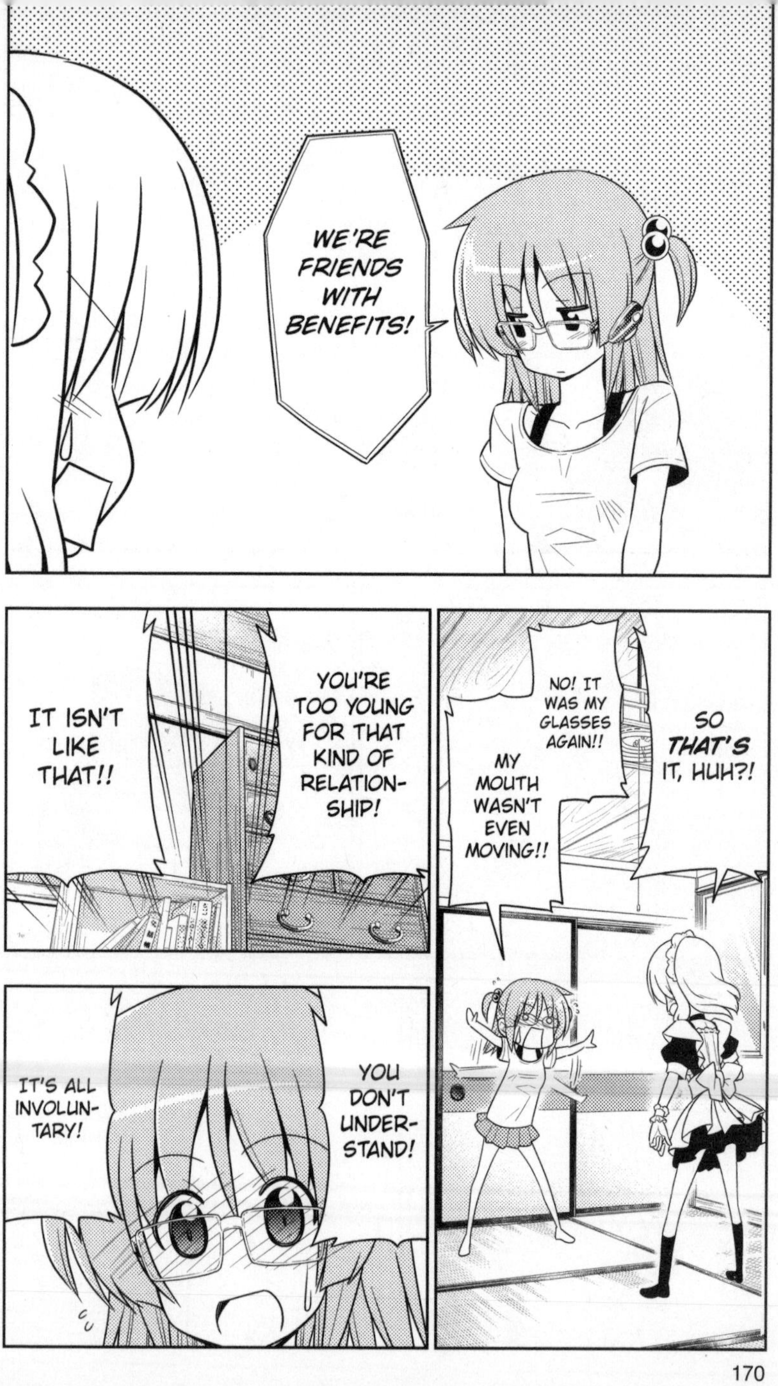
WE'RE FRIENDS WITH BENEFITS!
SO *THAT'S* IT, HUH?!
NO! IT WAS MY GLASSES AGAIN!!
MY MOUTH WASN'T EVEN MOVING!!
YOU'RE TOO YOUNG FOR THAT KIND OF RELATION-SHIP!
IT ISN'T LIKE THAT!!
YOU DON'T UNDER-STAND!
IT'S ALL INVOLUN-TARY!

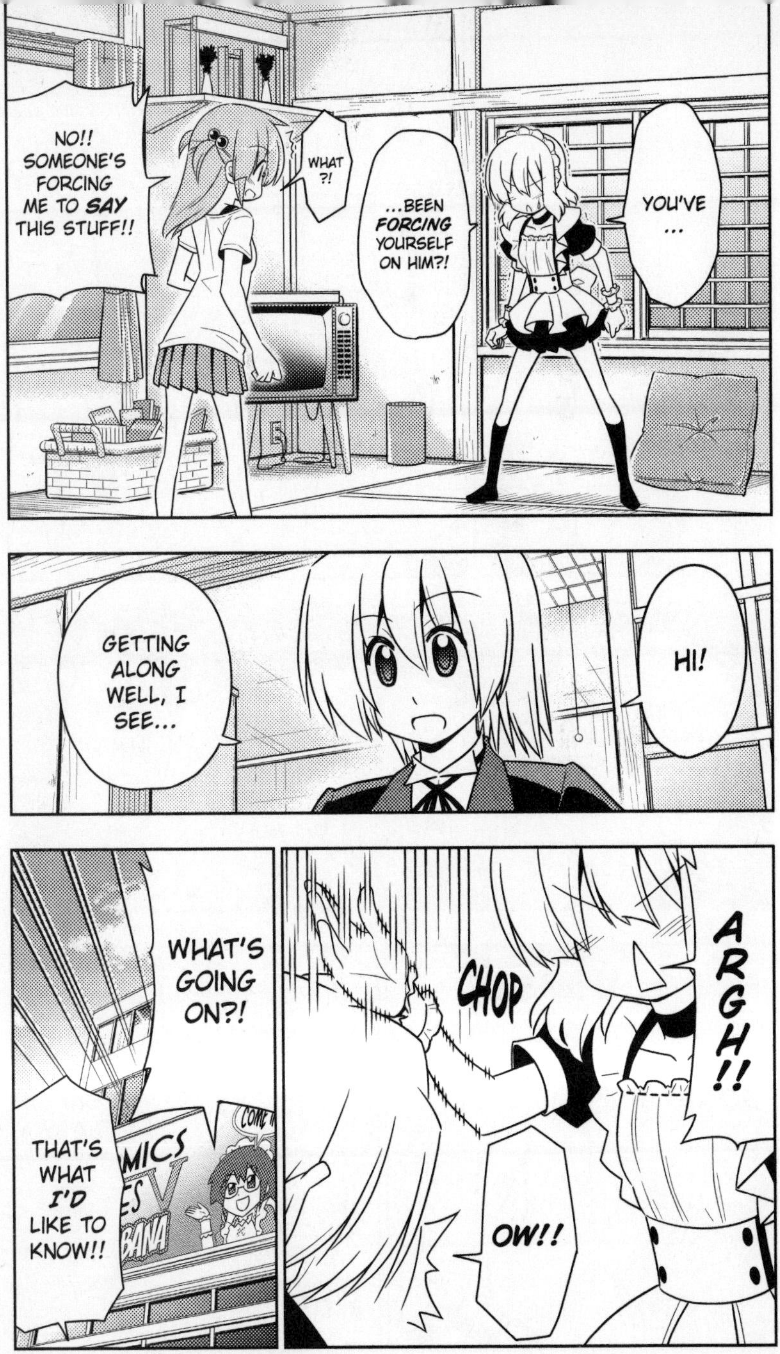
YOU'VE ...
...BEEN FORCING YOURSELF ON HIM?!
WHAT ?!
NO!! SOMEONE'S FORCING ME TO SAY THIS STUFF!!
HI!
GETTING ALONG WELL, I SEE...
ARGH!!
CHOP
OW!!
WHAT'S GOING ON?!
THAT'S WHAT I'D LIKE TO KNOW!!

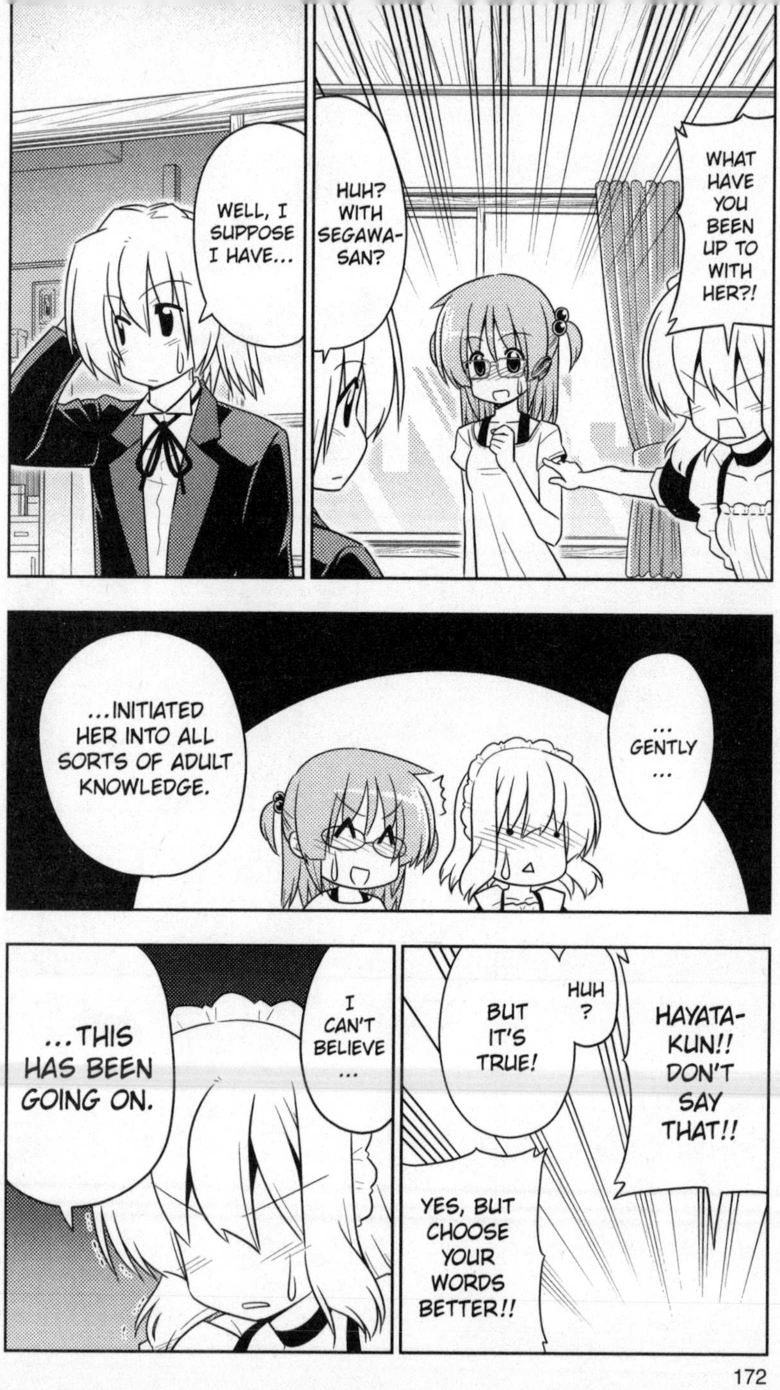
WHAT HAVE YOU BEEN UP TO WITH HER?!
HUH? WITH SEGAWA-SAN?
WELL, I SUPPOSE I HAVE...
... GENTLY ...
...INITIATED HER INTO ALL SORTS OF ADULT KNOWLEDGE.
HAYATA-KUN!! DON'T SAY THAT!!
HUH?
BUT IT'S TRUE!
YES, BUT CHOOSE YOUR WORDS BETTER!!
I CAN'T BELIEVE ...
...THIS HAS BEEN GOING ON.

HUH?

DO YOU CARE ABOUT HIM?

ARE YOU IN LOVE WITH HAYATE-KUN?

BLUSH

...

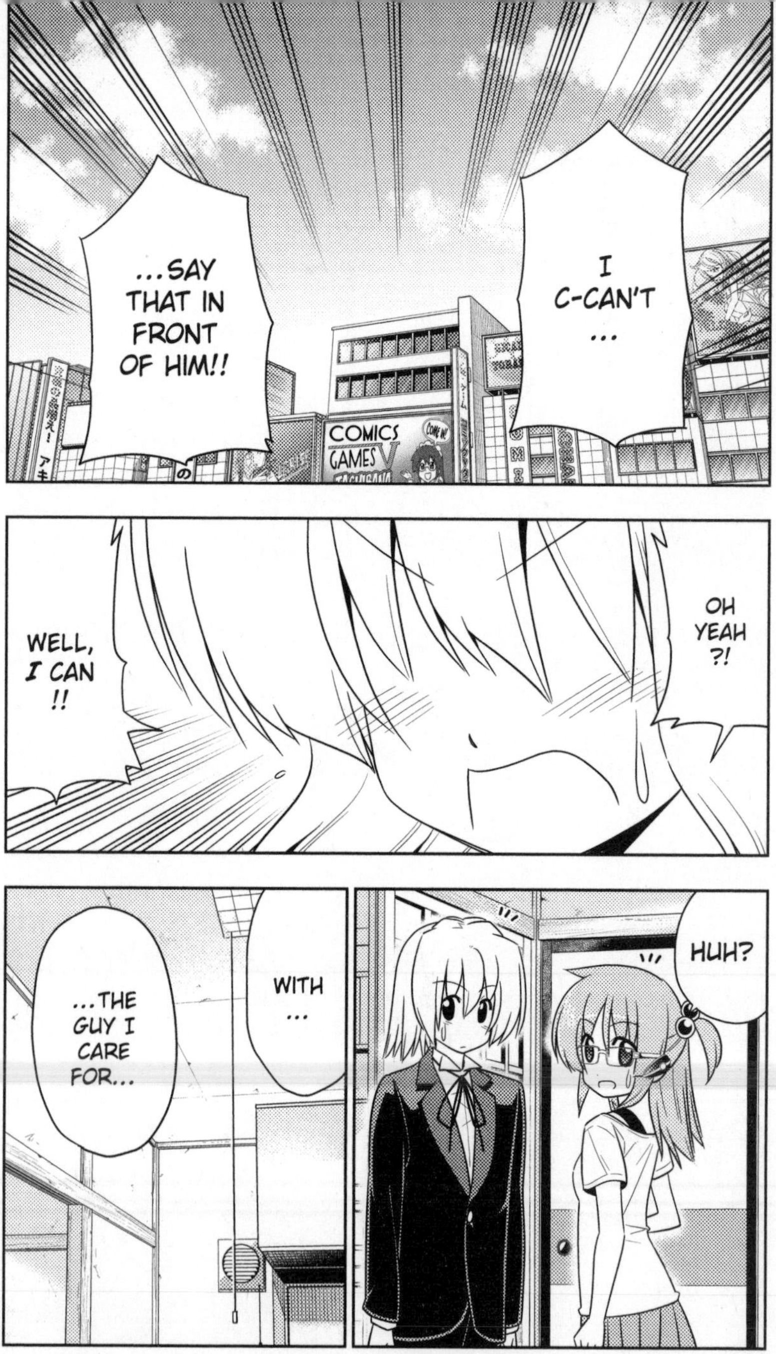
I C-CAN'T ...
...SAY THAT IN FRONT OF HIM!!
COME IN!
COMICS
GAMES
OH YEAH ?!
WELL, I CAN !!
HUH?
WITH ...
...THE GUY I CARE FOR...

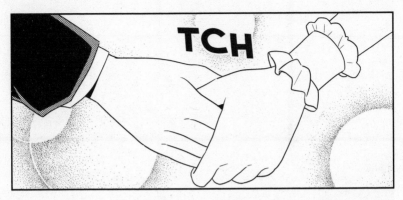

TCH

...MY FEELINGS.

...I CAN SHARE...

UM...

...ER...

HUH?!!

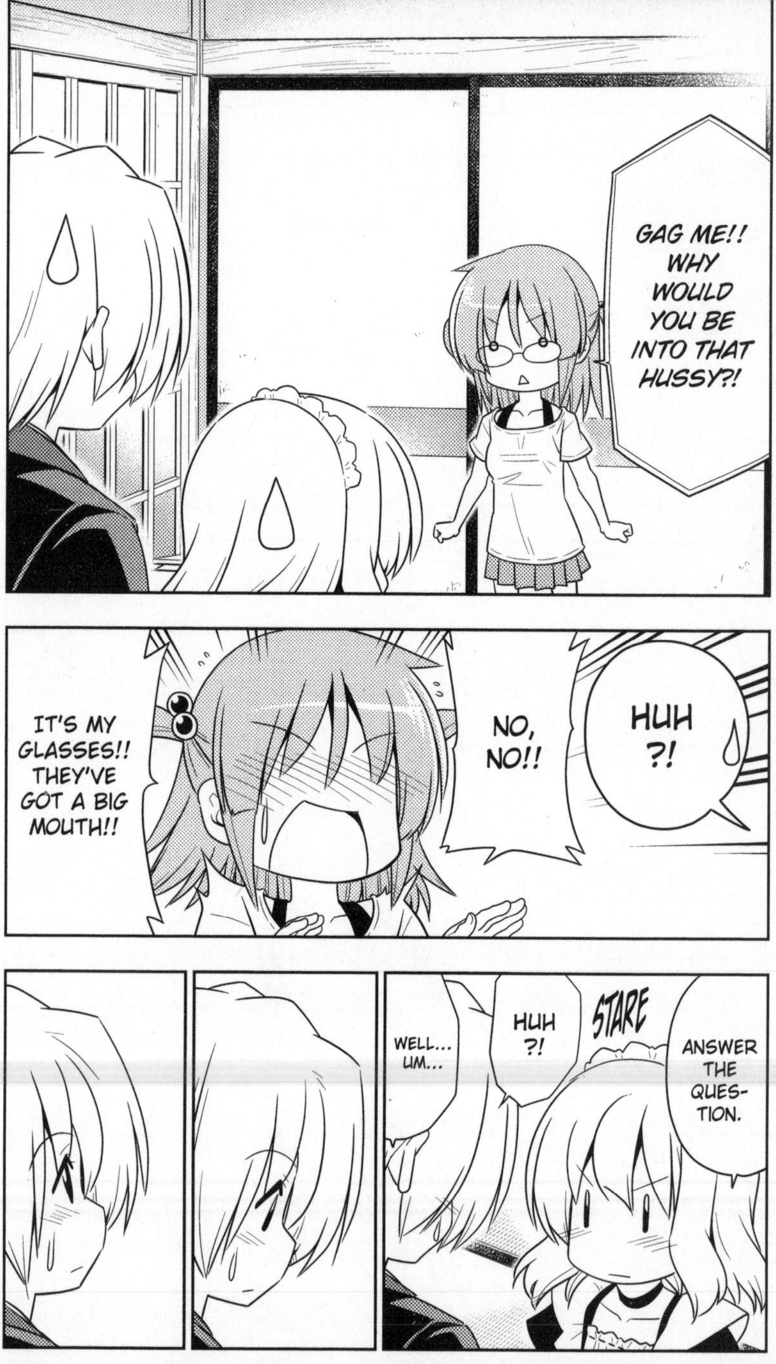
GAG ME!! WHY WOULD YOU BE INTO THAT HUSSY?!
HUH ?!
NO, NO!!
IT'S MY GLASSES!! THEY'VE GOT A BIG MOUTH!!
ANSWER THE QUES-TION.
STARE
HUH ?!
WELL... UM...

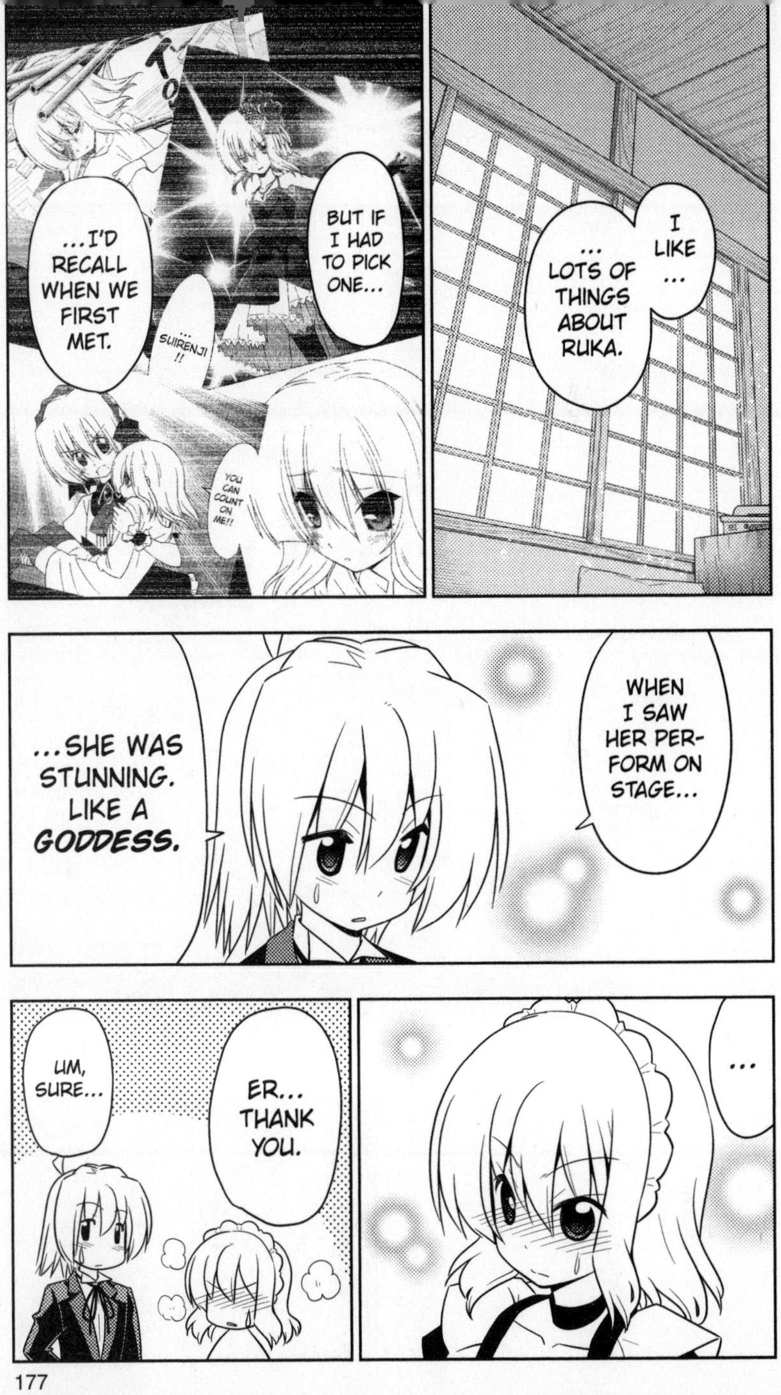
I LIKE ...
... LOTS OF THINGS ABOUT RUKA.
BUT IF I HAD TO PICK ONE...
...I'D RECALL WHEN WE FIRST MET.
... SUIRENJI!!
YOU CAN COUNT ON ME!!
WHEN I SAW HER PER-FORM ON STAGE...
...SHE WAS STUNNING. LIKE A GODDESS.
...
ER... THANK YOU.
UM, SURE...

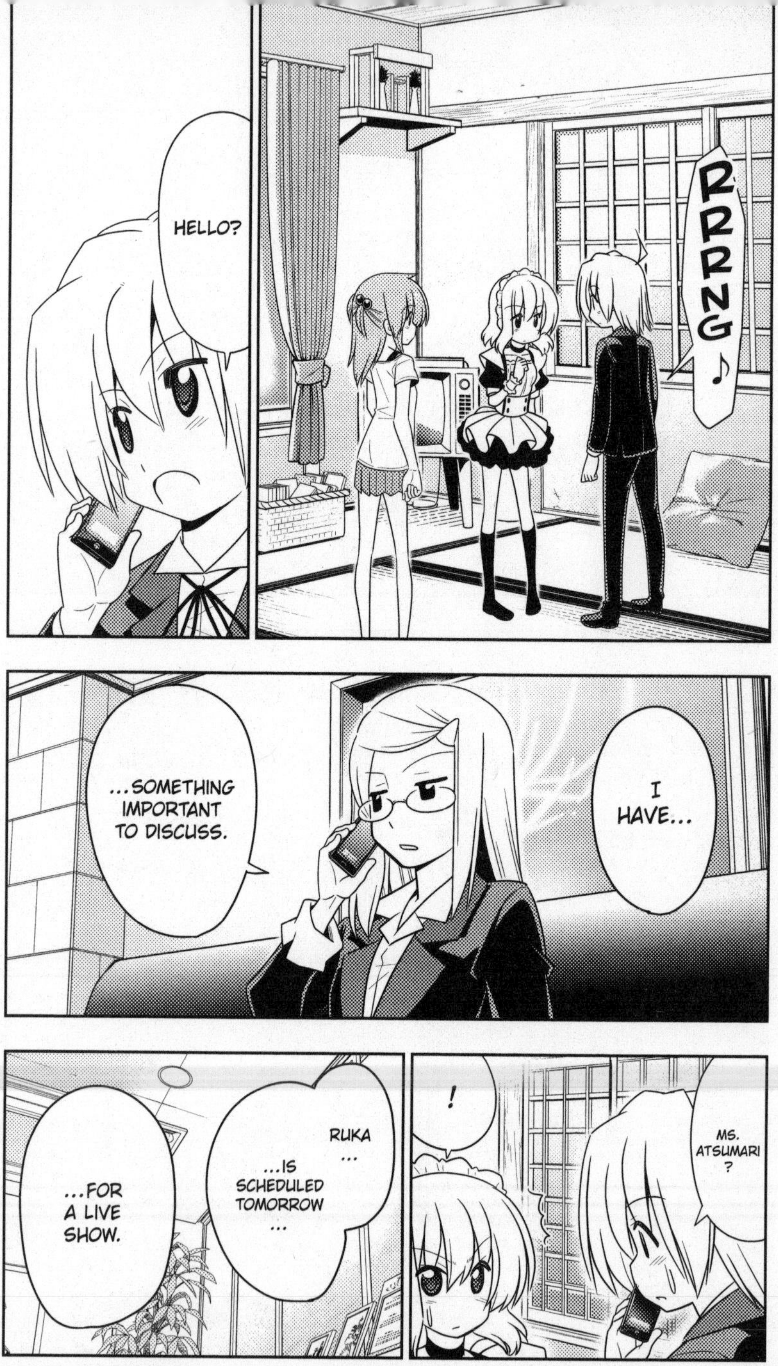
RRRNG ♪
HELLO?
I HAVE...
...SOMETHING IMPORTANT TO DISCUSS.
MS. ATSUMARI?
!
RUKA...
...IS SCHEDULED TOMORROW...
...FOR A LIVE SHOW.

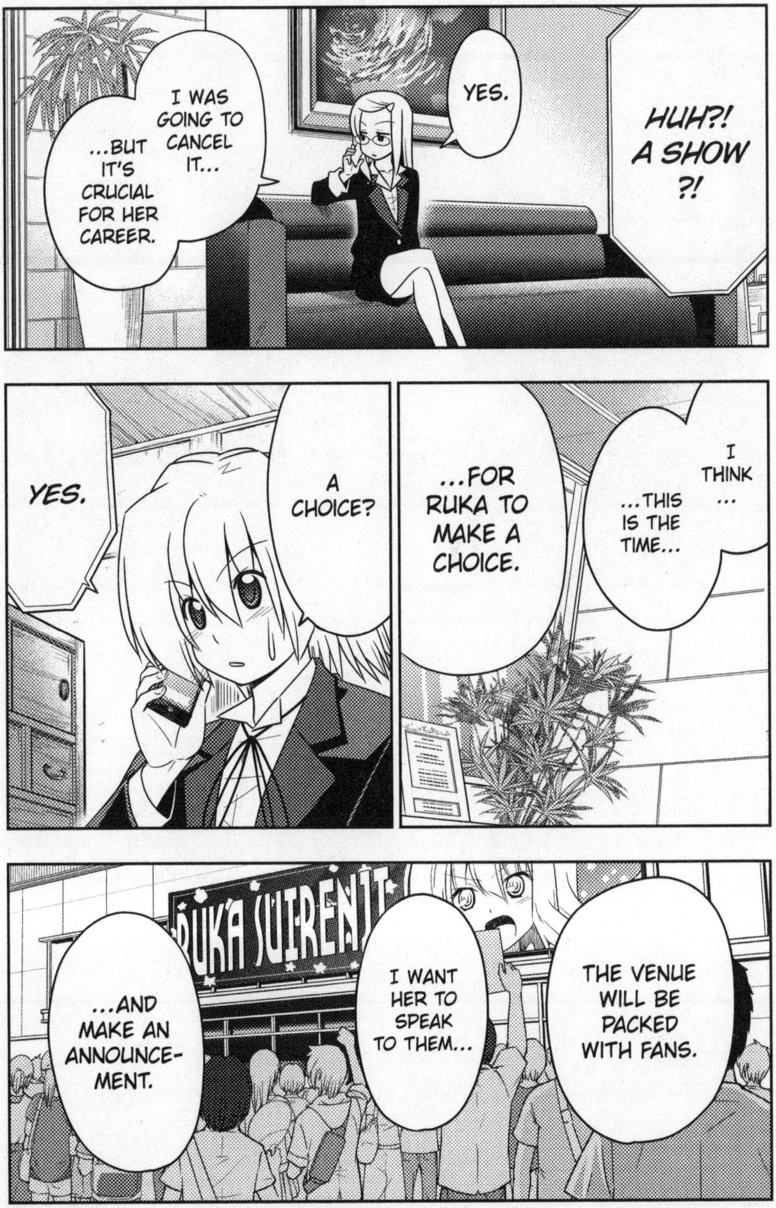
HUH?! A SHOW?!
YES.
I WAS GOING TO CANCEL IT...
...BUT IT'S CRUCIAL FOR HER CAREER.
I THINK...
...THIS IS THE TIME...
...FOR RUKA TO MAKE A CHOICE.
A CHOICE?
YES.
THE VENUE WILL BE PACKED WITH FANS.
I WANT HER TO SPEAK TO THEM...
...AND MAKE AN ANNOUNCE-MENT.
RUKA SUIRENJI

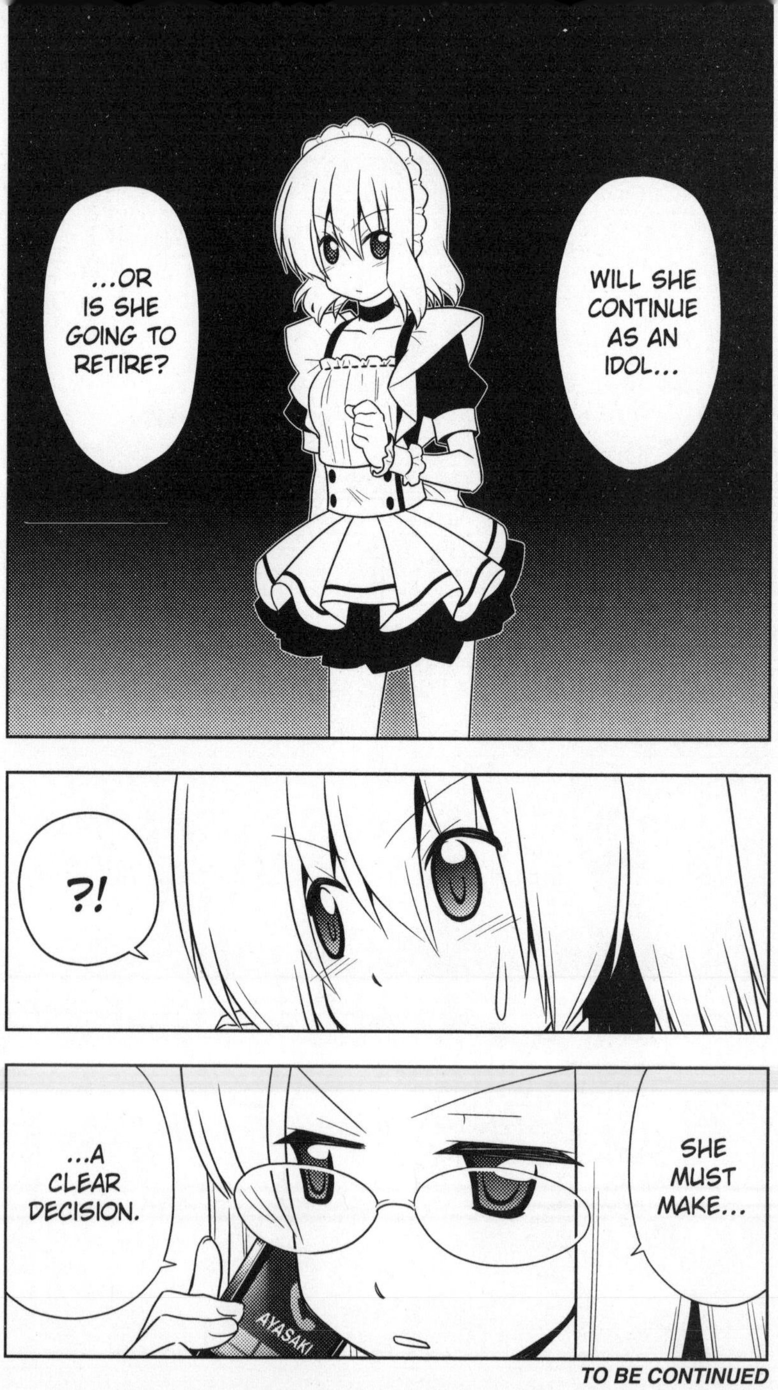
WILL SHE CONTINUE AS AN IDOL...
...OR IS SHE GOING TO RETIRE?
?!
SHE MUST MAKE...
...A CLEAR DECISION.
AYASAKI

TO BE CONTINUED

HAYATE THE COMBAT BUTLER

BONUS PAGES

Title by Ritsuko Hata (whose son is paying for her trip to France)

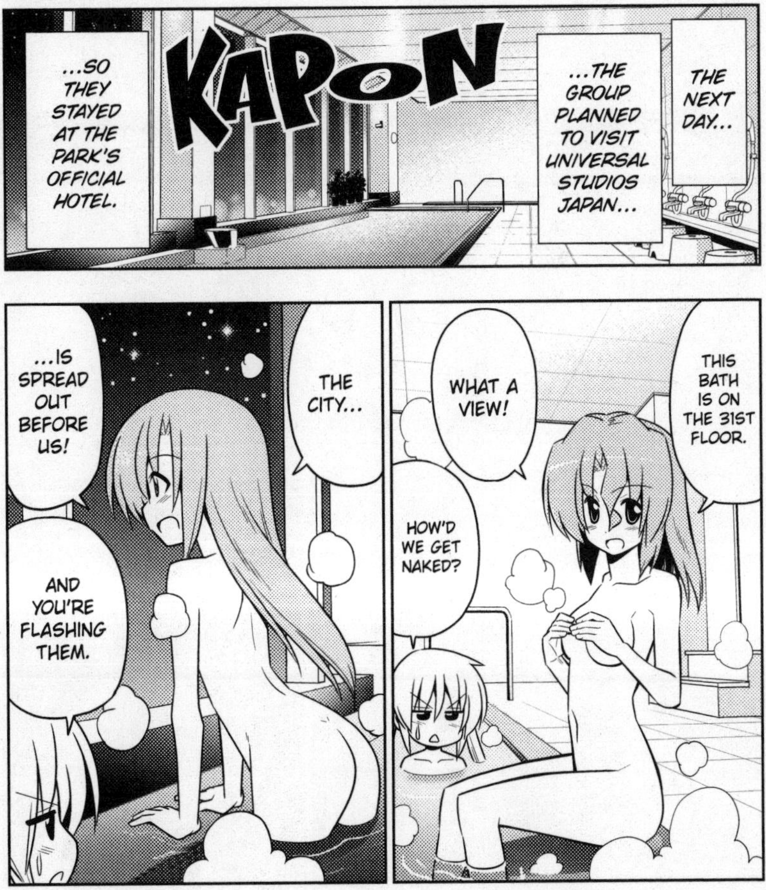
THE NEXT DAY...
...THE GROUP PLANNED TO VISIT UNIVERSAL STUDIOS JAPAN...
KAPON
...SO THEY STAYED AT THE PARK'S OFFICIAL HOTEL.
THIS BATH IS ON THE 31ST FLOOR.
WHAT A VIEW!
HOW'D WE GET NAKED?
THE CITY...
...IS SPREAD OUT BEFORE US!
AND YOU'RE FLASHING THEM.

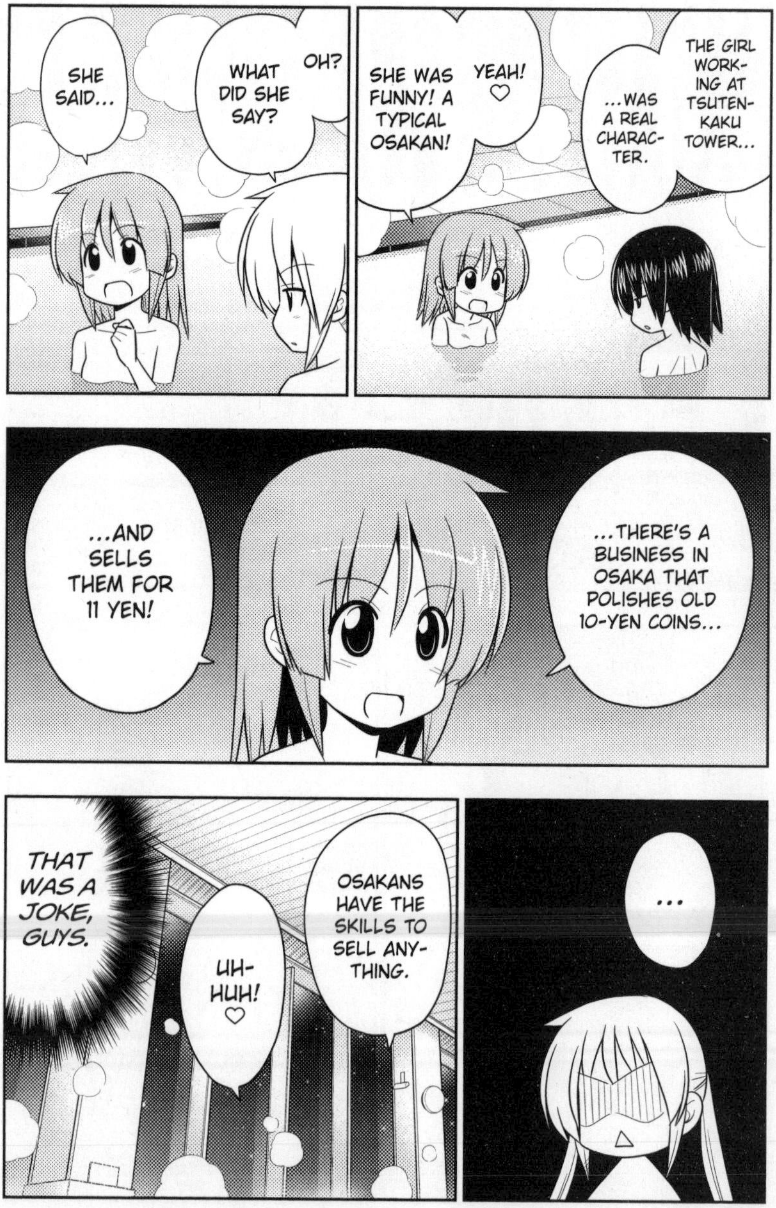
THE GIRL WORKING AT TSUTEN-KAKU TOWER...
...WAS A REAL CHARAC-TER.
YEAH! ♡
SHE WAS FUNNY! A TYPICAL OSAKAN!
OH?
WHAT DID SHE SAY?
SHE SAID...
...THERE'S A BUSINESS IN OSAKA THAT POLISHES OLD 10-YEN COINS...
...AND SELLS THEM FOR 11 YEN!
...
OSAKANS HAVE THE SKILLS TO SELL ANY-THING.
UH-HUH! ♡
THAT WAS A JOKE, GUYS.

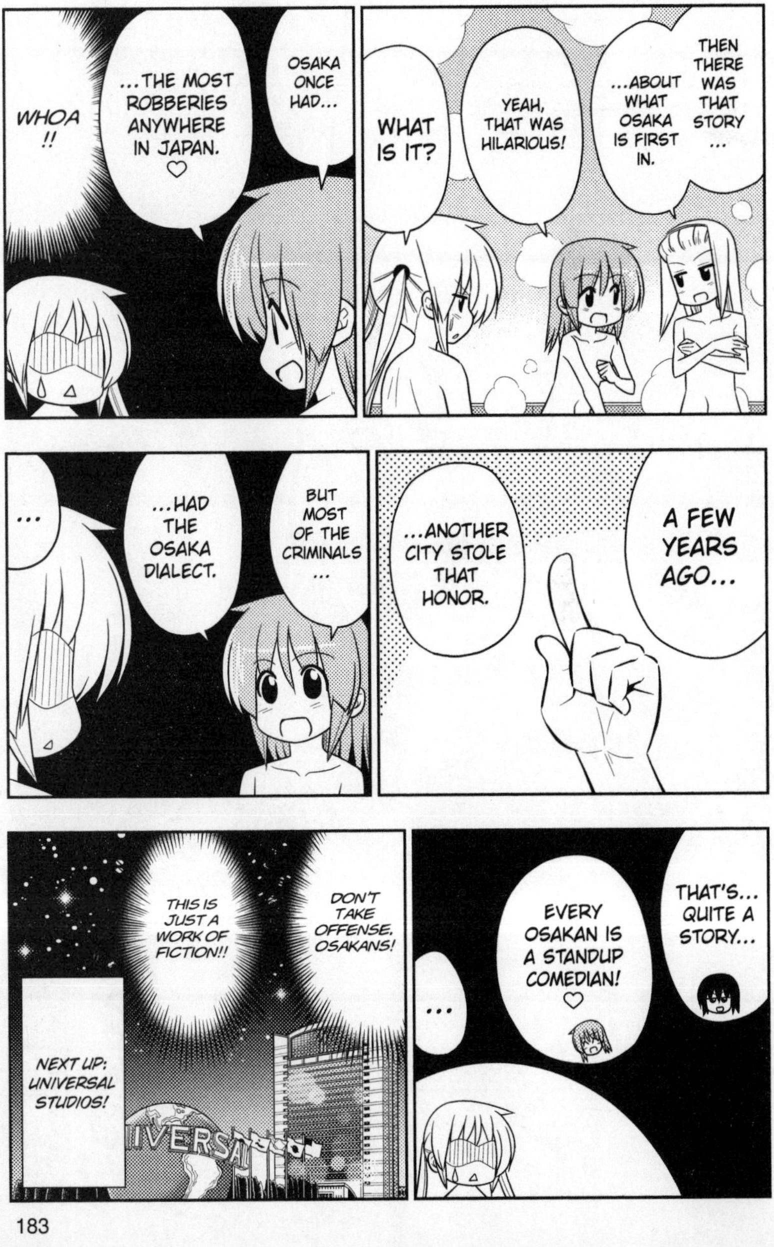
THEN THERE WAS THAT STORY...
...ABOUT WHAT OSAKA IS FIRST IN.
YEAH, THAT WAS HILARIOUS!
WHAT IS IT?
OSAKA ONCE HAD...
...THE MOST ROBBERIES ANYWHERE IN JAPAN. ♡
WHOA!!
A FEW YEARS AGO...
...ANOTHER CITY STOLE THAT HONOR.
BUT MOST OF THE CRIMINALS...
...HAD THE OSAKA DIALECT.
...
THAT'S... QUITE A STORY...
EVERY OSAKAN IS A STANDUP COMEDIAN! ♡
...
DON'T TAKE OFFENSE, OSAKANS!
THIS IS JUST A WORK OF FICTION!!
NEXT UP: UNIVERSAL STUDIOS!

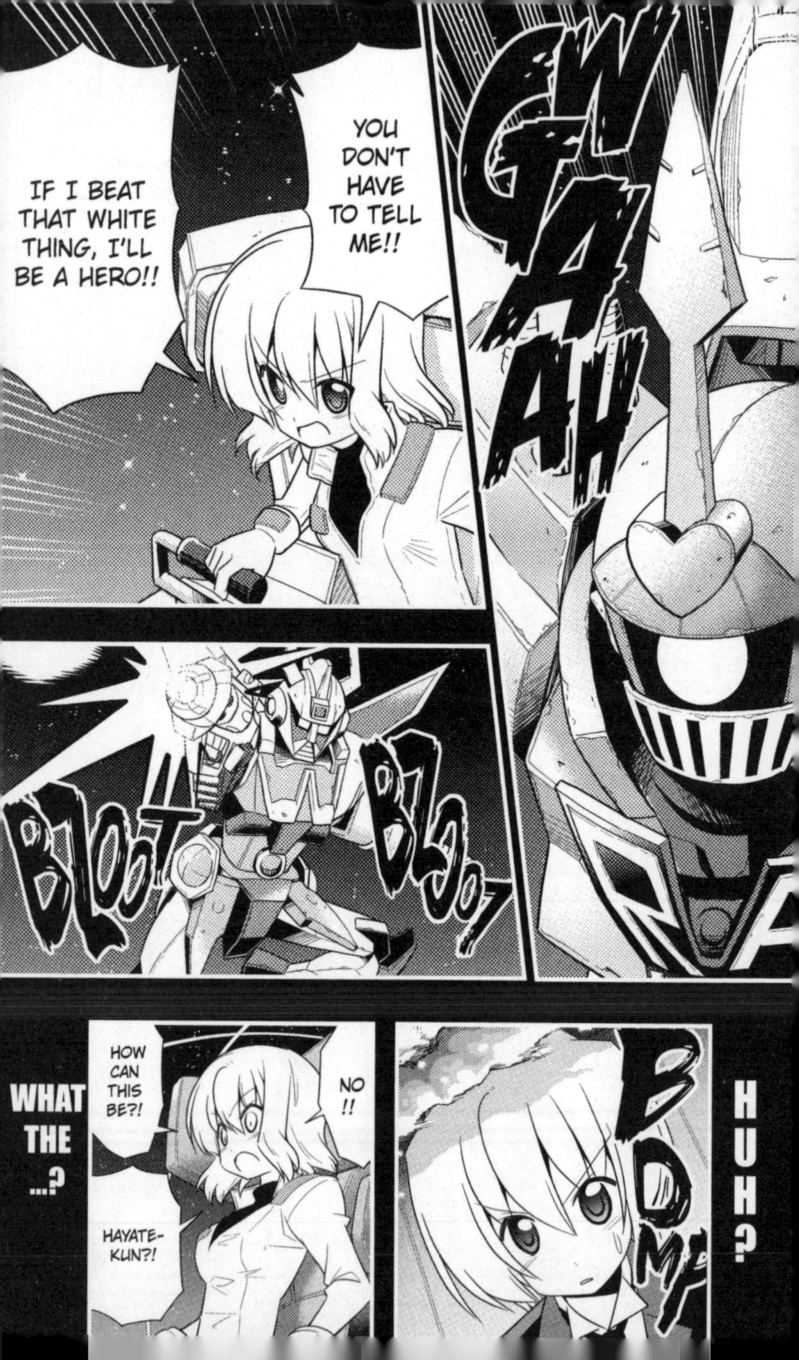
GWAAH
YOU DON'T HAVE TO TELL ME!!
IF I BEAT THAT WHITE THING, I'LL BE A HERO!!
BZOOT
BZOOT
HUH?
BDMP
NO!!
HOW CAN THIS BE?!
HAYATE-KUN?!
WHAT THE ...?

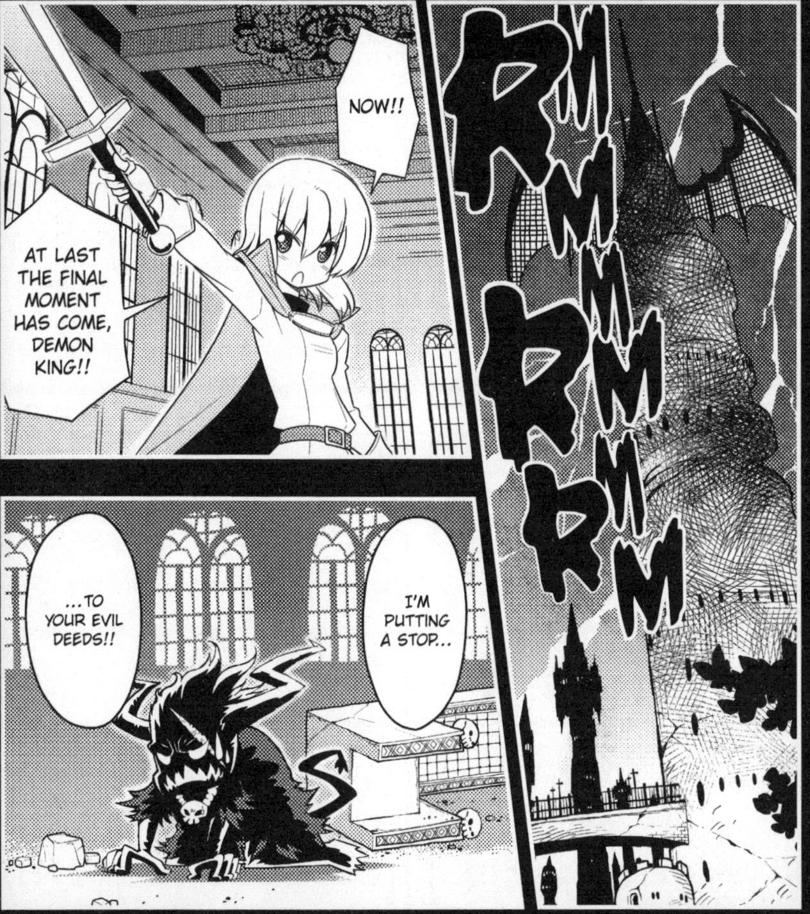
RMMM RMMM RMMM RM
NOW!!
AT LAST THE FINAL MOMENT HAS COME, DEMON KING!!
I'M PUTTING A STOP...
...TO YOUR EVIL DEEDS!!

WASN'T THIS A COMEDY MANGA ABOUT A BUTLER?

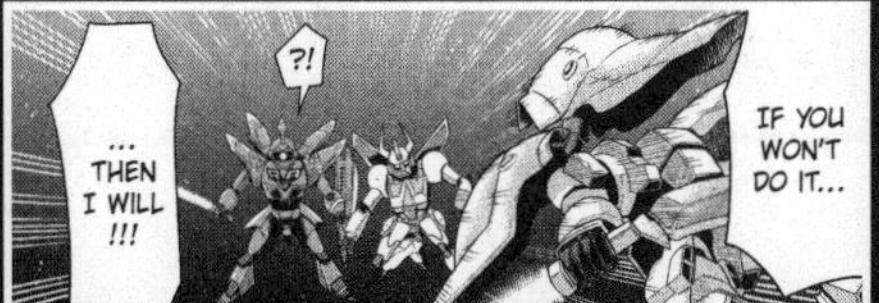
IF YOU WON'T DO IT...
?!
...THEN I WILL!!!

DON'T WORRY. NEXT VOLUME WILL BE A BUTLER COMEDY TOO.
DON'T MISS *HAYATE THE COMBAT BUTLER* VOLUME 39!

Getting a Pet

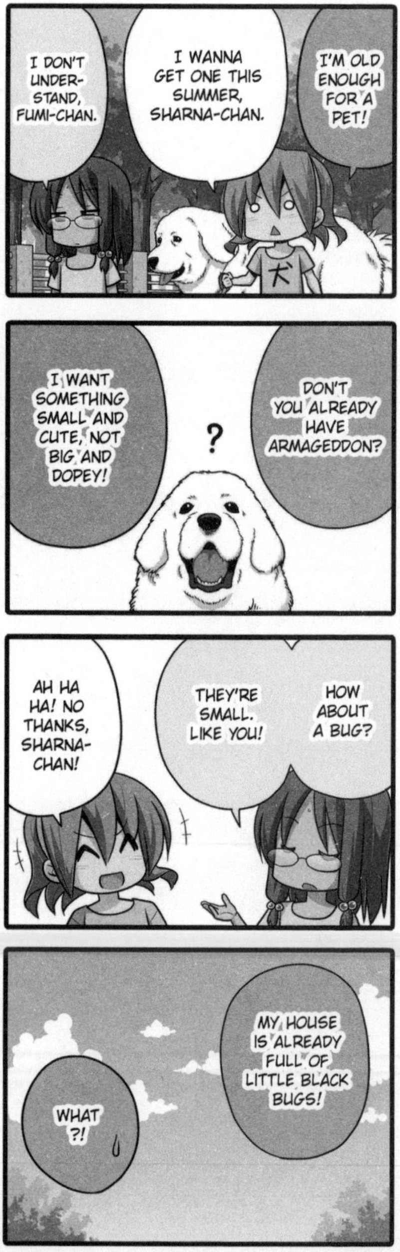
I'M OLD ENOUGH FOR A PET!
I WANNA GET ONE THIS SUMMER, SHARNA-CHAN.
I DON'T UNDERSTAND, FUMI-CHAN.
DON'T YOU ALREADY HAVE ARMAGEDDON?
?
I WANT SOMETHING SMALL AND CUTE, NOT BIG AND DOPEY!
HOW ABOUT A BUG?
THEY'RE SMALL. LIKE YOU!
AH HA HA! NO THANKS, SHARNA-CHAN!
MY HOUSE IS ALREADY FULL OF LITTLE BLACK BUGS!
WHAT?!

The Pet Goes "Peh!"

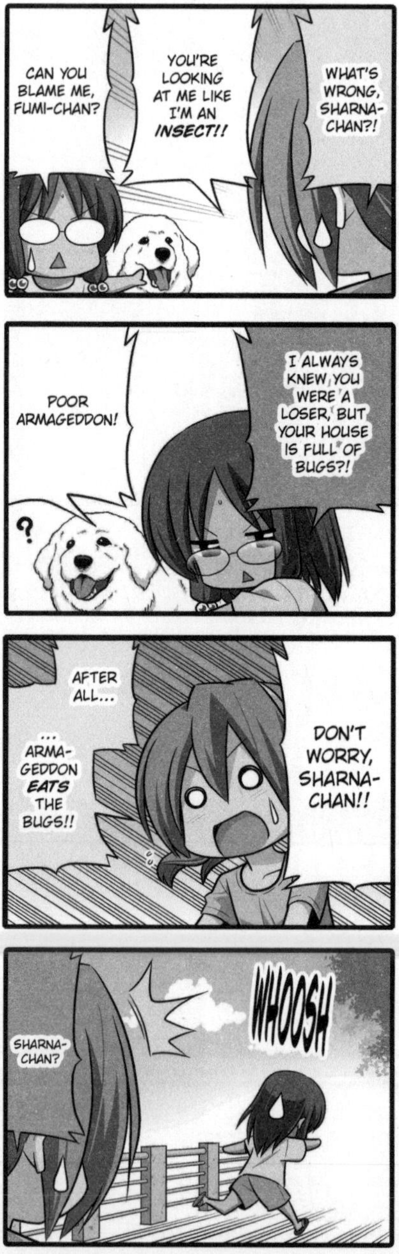
WHAT'S WRONG, SHARNA-CHAN?!
YOU'RE LOOKING AT ME LIKE I'M AN INSECT!!
CAN YOU BLAME ME, FUMI-CHAN?
I ALWAYS KNEW YOU WERE A LOSER, BUT YOUR HOUSE IS FULL OF BUGS?!
POOR ARMAGEDDON!
?
DON'T WORRY, SHARNA-CHAN!!
AFTER ALL...
...ARMAGEDDON EATS THE BUGS!!
WHOOSH
SHARNA-CHAN?

HAYATE THE COMBAT BUTLER

~SIDE STORY~

WITH NO ONE TO CARE FOR HER, NISHIZAWA HOVERED BETWEEN LIFE AND DEATH...

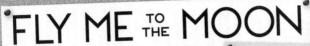

Komi Can't Communicate

Story & Art by Tomohito Oda

The journey to a hundred friends begins with a single conversation.

Socially anxious high school student Shoko Komi's greatest dream is to make some friends, but everyone at school mistakes her crippling social anxiety for cool reserve. With the whole student body keeping its distance and Komi unable to utter a single word, friendship might be forever beyond her reach.

Hey! You're Reading in the Wrong Direction!

This is the **end** of this graphic novel!

To properly enjoy this VIZ graphic novel, please turn it around and begin reading from **right to left.** Unlike English, Japanese is read right to left, so Japanese comics are read in reverse order from the way English comics are typically read.

Follow the action this way

This book has been printed in the original Japanese format in order to preserve the orientation of the original artwork. Have fun with it!